Panic x Panic

1

MIKA KAWAMURA

TRANSLATED AND ADAPTED BY
JOSHUA WEEKS

NORTH MARKET STREET GRAPHICS

Panic X Panic volume 1 is a work of fiction. Names, characters, places, and incidents are the products of the author's imagination or are used fictitiously. Any resemblance to actual events, locales, or persons, living or dead, is entirely coincidental.

A Del Rey Manga/Kodansha Trade Paperback Original

Published in the United States by Del Rey Books, an imprint of The Random House Publishing Group, a division of Random House, Inc., New York.

Publication rights arranged through Kodansha Ltd.

First published in Japan in 2005 by Kodansha Ltd., Tokyo

ISBN 978-0-345-51463-9

Printed in the United States of America

www.delreymanga.com

2 4 6 8 9 7 5 3 1

Translator/Adapter: Joshua Weeks
Lettering: North Market Street Graphics

CONTENTS

HONORIFICS EXPLAINED

Throughout the Del Rey Manga books, you will find Japanese honorifics left intact in the translations. For those not familiar with how the Japanese use honorifics and, more important, how they differ from American honorifics, we present this brief overview.

Politeness has always been a critical facet of Japanese culture. Ever since the feudal era, when Japan was a highly stratified society, use of honorifics—which can be defined as polite speech that indicates relationship or status—has played an essential role in the Japanese language. When addressing someone in Japanese, an honorific usually takes the form of a suffix attached to one's name (example: "Asuna-san"), is used as a title at the end of one's name, or appears in place of the name itself (example: "Negi-sensei," or simply "Sensei!").

Honorifics can be expressions of respect or endearment. In the context of manga and anime, honorifics give insight into the nature of the relationship between characters. Many English translations leave out these important honorifics and therefore distort the feel of the original Japanese. Because Japanese honorifics contain nuances that English honorifics lack, it is our policy at Del Rey not to translate them. Here, instead, is a guide to some of the honorifics you may encounter in Del Rey Manga.

-san: This is the most common honorific and is equivalent to Mr., Miss, Ms., or Mrs. It is the all-purpose honorific and can be used in any situation where politeness is required.

-sama: This is one level higher than "-san" and is used to confer great respect.

-dono: This comes from the word "tono," which means "lord." It is an even higher level than "-sama" and confers utmost respect.

-kun: This suffix is used at the end of boys' names to express familiarity or endearment. It is also sometimes used by men among friends, or when addressing someone younger or of a lower station.

-chan: This is used to express endearment, mostly toward girls. It is also used for little boys, pets, and even among lovers. It gives a sense of childish cuteness.

Bozu: This is an informal way to refer to a boy, similar to the English terms "kid" and "squirt."

Sempai/
Senpai: This title suggests that the addressee is one's senior in a group or organization. It is most often used in a school setting, where underclassmen refer to their upperclassmen as "sempai." It can also be used in the workplace, such as when a newer employee addresses an employee who has seniority in the company.

Kohai: This is the opposite of "sempai" and is used toward underclassmen in school or newcomers in the workplace. It connotes that the addressee is of a lower station.

Sensei: Literally meaning "one who has come before," this title is used for teachers, doctors, or masters of any profession or art.

-[blank]:   This is usually forgotten in these lists, but it is perhaps the most significant difference between Japanese and English. The lack of honorific means that the speaker has permission to address the person in a very intimate way. Usually, only family, spouses, or very close friends have this kind of permission. Known as *yobisute,* it can be gratifying when someone who has earned the intimacy starts to call one by one's name without an honorific. But when that intimacy hasn't been earned, it can be very insulting.

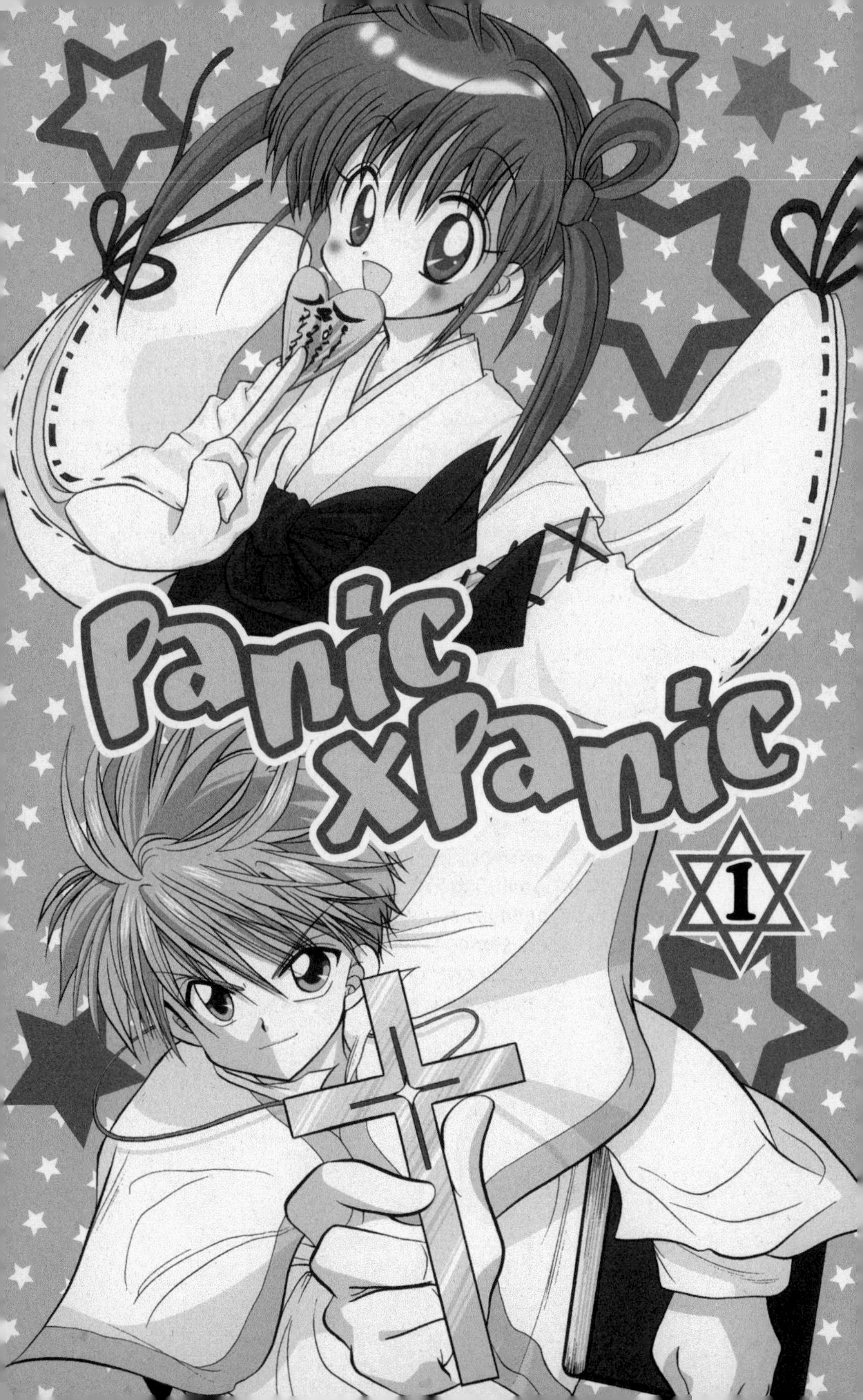
Panic
xPanic
1

Panic x Panic

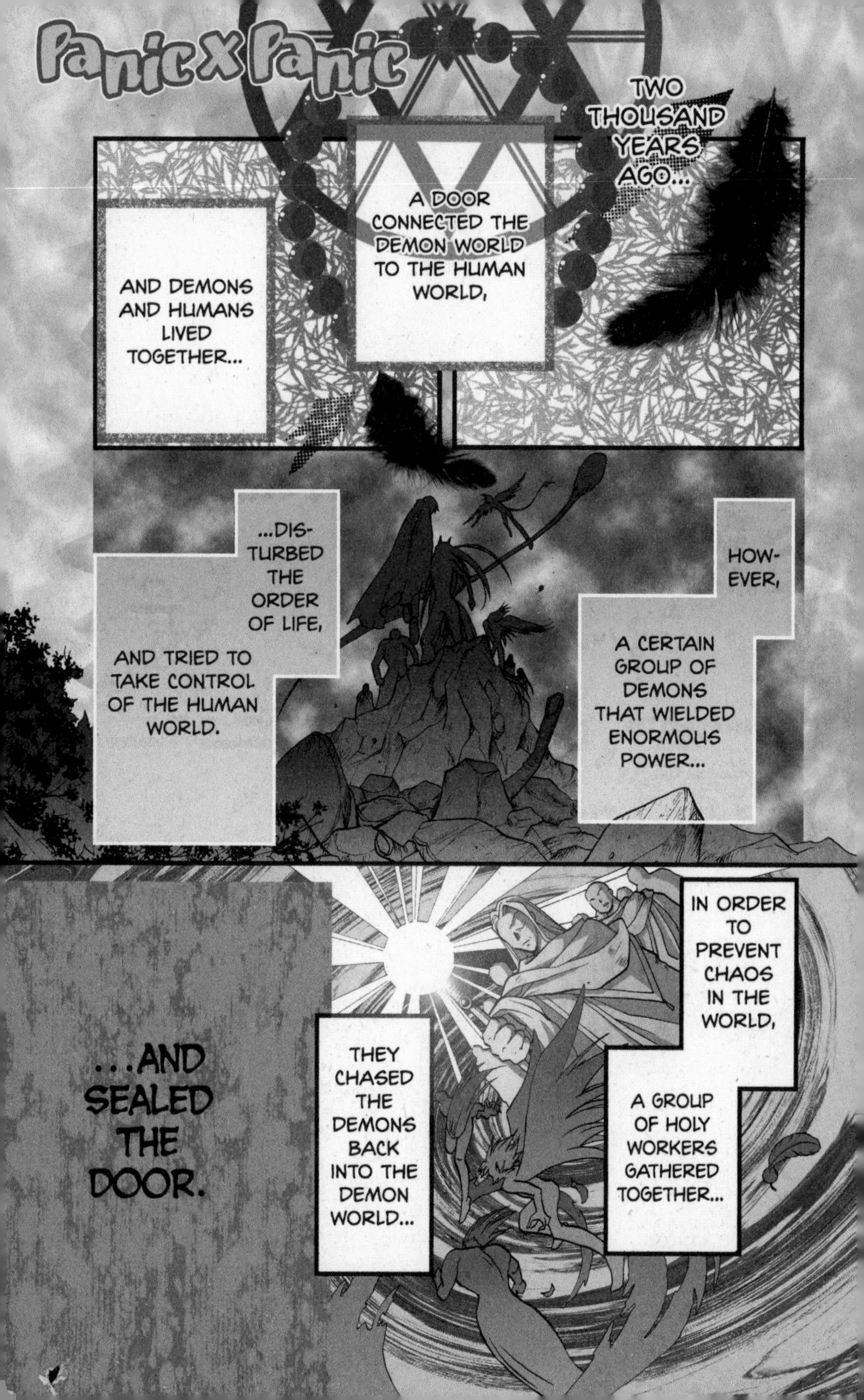
Panic x Panic
TWO THOUSAND YEARS AGO...
A DOOR CONNECTED THE DEMON WORLD TO THE HUMAN WORLD,
AND DEMONS AND HUMANS LIVED TOGETHER...
HOW-EVER,
A CERTAIN GROUP OF DEMONS THAT WIELDED ENORMOUS POWER...
...DIS-TURBED THE ORDER OF LIFE,
AND TRIED TO TAKE CONTROL OF THE HUMAN WORLD.
IN ORDER TO PREVENT CHAOS IN THE WORLD,
A GROUP OF HOLY WORKERS GATHERED TOGETHER...
THEY CHASED THE DEMONS BACK INTO THE DEMON WORLD...
...AND SEALED THE DOOR.

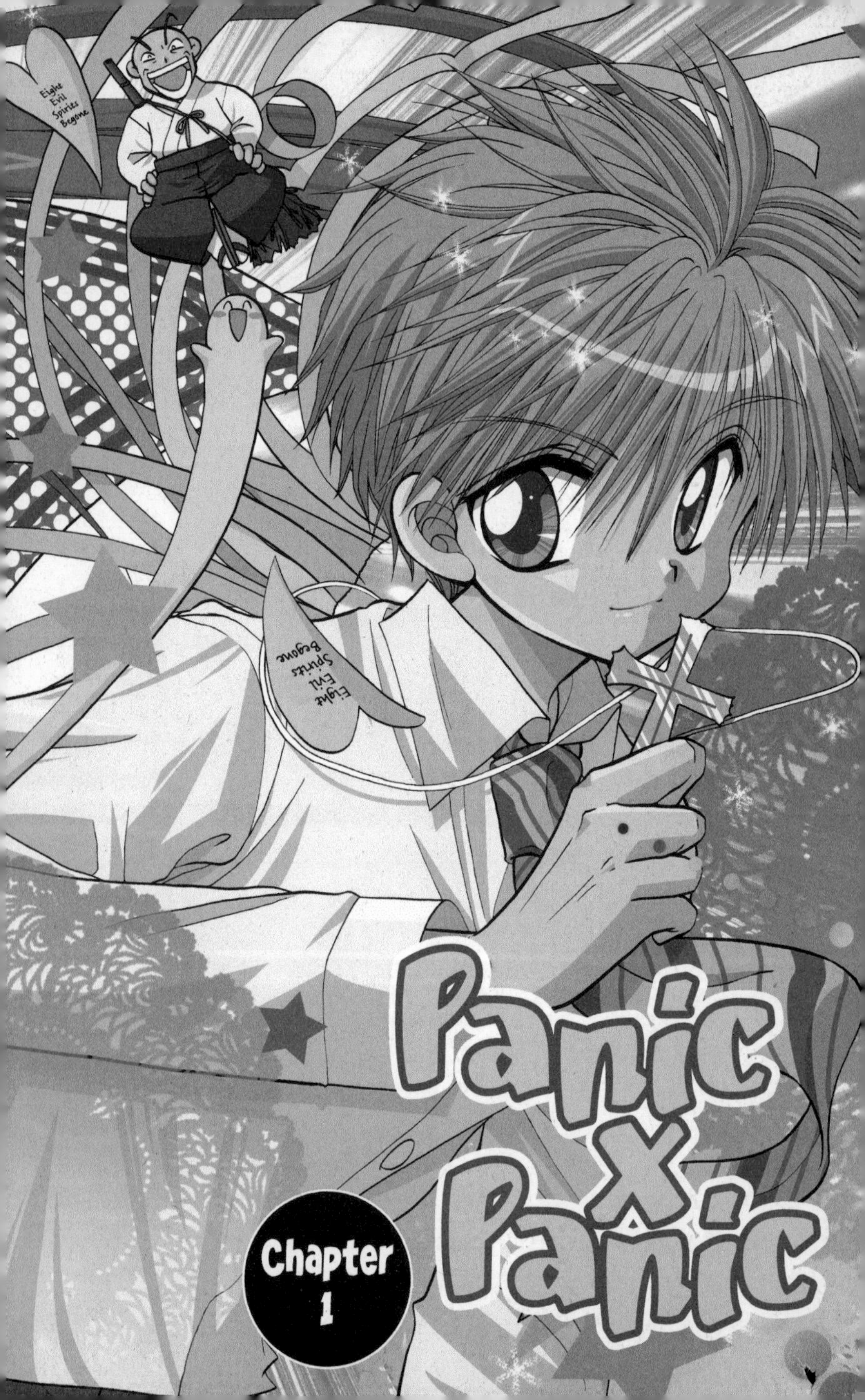
Eight Evil Spirits Begone
Eight Evil Spirits Begone
Panic X Panic
Chapter 1

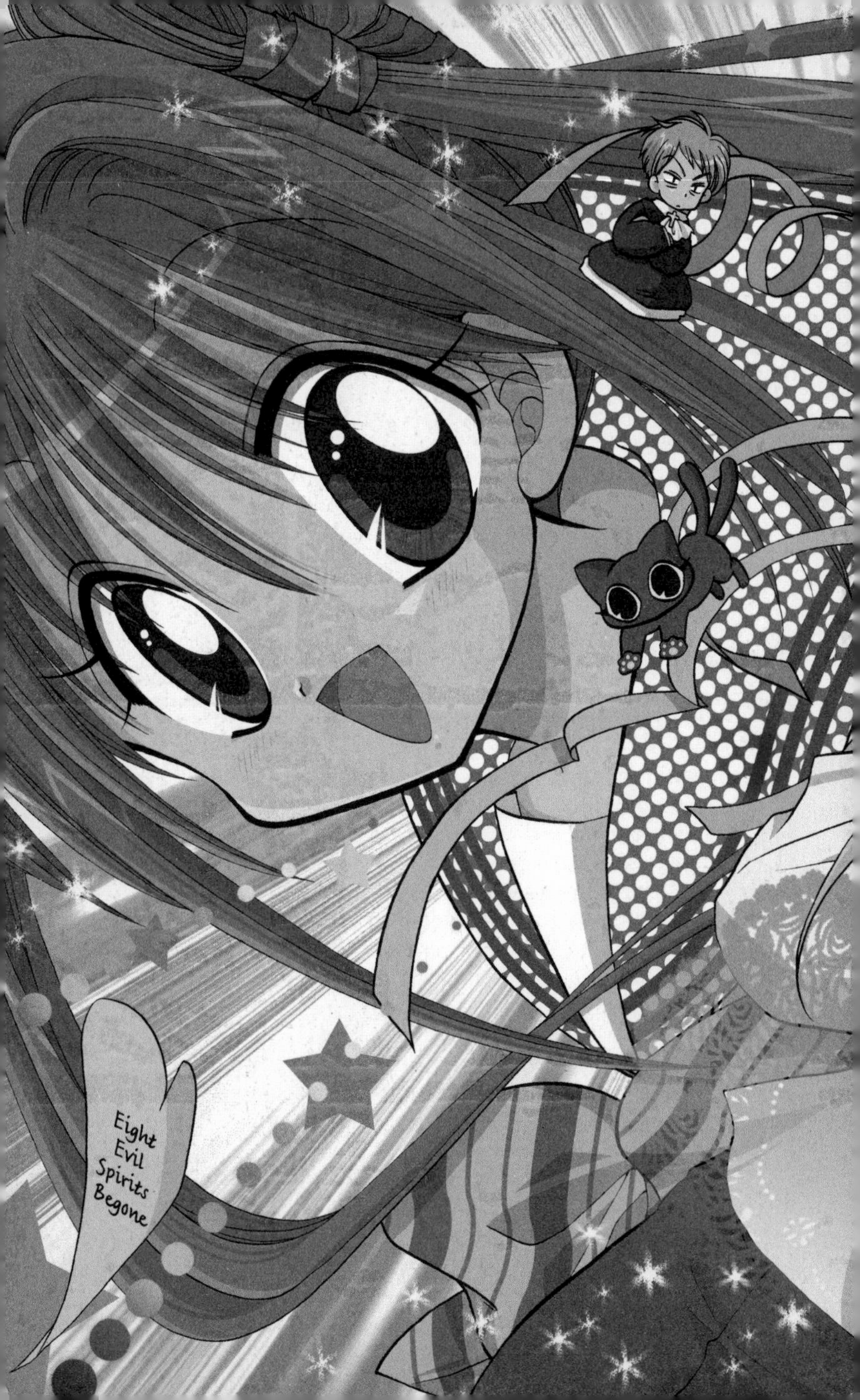
Eight Evil Spirits Begone

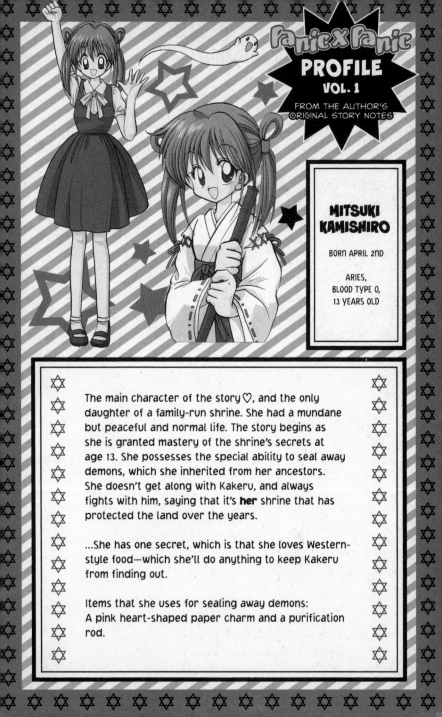

PanicXPanic
PROFILE
VOL. 1

FROM THE AUTHOR'S
ORIGINAL STORY NOTES

MITSUKI KAMISHIRO

BORN APRIL 2ND

ARIES,
BLOOD TYPE O,
13 YEARS OLD

The main character of the story ♡, and the only daughter of a family-run shrine. She had a mundane but peaceful and normal life. The story begins as she is granted mastery of the shrine's secrets at age 13. She possesses the special ability to seal away demons, which she inherited from her ancestors. She doesn't get along with Kakeru, and always fights with him, saying that it's **her** shrine that has protected the land over the years.

...She has one secret, which is that she loves Western-style food—which she'll do anything to keep Kakeru from finding out.

Items that she uses for sealing away demons:
A pink heart-shaped paper charm and a purification rod.

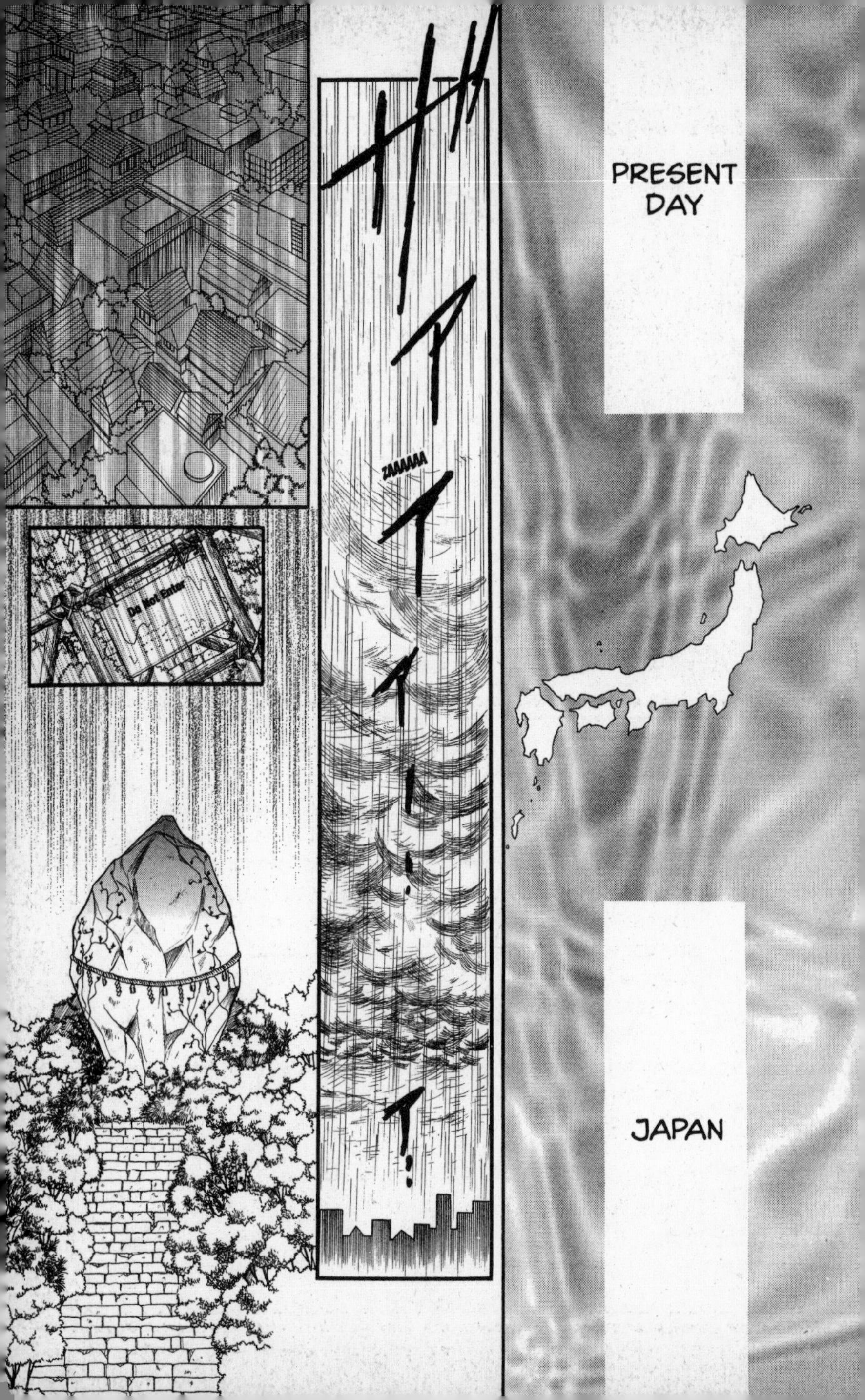
PRESENT DAY
JAPAN
ZAAAAAA
Do Not Enter

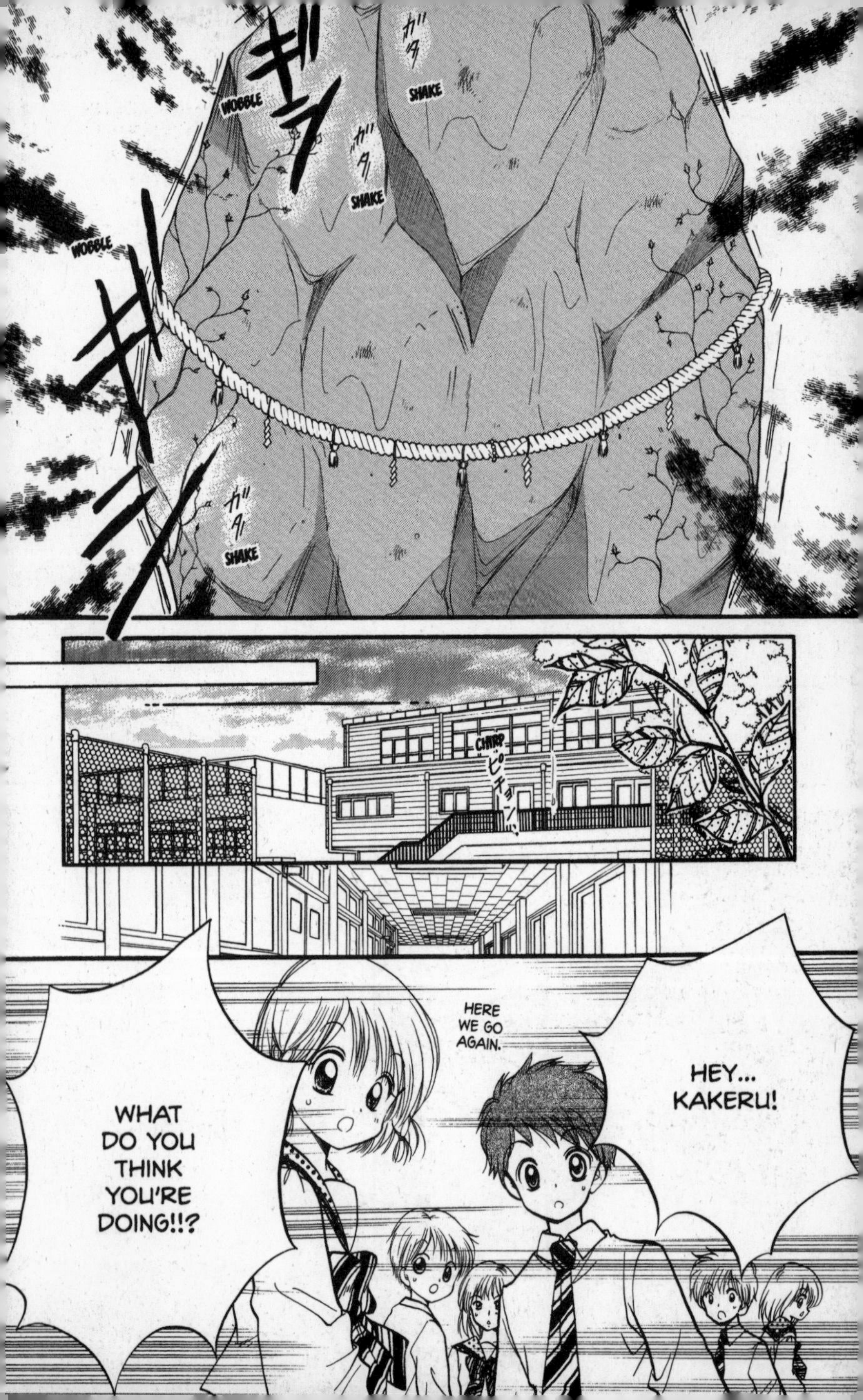
ガタ
SHAKE
WOBBLE
ガタ
SHAKE
WOBBLE
ガタ
SHAKE
CHIRP
ピチョン…
HEY... KAKERU!
HERE WE GO AGAIN.
WHAT DO YOU THINK YOU'RE DOING!!?

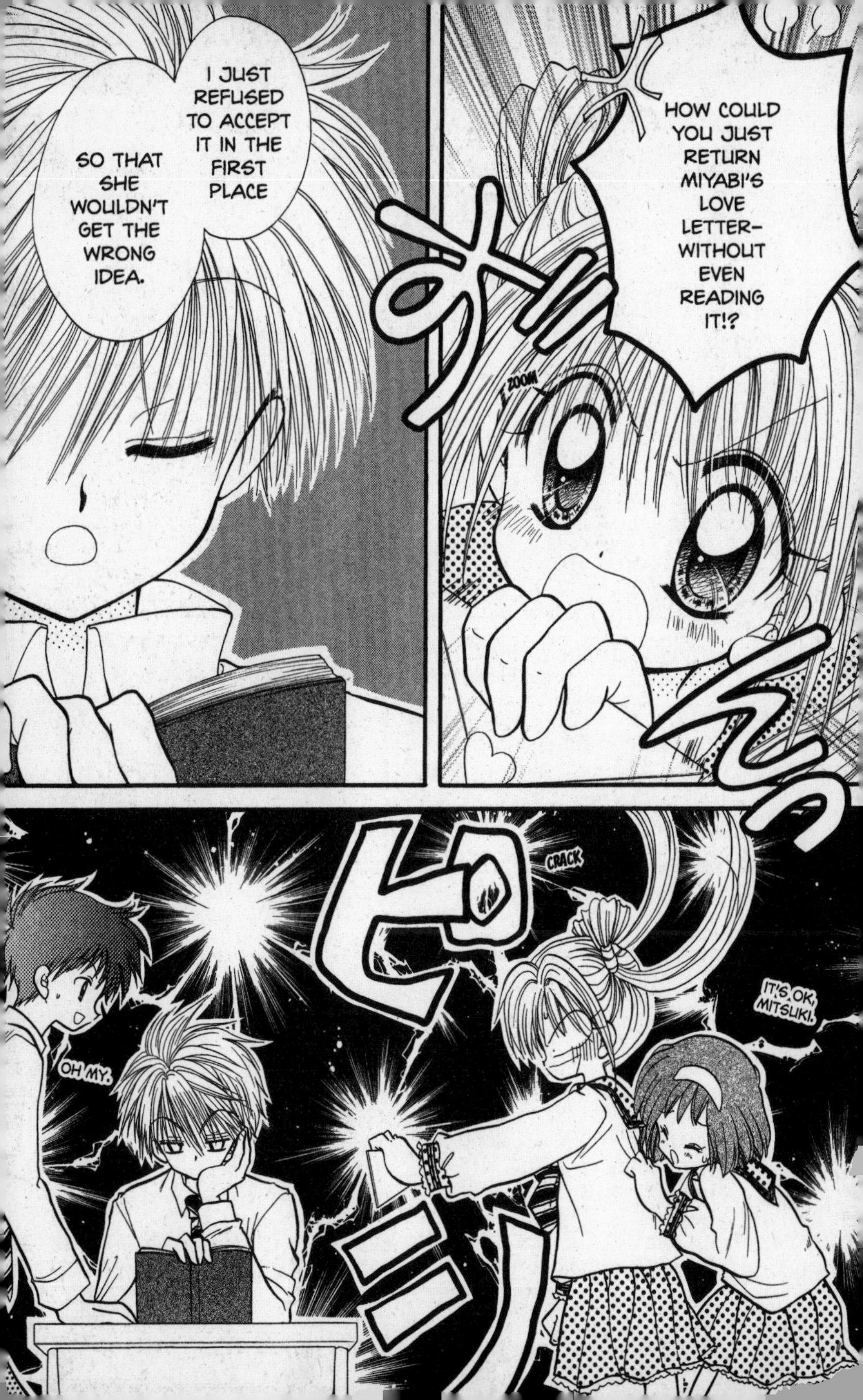
HOW COULD YOU JUST RETURN MIYABI'S LOVE LETTER–WITHOUT EVEN READING IT!?
ZOOM
I JUST REFUSED TO ACCEPT IT IN THE FIRST PLACE
SO THAT SHE WOULDN'T GET THE WRONG IDEA.
IT'S OK, MITSUKI.
CRACK
OH MY.

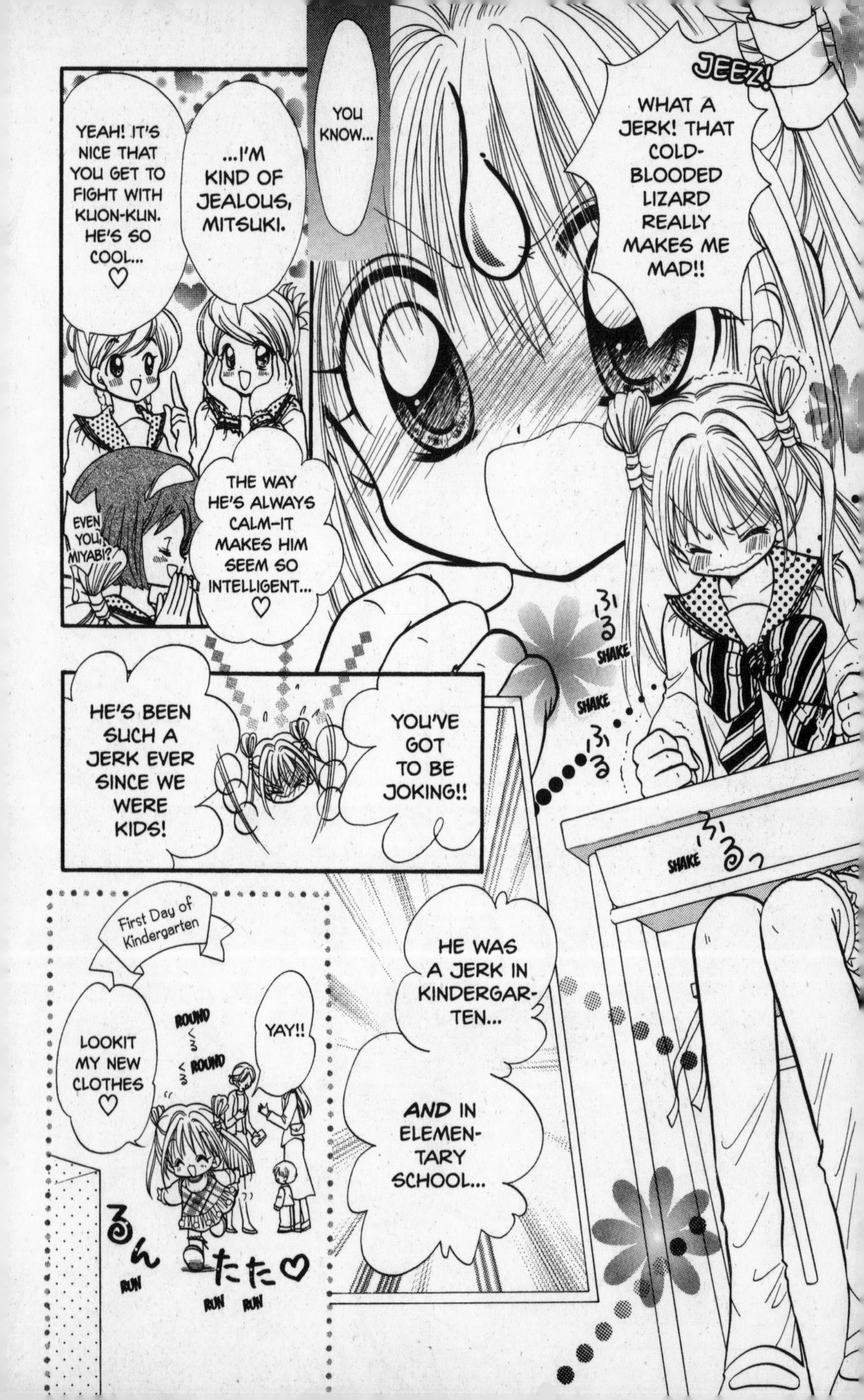
JEEZ!
WHAT A JERK! THAT COLD-BLOODED LIZARD REALLY MAKES ME MAD!!
ふる SHAKE
SHAKE ふる
ふるっ SHAKE
YOU KNOW...
...I'M KIND OF JEALOUS, MITSUKI.
YEAH! IT'S NICE THAT YOU GET TO FIGHT WITH KUON-KUN. HE'S SO COOL... ♡
THE WAY HE'S ALWAYS CALM—IT MAKES HIM SEEM SO INTELLIGENT... ♡
EVEN YOU, MIYABI!?
YOU'VE GOT TO BE JOKING!!
HE'S BEEN SUCH A JERK EVER SINCE WE WERE KIDS!
HE WAS A JERK IN KINDERGARTEN...
AND IN ELEMENTARY SCHOOL...
First Day of Kindergarten
YAY!!
LOOKIT MY NEW CLOTHES ♡
ROUND くる くる ROUND
るん RUN たた♡ RUN RUN

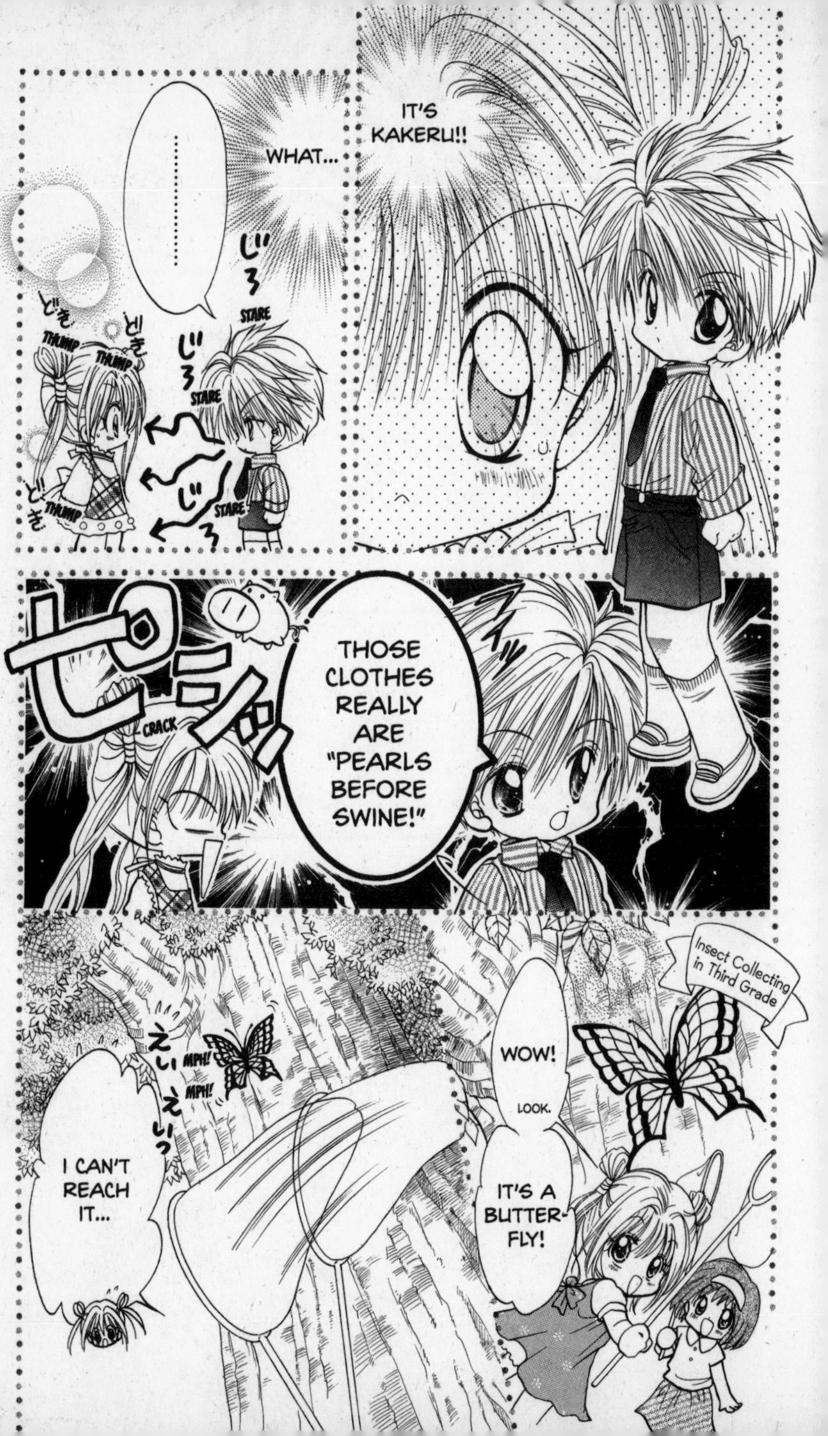

IT'S KAKERU!!
WHAT...
......
STARE
STARE
STARE
THUMP
THUMP
THUMP
THOSE CLOTHES REALLY ARE "PEARLS BEFORE SWINE!"
CRACK
Insect Collecting in Third Grade
WOW!
LOOK.
IT'S A BUTTERFLY!
MPH!
MPH!
I CAN'T REACH IT...

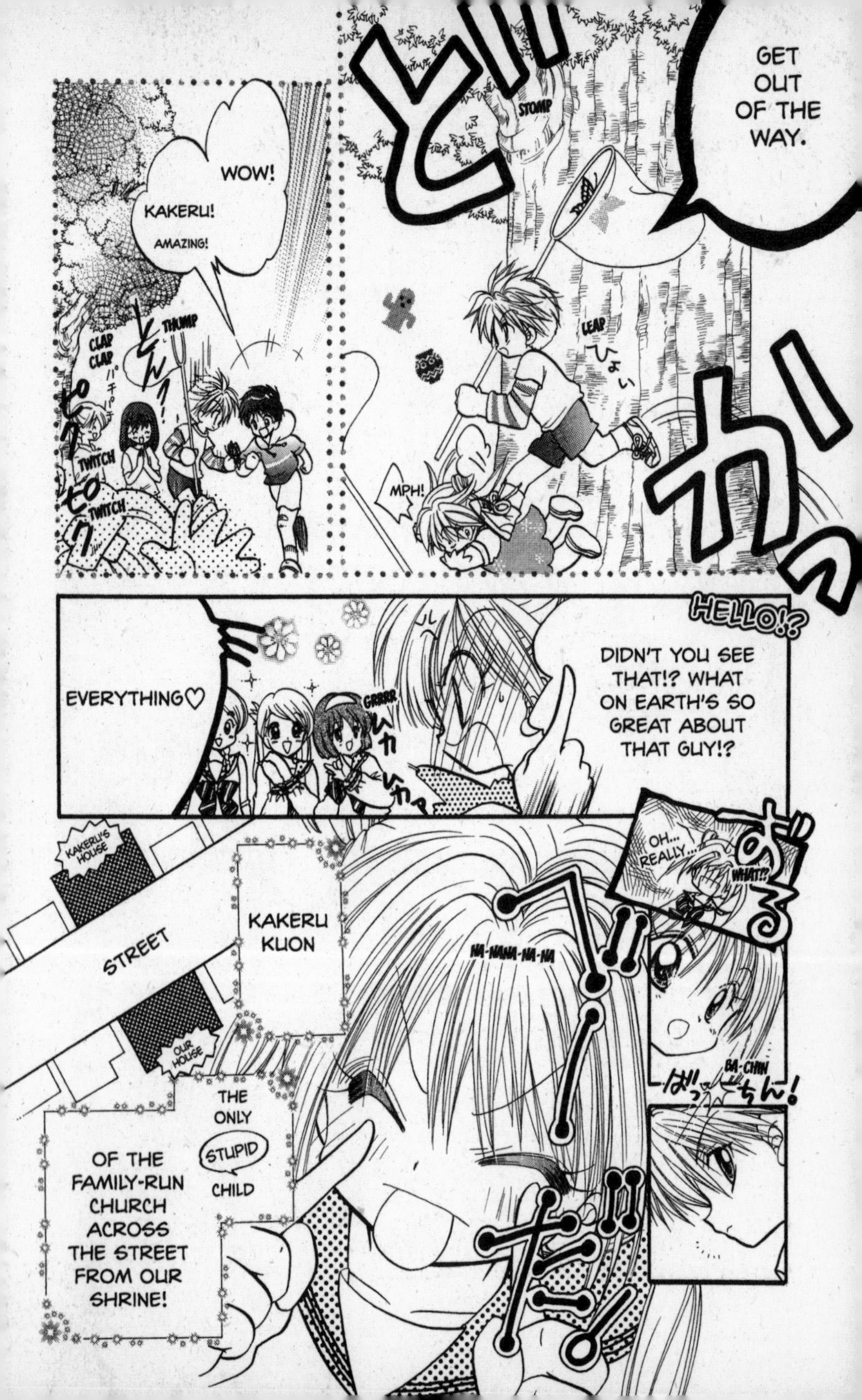
GET OUT OF THE WAY.
STOMP
LEAP
MPH!
WOW!
KAKERU!
AMAZING!
THUMP
CLAP CLAP
TWITCH
TWITCH
HELLO!?
DIDN'T YOU SEE THAT!? WHAT ON EARTH'S SO GREAT ABOUT THAT GUY!?
GRRRR
EVERYTHING♡
OH... REALLY...
WHAT!?
BA-CHIN
NA-NANA-NA-NA
KAKERU KUON
THE ONLY STUPID CHILD
OF THE FAMILY-RUN CHURCH ACROSS THE STREET FROM OUR SHRINE!
KAKERU'S HOUSE
STREET
OUR HOUSE

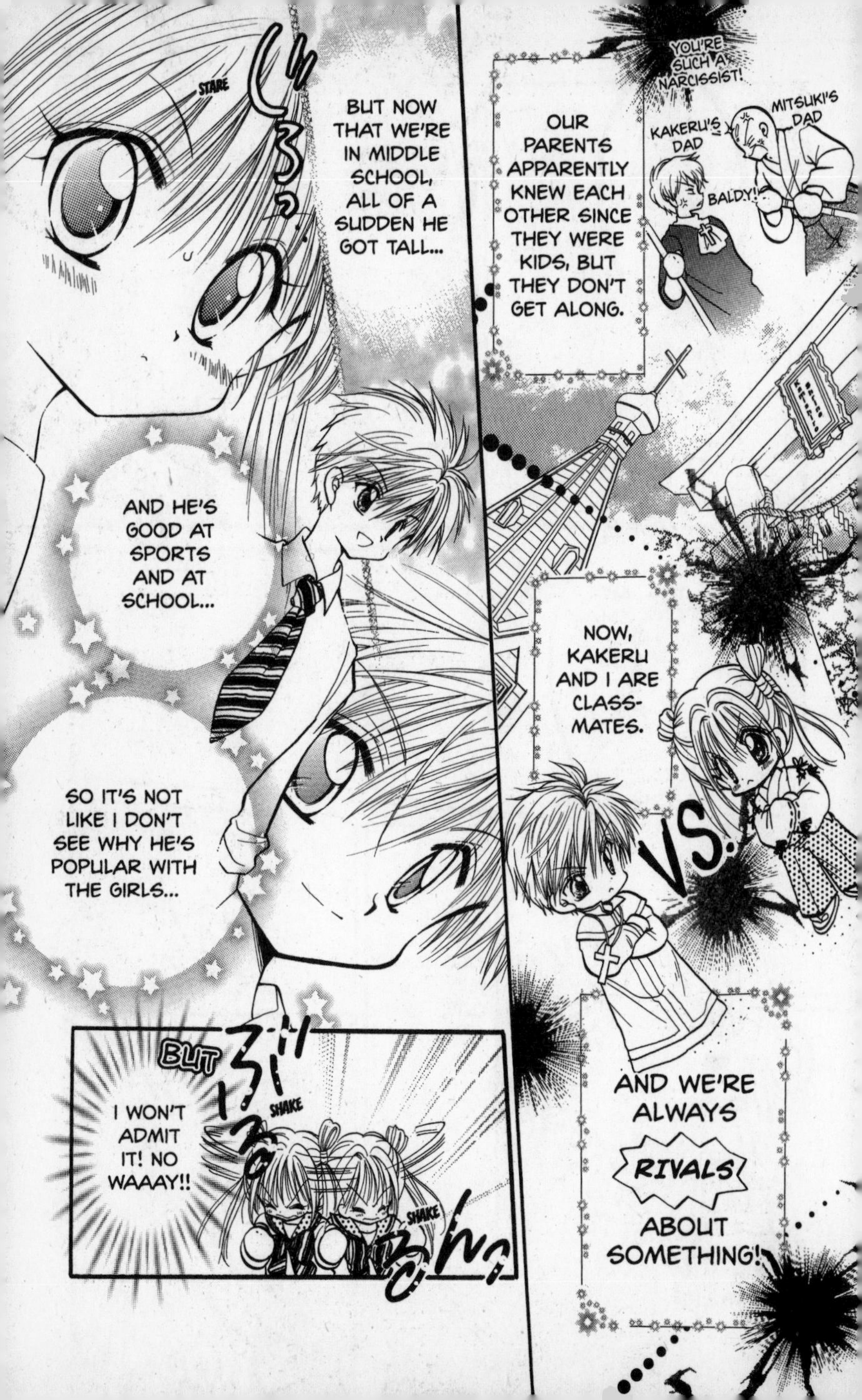
YOU'RE SUCH A NARCISSIST!
MITSUKI'S DAD
KAKERU'S DAD
BALDY!
OUR PARENTS APPARENTLY KNEW EACH OTHER SINCE THEY WERE KIDS, BUT THEY DON'T GET ALONG.
NOW, KAKERU AND I ARE CLASSMATES.
VS.
AND WE'RE ALWAYS RIVALS ABOUT SOMETHING!
STARE
BUT NOW THAT WE'RE IN MIDDLE SCHOOL, ALL OF A SUDDEN HE GOT TALL...
AND HE'S GOOD AT SPORTS AND AT SCHOOL...
SO IT'S NOT LIKE I DON'T SEE WHY HE'S POPULAR WITH THE GIRLS...
BUT
I WON'T ADMIT IT! NO WAAAY!!
SHAKE
SHAKE

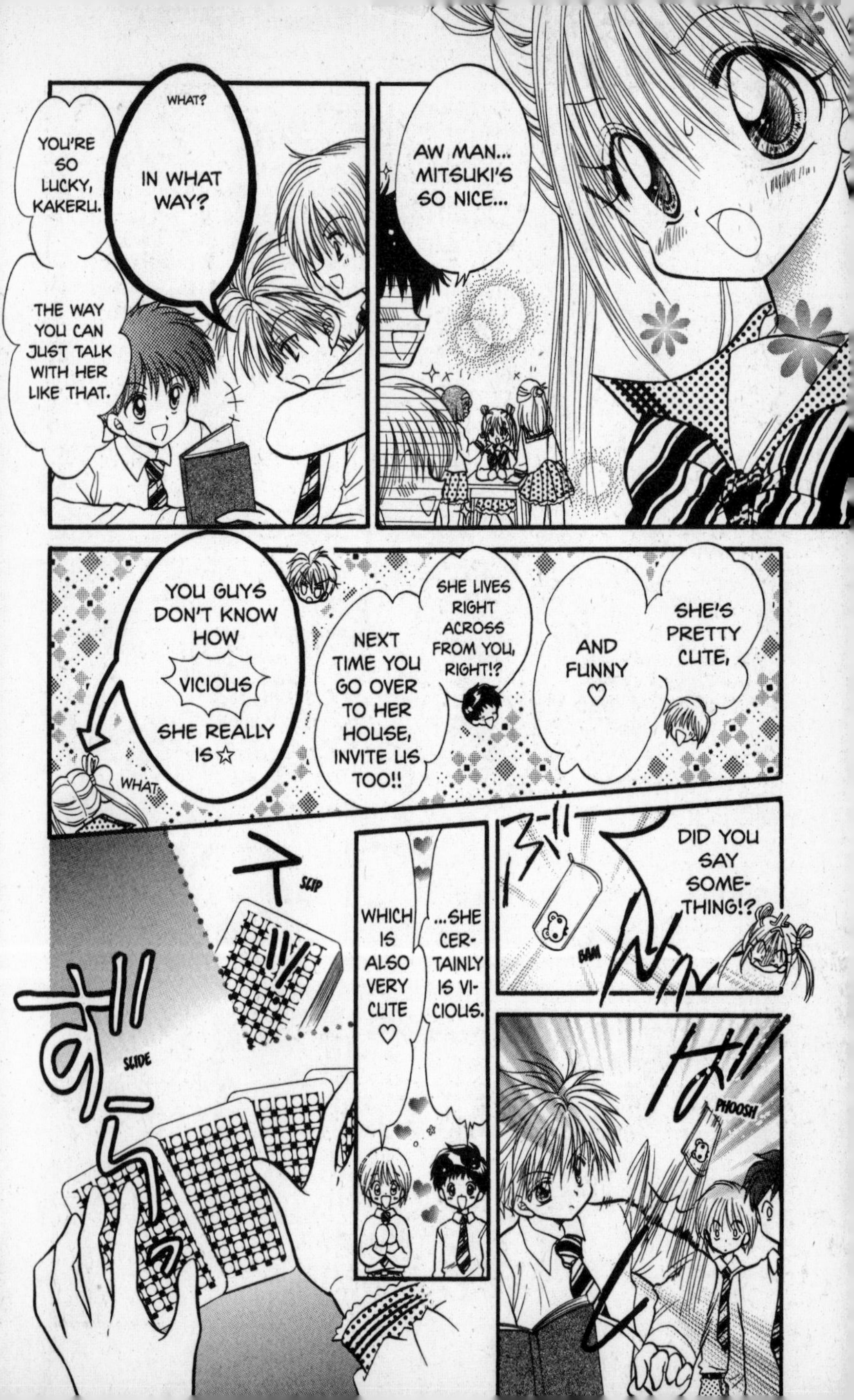
AW MAN... MITSUKI'S SO NICE...
YOU'RE SO LUCKY, KAKERU.
WHAT?
IN WHAT WAY?
THE WAY YOU CAN JUST TALK WITH HER LIKE THAT.
SHE'S PRETTY CUTE,
AND FUNNY ♡
SHE LIVES RIGHT ACROSS FROM YOU, RIGHT!?
NEXT TIME YOU GO OVER TO HER HOUSE, INVITE US TOO!!
YOU GUYS DON'T KNOW HOW VICIOUS SHE REALLY IS☆
WHAT
DID YOU SAY SOME-THING!?
BAM
PHOOSH
...SHE CER-TAINLY IS VI-CIOUS.
WHICH IS ALSO VERY CUTE ♡
SLIP
SLIDE

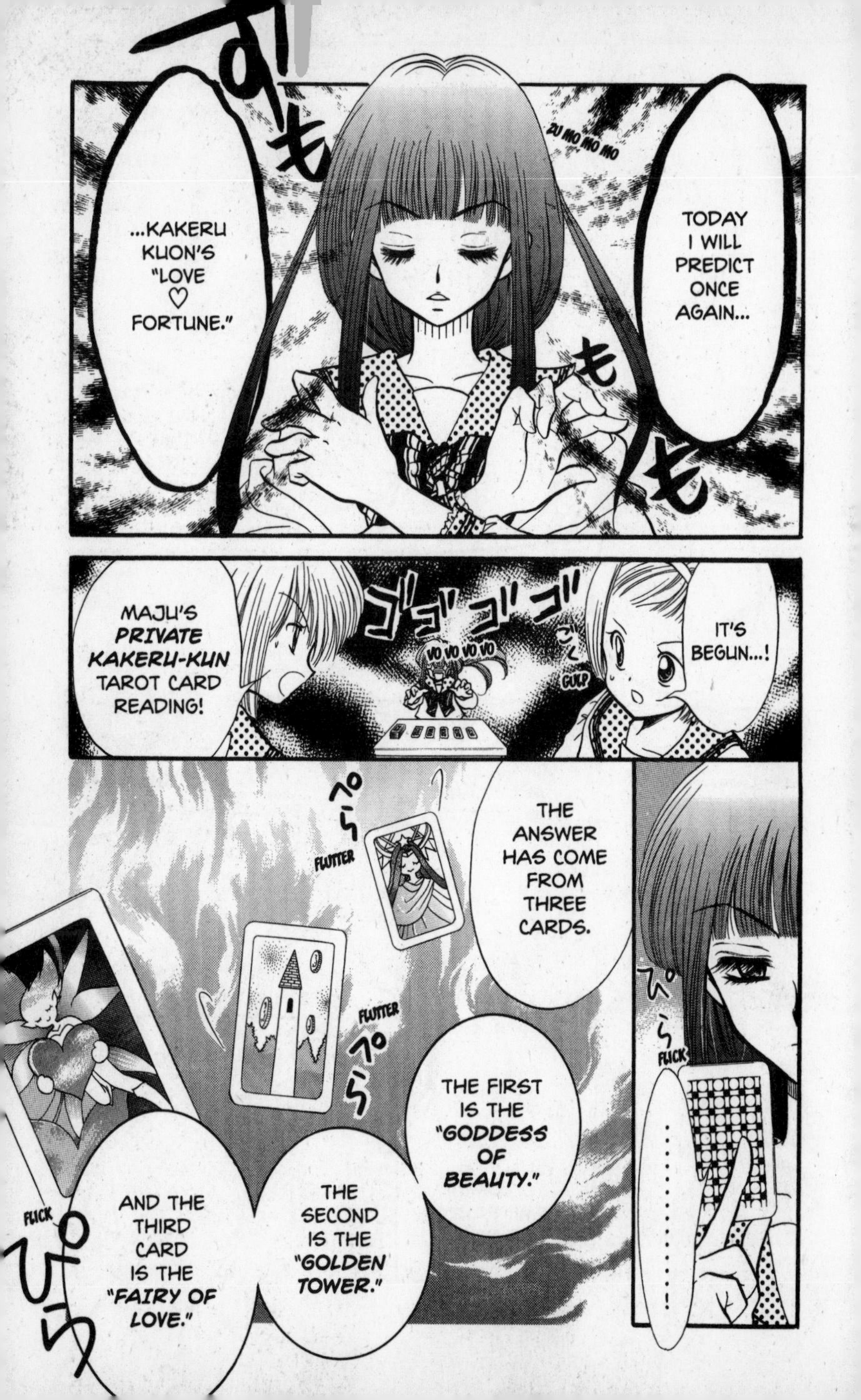
TODAY I WILL PREDICT ONCE AGAIN...
ZU MO MO MO
...KAKERU KUON'S "LOVE ♡ FORTUNE."
IT'S BEGUN...!
GULP
VO VO VO VO
MAJU'S *PRIVATE KAKERU-KUN* TAROT CARD READING!
......!
FLICK
THE ANSWER HAS COME FROM THREE CARDS.
FLUTTER
FLUTTER
THE FIRST IS THE "*GODDESS OF BEAUTY.*"
THE SECOND IS THE "*GOLDEN TOWER.*"
FLICK
AND THE THIRD CARD IS THE "*FAIRY OF LOVE.*"

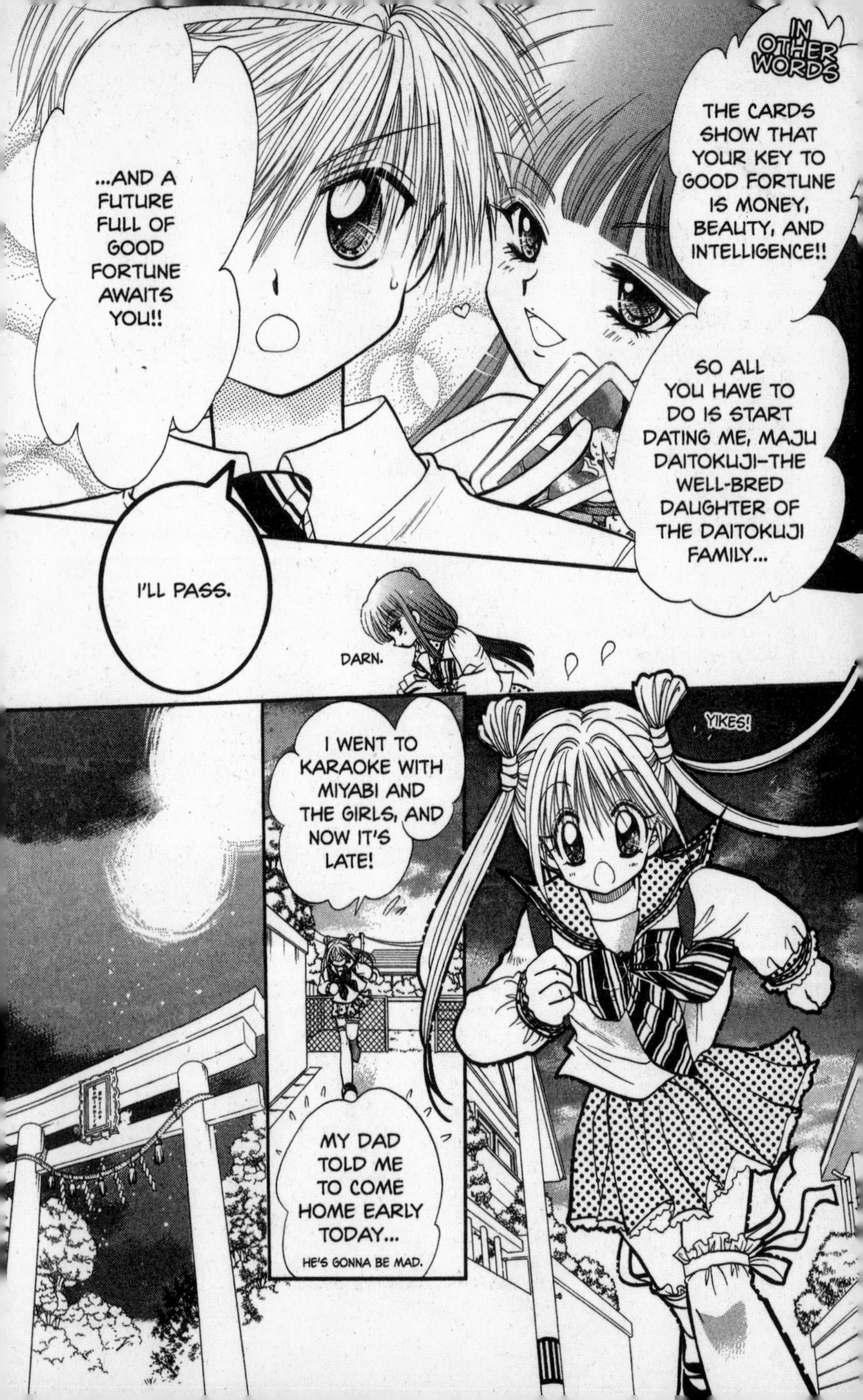
IN OTHER WORDS
THE CARDS SHOW THAT YOUR KEY TO GOOD FORTUNE IS MONEY, BEAUTY, AND INTELLIGENCE!!
...AND A FUTURE FULL OF GOOD FORTUNE AWAITS YOU!!
SO ALL YOU HAVE TO DO IS START DATING ME, MAJU DAITOKUJI–THE WELL-BRED DAUGHTER OF THE DAITOKUJI FAMILY...
I'LL PASS.
DARN.
YIKES!
I WENT TO KARAOKE WITH MIYABI AND THE GIRLS, AND NOW IT'S LATE!
MY DAD TOLD ME TO COME HOME EARLY TODAY...
HE'S GONNA BE MAD.

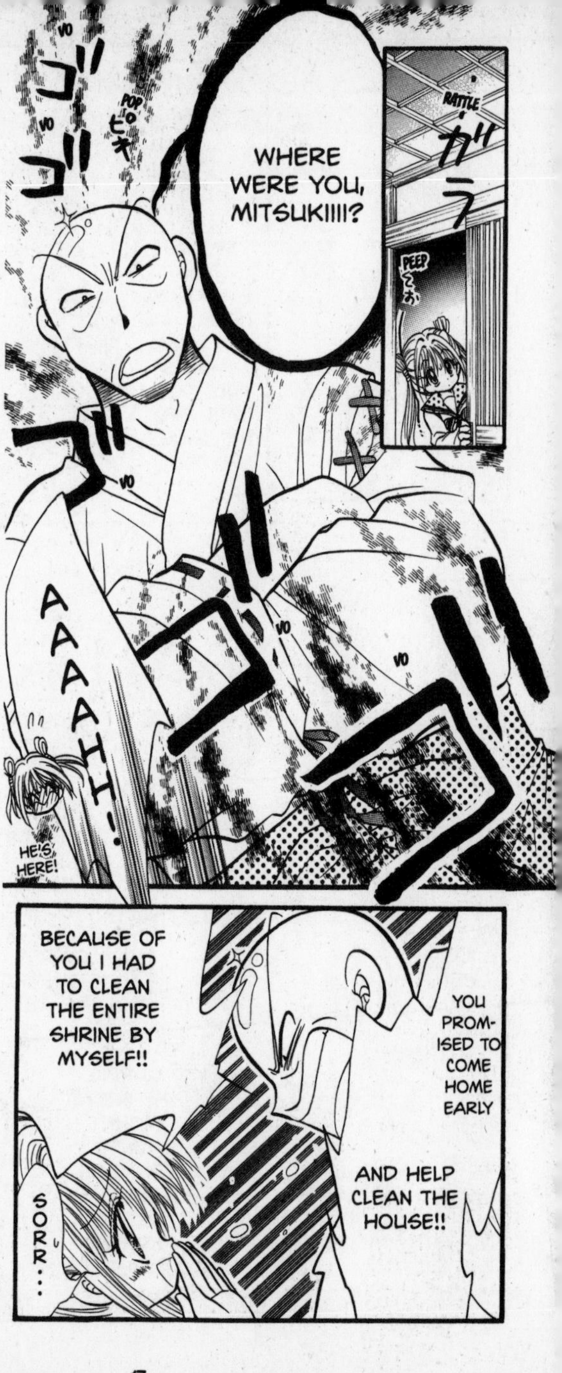
RATTLE
ガラ
PEEP
そお
WHERE WERE YOU, MITSUKI!!!!?
VO
ゴゴ
VO
POP
ピキ
VO
VO
VO
AAAAHH!!
HE'S HERE!
YOU PROM-ISED TO COME HOME EARLY
AND HELP CLEAN THE HOUSE!!
BECAUSE OF YOU I HAD TO CLEAN THE ENTIRE SHRINE BY MYSELF!!
SORR...

Nobody Cares The Author's Favorite Foods!

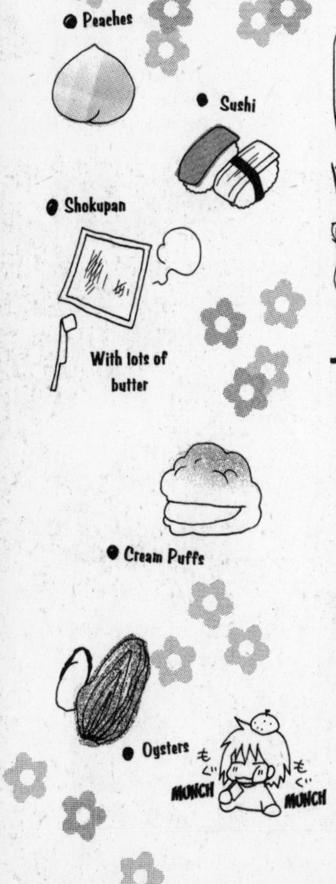
Peaches
Sushi
Shokupan
With lots of butter
Cream Puffs
Oysters
もぐ
MUNCH
もぐ
MUNCH

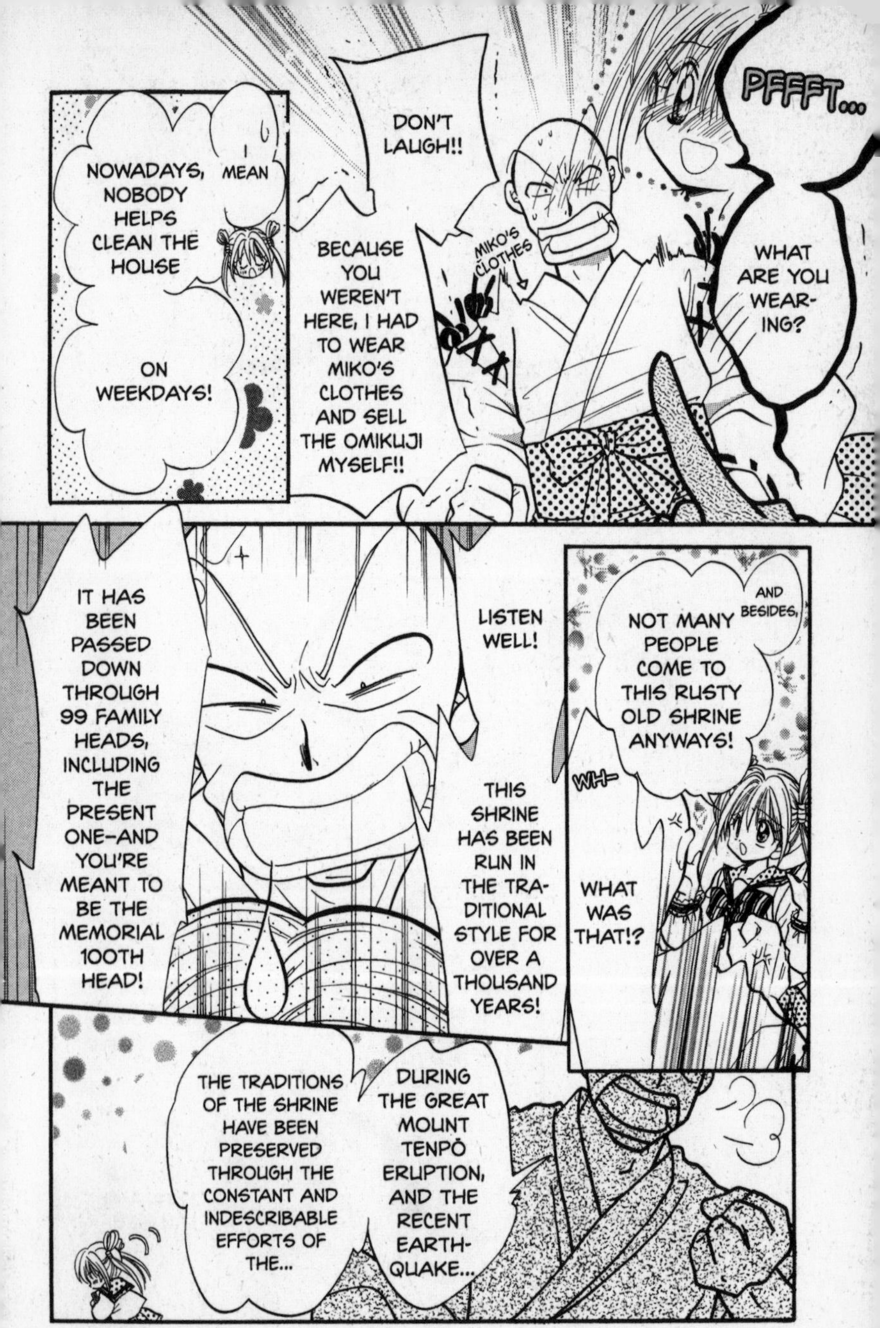
PFFFT...
WHAT ARE YOU WEAR-ING?
DON'T LAUGH!!
BECAUSE YOU WEREN'T HERE, I HAD TO WEAR MIKO'S CLOTHES AND SELL THE OMIKUJI MYSELF!!
MIKO'S CLOTHES
I MEAN
NOWADAYS, NOBODY HELPS CLEAN THE HOUSE
ON WEEKDAYS!
AND BESIDES,
NOT MANY PEOPLE COME TO THIS RUSTY OLD SHRINE ANYWAYS!
WH-
WHAT WAS THAT!?
LISTEN WELL!
THIS SHRINE HAS BEEN RUN IN THE TRA-DITIONAL STYLE FOR OVER A THOUSAND YEARS!
IT HAS BEEN PASSED DOWN THROUGH 99 FAMILY HEADS, INCLUDING THE PRESENT ONE–AND YOU'RE MEANT TO BE THE MEMORIAL 100TH HEAD!
DURING THE GREAT MOUNT TENPŌ ERUPTION, AND THE RECENT EARTH-QUAKE...
THE TRADITIONS OF THE SHRINE HAVE BEEN PRESERVED THROUGH THE CONSTANT AND INDESCRIBABLE EFFORTS OF THE...

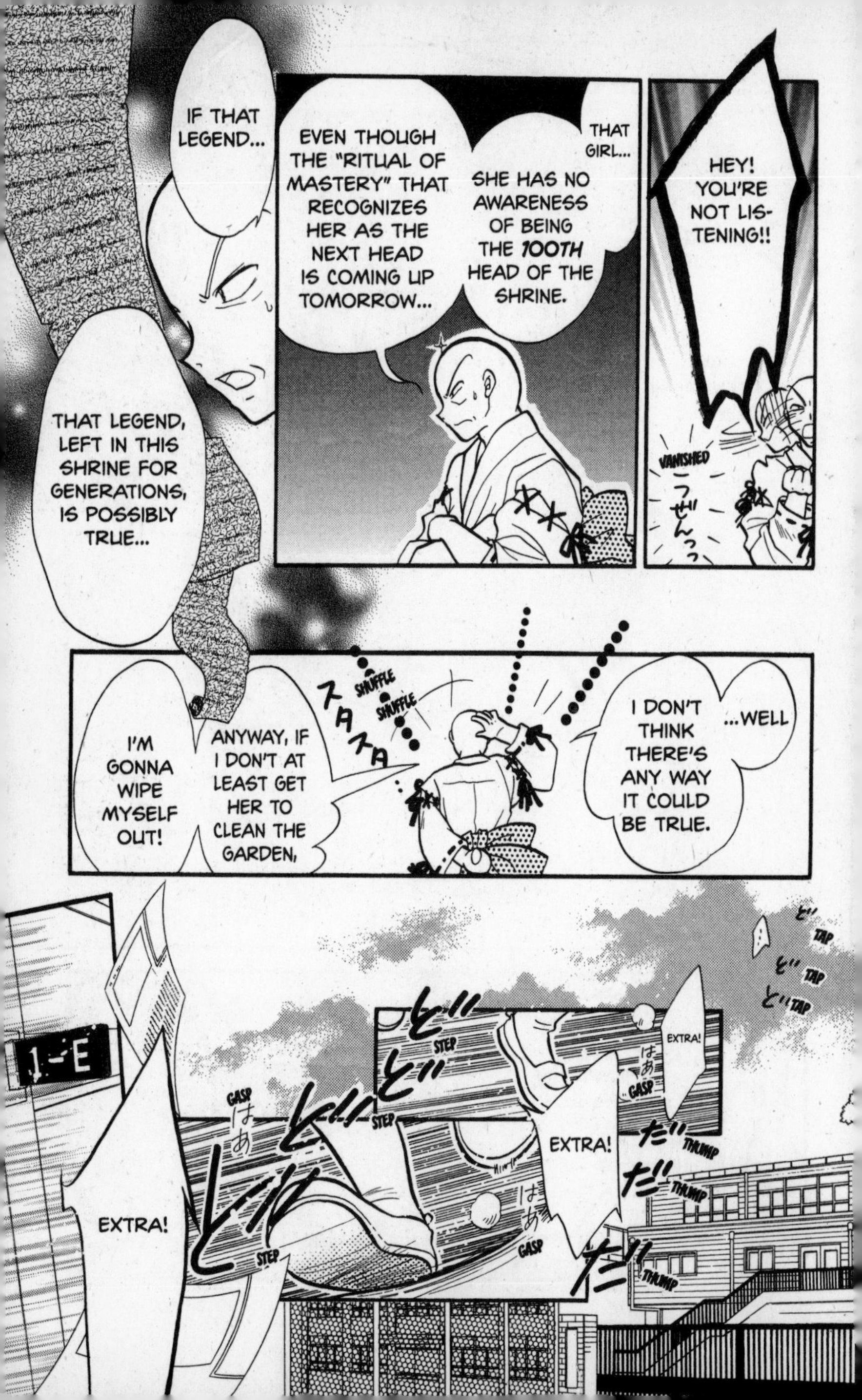

HEY! YOU'RE NOT LIS-TENING!!
VANISHED
つぜんっっ
THAT GIRL...
SHE HAS NO AWARENESS OF BEING THE *100TH* HEAD OF THE SHRINE.
EVEN THOUGH THE "RITUAL OF MASTERY" THAT RECOGNIZES HER AS THE NEXT HEAD IS COMING UP TOMORROW...
IF THAT LEGEND...
THAT LEGEND, LEFT IN THIS SHRINE FOR GENERATIONS, IS POSSIBLY TRUE...
...WELL
I DON'T THINK THERE'S ANY WAY IT COULD BE TRUE.
SHUFFLE SHUFFLE
スタスタ
ANYWAY, IF I DON'T AT LEAST GET HER TO CLEAN THE GARDEN,
I'M GONNA WIPE MYSELF OUT!
ど TAP ど TAP ど TAP
EXTRA!
はあ GASP
だ THUMP だ THUMP だ THUMP
EXTRA!
ど STEP ど STEP ど STEP
はあ GASP
はあ GASP
1-E
EXTRA!

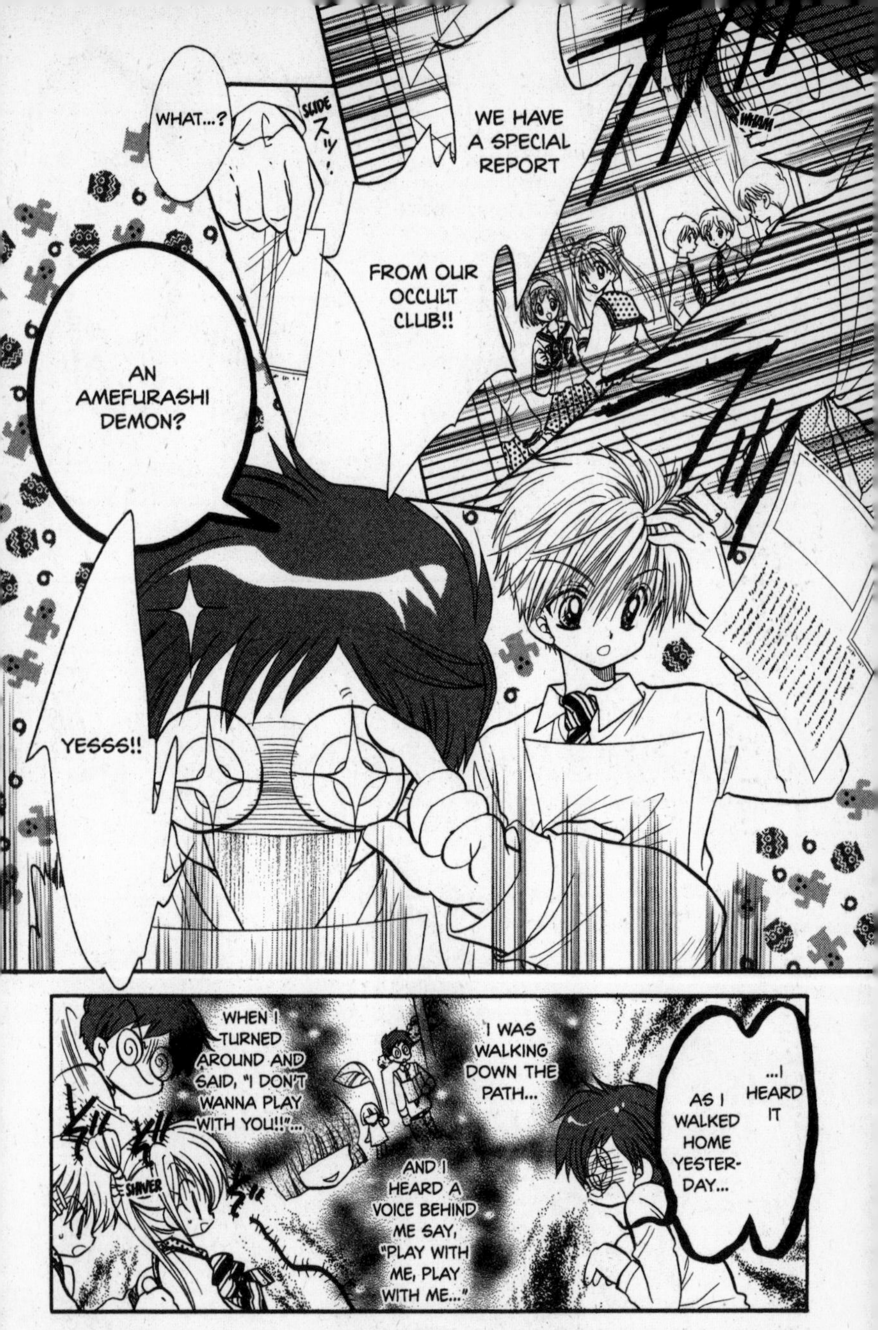
WHAM
WE HAVE A SPECIAL REPORT
FROM OUR OCCULT CLUB!!
SLIDE
WHAT...?
AN AMEFURASHI DEMON?
YESSS!!
AS I WALKED HOME YESTER-DAY... ...I HEARD IT
I WAS WALKING DOWN THE PATH...
AND I HEARD A VOICE BEHIND ME SAY, "PLAY WITH ME, PLAY WITH ME..."
WHEN I TURNED AROUND AND SAID, "I DON'T WANNA PLAY WITH YOU!!"...
SHIVER

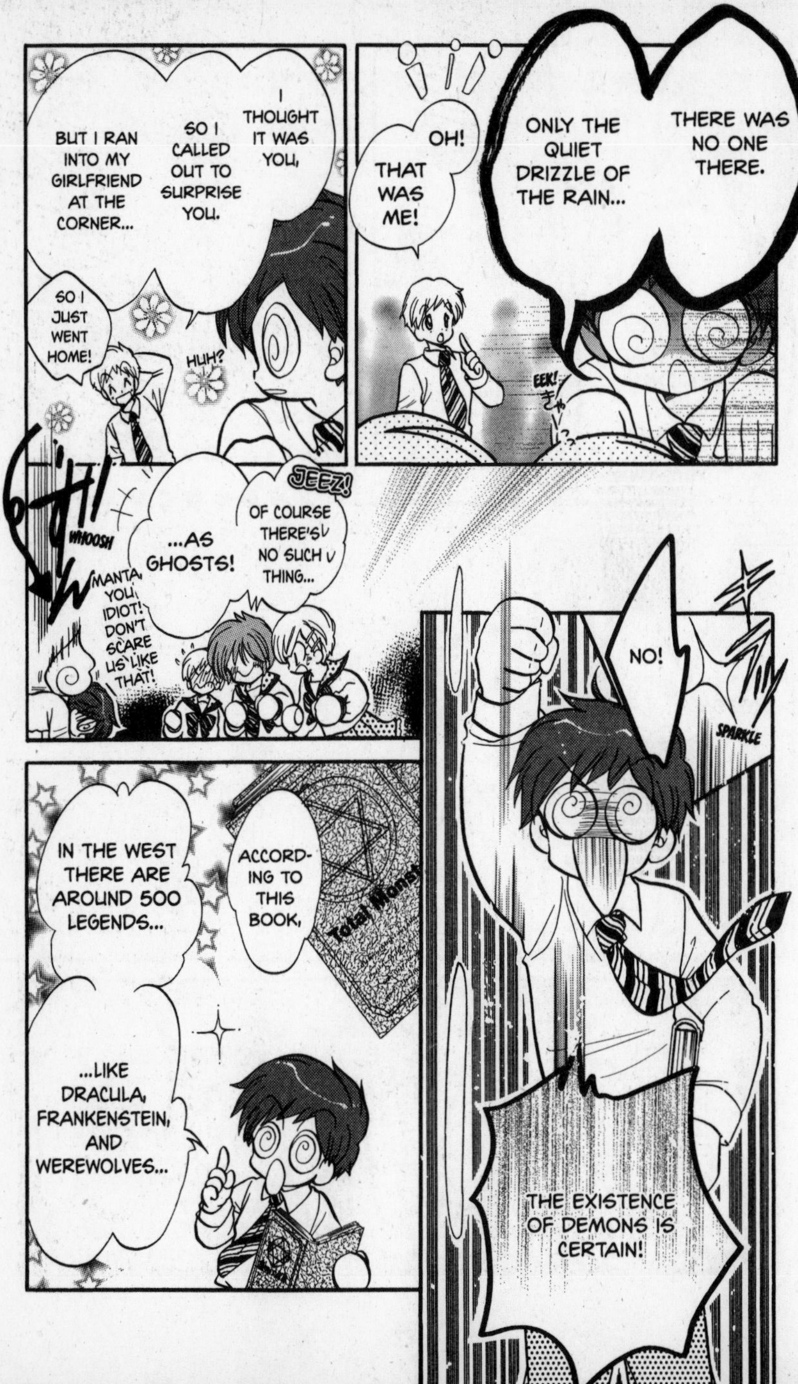
THERE WAS NO ONE THERE.
ONLY THE QUIET DRIZZLE OF THE RAIN...
OH!
THAT WAS ME!
EEK!
I THOUGHT IT WAS YOU,
SO I CALLED OUT TO SURPRISE YOU.
BUT I RAN INTO MY GIRLFRIEND AT THE CORNER...
HUH?
SO I JUST WENT HOME!
JEEZ!
OF COURSE THERE'S NO SUCH THING...
...AS GHOSTS!
WHOOSH
MANTA, YOU IDIOT! DON'T SCARE US LIKE THAT!
NO!
SPARKLE
THE EXISTENCE OF DEMONS IS CERTAIN!
ACCORDING TO THIS BOOK,
IN THE WEST THERE ARE AROUND 500 LEGENDS...
...LIKE DRACULA, FRANKENSTEIN, AND WEREWOLVES...

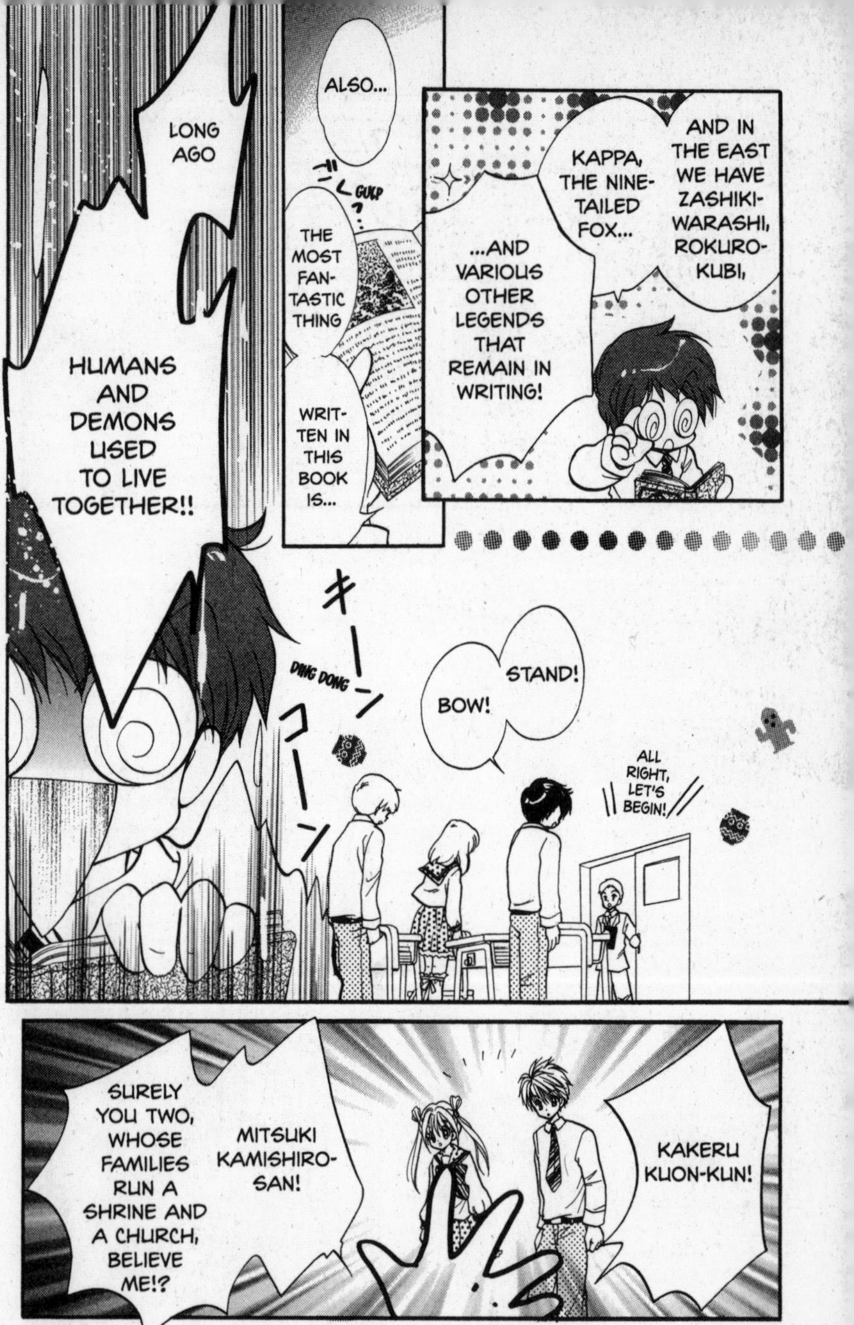
ALSO...
GULP
THE MOST FANTASTIC THING
WRITTEN IN THIS BOOK IS...
AND IN THE EAST WE HAVE ZASHIKI-WARASHI, ROKURO-KUBI,
KAPPA, THE NINE-TAILED FOX...
...AND VARIOUS OTHER LEGENDS THAT REMAIN IN WRITING!
LONG AGO
HUMANS AND DEMONS USED TO LIVE TOGETHER!!
DING DONG
STAND!
BOW!
ALL RIGHT, LET'S BEGIN!
KAKERU KUON-KUN!
MITSUKI KAMISHIRO-SAN!
SURELY YOU TWO, WHOSE FAMILIES RUN A SHRINE AND A CHURCH, BELIEVE ME!?

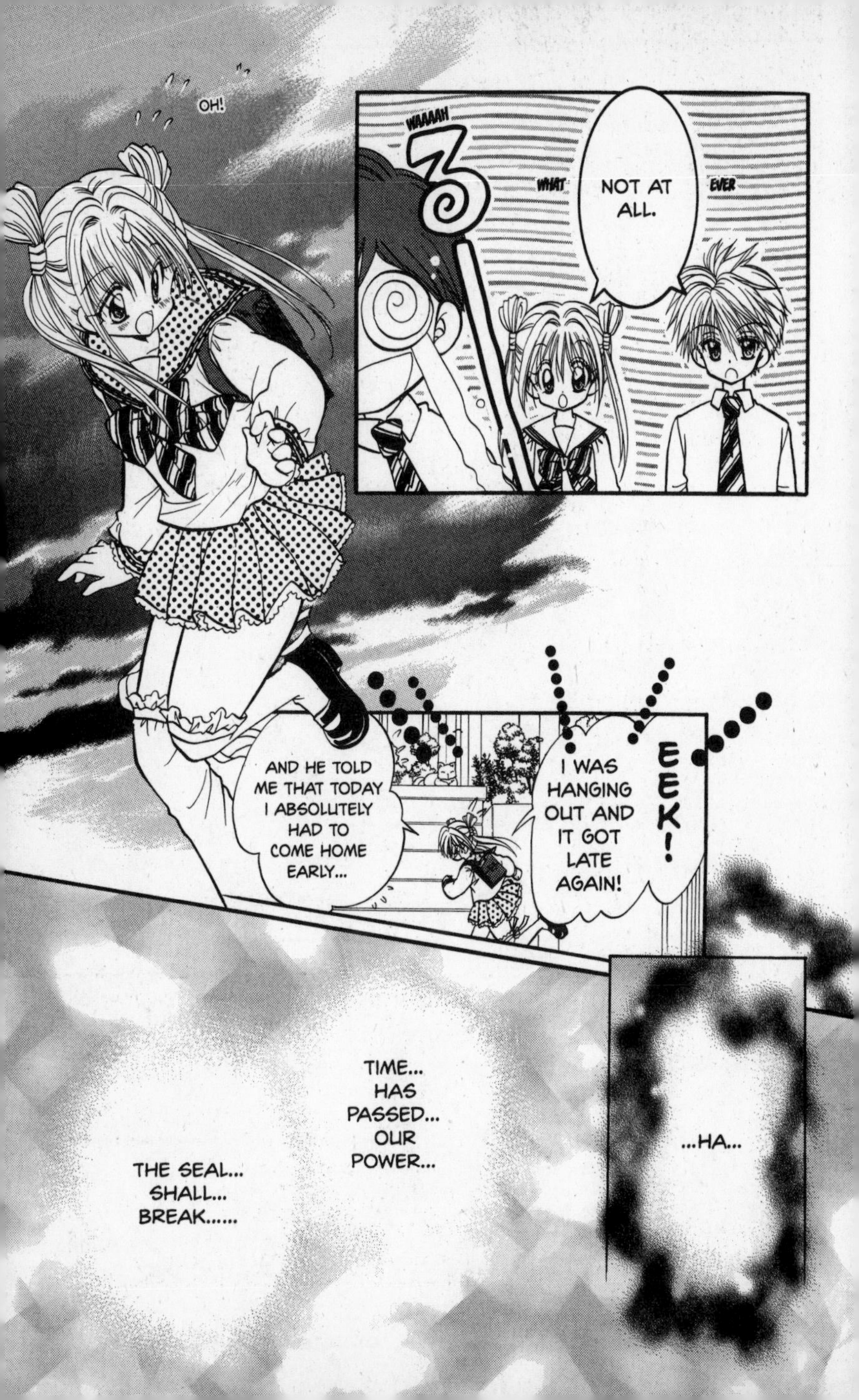
WAAAAH
WHAT
NOT AT ALL.
EVER
EEK!
I WAS HANGING OUT AND IT GOT LATE AGAIN!
AND HE TOLD ME THAT TODAY I ABSOLUTELY HAD TO COME HOME EARLY...
OH!
...HA...
TIME... HAS PASSED... OUR POWER...
THE SEAL... SHALL... BREAK......

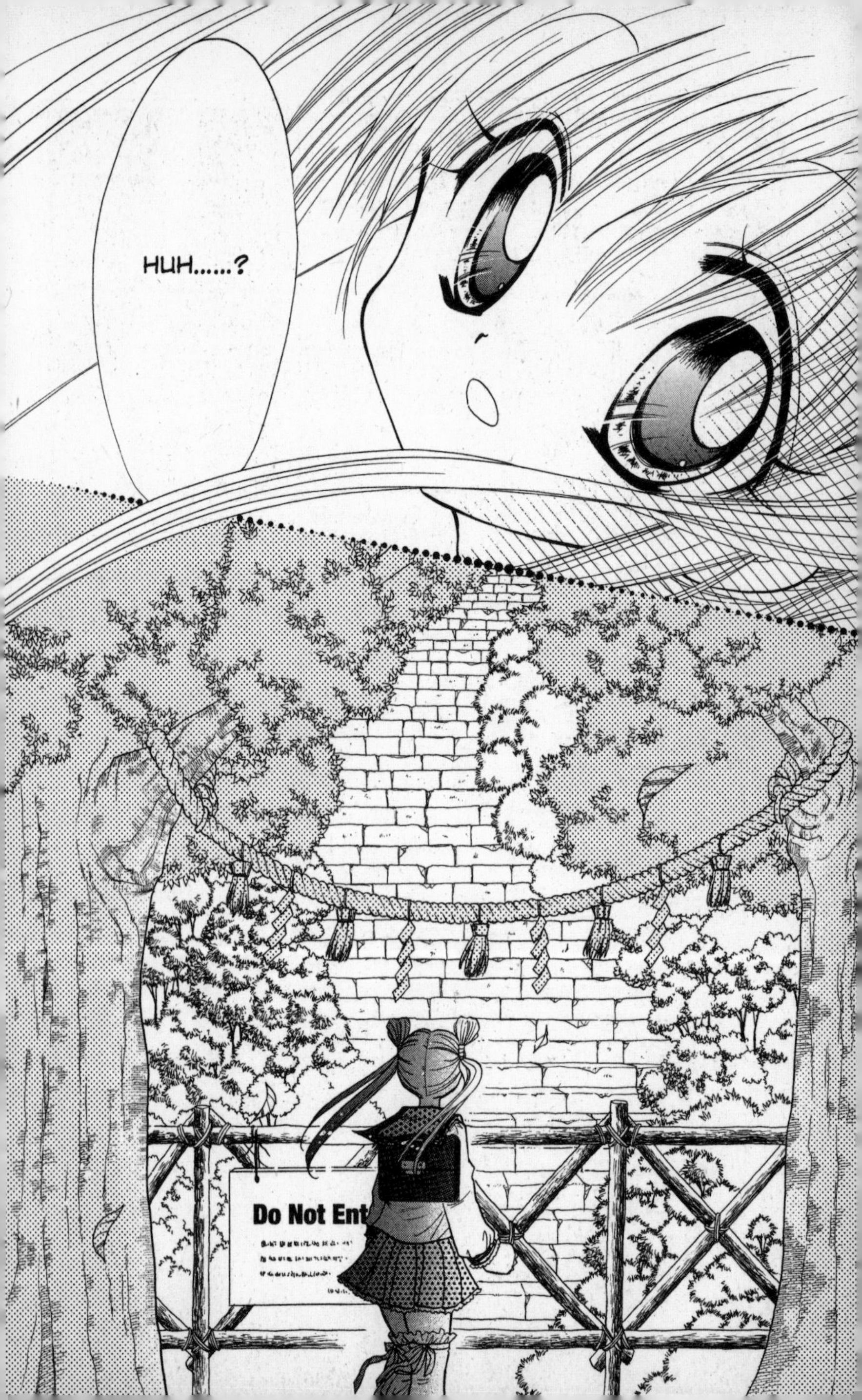
HUH......?
Do Not Ent

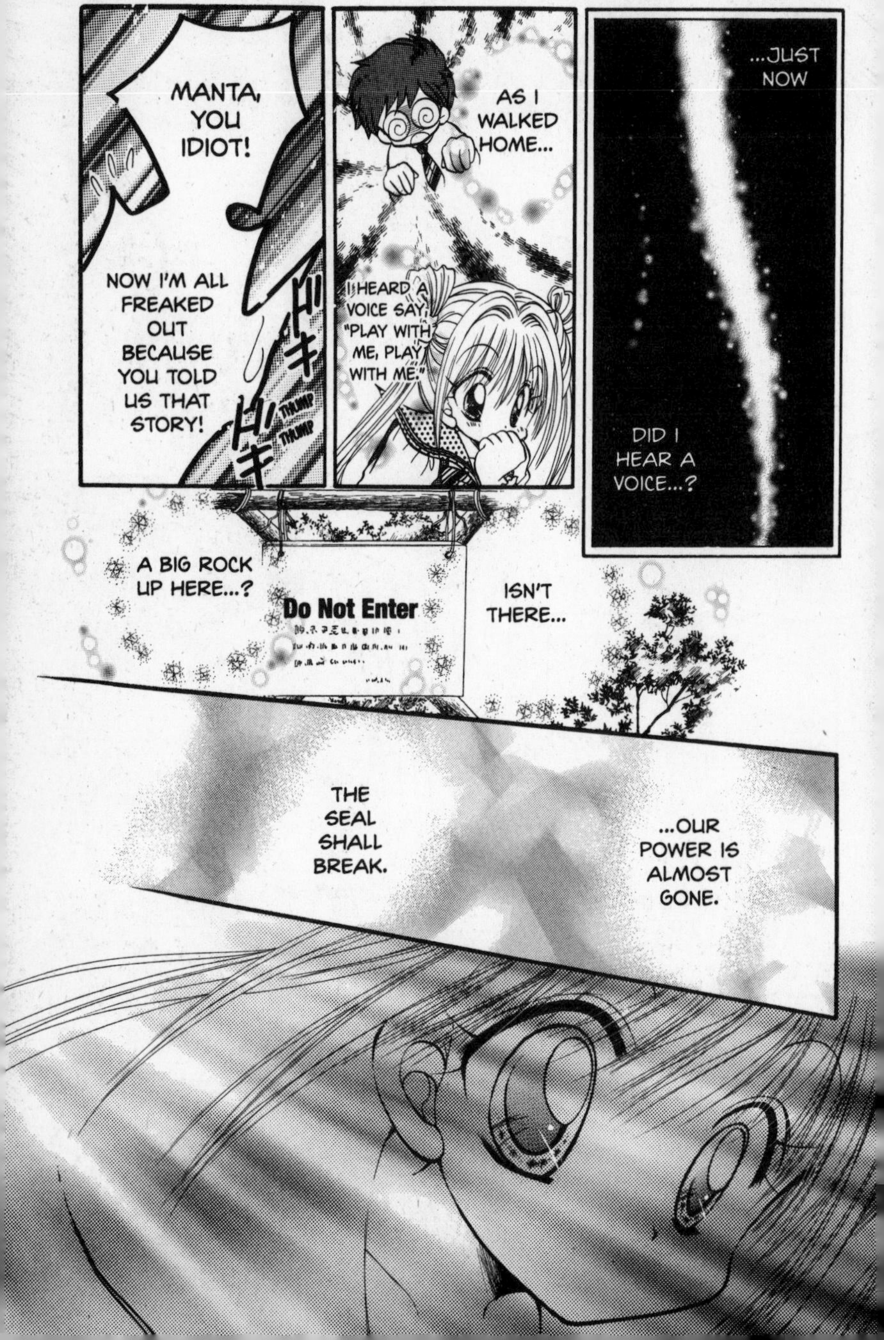
...JUST NOW
DID I HEAR A VOICE...?
AS I WALKED HOME...
I HEARD A VOICE SAY, "PLAY WITH ME, PLAY WITH ME."
MANTA, YOU IDIOT!
NOW I'M ALL FREAKED OUT BECAUSE YOU TOLD US THAT STORY!
THUMP THUMP
ISN'T THERE...
Do Not Enter
A BIG ROCK UP HERE...?
...OUR POWER IS ALMOST GONE.
THE SEAL SHALL BREAK.

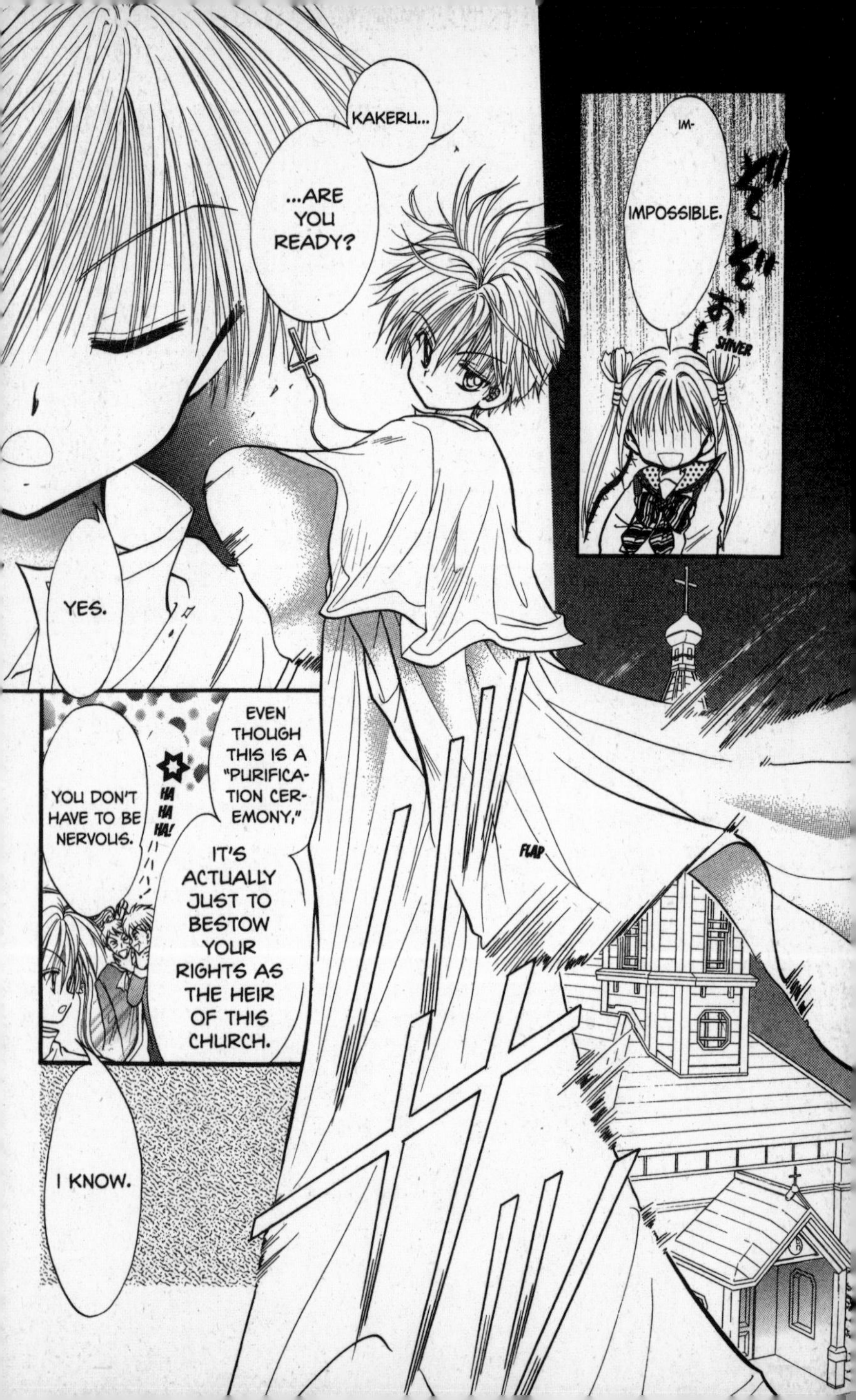
IM-
IMPOSSIBLE.
SHIVER
KAKERU...
...ARE YOU READY?
YES.
FLAP
EVEN THOUGH THIS IS A "PURIFICATION CEREMONY,"
IT'S ACTUALLY JUST TO BESTOW YOUR RIGHTS AS THE HEIR OF THIS CHURCH.
HA HA HA!
YOU DON'T HAVE TO BE NERVOUS.
I KNOW.

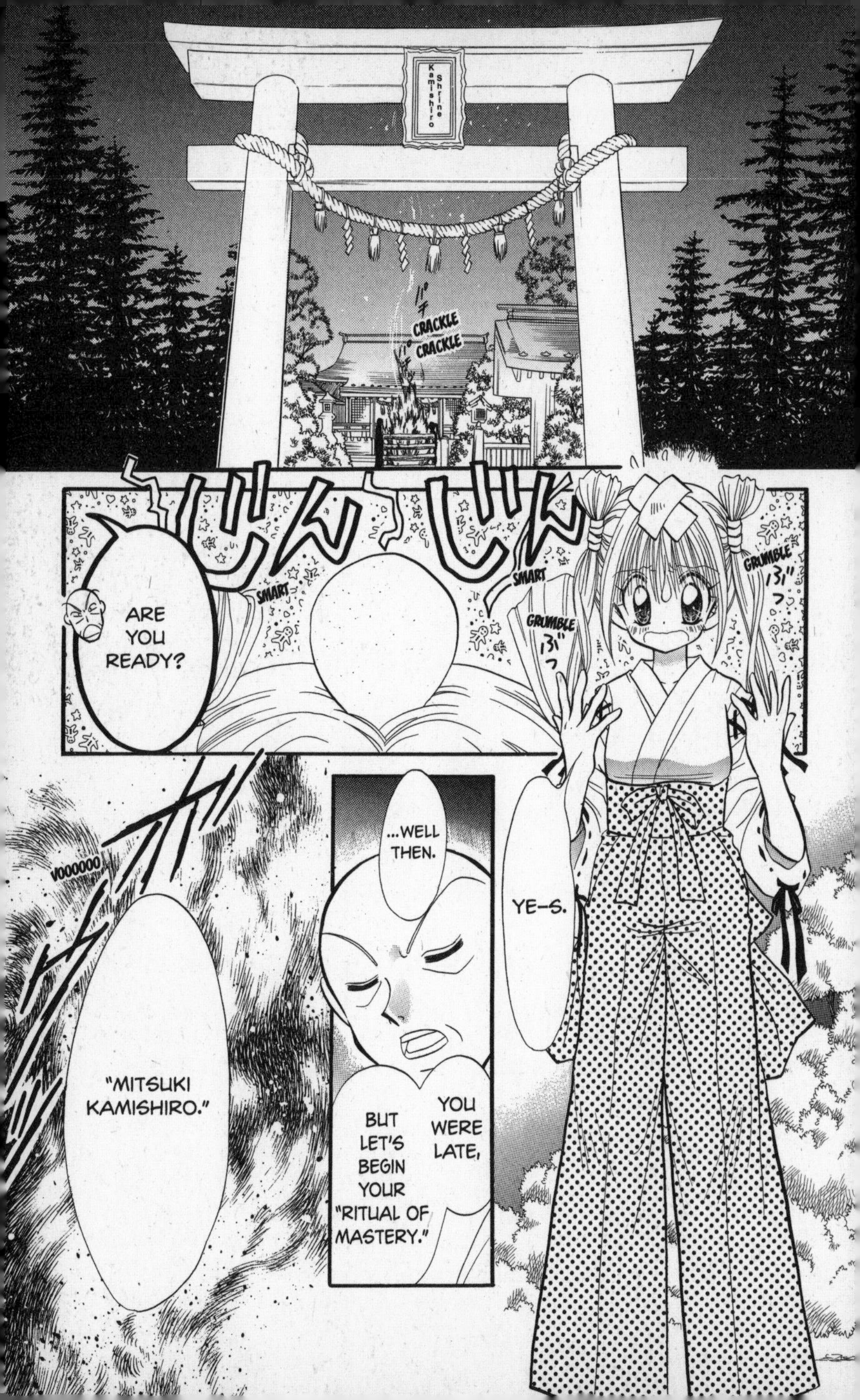
Kamishiro Shrine
CRACKLE
CRACKLE
じんじん
GRUMBLE
ぶつ
SMART
GRUMBLE
ぶつ
SMART
ARE YOU READY?
YE-S.
...WELL THEN.
YOU WERE LATE,
BUT LET'S BEGIN YOUR "RITUAL OF MASTERY."
VOOOOOO
"MITSUKI KAMISHIRO."

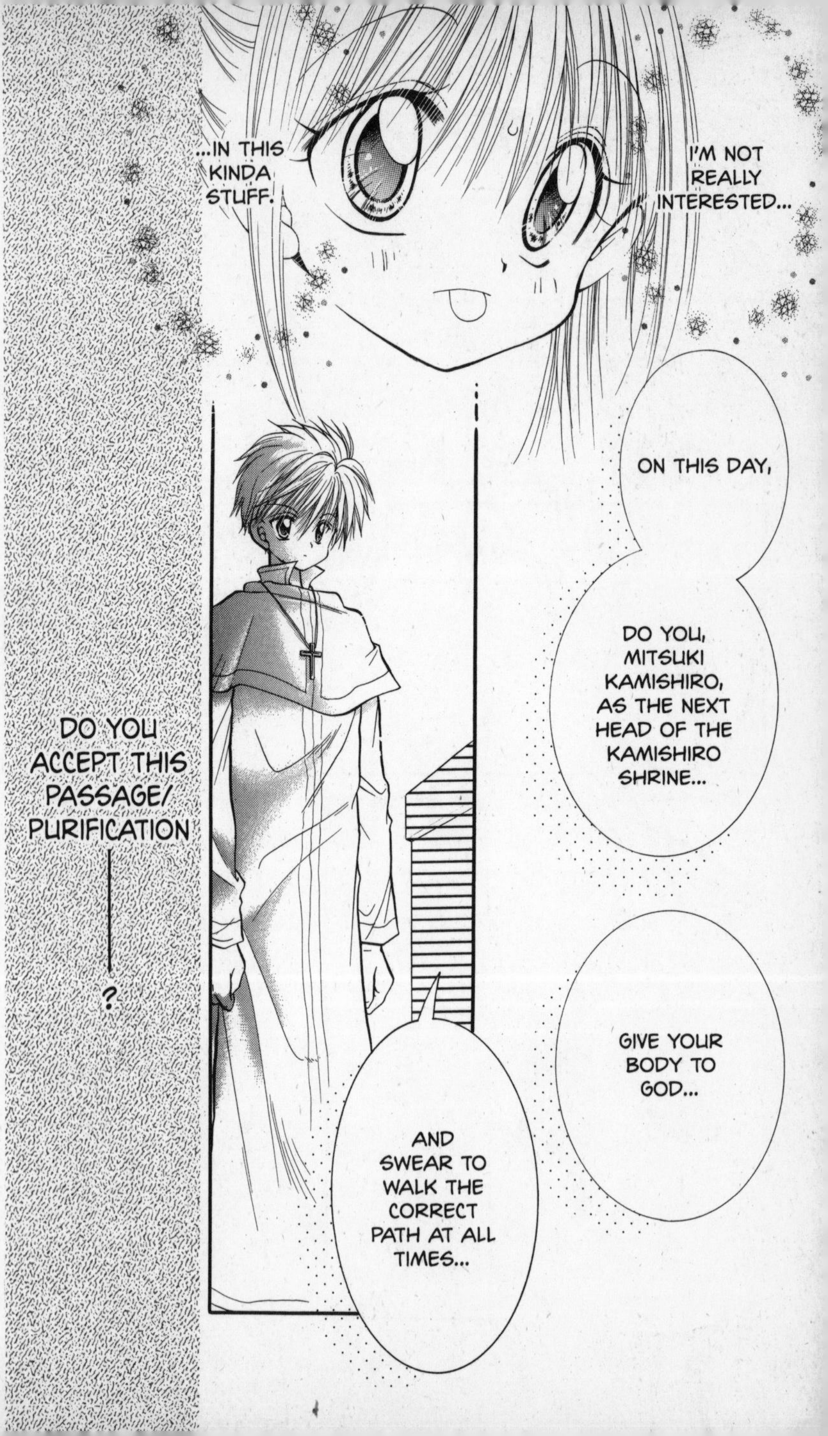
I'M NOT REALLY INTERESTED...
...IN THIS KINDA STUFF.
ON THIS DAY,
DO YOU, MITSUKI KAMISHIRO, AS THE NEXT HEAD OF THE KAMISHIRO SHRINE...
GIVE YOUR BODY TO GOD...
AND SWEAR TO WALK THE CORRECT PATH AT ALL TIMES...
DO YOU ACCEPT THIS PASSAGE/PURIFICATION
?

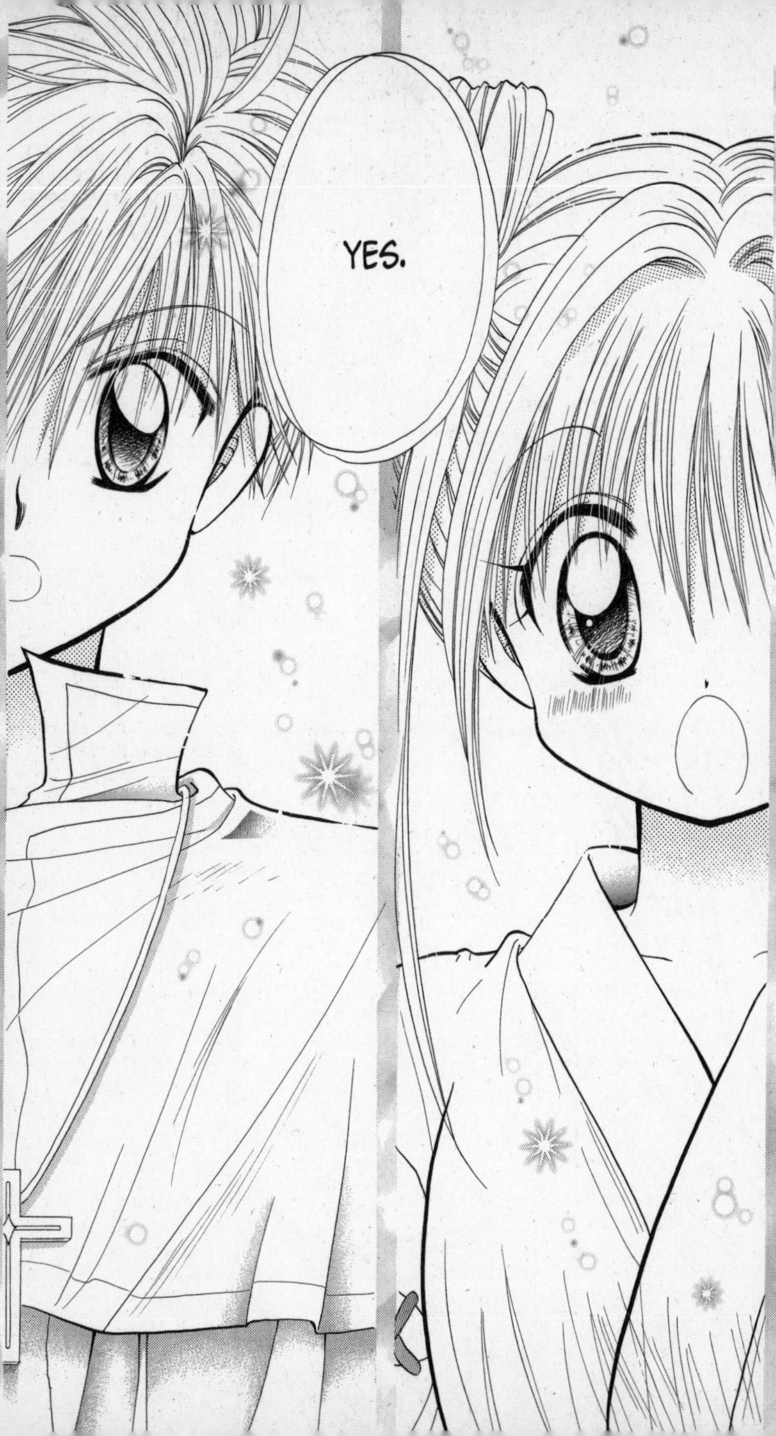
YES.

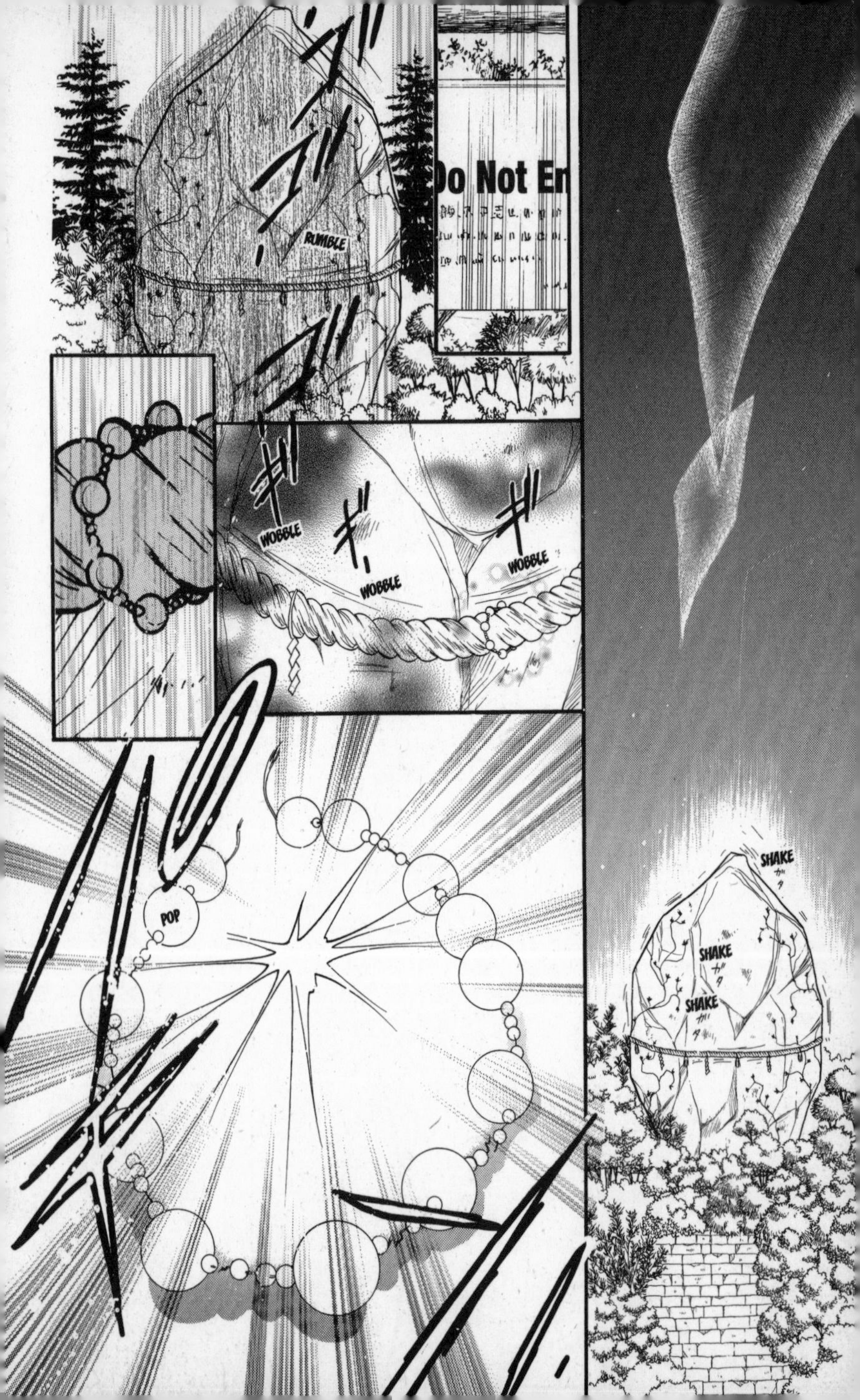
SHAKE
SHAKE
SHAKE
Do Not En
RUMBLE
WOBBLE
WOBBLE
WOBBLE
POP

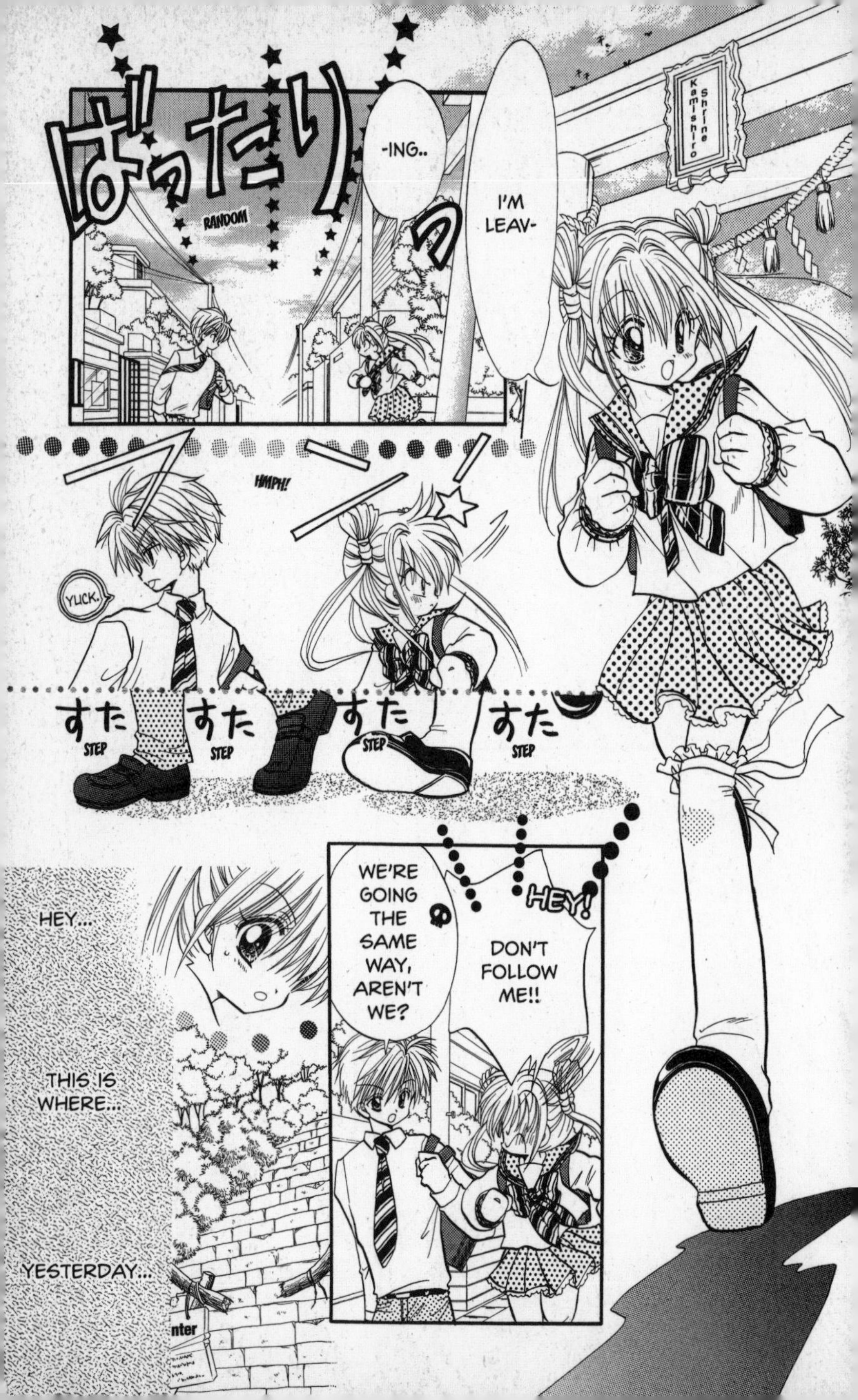
Kamishiro Shrine
I'M LEAV-
-ING..
ぱったり
RANDOM
HMPH!
YUCK.
すた
STEP
すた
STEP
すた
STEP
すた
STEP
HEY!
DON'T FOLLOW ME!!
WE'RE GOING THE SAME WAY, AREN'T WE?
HEY...
THIS IS WHERE...
YESTERDAY...

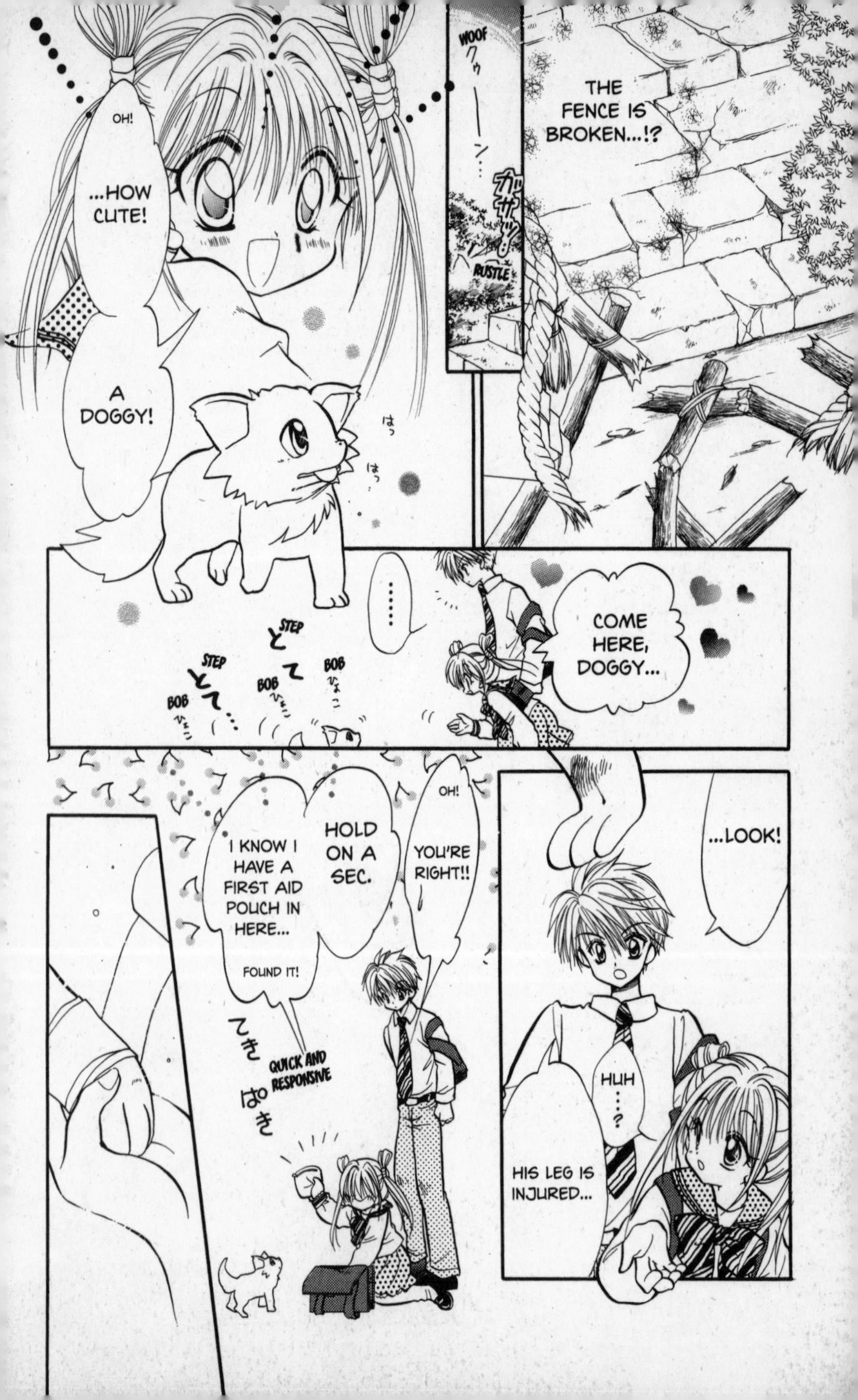
THE FENCE IS BROKEN...!?
WOOF
クゥーン…
ガサッ
RUSTLE
OH!
...HOW CUTE!
A DOGGY!
はっ はっ
COME HERE, DOGGY...
......
STEP
とて
STEP
とて…
BOB
ひょこ
BOB
ひょこ
BOB
ひょこ
...LOOK!
HUH...?
HIS LEG IS INJURED...
OH!
YOU'RE RIGHT!!
HOLD ON A SEC.
I KNOW I HAVE A FIRST AID POUCH IN HERE...
FOUND IT!
てきぱき
QUICK AND RESPONSIVE

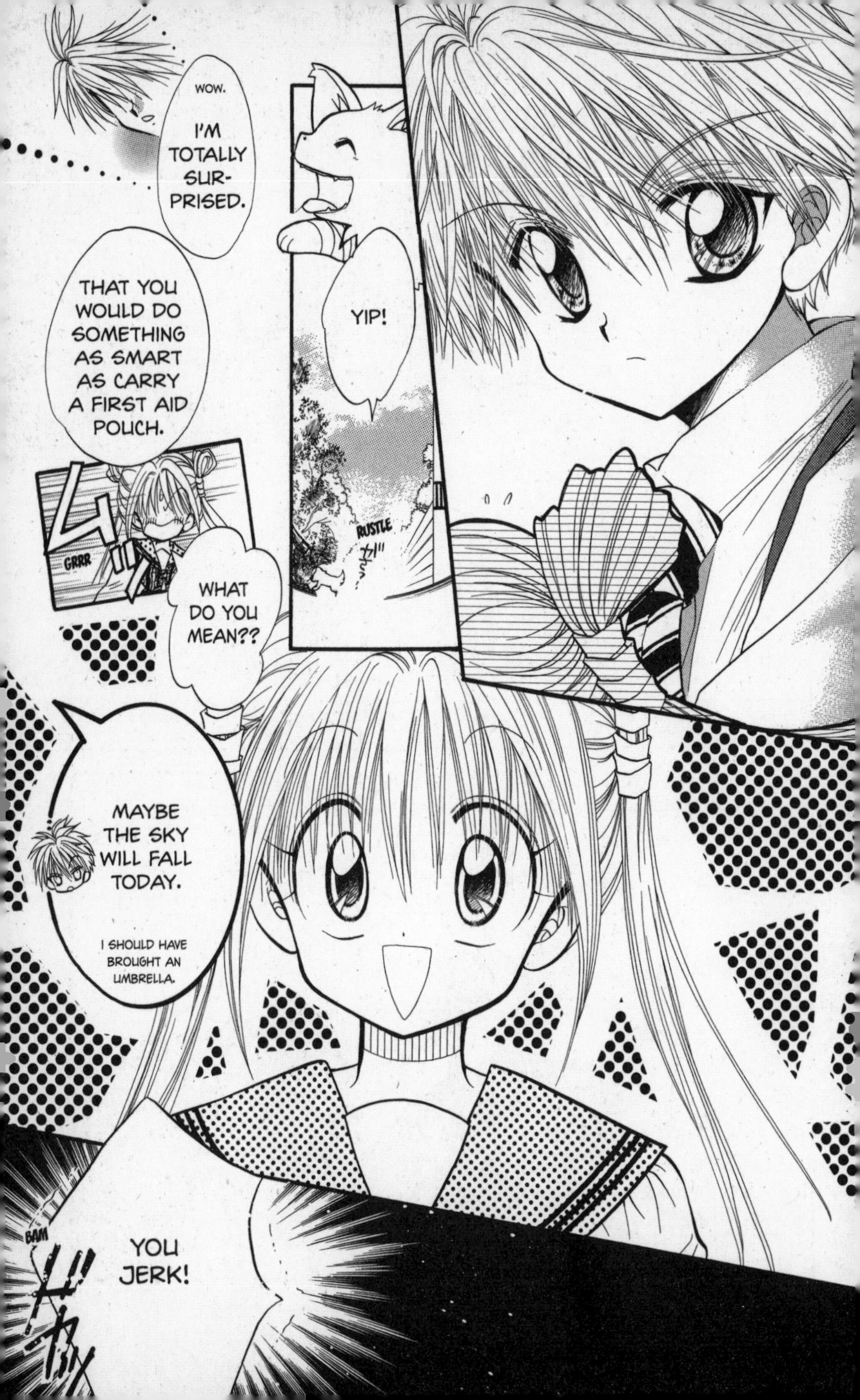
WOW.
I'M TOTALLY SUR-PRISED.
THAT YOU WOULD DO SOMETHING AS SMART AS CARRY A FIRST AID POUCH.
YIP!
RUSTLE
GRRR
WHAT DO YOU MEAN??
MAYBE THE SKY WILL FALL TODAY.
I SHOULD HAVE BROUGHT AN UMBRELLA.
BAM
YOU JERK!

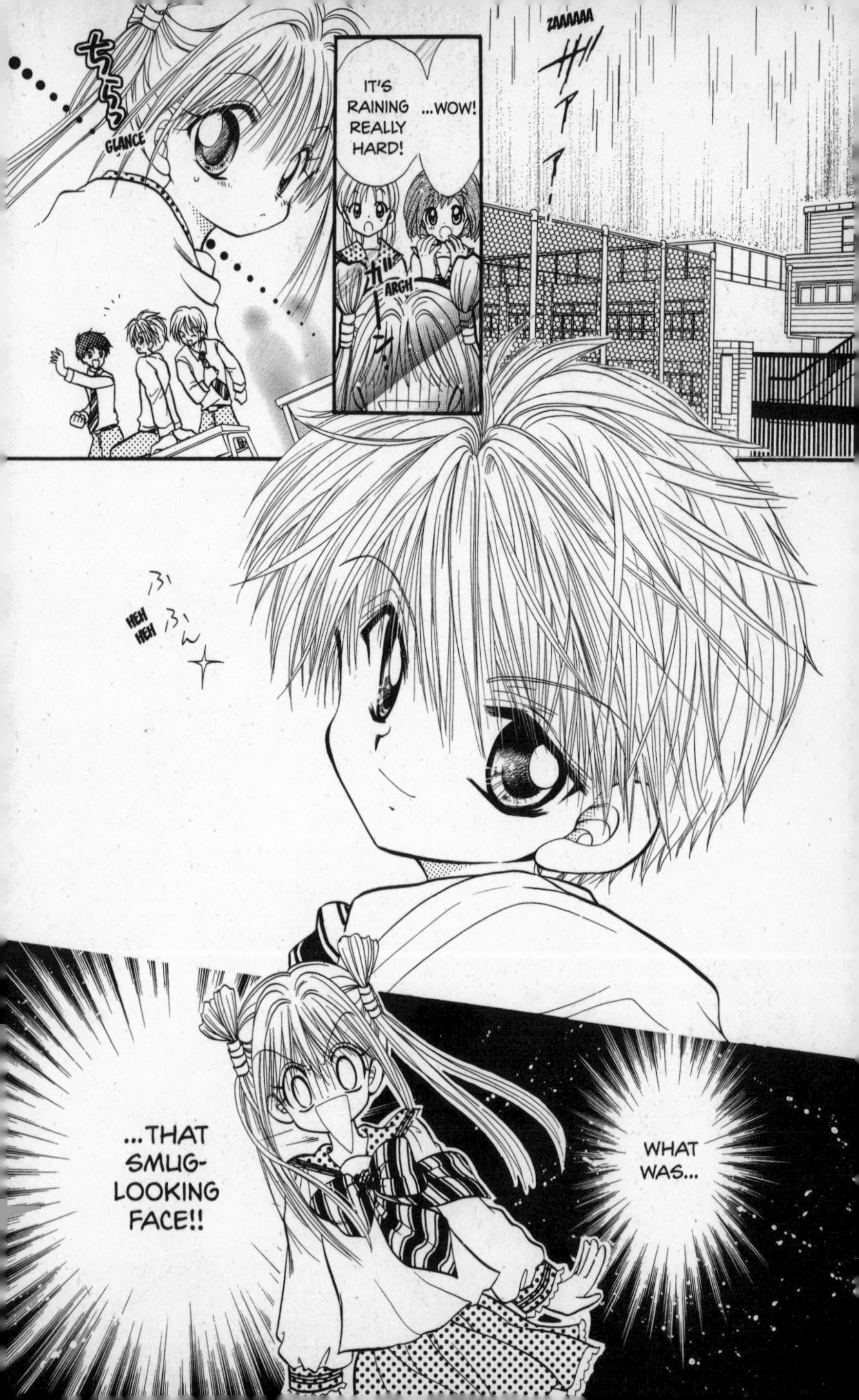
ZAAAAAA
IT'S RAINING REALLY HARD!
...WOW!
ARGH
GLANCE
HEH HEH
WHAT WAS...
...THAT SMUG-LOOKING FACE!!

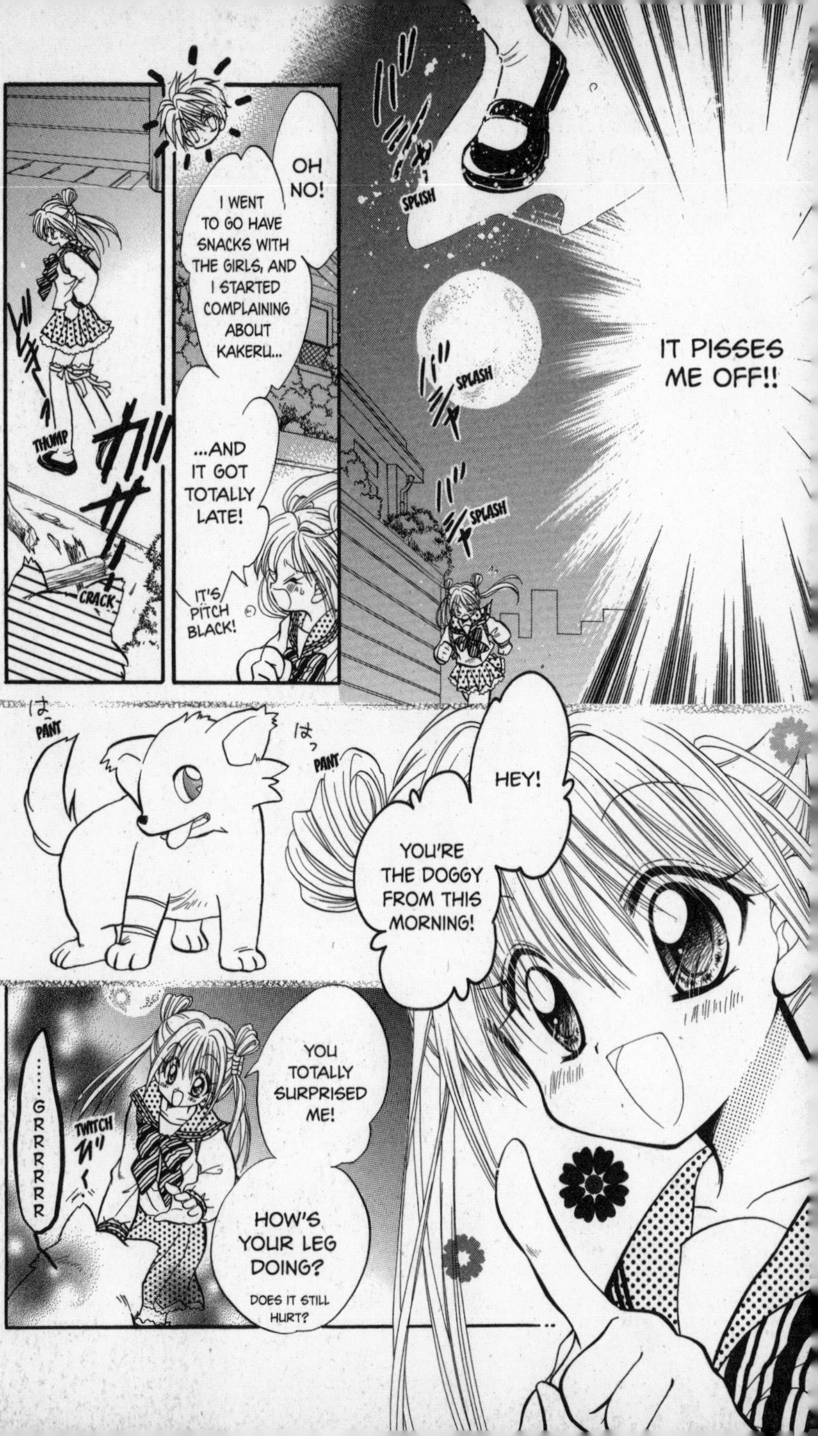
SPLISH
IT PISSES ME OFF!!
SPLASH
SPLASH
OH NO!
I WENT TO GO HAVE SNACKS WITH THE GIRLS, AND I STARTED COMPLAINING ABOUT KAKERU...
...AND IT GOT TOTALLY LATE!
IT'S PITCH BLACK!
THUMP
CRACK
HEY!
YOU'RE THE DOGGY FROM THIS MORNING!
PANT
PANT
YOU TOTALLY SURPRISED ME!
HOW'S YOUR LEG DOING?
DOES IT STILL HURT?
TWITCH
.....GRRRRR

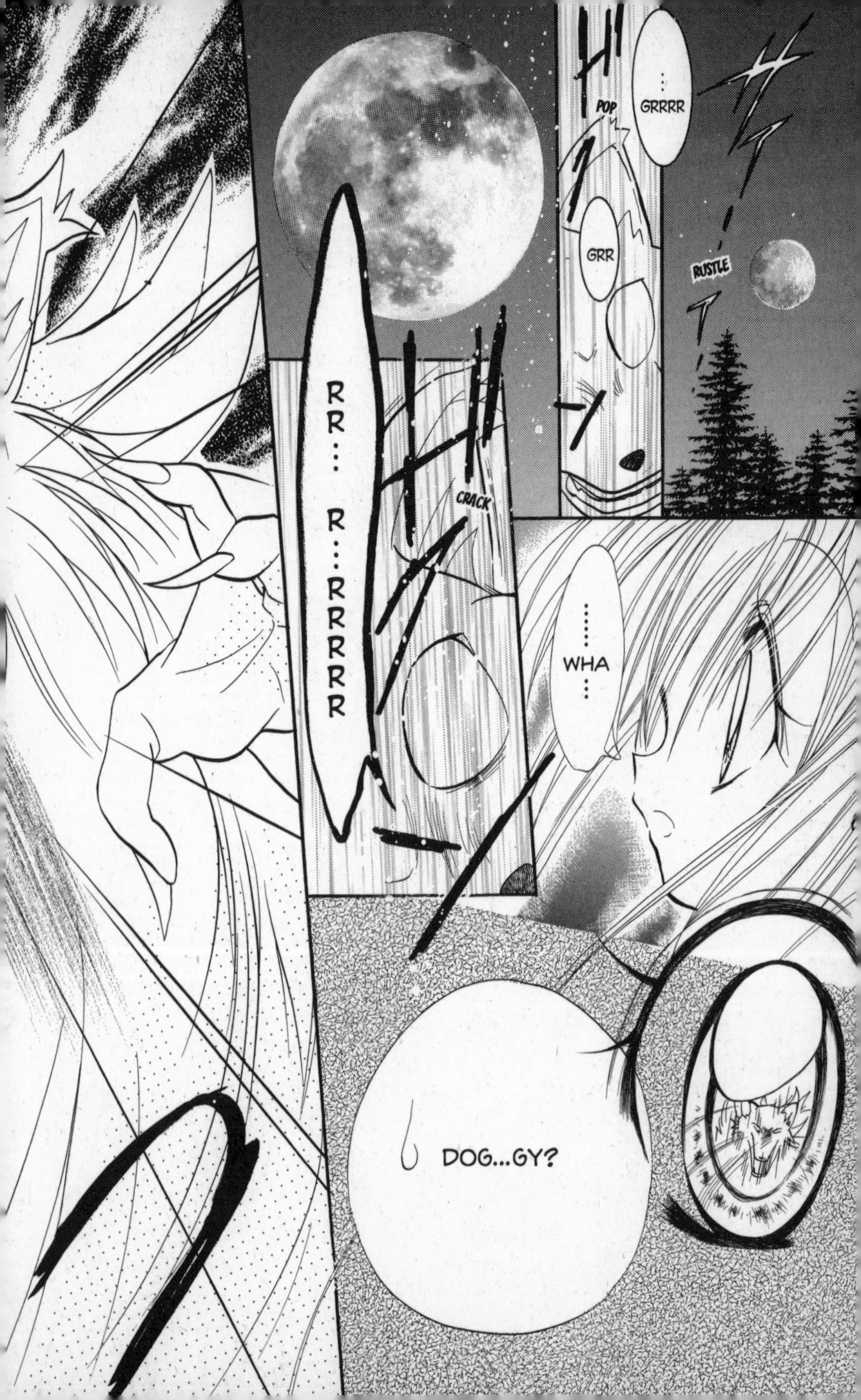
RUSTLE
…GRRRR
POP
GRR
CRACK
RR… R…RRRRR
…WHA…
DOG…GY?

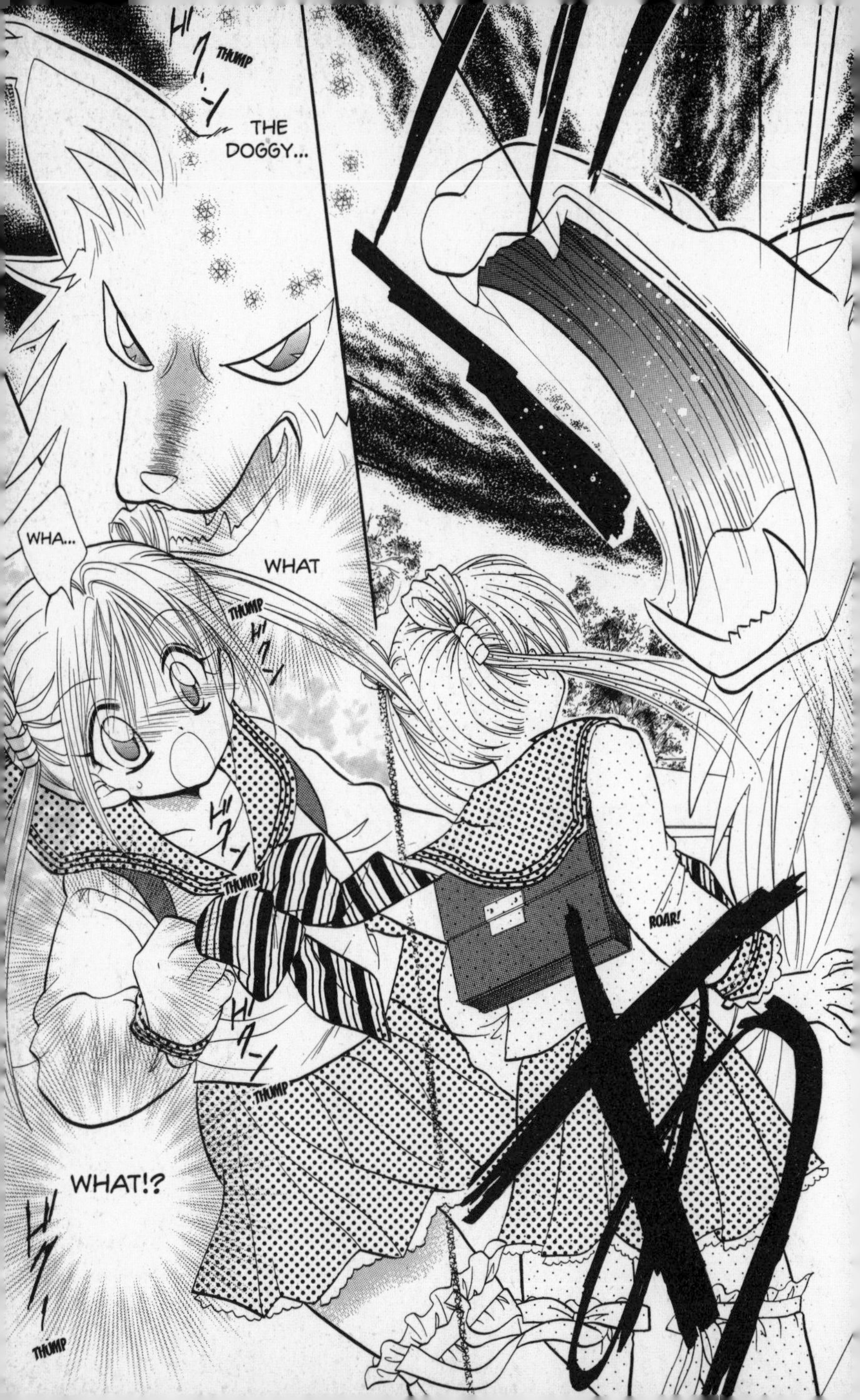
THUMP
THE DOGGY...
ROAR!
WHA...
WHAT
THUMP
THUMP
THUMP
WHAT!?
THUMP

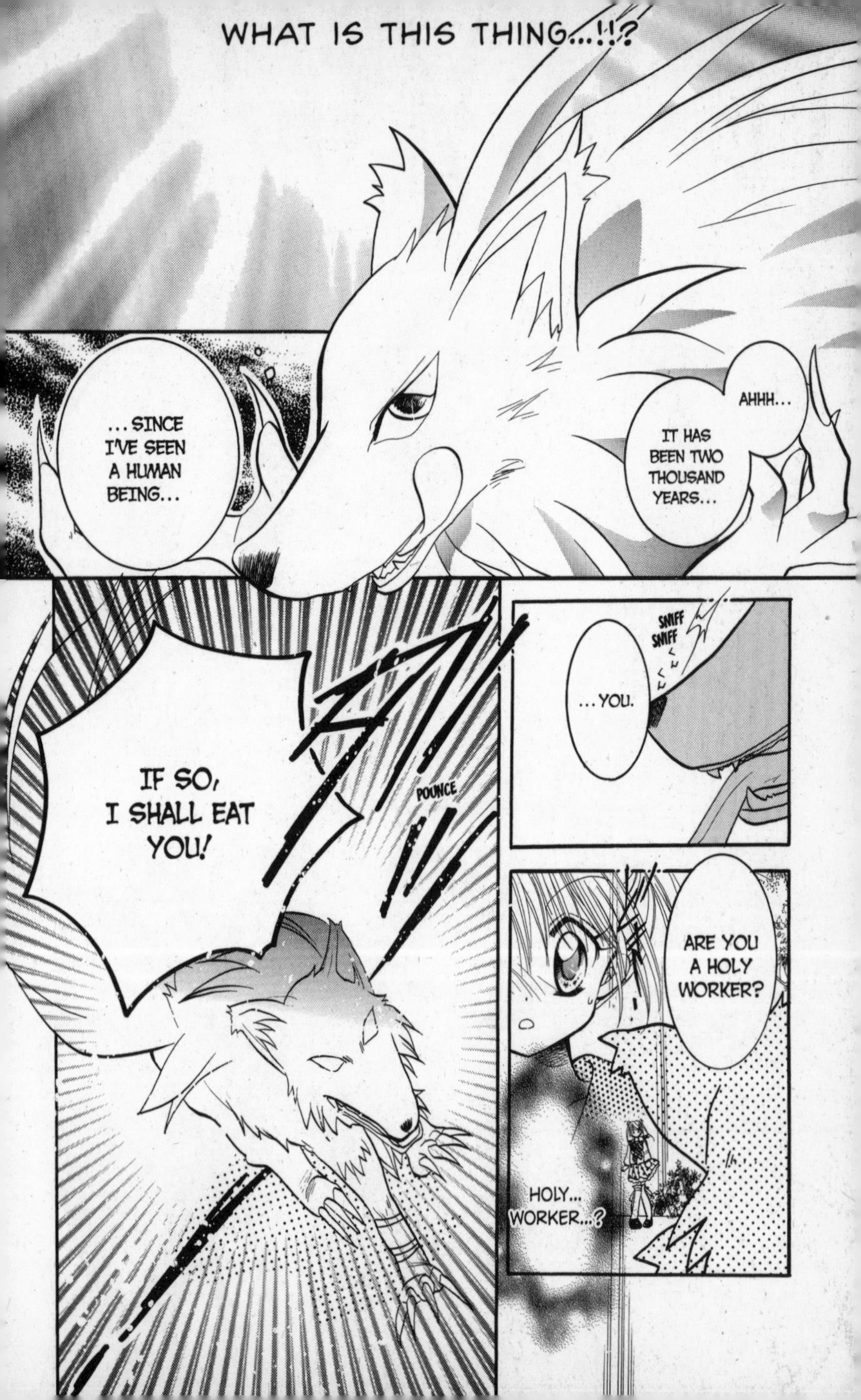
WHAT IS THIS THING...!!?
AHHH...
IT HAS BEEN TWO THOUSAND YEARS...
...SINCE I'VE SEEN A HUMAN BEING...
SNIFF SNIFF
...YOU.
ARE YOU A HOLY WORKER?
HOLY... WORKER...?
POUNCE
IF SO, I SHALL EAT YOU!

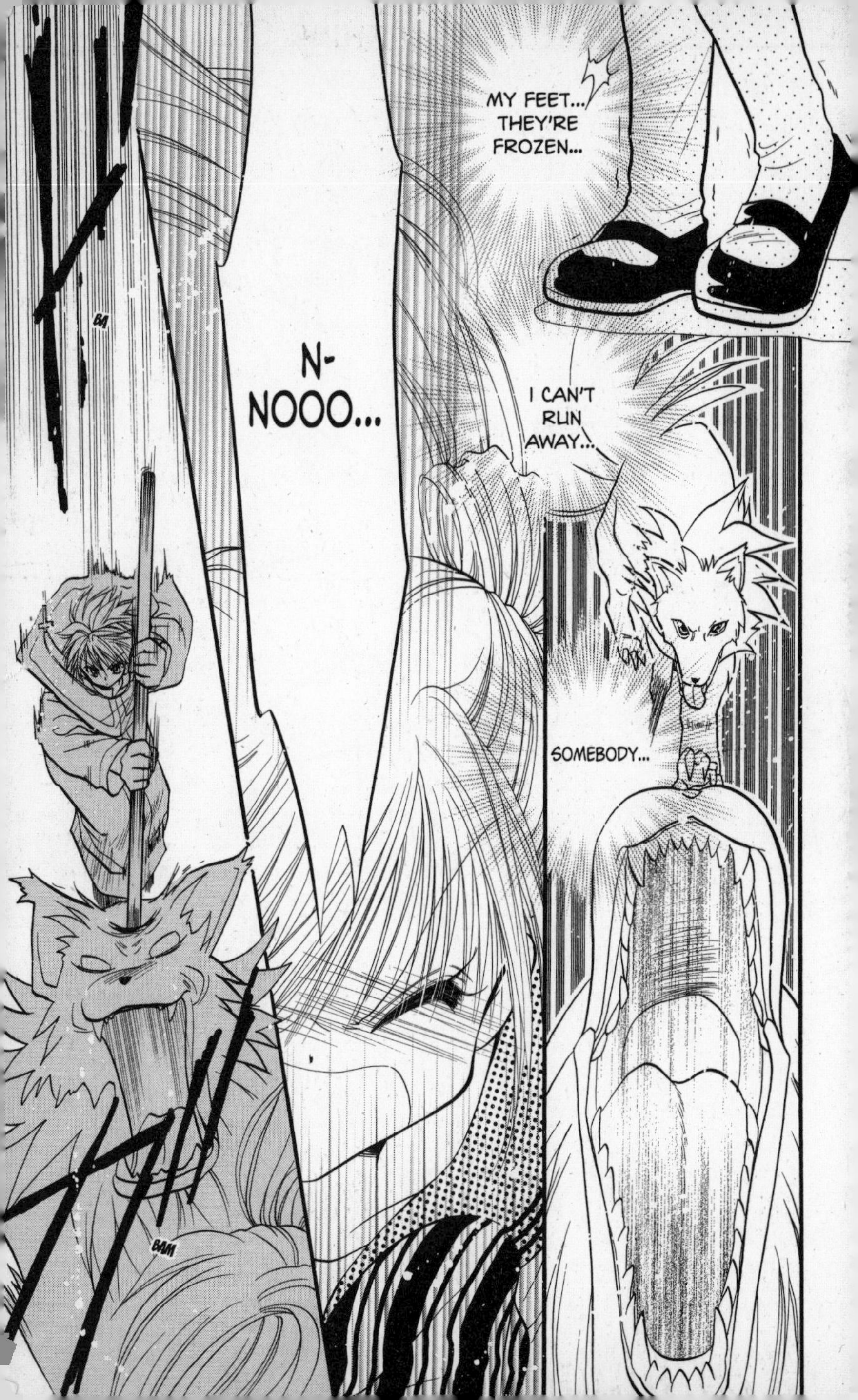
MY FEET... THEY'RE FROZEN...
I CAN'T RUN AWAY...
SOMEBODY...
N- NOOO...
BA
BAM

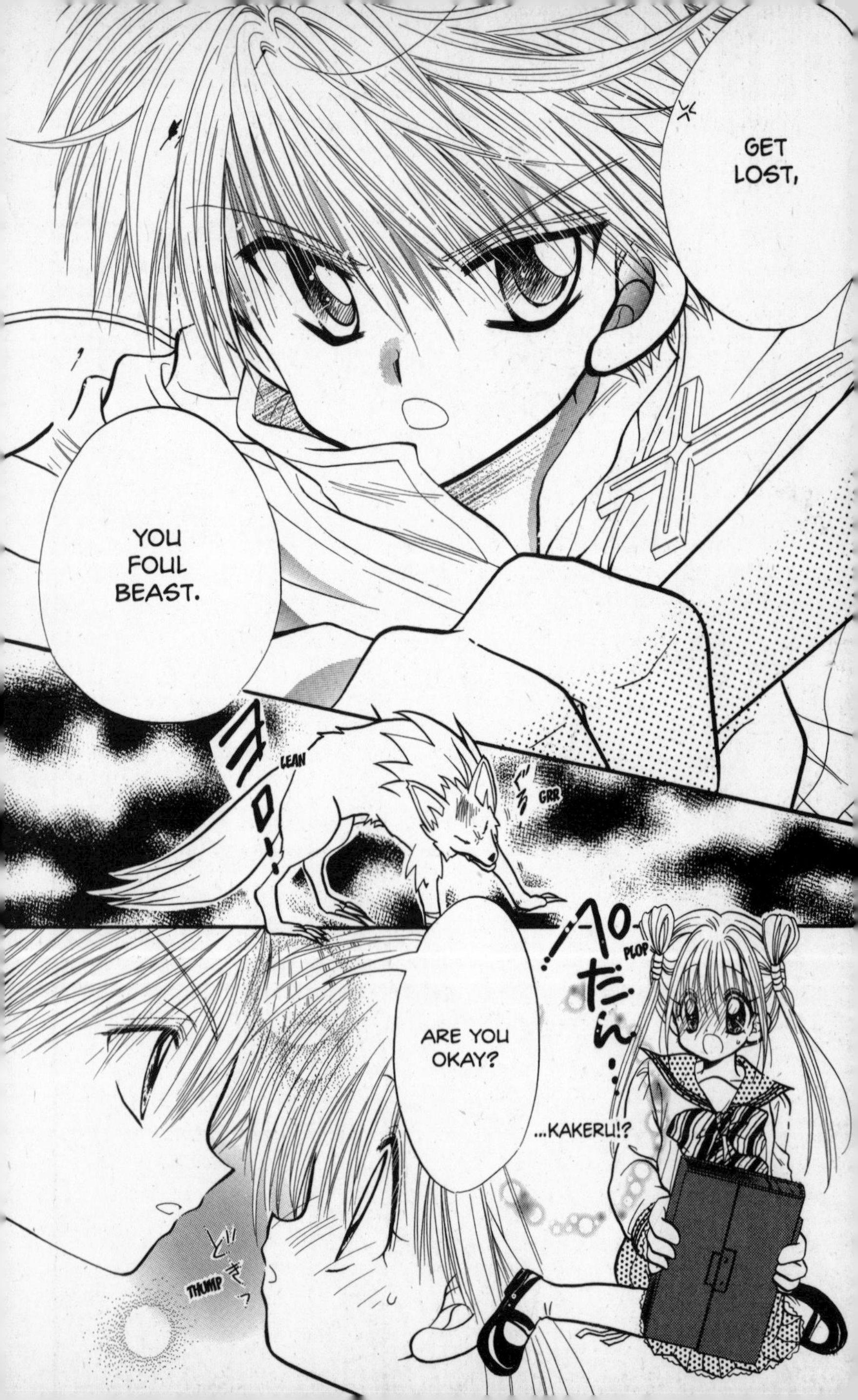
GET LOST,
YOU FOUL BEAST.
GRR
LEAN
PLOP
ARE YOU OKAY?
...KAKERU!?
THUMP

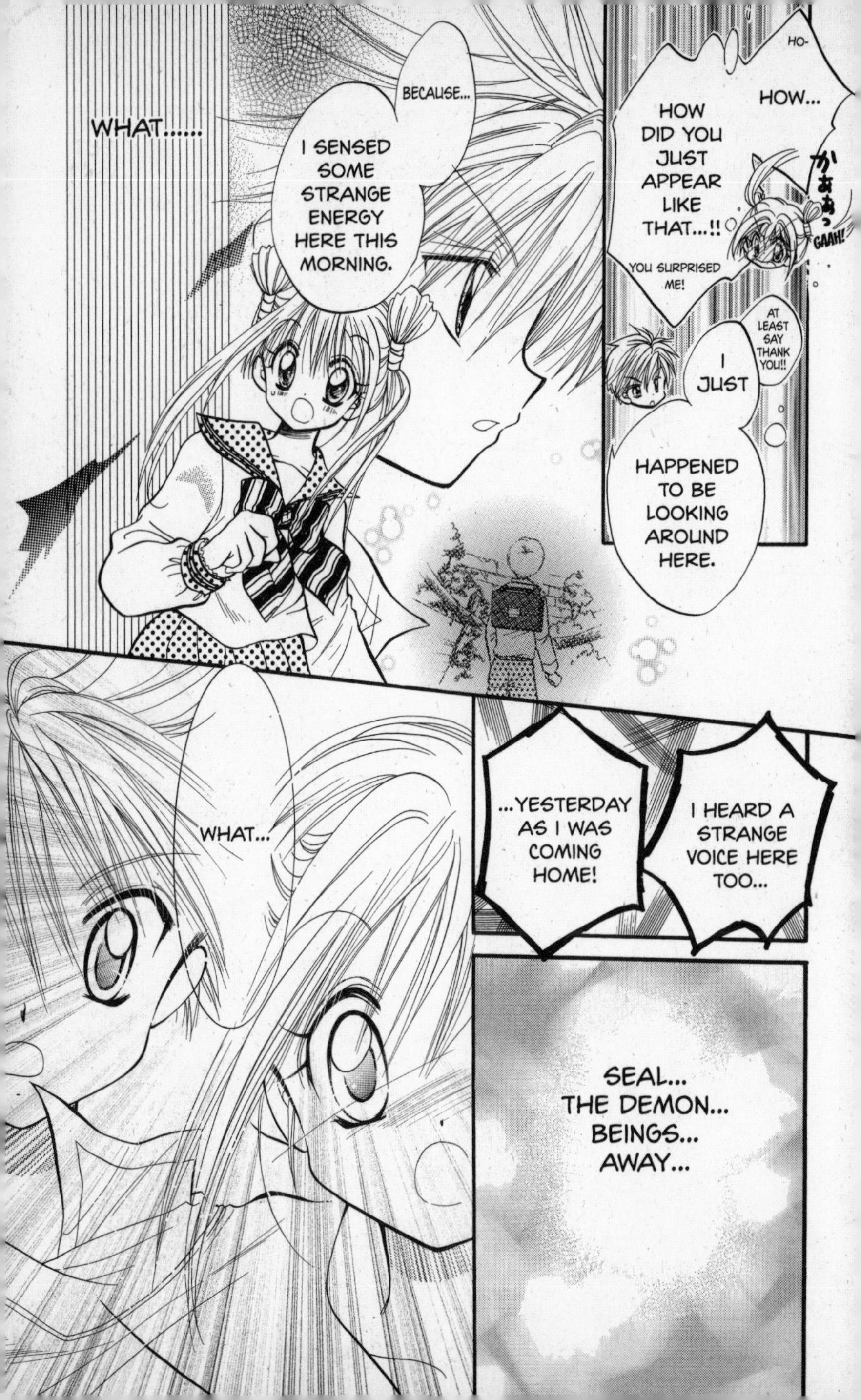
HO-
HOW...
HOW DID YOU JUST APPEAR LIKE THAT...!!
かああっ
GAAH!
YOU SURPRISED ME!
AT LEAST SAY THANK YOU!!
I JUST
HAPPENED TO BE LOOKING AROUND HERE.
BECAUSE...
I SENSED SOME STRANGE ENERGY HERE THIS MORNING.
WHAT......
I HEARD A STRANGE VOICE HERE TOO...
...YESTERDAY AS I WAS COMING HOME!
SEAL... THE DEMON... BEINGS... AWAY...
WHAT...

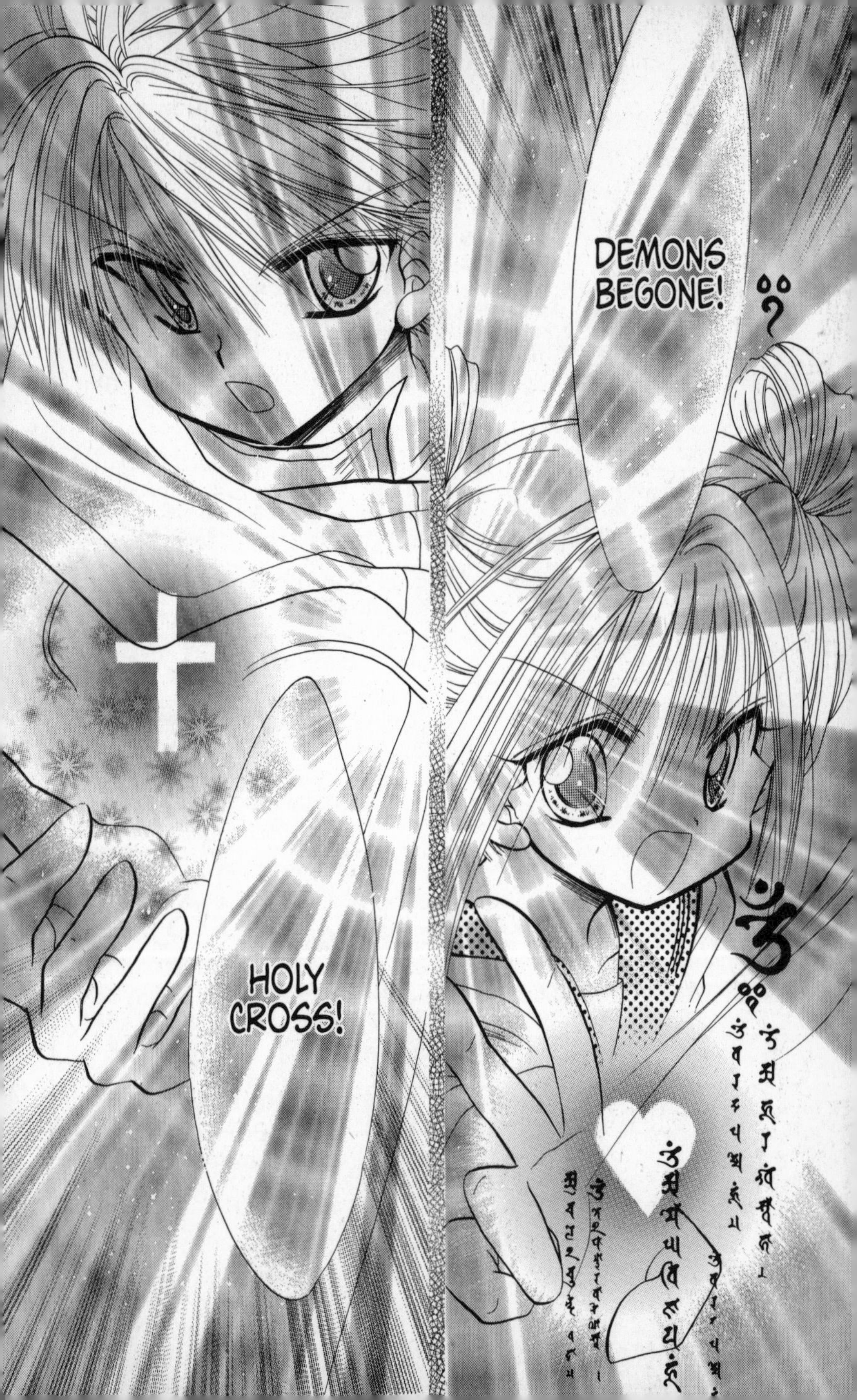
DEMONS BEGONE!
HOLY CROSS!

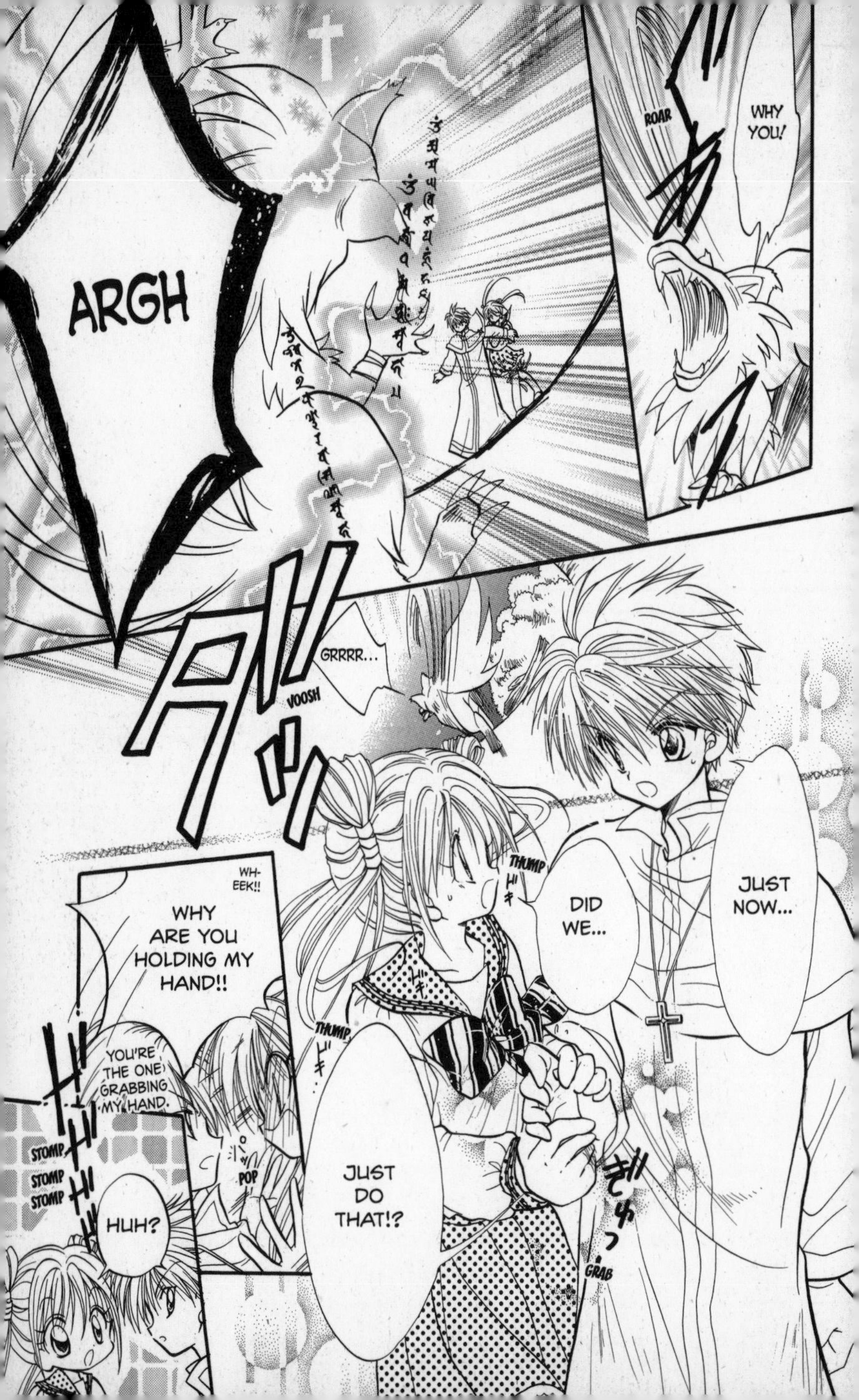
WHY YOU!
ROAR
ARGH
GRRRR...
VOOSH
JUST NOW...
THUMP
DID WE...
JUST DO THAT!?
THUMP
GRAB
WH-EEK!!
WHY ARE YOU HOLDING MY HAND!!
YOU'RE THE ONE GRABBING MY HAND.
STOMP
STOMP
STOMP
POP
HUH?

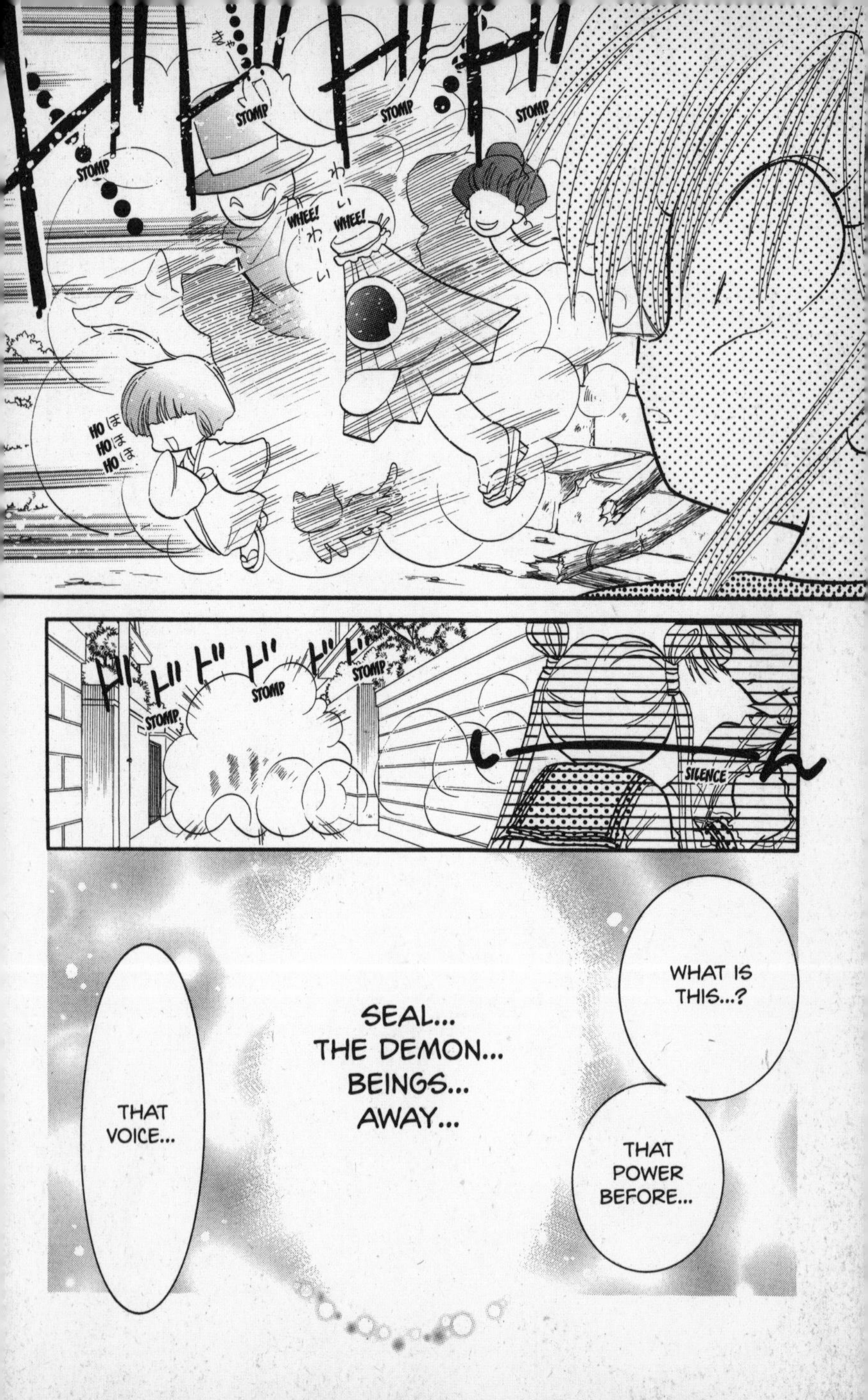
STOMP
STOMP
きゃ
STOMP
STOMP
わーい
WHEE!
わーい
WHEE!
HO HO HO
ほほほ
STOMP
STOMP
STOMP
しーん
SILENCE
WHAT IS THIS...?
THAT POWER BEFORE...
SEAL... THE DEMON... BEINGS... AWAY...
THAT VOICE...

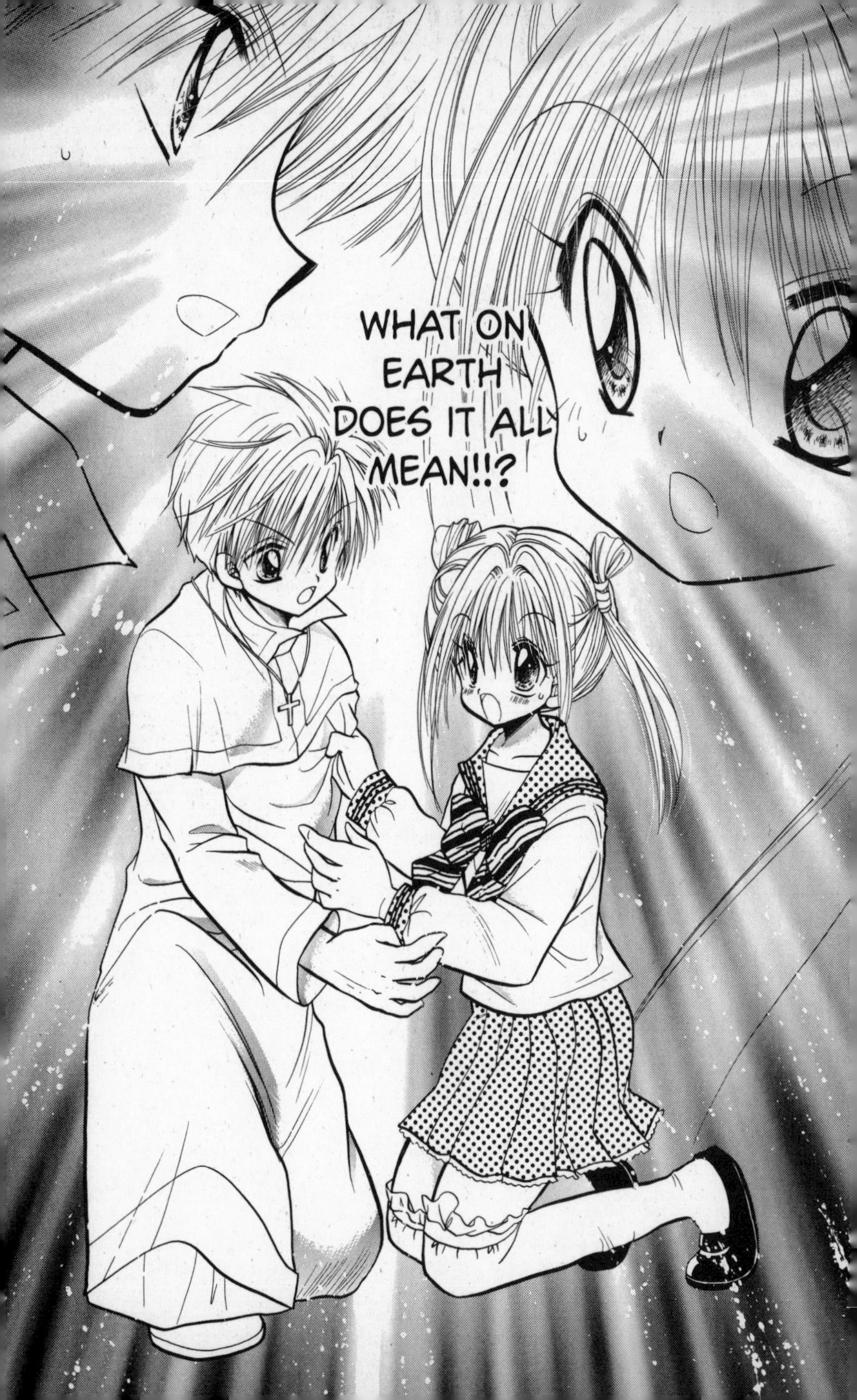
WHAT ON EARTH DOES IT ALL MEAN!!?

Panic x Panic

PROFILE

VOL. 2

FROM THE AUTHOR'S ORIGINAL STORY NOTES

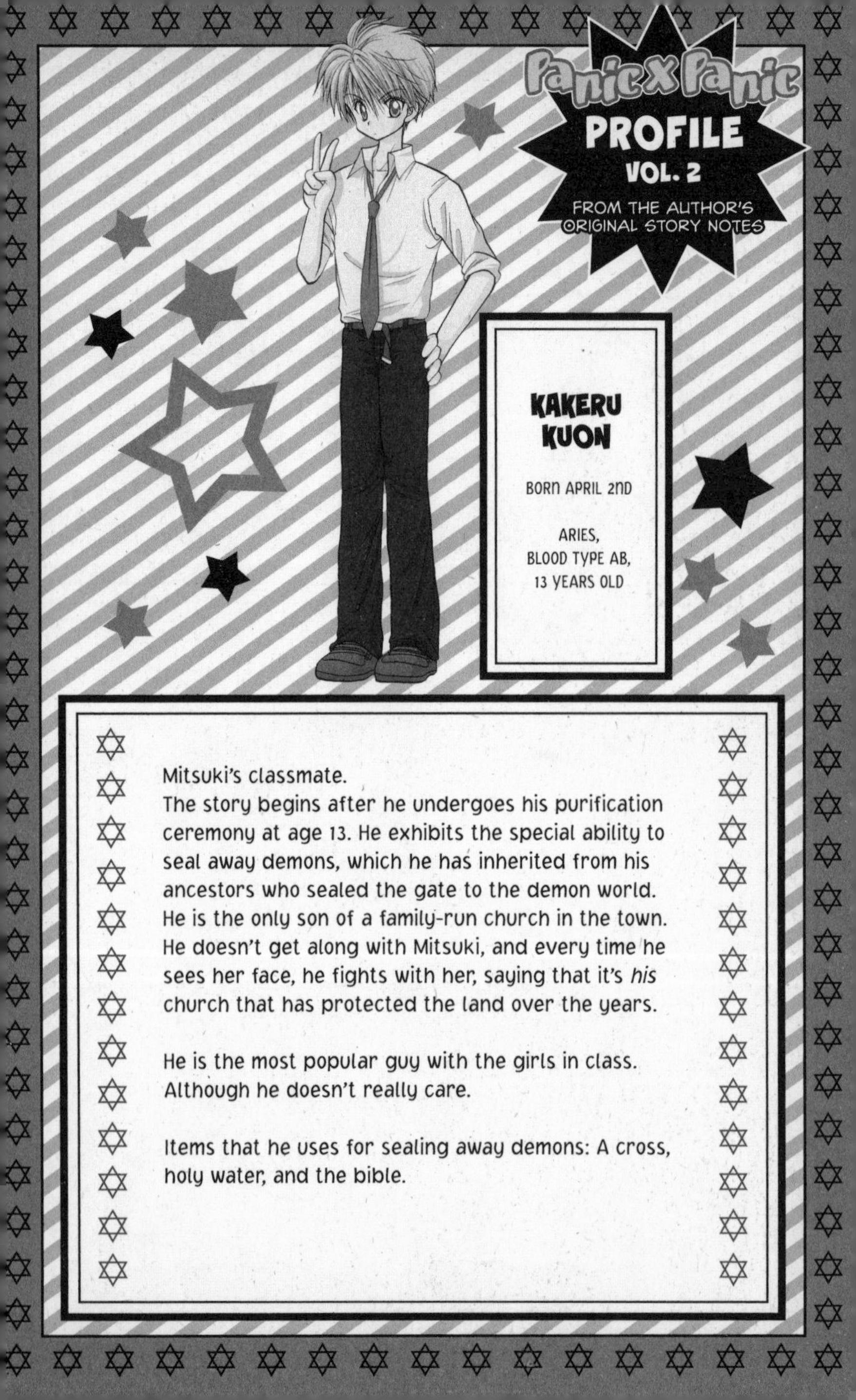

KAKERU KUON

BORN APRIL 2ND

ARIES,
BLOOD TYPE AB,
13 YEARS OLD

Mitsuki's classmate.
The story begins after he undergoes his purification ceremony at age 13. He exhibits the special ability to seal away demons, which he has inherited from his ancestors who sealed the gate to the demon world. He is the only son of a family-run church in the town. He doesn't get along with Mitsuki, and every time he sees her face, he fights with her, saying that it's *his* church that has protected the land over the years.

He is the most popular guy with the girls in class. Although he doesn't really care.

Items that he uses for sealing away demons: A cross, holy water, and the bible.

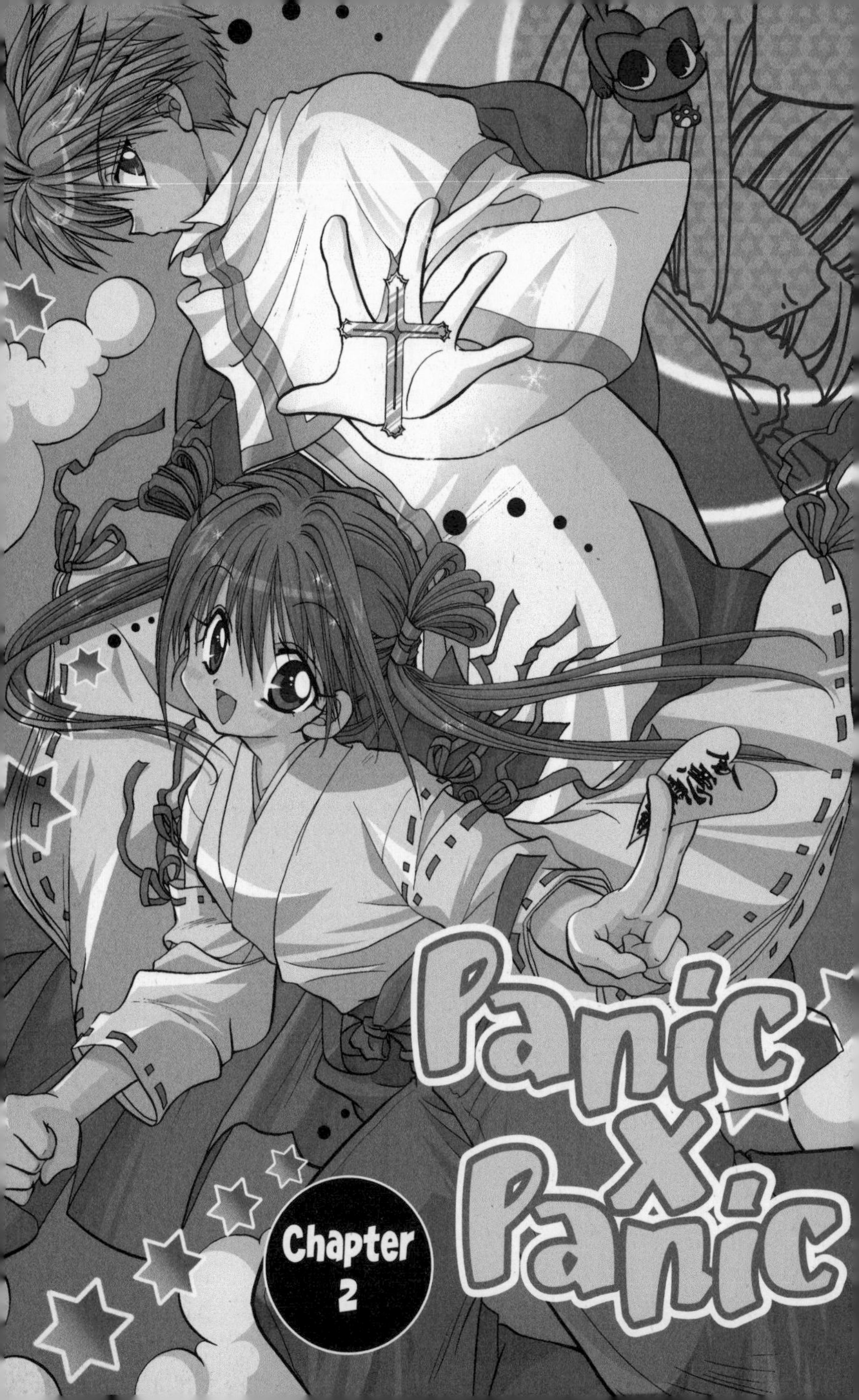
Panic X Panic
Chapter 2

Panic x Panic
PROFILE
VOL. 3
FROM THE AUTHOR'S ORIGINAL STORY NOTES

A furry demon.
He has haunted Benkei's head, so he looks like a wig for Benkei, who is bald.
Benkei mistakenly believes he has grown hair and rejoices♡

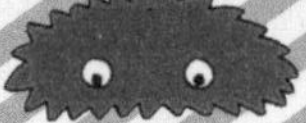

MOJA

DATE OF BIRTH
unknown

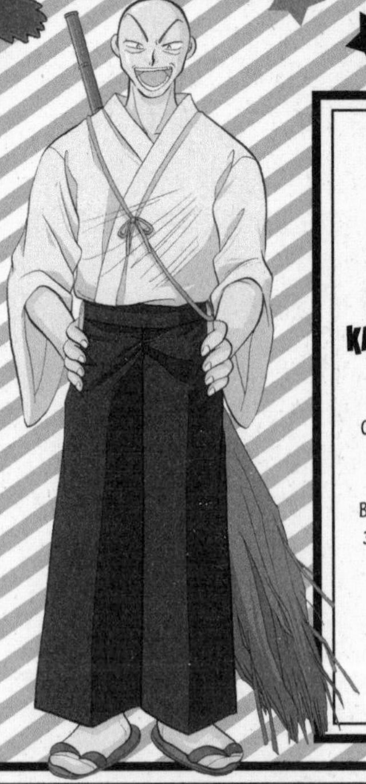

BENKEI KAMISHIRO

BORN
OCTOBER 25TH

SCORPIO,
BLOOD TYPE A,
39 YEARS OLD

Mitsuki's father. Guardian of the family shrine.
He has a wonderfully carefree personality.
He lost his wife five years ago, and now is single.
Although he is the same age as Kakeru's father, they have a cat-and-dog relationship.
They are always cursing at each other like children.
Since he is a holy worker, he can see demons.

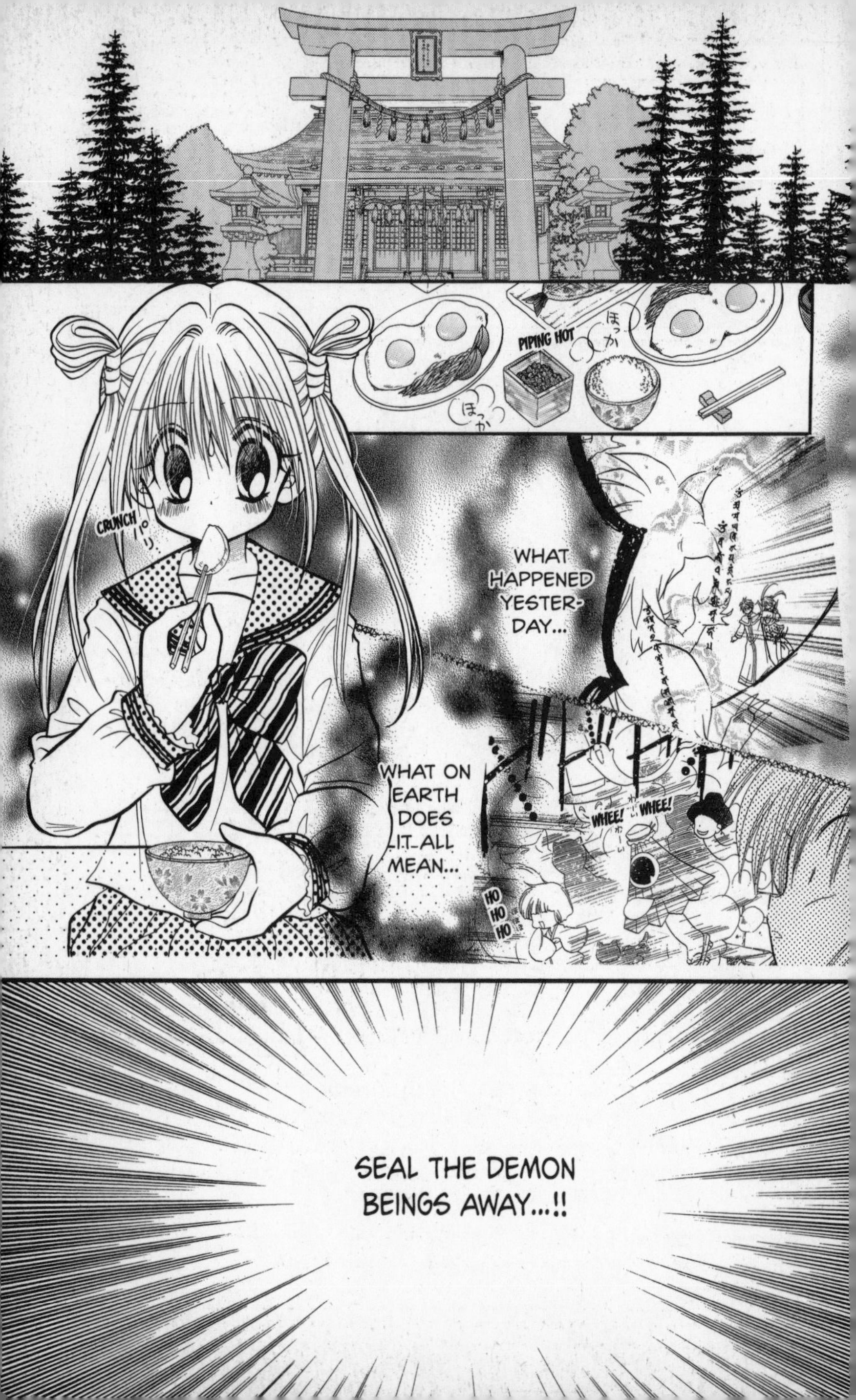
PIPING HOT
WHAT HAPPENED YESTER-DAY...
WHAT ON EARTH DOES IT ALL MEAN...
WHEE!
WHEE!
HO HO HO
CRUNCH
SEAL THE DEMON BEINGS AWAY...!!

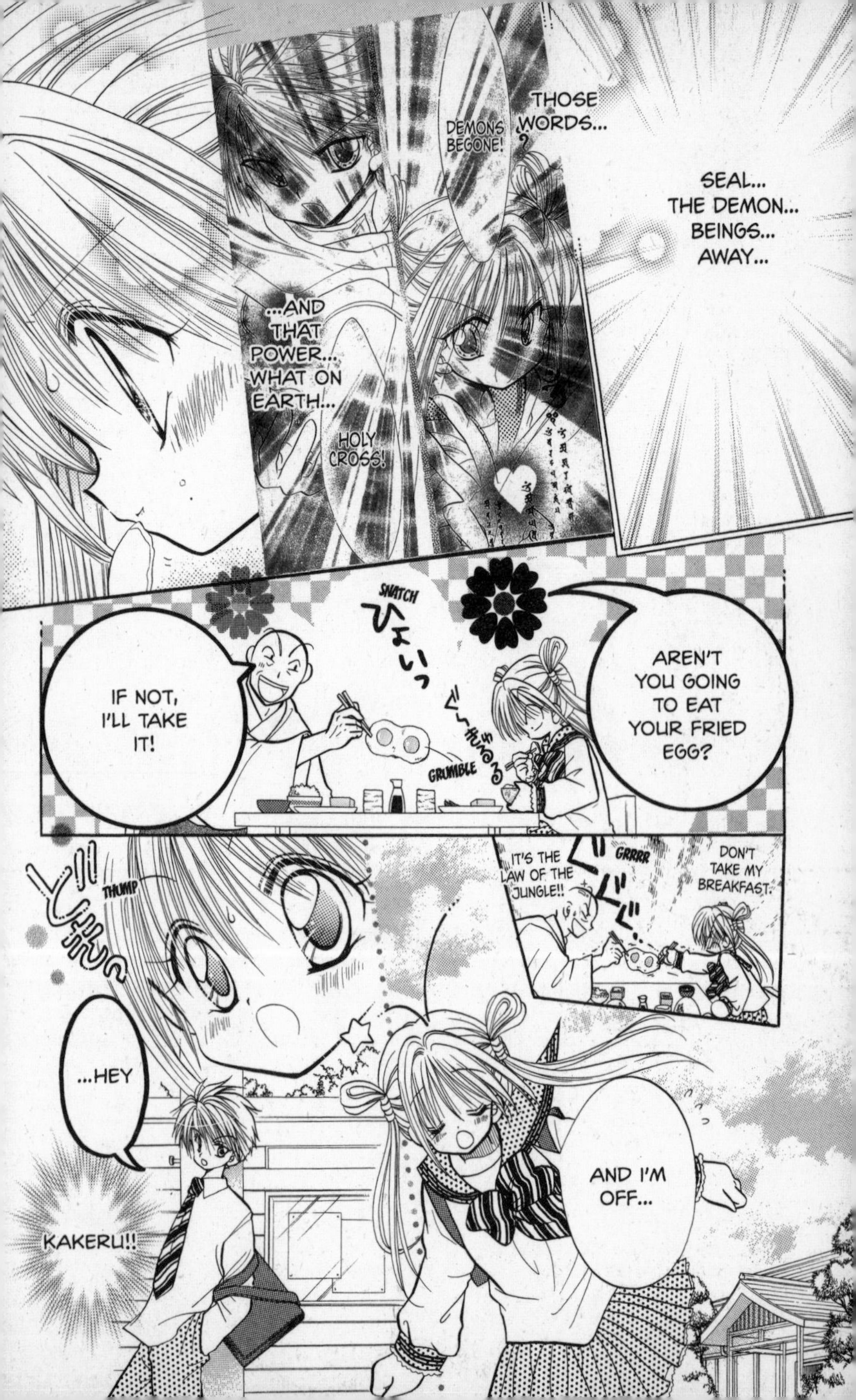
SEAL... THE DEMON... BEINGS... AWAY...
THOSE WORDS...?
DEMONS BEGONE!
...AND THAT POWER... WHAT ON EARTH...
HOLY CROSS!
AREN'T YOU GOING TO EAT YOUR FRIED EGG?
SNATCH
ひょいっ
GRUMBLE
IF NOT, I'LL TAKE IT!
DON'T TAKE MY BREAKFAST.
GRRRR
IT'S THE LAW OF THE JUNGLE!!
AND I'M OFF...
THUMP
...HEY
KAKERU!!

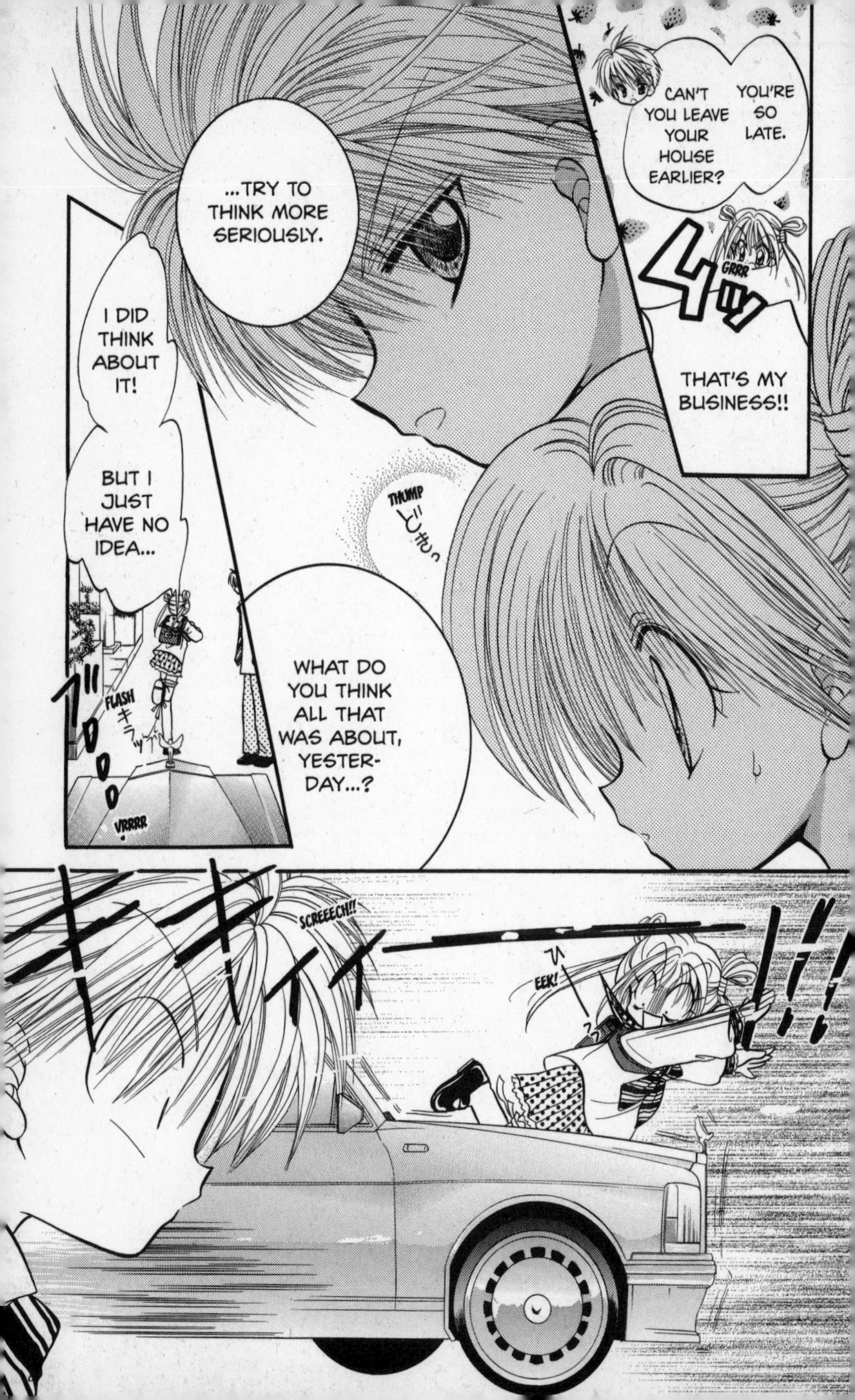
YOU'RE SO LATE.
CAN'T YOU LEAVE YOUR HOUSE EARLIER?
GRRR
THAT'S MY BUSINESS!!
...TRY TO THINK MORE SERIOUSLY.
THUMP
WHAT DO YOU THINK ALL THAT WAS ABOUT, YESTER-DAY...?
I DID THINK ABOUT IT!
BUT I JUST HAVE NO IDEA...
FLASH
VRRRR
SCREEECH!!
EEK!
!!

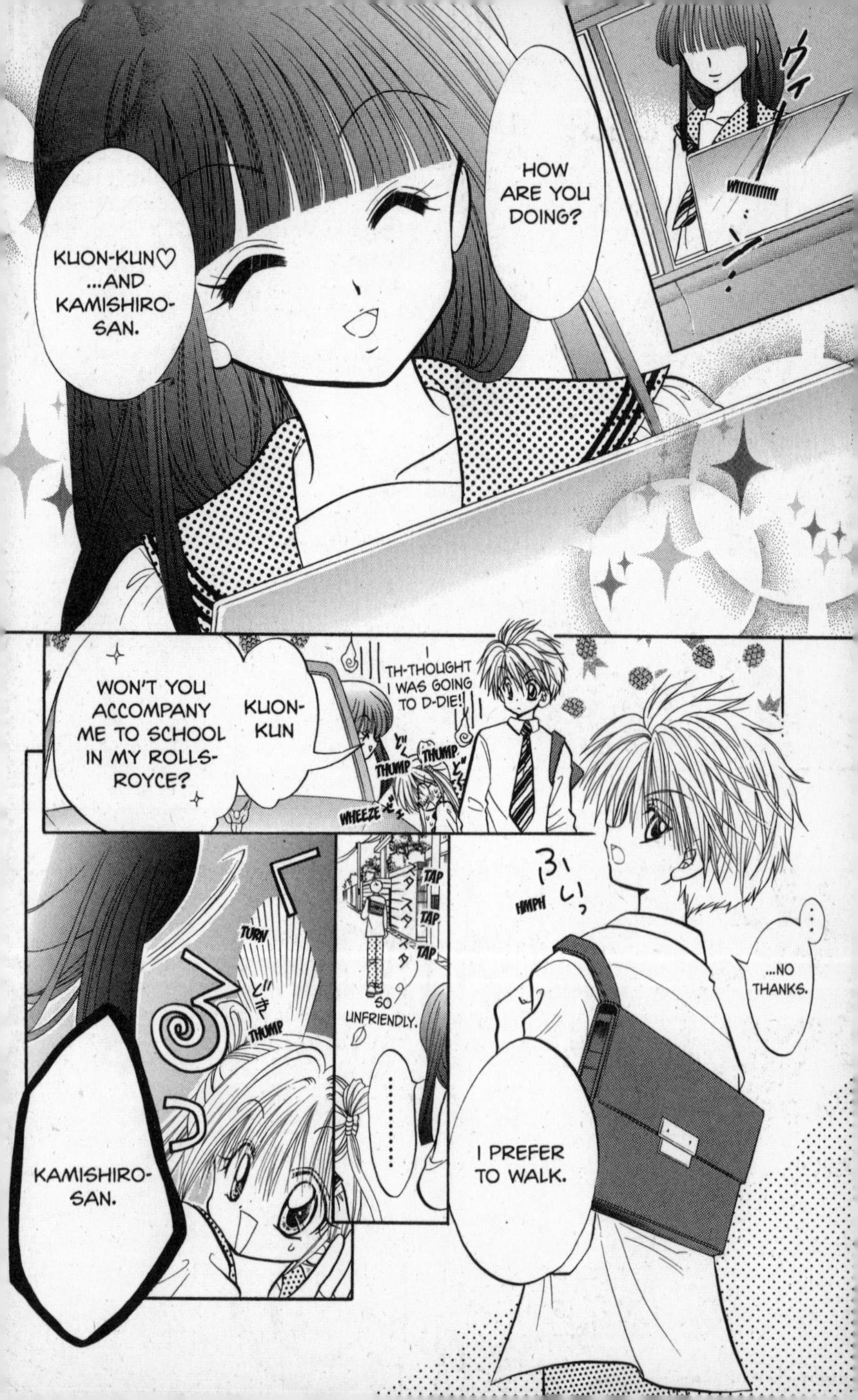
HOW ARE YOU DOING?
KUON-KUN♡ ...AND KAMISHIRO-SAN.
I TH-THOUGHT I WAS GOING TO D-DIE!!
THUMP
THUMP
WHEEZE
KUON-KUN
WON'T YOU ACCOMPANY ME TO SCHOOL IN MY ROLLS-ROYCE?
HMPH
...
...NO THANKS.
I PREFER TO WALK.
TAP
TAP
TAP
SO UNFRIENDLY.
......
TURN
THUMP
KAMISHIRO-SAN.

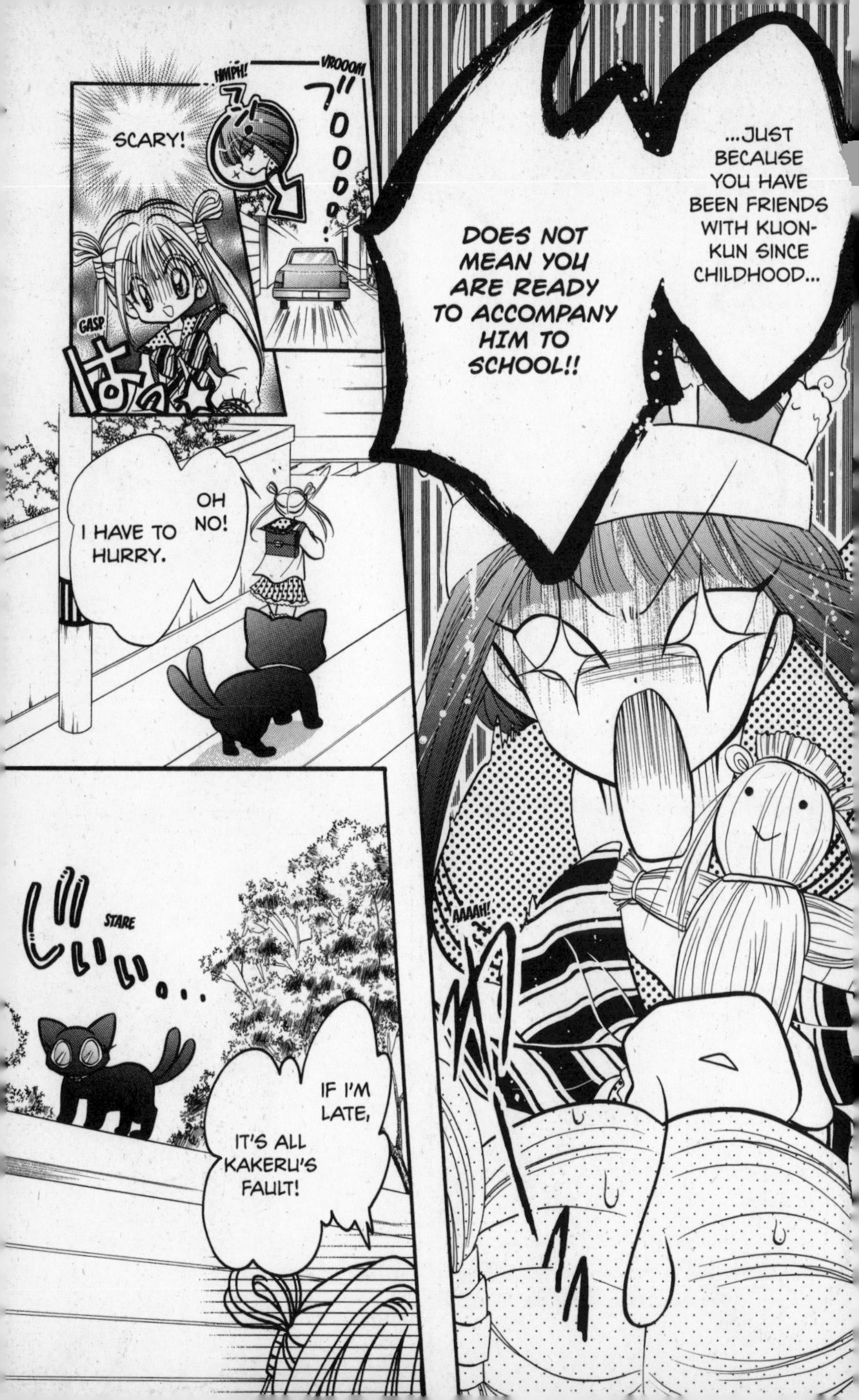
...JUST BECAUSE YOU HAVE BEEN FRIENDS WITH KUON-KUN SINCE CHILDHOOD...
DOES NOT MEAN YOU ARE READY TO ACCOMPANY HIM TO SCHOOL!!
AAAAH!
VROOOM
HMPH!
SCARY!
GASP
OH NO!
I HAVE TO HURRY.
STARE
IF I'M LATE,
IT'S ALL KAKERU'S FAULT!

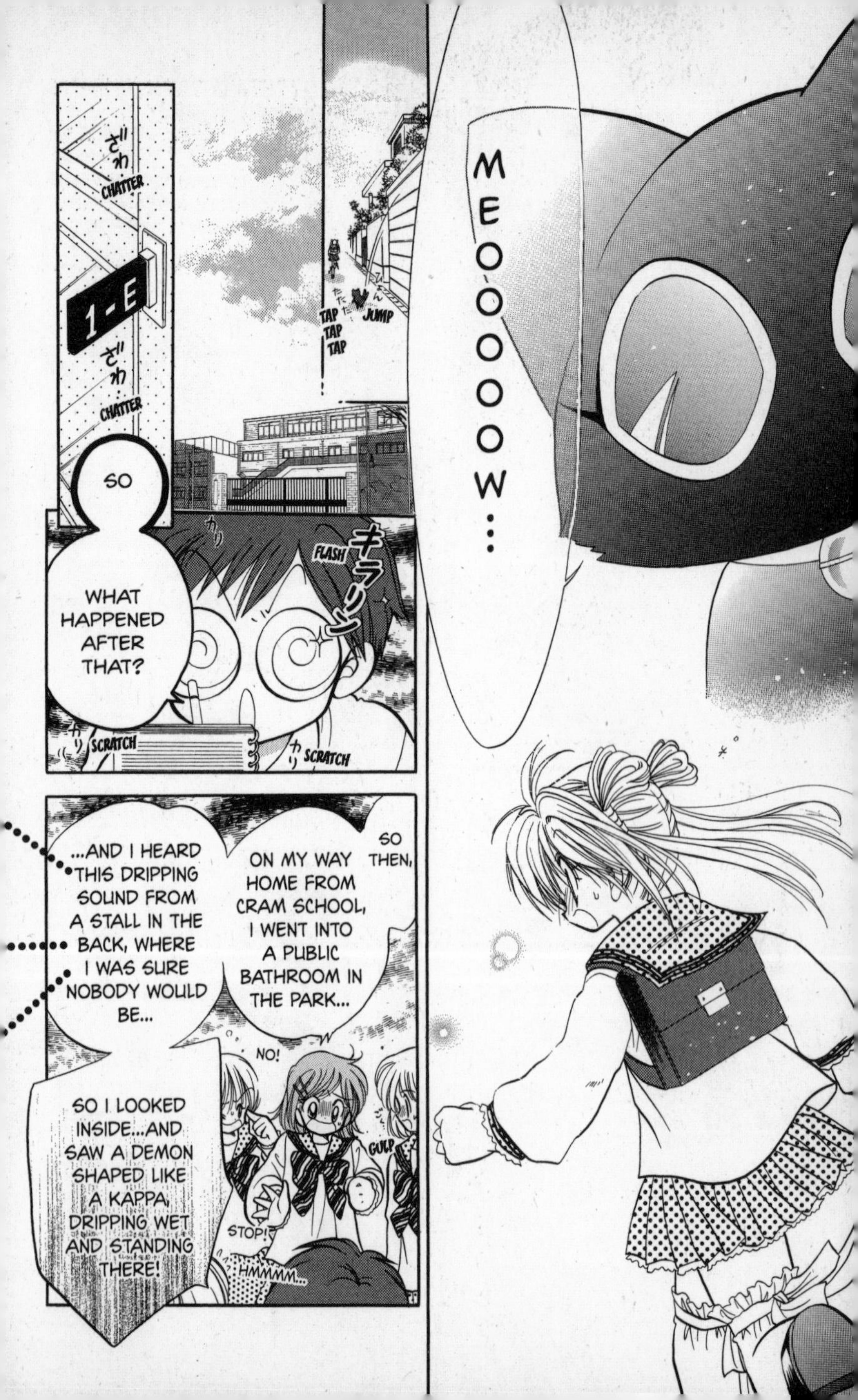
MEOOOOOW...
ぴょん
JUMP
たたた
TAP TAP TAP
ざわ
CHATTER
ざわ
CHATTER
SO
WHAT HAPPENED AFTER THAT?
キラリン
FLASH
カリ
SCRATCH
カリ
SCRATCH
SO THEN,
ON MY WAY HOME FROM CRAM SCHOOL, I WENT INTO A PUBLIC BATHROOM IN THE PARK...
...AND I HEARD THIS DRIPPING SOUND FROM A STALL IN THE BACK, WHERE I WAS SURE NOBODY WOULD BE...
SO I LOOKED INSIDE...AND SAW A DEMON SHAPED LIKE A KAPPA, DRIPPING WET AND STANDING THERE!
NO!
GULP
STOP!
HMMMM...

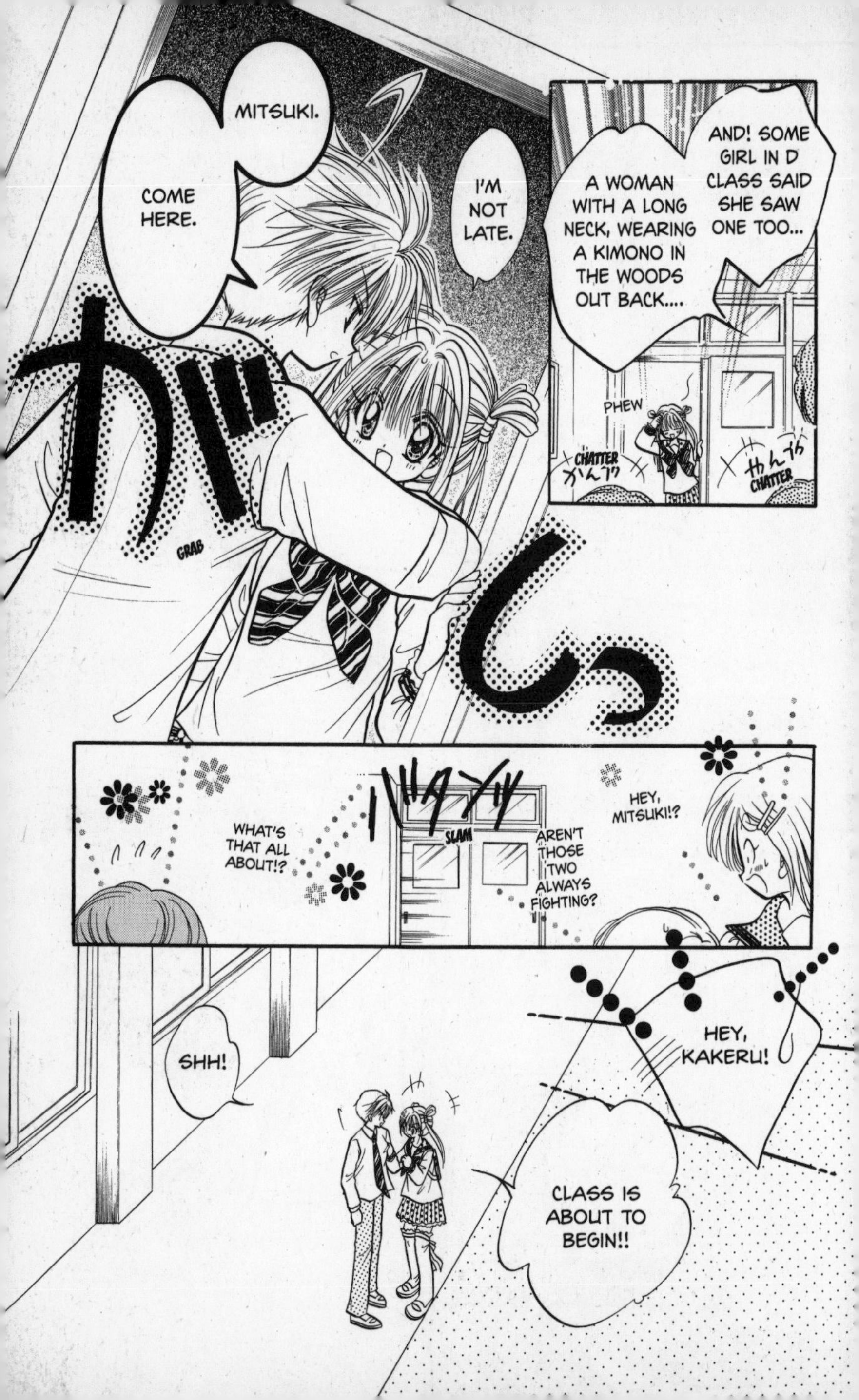
AND! SOME GIRL IN D CLASS SAID SHE SAW ONE TOO...
A WOMAN WITH A LONG NECK, WEARING A KIMONO IN THE WOODS OUT BACK....
PHEW
CHATTER
CHATTER
I'M NOT LATE.
MITSUKI.
COME HERE.
GRAB
HEY, MITSUKI!?
AREN'T THOSE TWO ALWAYS FIGHTING?
SLAM
WHAT'S THAT ALL ABOUT!?
HEY, KAKERU!
CLASS IS ABOUT TO BEGIN!!
SHH!

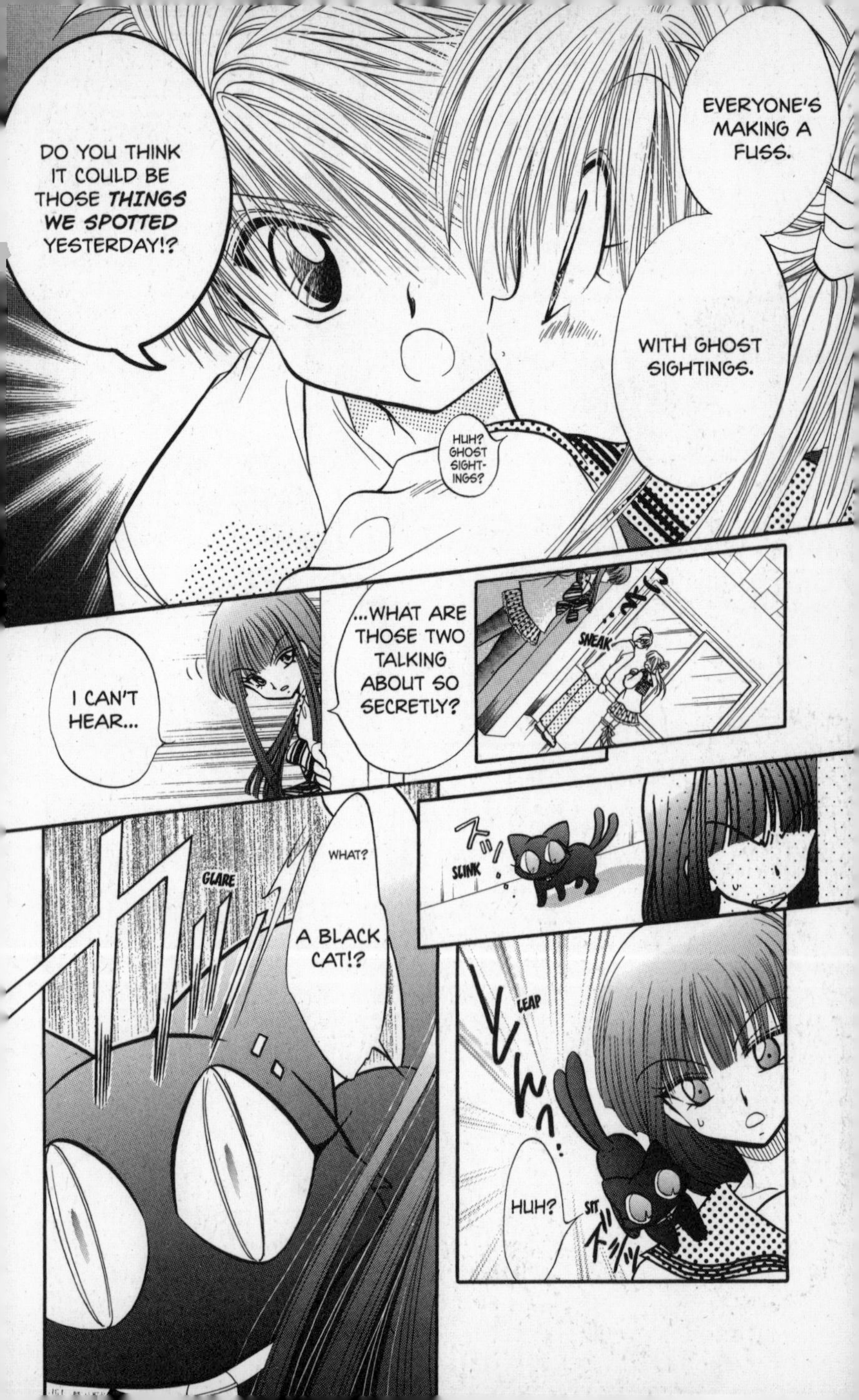
EVERYONE'S MAKING A FUSS.
WITH GHOST SIGHTINGS.
HUH? GHOST SIGHT-INGS?
DO YOU THINK IT COULD BE THOSE *THINGS WE SPOTTED* YESTERDAY!?
SNEAK
...WHAT ARE THOSE TWO TALKING ABOUT SO SECRETLY?
I CAN'T HEAR...
SLINK
LEAP
HUH?
SIT
WHAT?
A BLACK CAT!?
GLARE

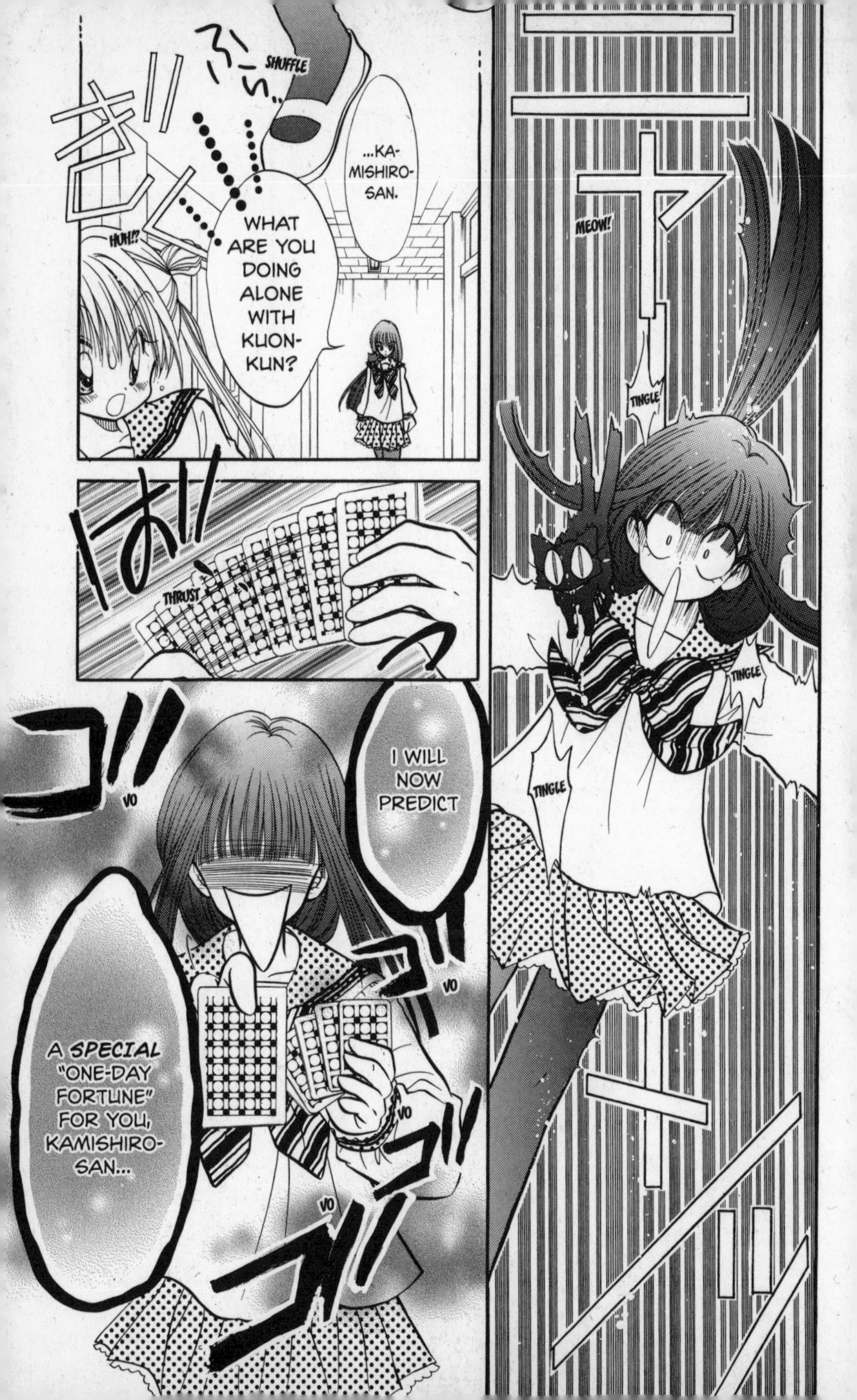
MEOW!
TINGLE
TINGLE
TINGLE
SHUFFLE
...KA-MISHIRO-SAN.
WHAT ARE YOU DOING ALONE WITH KUON-KUN?
HUH!?
THRUST
I WILL NOW PREDICT
A SPECIAL "ONE-DAY FORTUNE" FOR YOU, KAMISHIRO-SAN...
VO
VO
VO
VO

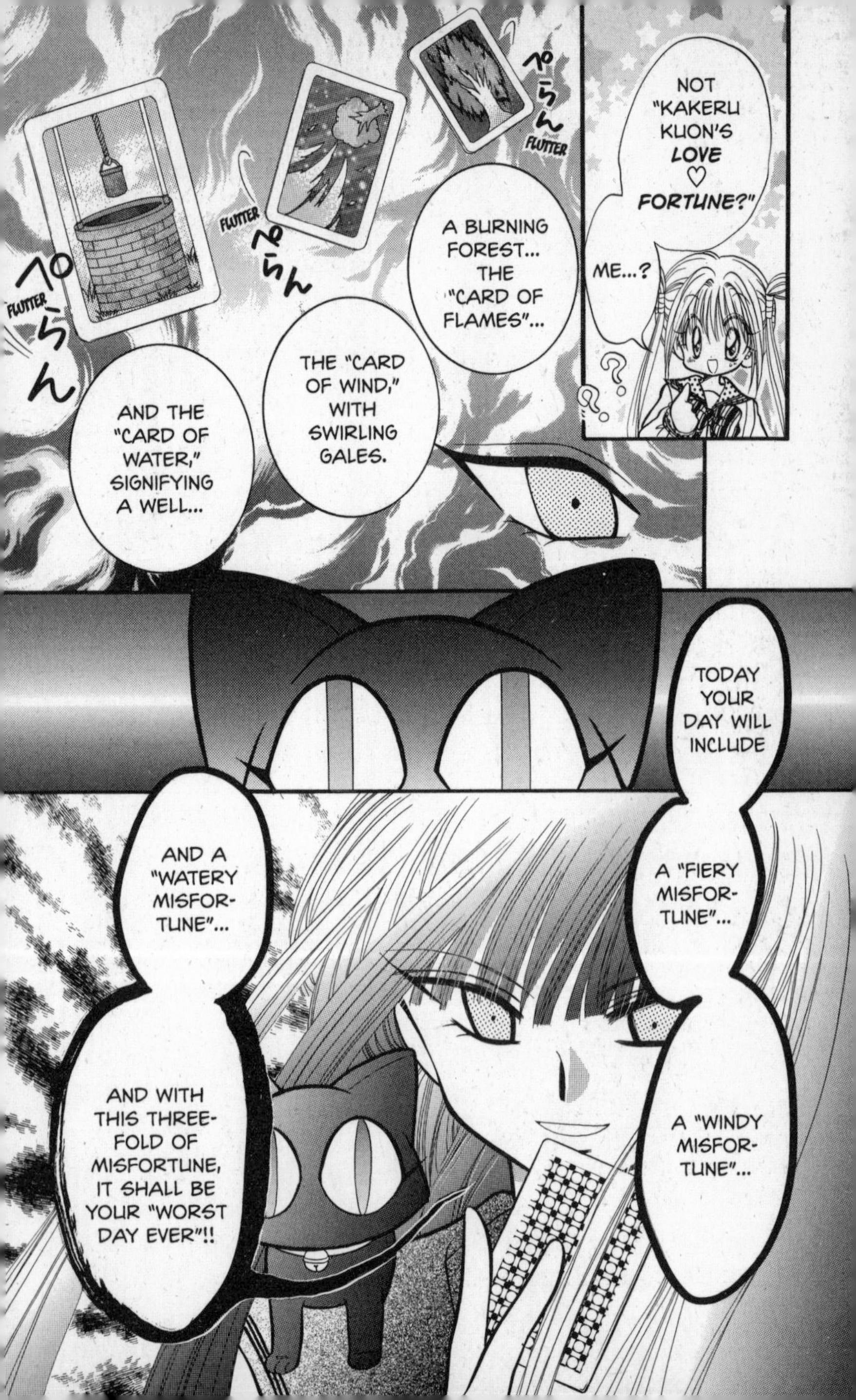
NOT "KAKERU KUON'S **LOVE** ♡ **FORTUNE?**"
ME...?
ぺらん
FLUTTER
A BURNING FOREST... THE "CARD OF FLAMES"...
ぺらん
FLUTTER
THE "CARD OF WIND," WITH SWIRLING GALES.
ぺらん
FLUTTER
AND THE "CARD OF WATER," SIGNIFYING A WELL...
TODAY YOUR DAY WILL INCLUDE
A "FIERY MISFORTUNE"...
A "WINDY MISFORTUNE"...
AND A "WATERY MISFORTUNE"...
AND WITH THIS THREE-FOLD OF MISFORTUNE, IT SHALL BE YOUR "WORST DAY EVER"!!

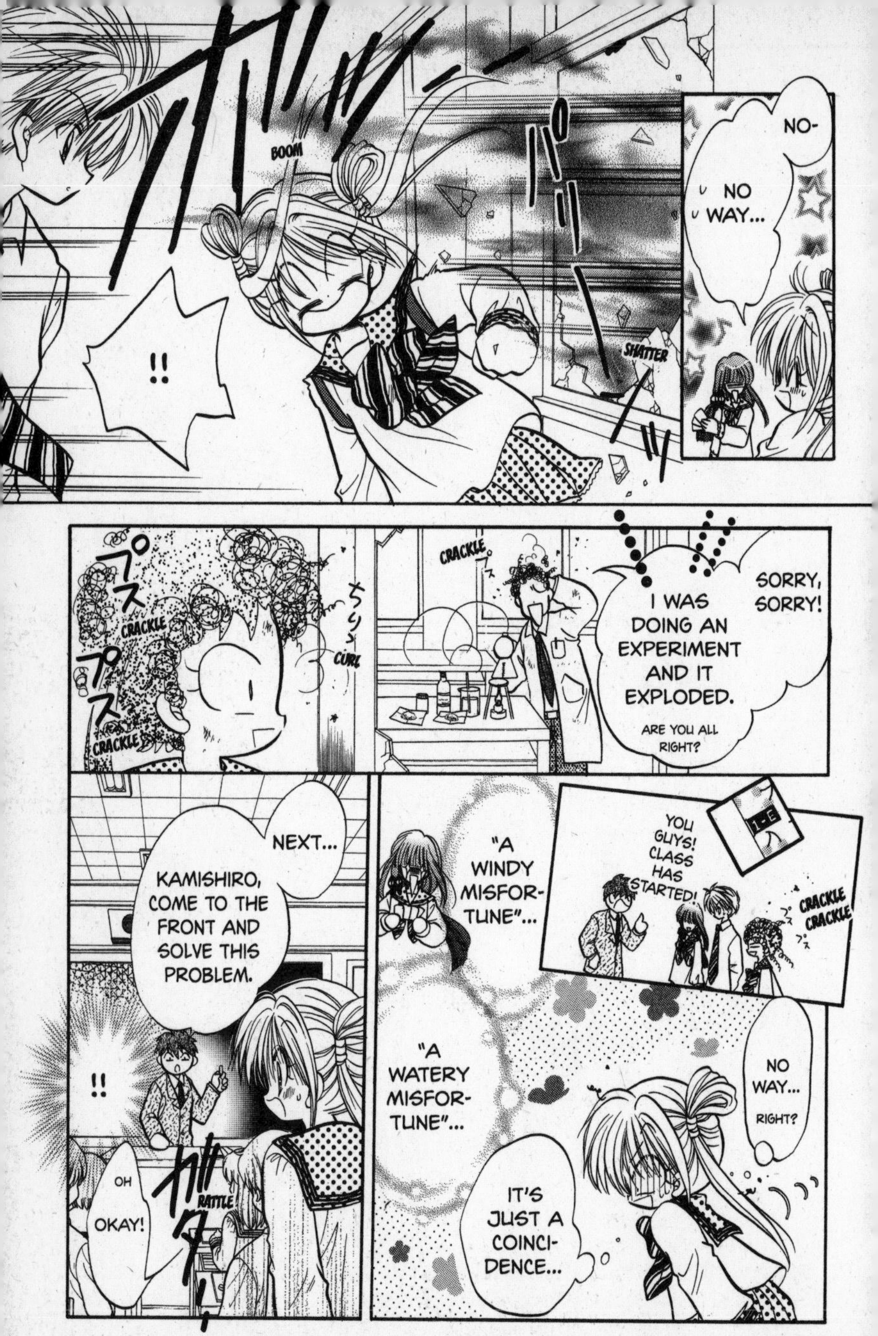
NO- NO WAY...
BOOM
SHATTER
!!
SORRY, SORRY!
I WAS DOING AN EXPERIMENT AND IT EXPLODED.
ARE YOU ALL RIGHT?
CRACKLE
CURL
CRACKLE
CRACKLE
YOU GUYS! CLASS HAS STARTED!
CRACKLE CRACKLE
"A WINDY MISFORTUNE"...
"A WATERY MISFORTUNE"...
NO WAY... RIGHT?
IT'S JUST A COINCIDENCE...
NEXT...
KAMISHIRO, COME TO THE FRONT AND SOLVE THIS PROBLEM.
!!
OH OKAY!
RATTLE

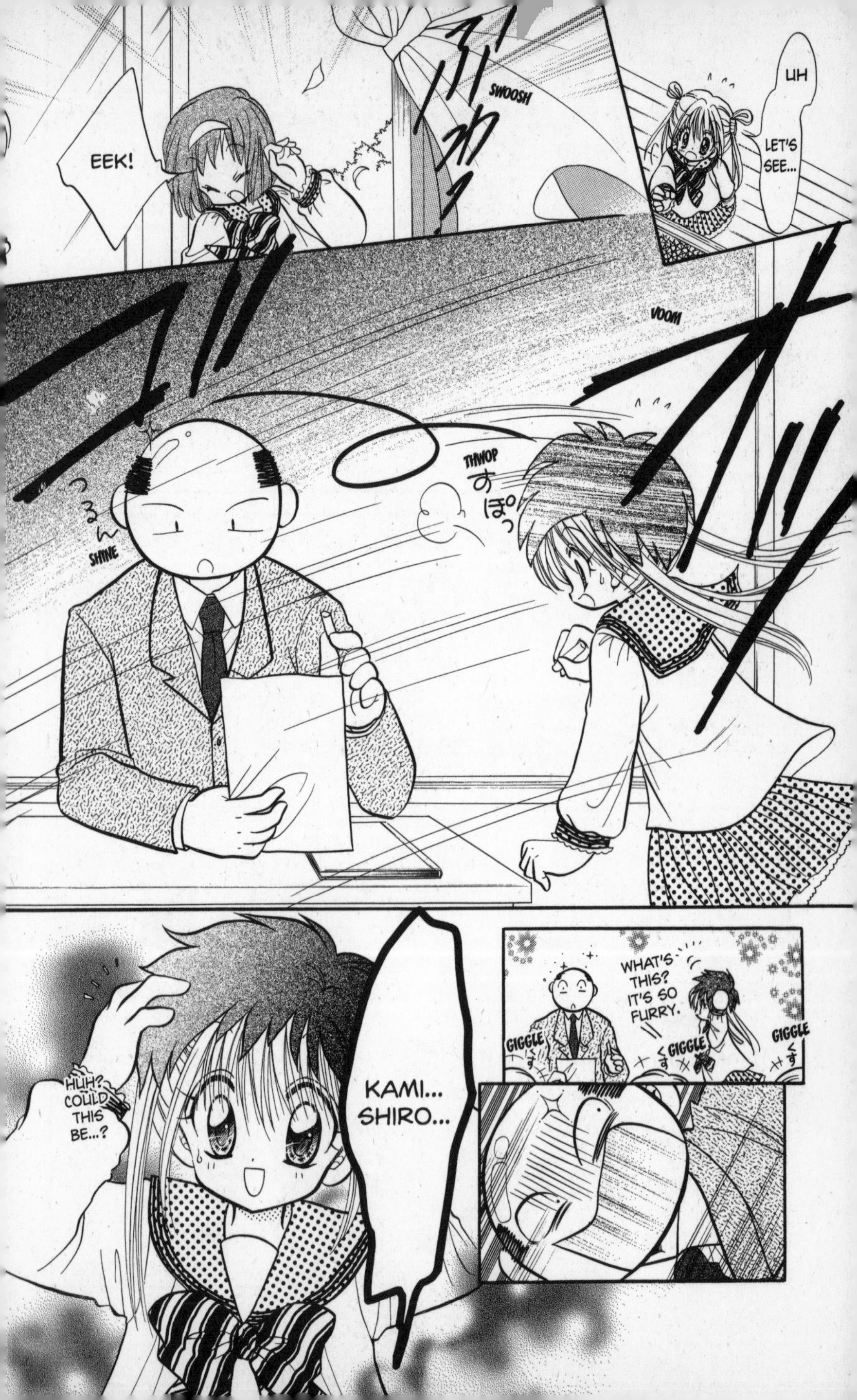
UH
LET'S SEE...
SWOOSH
EEK!
VOOM
THWOP
すぽっ
つるん
SHINE
WHAT'S THIS? IT'S SO FURRY.
GIGGLE
くす
GIGGLE
くす
GIGGLE
くす
KAMI... SHIRO...
HUH? COULD THIS BE...?

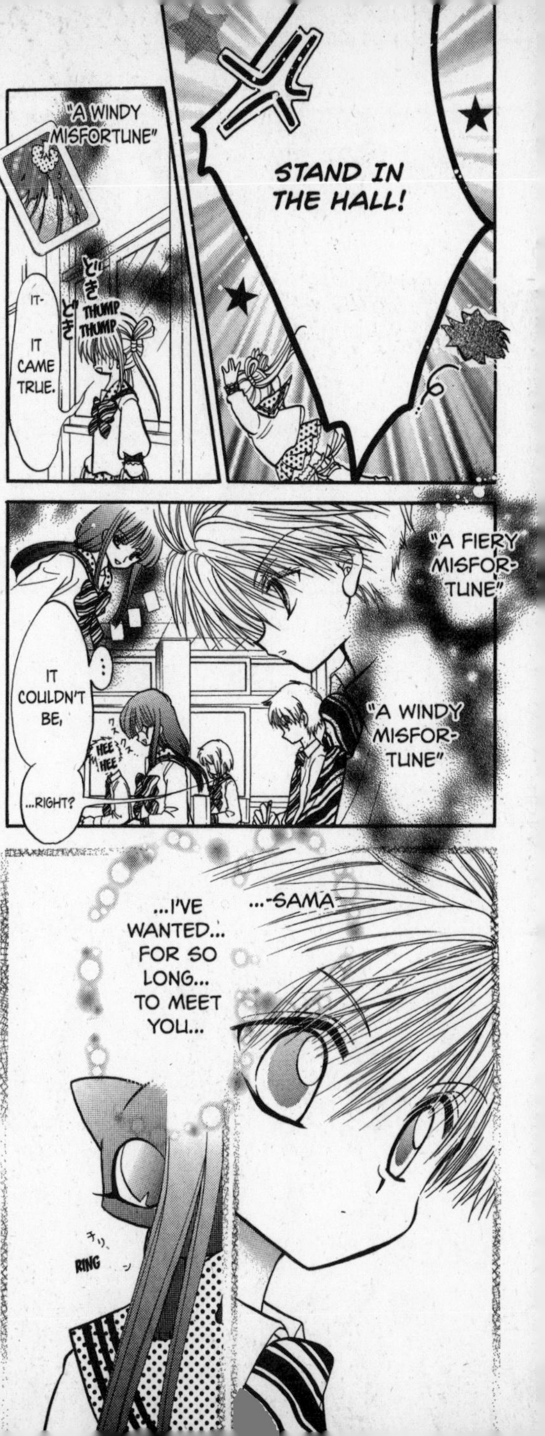
STAND IN THE HALL!
"A WINDY MISFORTUNE"
どきどき
THUMP THUMP
IT-
IT CAME TRUE.
"A FIERY MISFOR-TUNE"
"A WINDY MISFOR-TUNE"
...
IT COULDN'T BE,
...RIGHT?
HEE HEE
...-SAMA
...I'VE WANTED... FOR SO LONG... TO MEET YOU...
RING

Nobody Cares The Author's Favorite Music!!

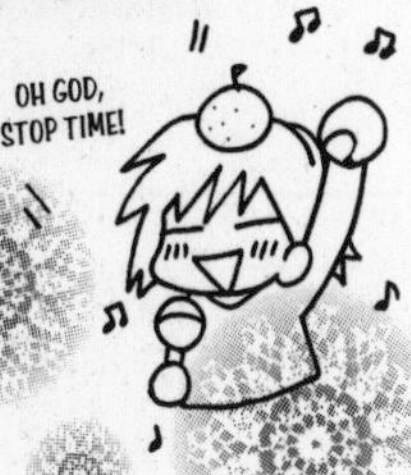
OH GOD, STOP TIME!

THE SONGS I SING MOST AT KARAOKE (ALTHOUGH I RARELY GO) ARE:

THE COLLECTORS

MR. CHILDREN

AS WELL AS HIKARU UTADA

AND OTHERS!!

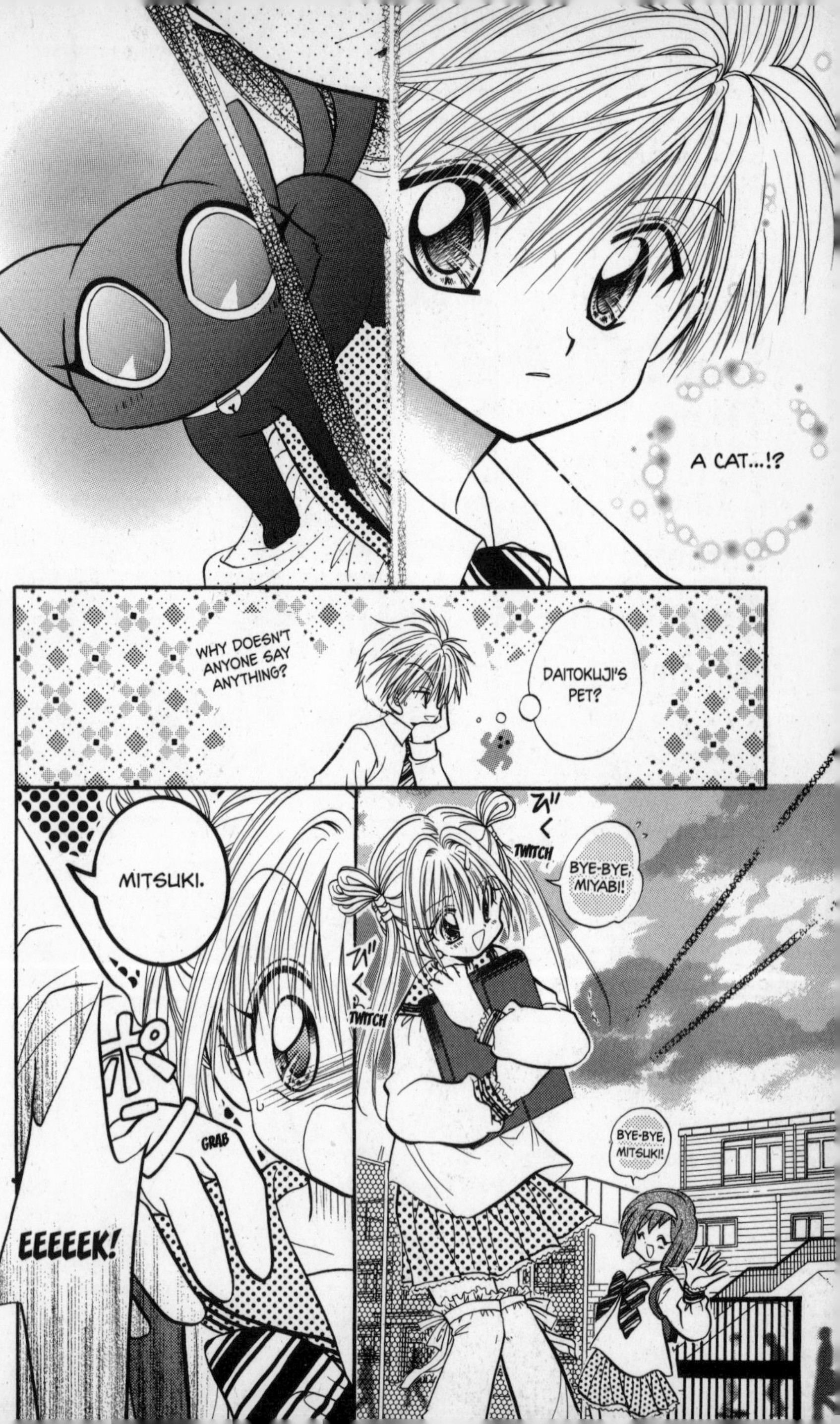
A CAT...!?
DAITOKUJI'S PET?
WHY DOESN'T ANYONE SAY ANYTHING?
TWITCH
BYE-BYE, MIYABI!
TWITCH
BYE-BYE, MITSUKI!
MITSUKI.
GRAB
EEEEEK!

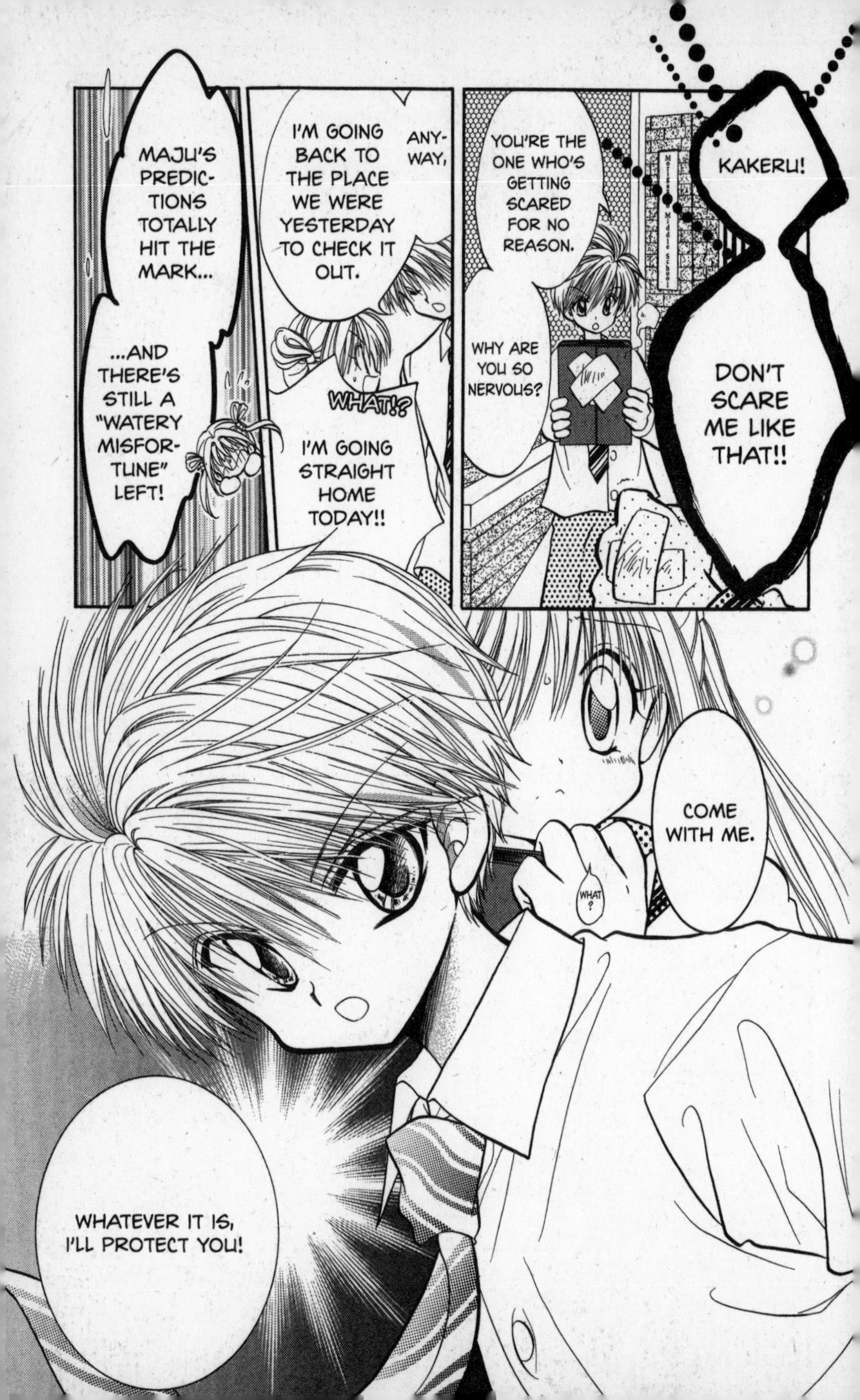
KAKERU!
DON'T SCARE ME LIKE THAT!!
YOU'RE THE ONE WHO'S GETTING SCARED FOR NO REASON.
WHY ARE YOU SO NERVOUS?
ANYWAY,
I'M GOING BACK TO THE PLACE WE WERE YESTERDAY TO CHECK IT OUT.
WHAT!?
I'M GOING STRAIGHT HOME TODAY!!
MAJU'S PREDICTIONS TOTALLY HIT THE MARK...
...AND THERE'S STILL A "WATERY MISFORTUNE" LEFT!
COME WITH ME.
WHAT?
WHATEVER IT IS, I'LL PROTECT YOU!

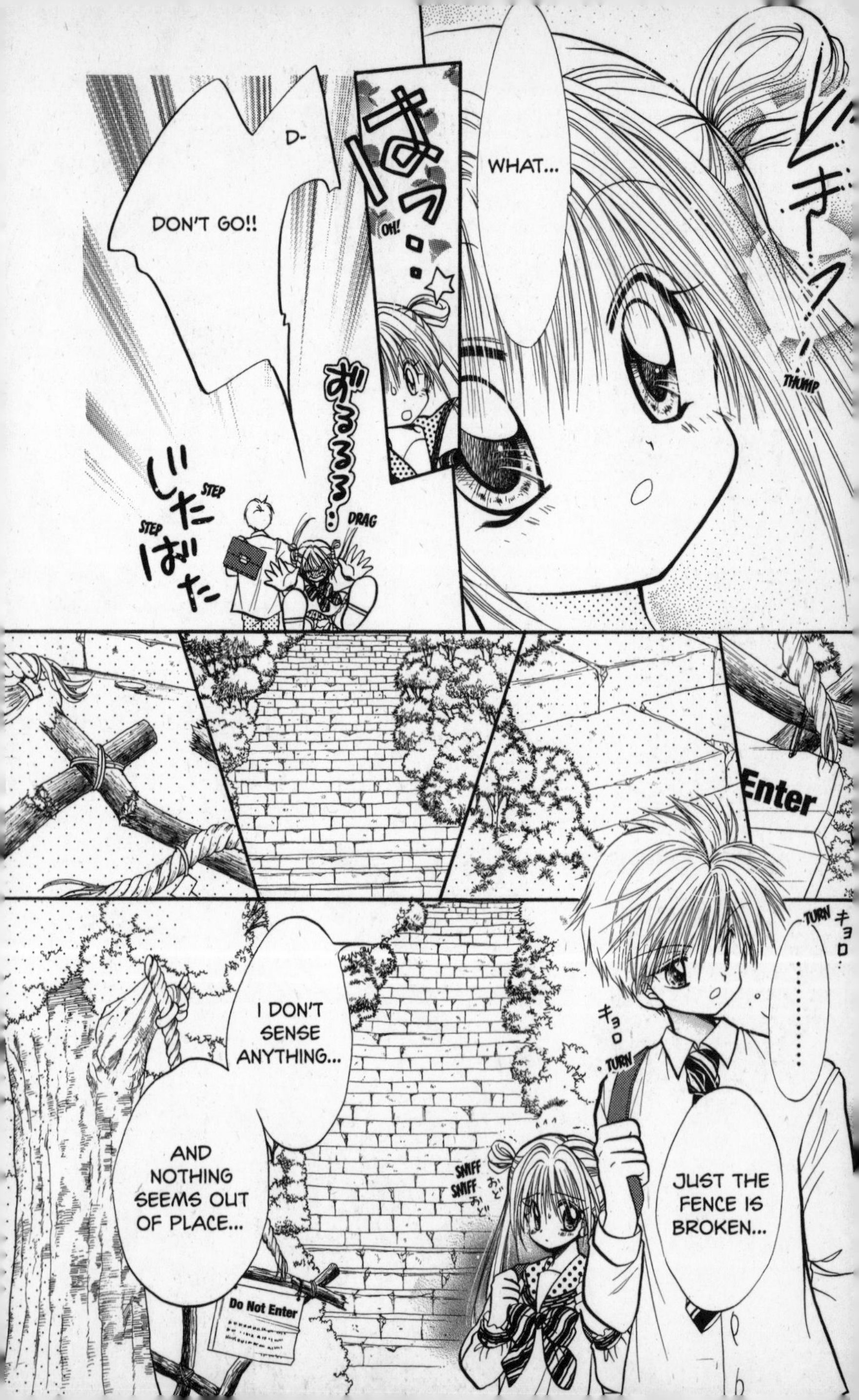
THUMP
WHAT...
はっ
OH!
ずるるる
DRAG
D-
DON'T GO!!
じたばた
STEP
STEP
Enter
キョロ
TURN
......
キョロ
TURN
I DON'T SENSE ANYTHING...
AND NOTHING SEEMS OUT OF PLACE...
JUST THE FENCE IS BROKEN...
SNIFF SNIFF
Do Not Enter

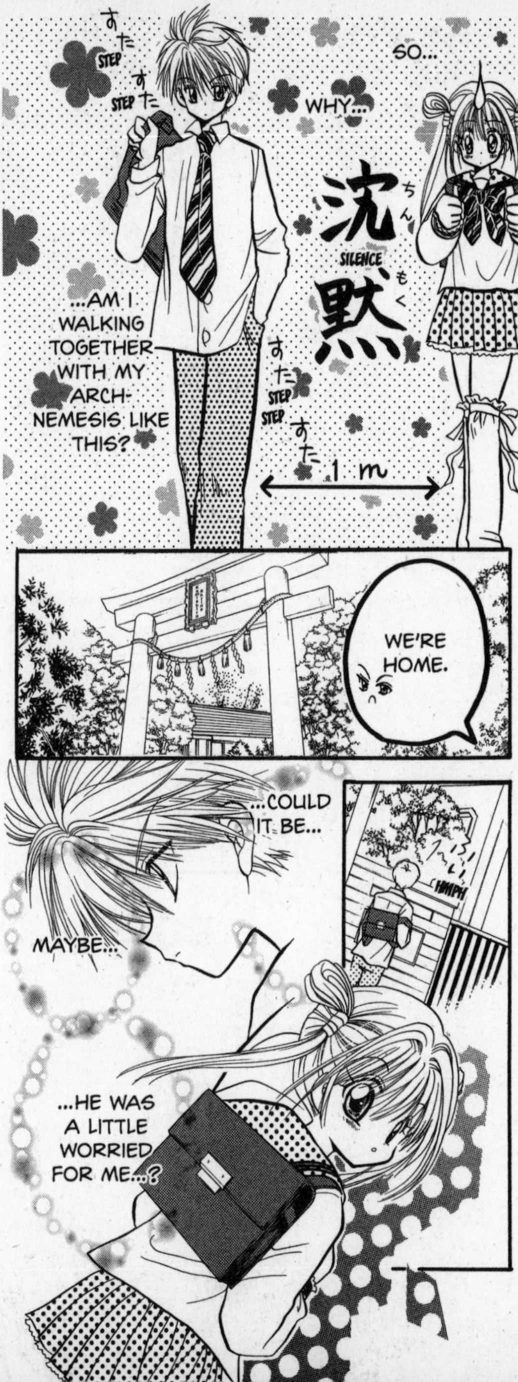
SO...
WHY...
すた STEP すた STEP
沈黙 ちん もく SILENCE
...AM I WALKING TOGETHER WITH MY ARCH-NEMESIS LIKE THIS?
すた STEP すた STEP
1 m
WE'RE HOME.
HMPH
...COULD IT BE...
MAYBE...
...HE WAS A LITTLE WORRIED FOR ME...?

Nobody Cares The Author's Favorite Painter!

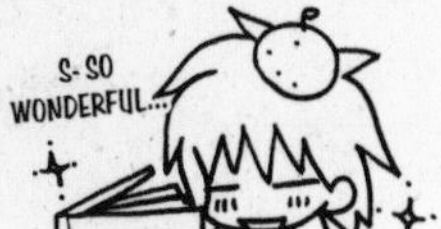
S-SO WONDERFUL...
Egon Schiele
ART BOOK

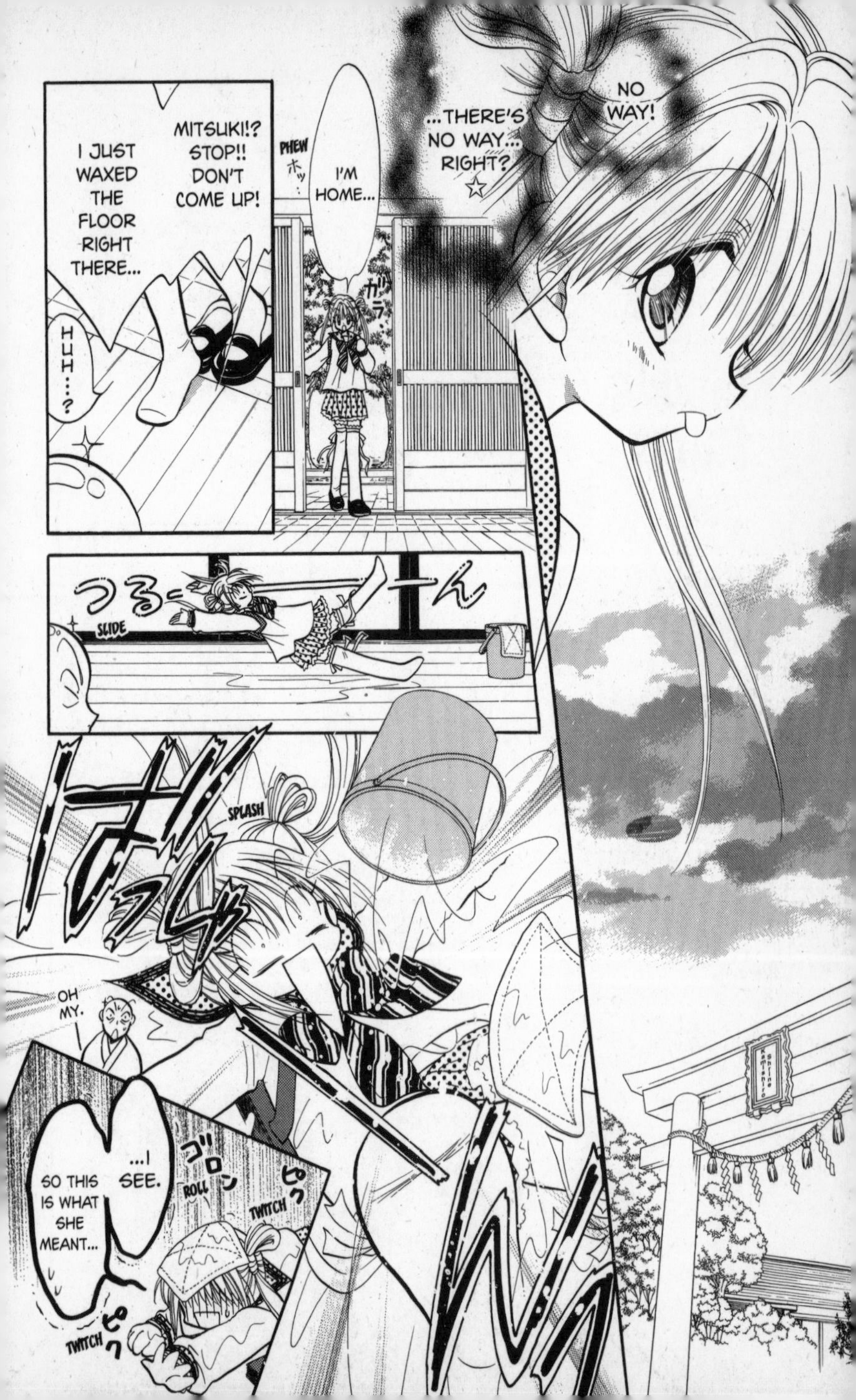
Kamishiro Shrine
NO WAY!
...THERE'S NO WAY... RIGHT? ☆
ガラ
PHEW
ホッ
I'M HOME...
MITSUKI!? STOP!! DON'T COME UP!
I JUST WAXED THE FLOOR RIGHT THERE...
HUH...?
つるーーん
SLIDE
SPLASH
OH MY.
ピク
TWITCH
ゴロン
ROLL
...I SEE.
SO THIS IS WHAT SHE MEANT...
ピク
TWITCH

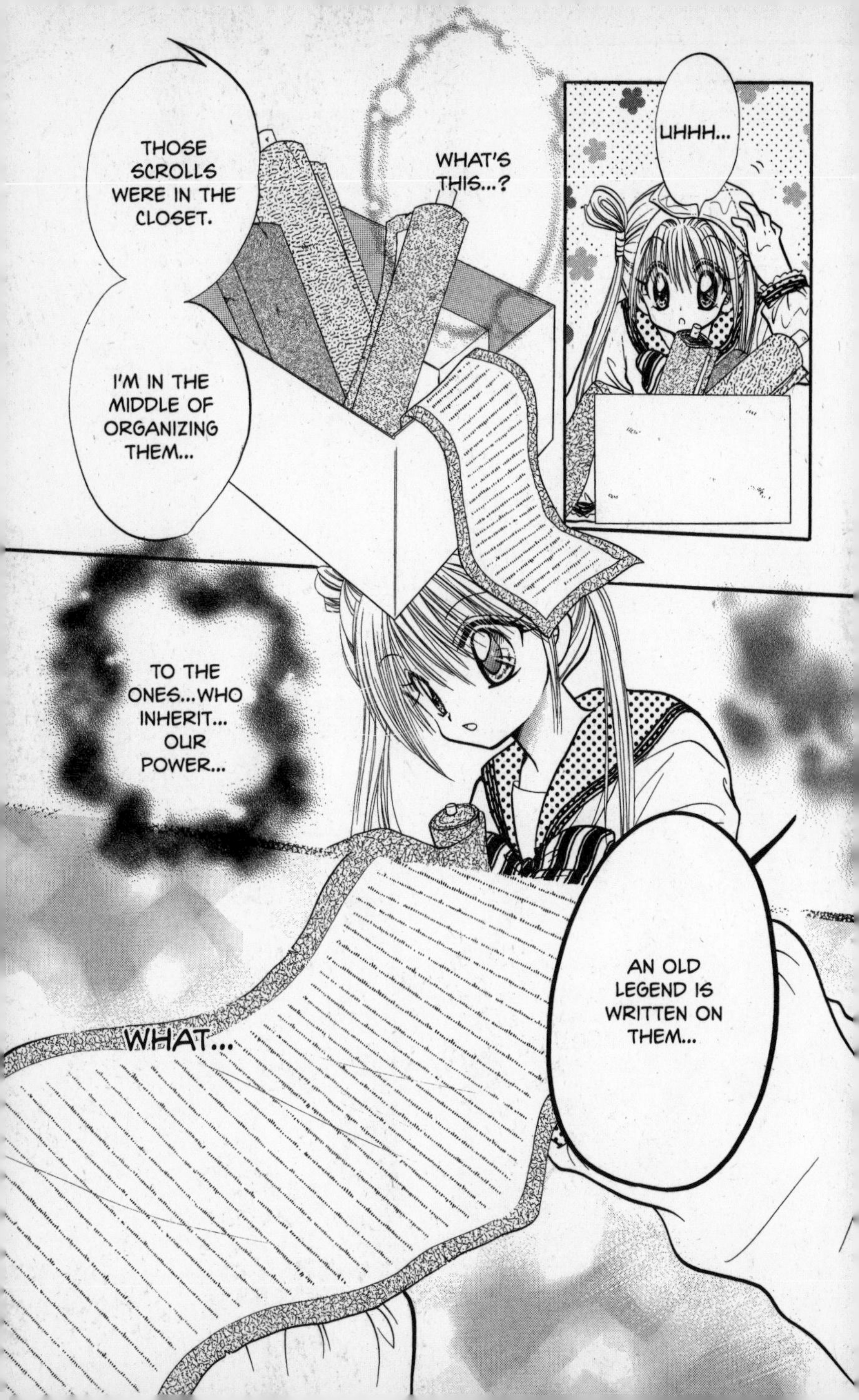
UHHH...
WHAT'S THIS...?
THOSE SCROLLS WERE IN THE CLOSET.
I'M IN THE MIDDLE OF ORGANIZING THEM...
AN OLD LEGEND IS WRITTEN ON THEM...
TO THE ONES...WHO INHERIT... OUR POWER...
WHAT...

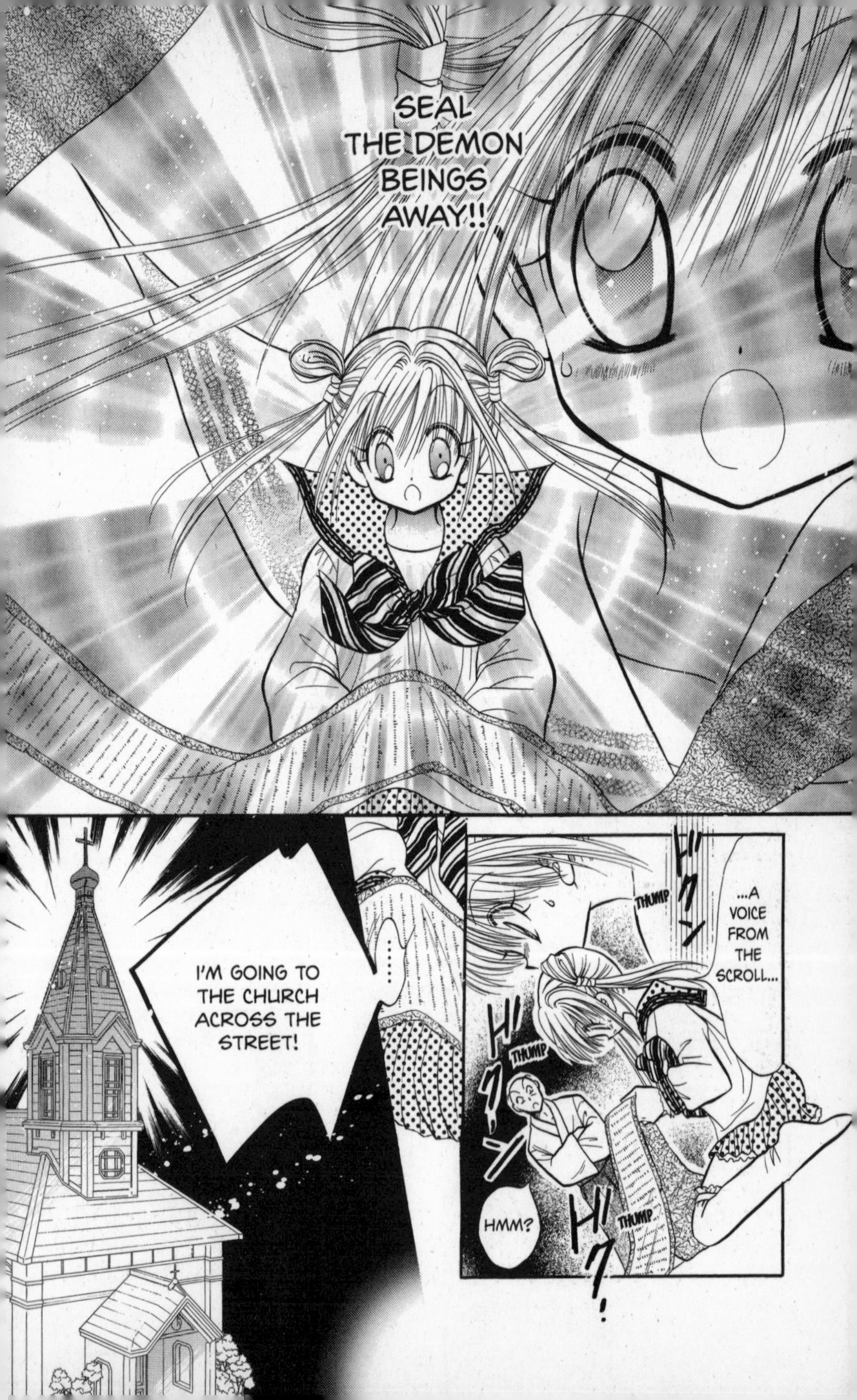
SEAL THE DEMON BEINGS AWAY!!
...A VOICE FROM THE SCROLL...
THUMP
THUMP
THUMP
HMM?
......
I'M GOING TO THE CHURCH ACROSS THE STREET!

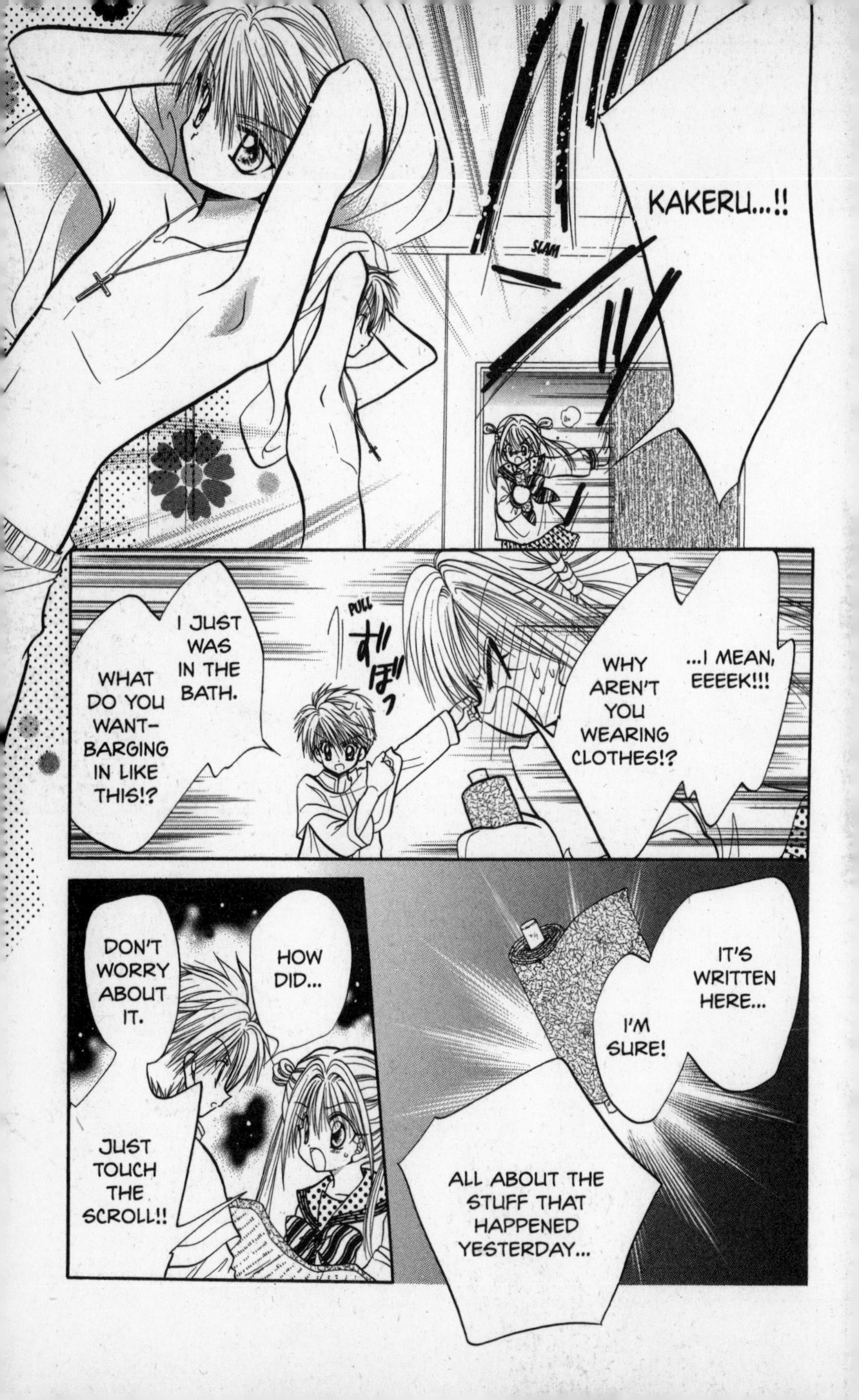
KAKERU...!!
SLAM
WHY AREN'T YOU WEARING CLOTHES!?
...I MEAN, EEEEK!!!
PULL
ずぼっ
I JUST WAS IN THE BATH.
WHAT DO YOU WANT-BARGING IN LIKE THIS!?
IT'S WRITTEN HERE...
I'M SURE!
ALL ABOUT THE STUFF THAT HAPPENED YESTERDAY...
HOW DID...
DON'T WORRY ABOUT IT.
JUST TOUCH THE SCROLL!!

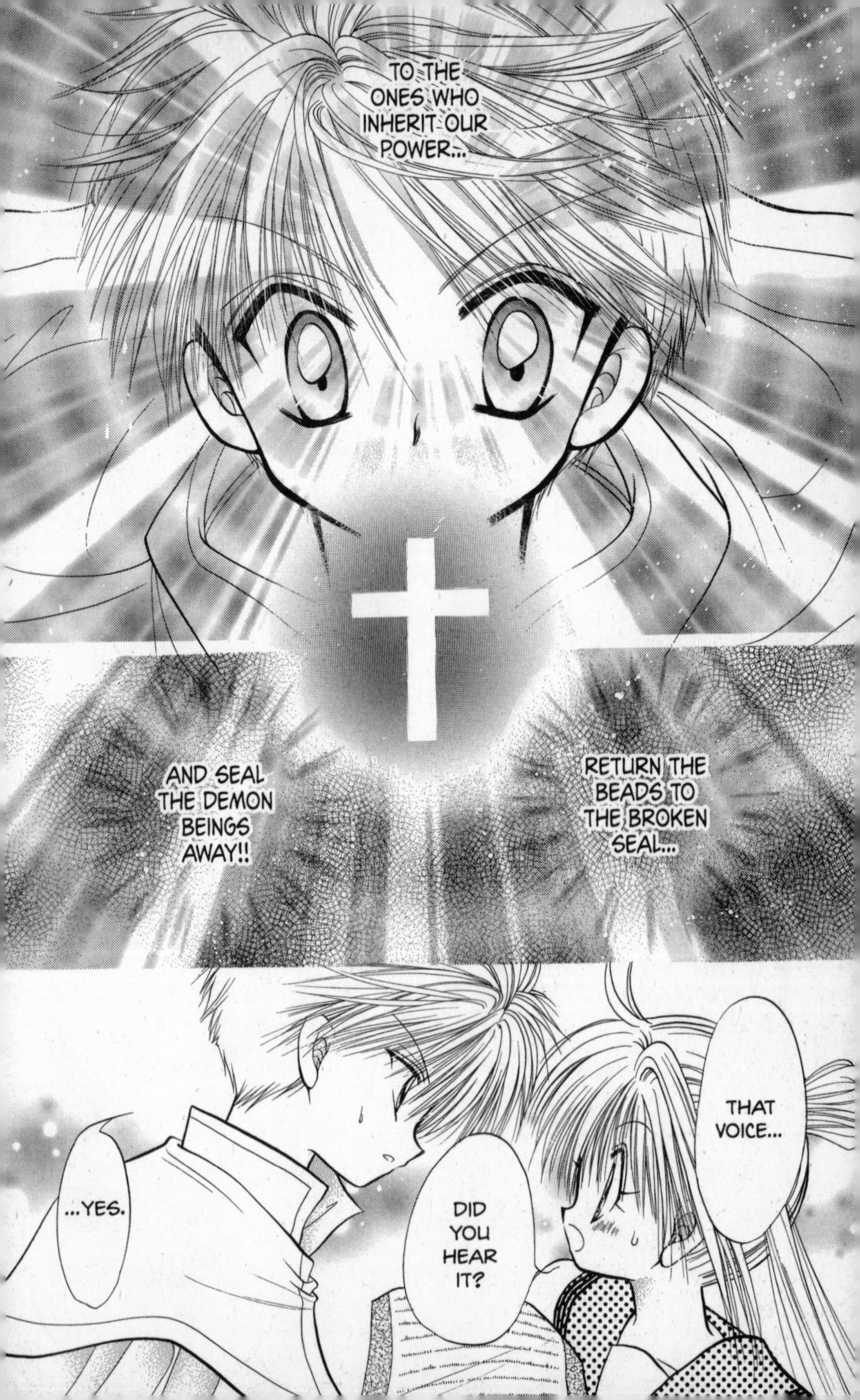
TO THE ONES WHO INHERIT OUR POWER...
RETURN THE BEADS TO THE BROKEN SEAL...
AND SEAL THE DEMON BEINGS AWAY!!
THAT VOICE...
DID YOU HEAR IT?
...YES.

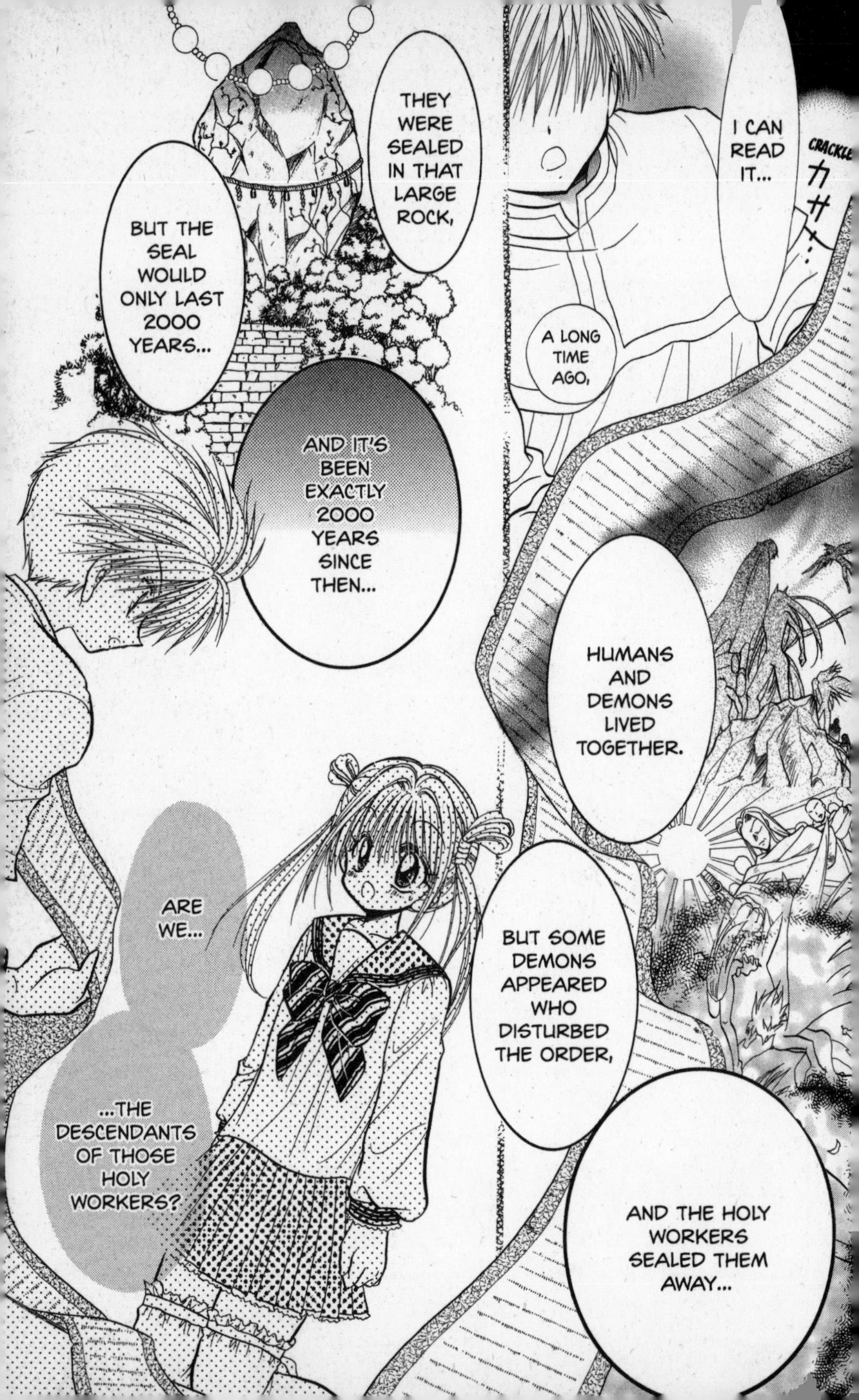
I CAN READ IT...
CRACKLE
カサ
A LONG TIME AGO,
HUMANS AND DEMONS LIVED TOGETHER.
BUT SOME DEMONS APPEARED WHO DISTURBED THE ORDER,
AND THE HOLY WORKERS SEALED THEM AWAY...
THEY WERE SEALED IN THAT LARGE ROCK,
BUT THE SEAL WOULD ONLY LAST 2000 YEARS...
AND IT'S BEEN EXACTLY 2000 YEARS SINCE THEN...
ARE WE...
...THE DESCENDANTS OF THOSE HOLY WORKERS?

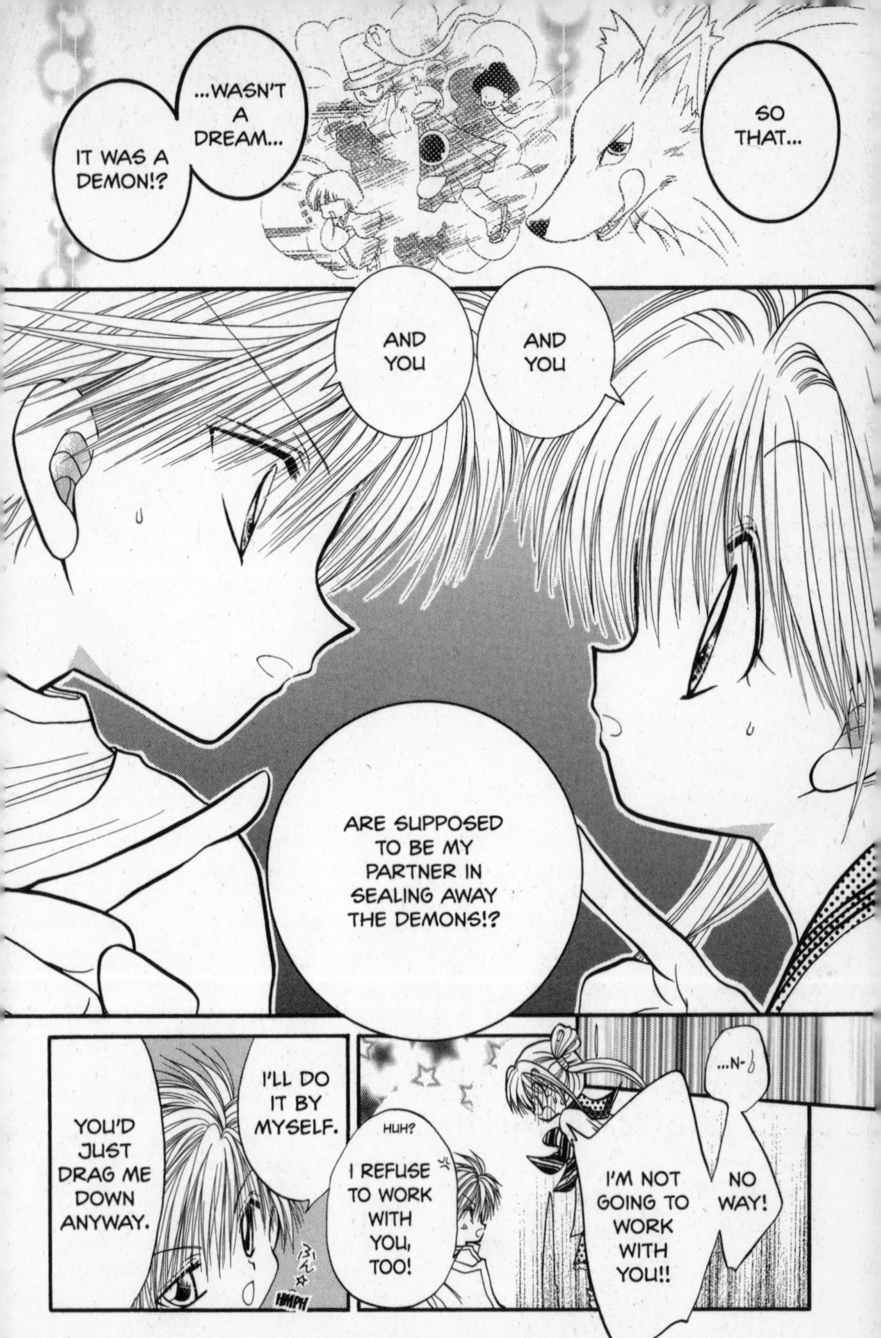
SO THAT...
...WASN'T A DREAM...
IT WAS A DEMON!?
AND YOU
AND YOU
ARE SUPPOSED TO BE MY PARTNER IN SEALING AWAY THE DEMONS!?
...N-
NO WAY!
I'M NOT GOING TO WORK WITH YOU!!
HUH?
I REFUSE TO WORK WITH YOU, TOO!
HMPH
I'LL DO IT BY MYSELF.
YOU'D JUST DRAG ME DOWN ANYWAY.

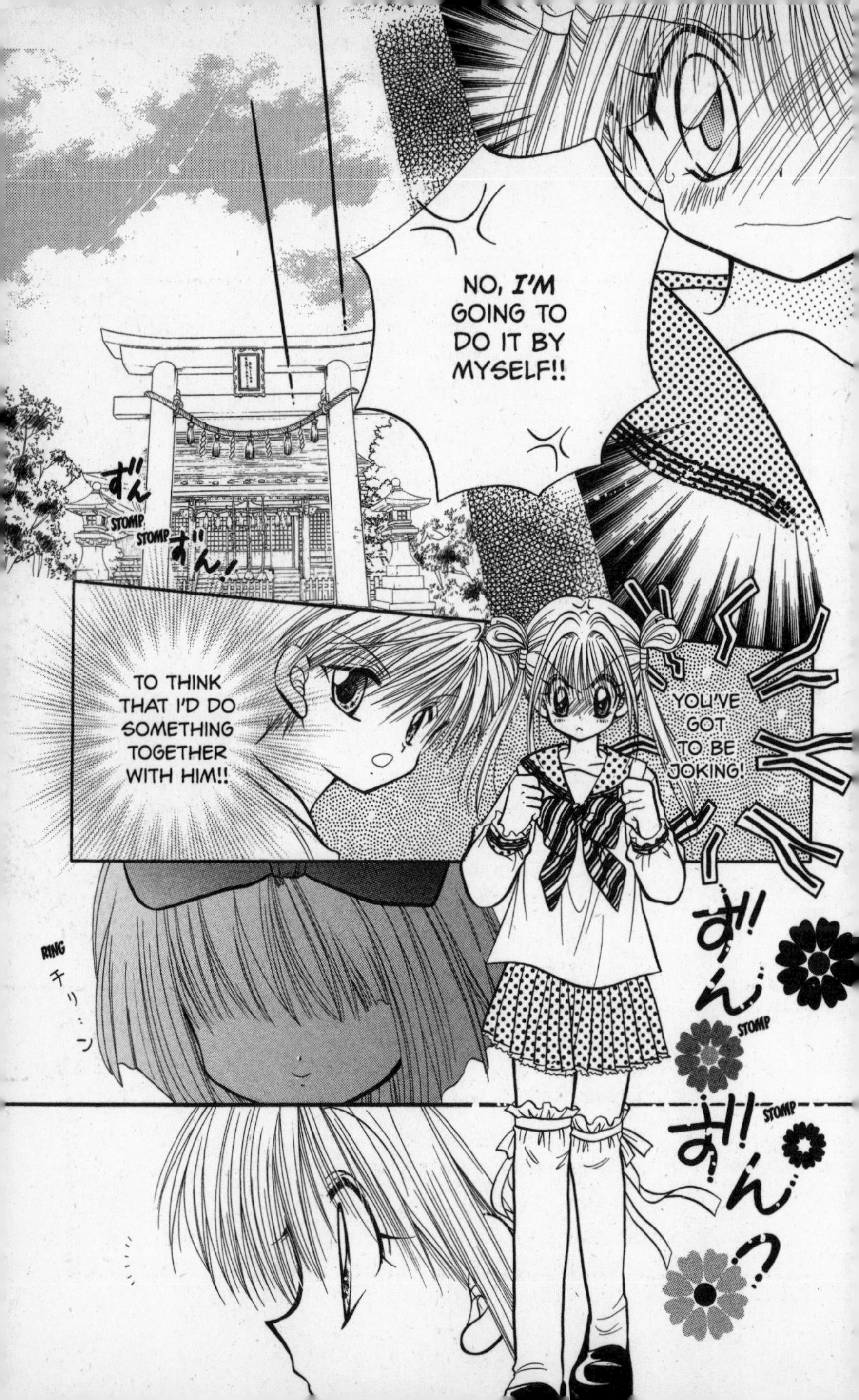
NO, I'M GOING TO DO IT BY MYSELF!!
ずん
STOMP
STOMP
ずん!
YOU'VE GOT TO BE JOKING!
ず!ん
STOMP
ず!ん
STOMP
ずんっ?
TO THINK THAT I'D DO SOMETHING TOGETHER WITH HIM!!
RING
チリ…ン

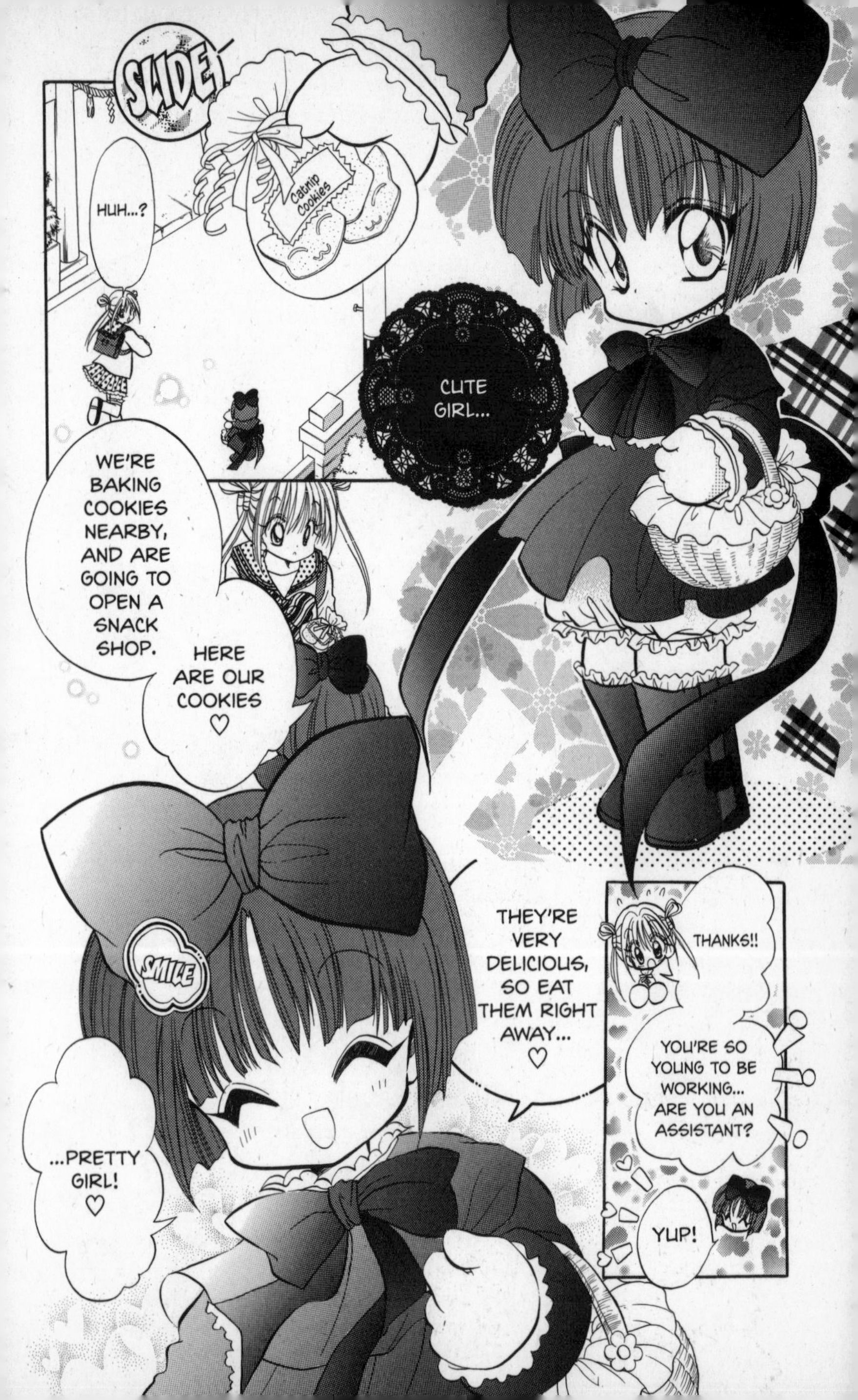
SLIDE
HUH...?
Catnip Cookies
CUTE GIRL...
WE'RE BAKING COOKIES NEARBY, AND ARE GOING TO OPEN A SNACK SHOP.
HERE ARE OUR COOKIES ♡
THEY'RE VERY DELICIOUS, SO EAT THEM RIGHT AWAY... ♡
THANKS!!
YOU'RE SO YOUNG TO BE WORKING... ARE YOU AN ASSISTANT?
YUP!
SMILE
...PRETTY GIRL! ♡

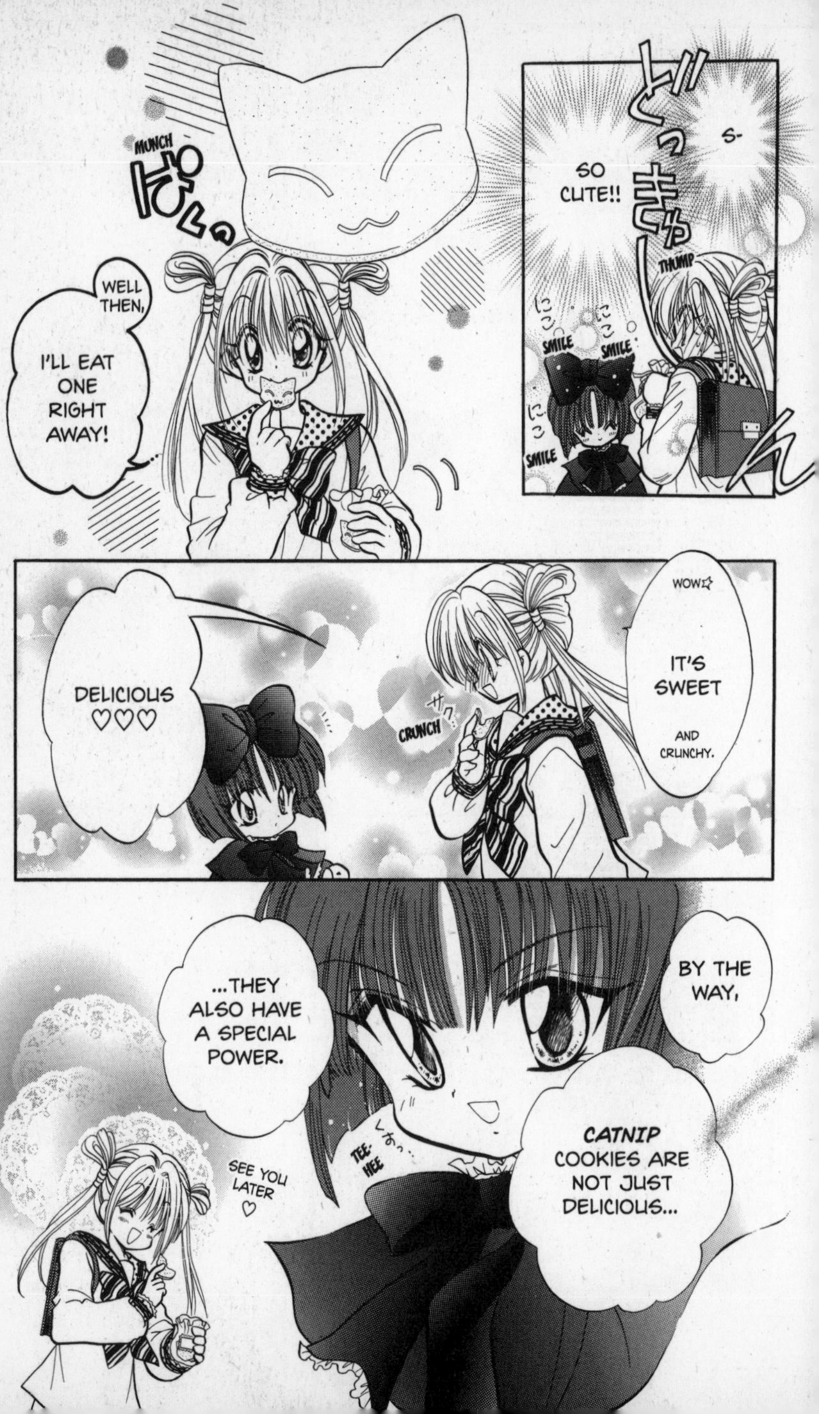
S-
SO CUTE!!
どっきゅん
THUMP
にこ SMILE
にこ SMILE
にこ SMILE
MUNCH ぱくっ
WELL THEN,
I'LL EAT ONE RIGHT AWAY!
WOW☆
IT'S SWEET
AND CRUNCHY.
サク… CRUNCH
DELICIOUS ♡♡♡
BY THE WAY,
CATNIP COOKIES ARE NOT JUST DELICIOUS...
...THEY ALSO HAVE A SPECIAL POWER.
くすっ… TEE-HEE
SEE YOU LATER ♡

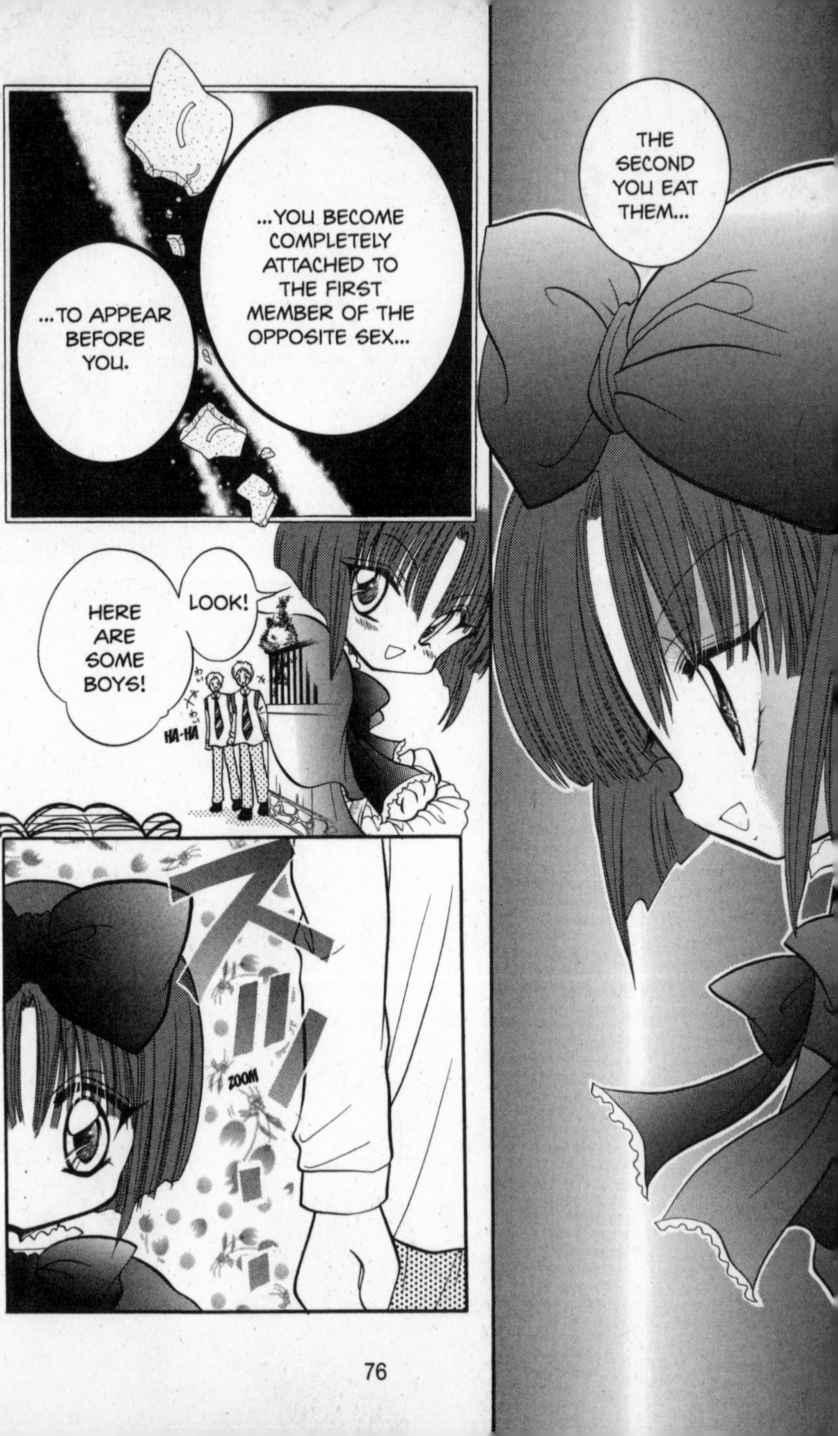
THE SECOND YOU EAT THEM...
...YOU BECOME COMPLETELY ATTACHED TO THE FIRST MEMBER OF THE OPPOSITE SEX...
...TO APPEAR BEFORE YOU.
LOOK!
HERE ARE SOME BOYS!
HA-HA
ZOOM

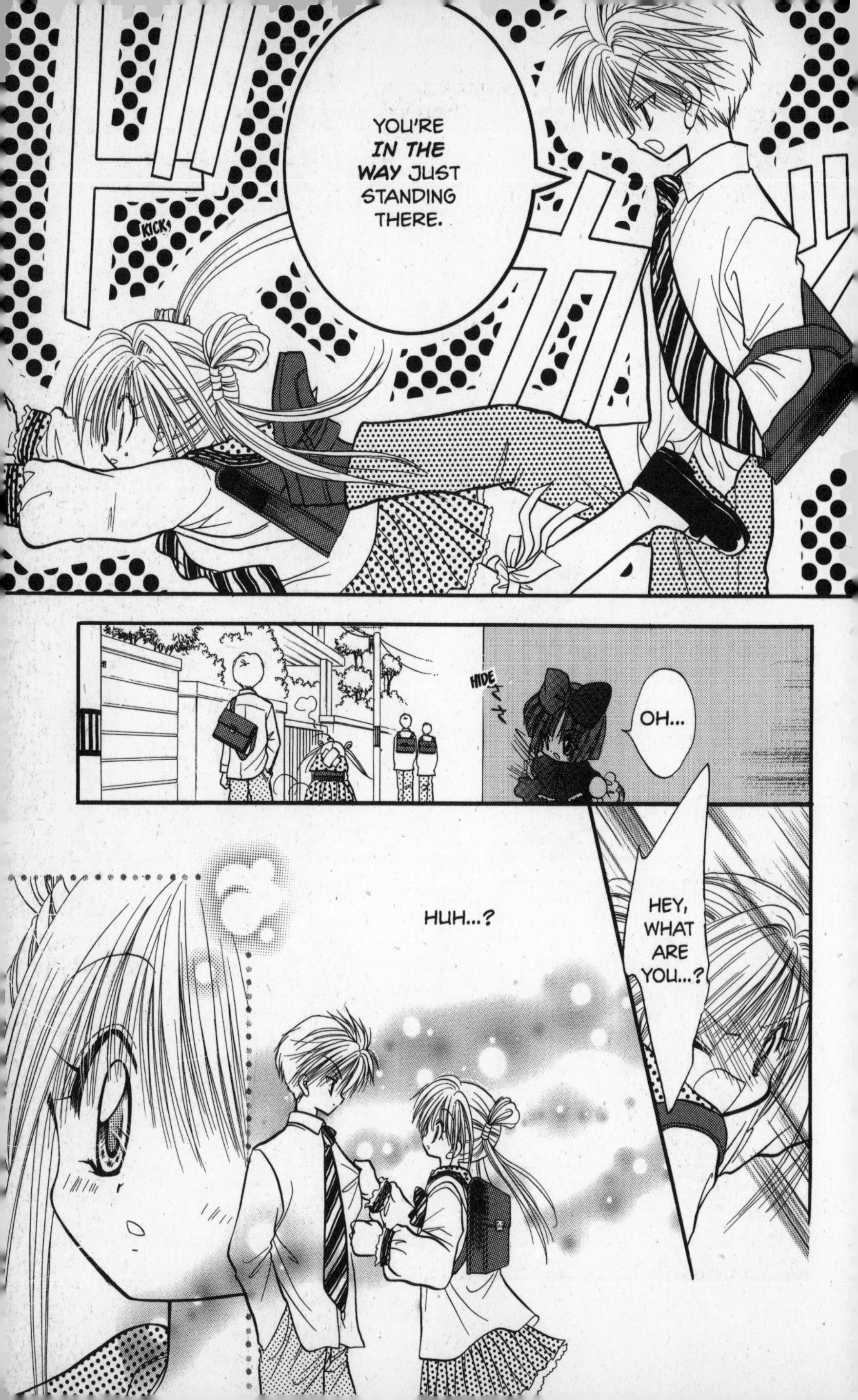
YOU'RE IN THE WAY JUST STANDING THERE.
KICK
HIDE
OH...
HEY, WHAT ARE YOU...?
HUH...?

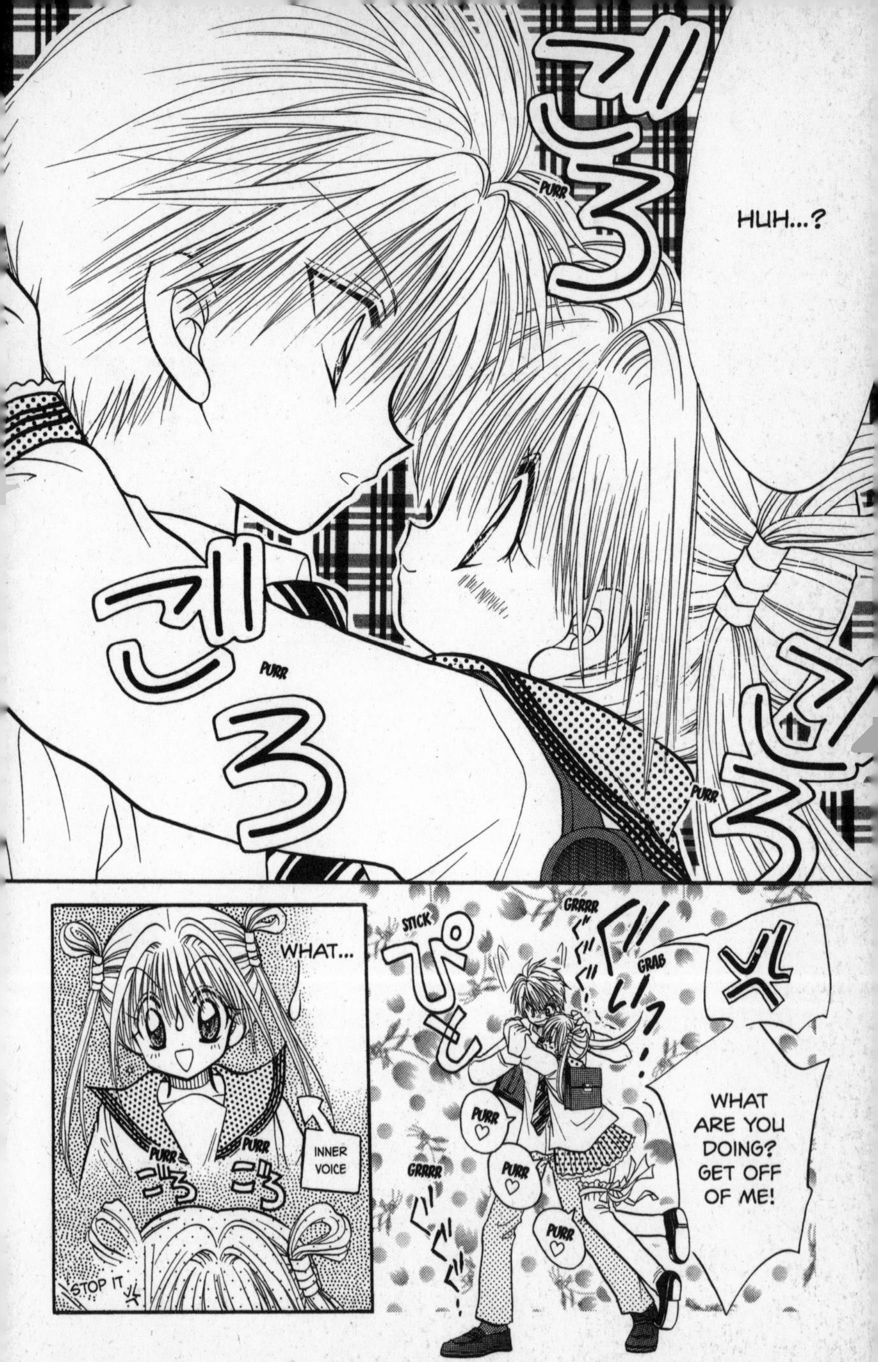
HUH...?
PURR
ごろ
PURR
ごろ
PURR
ごろ
GRRRR
GRAB
WHAT ARE YOU DOING? GET OFF OF ME!
STICK
ぴと
PURR ♡
PURR ♡
PURR ♡
GRRRR
WHAT...
INNER VOICE
PURR
PURR
ごろ ごろ
STOP IT

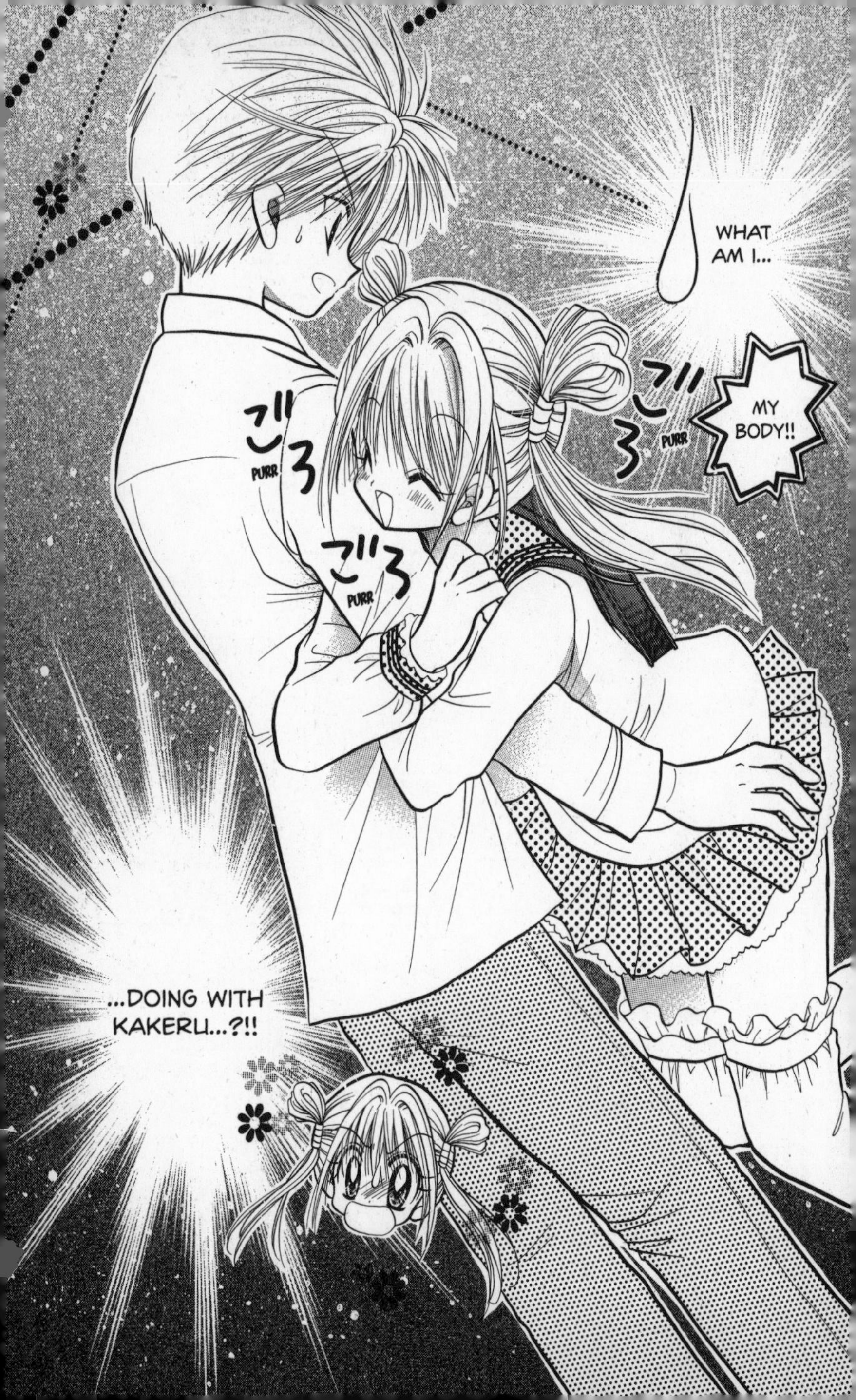
WHAT AM I...
MY BODY!!
ごろ
PURR
ごろ
PURR
ごろ
PURR
...DOING WITH KAKERU...?!!

Panic X Panic

PROFILE

VOL. 4

FROM THE AUTHOR'S ORIGINAL STORY NOTES

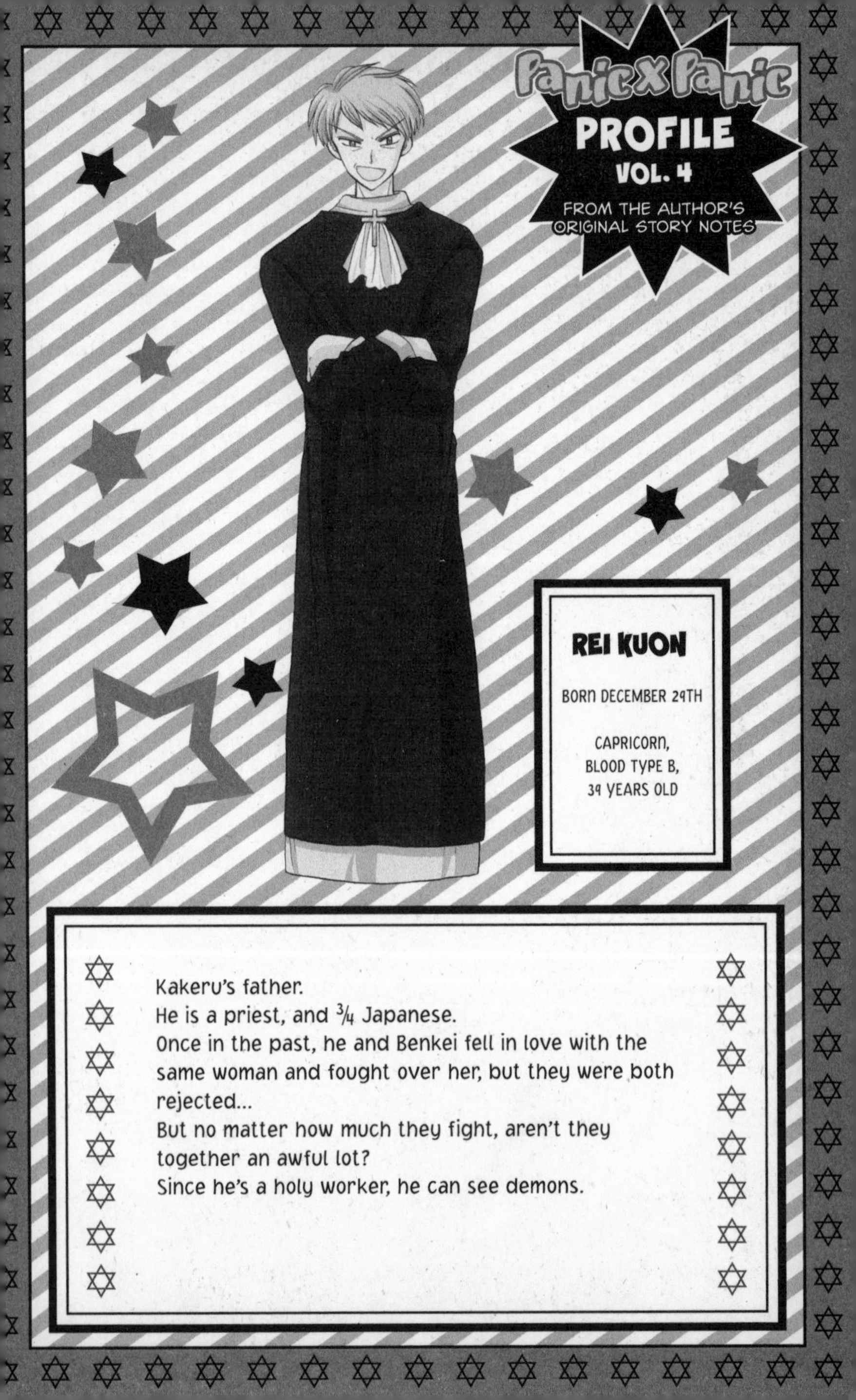

REI KUON

BORN DECEMBER 29TH

CAPRICORN,
BLOOD TYPE B,
39 YEARS OLD

Kakeru's father.
He is a priest, and 3/4 Japanese.
Once in the past, he and Benkei fell in love with the same woman and fought over her, but they were both rejected...
But no matter how much they fight, aren't they together an awful lot?
Since he's a holy worker, he can see demons.

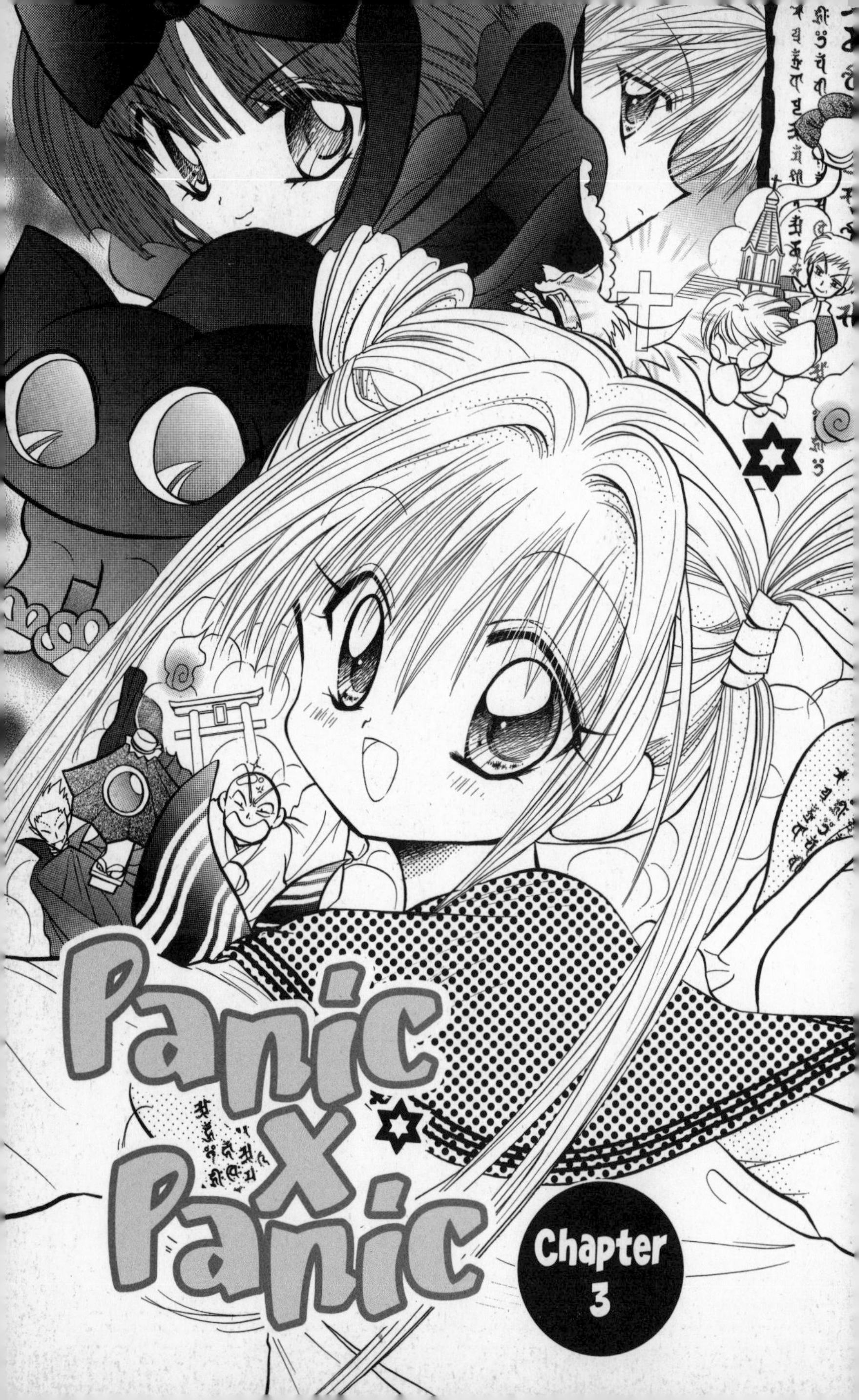
Panic X Panic
Chapter 3

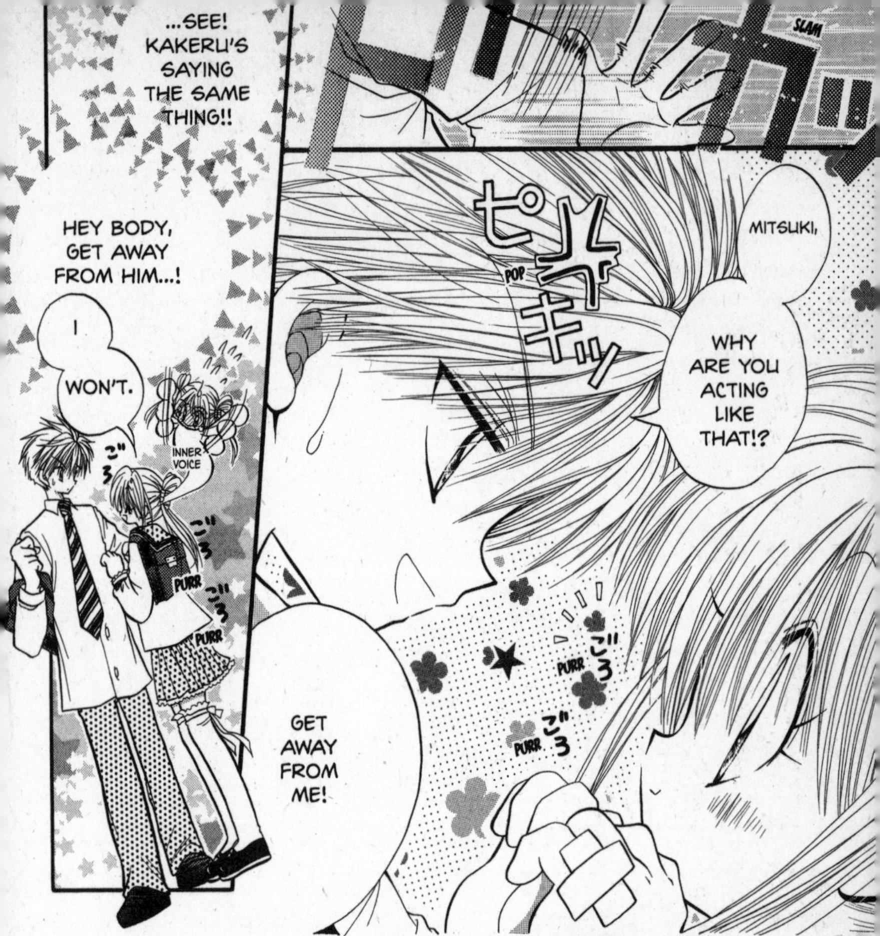
SLAM
MITSUKI,
WHY ARE YOU ACTING LIKE THAT!?
POP
GET AWAY FROM ME!
PURR
PURR
...SEE! KAKERU'S SAYING THE SAME THING!!
HEY BODY, GET AWAY FROM HIM...!
I WON'T.
INNER VOICE
PURR
PURR

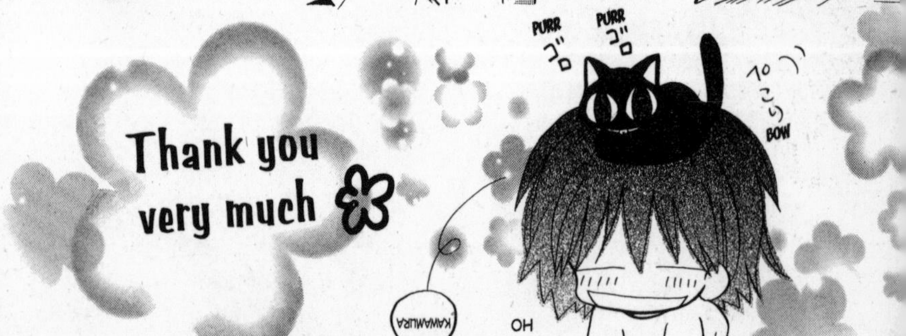
PURR
PURR
BOW
Thank you very much
KAWAMURA
HO

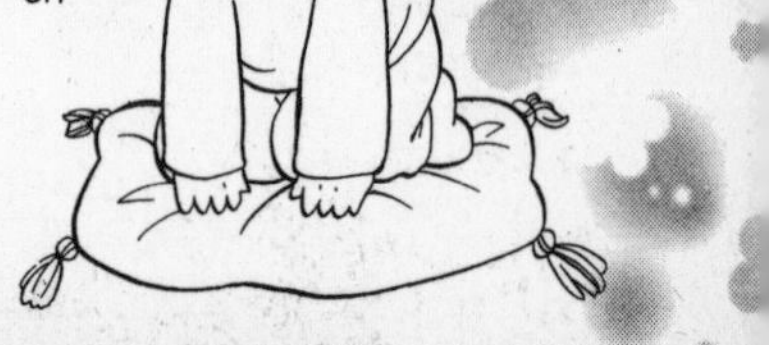

THE FIRST VOLUME OF "PANIC X PANIC" (!!) HAS MADE IT TO PRINT♡ IT'S REALLY BECAUSE OF EVERYONE'S SUPPORT—THOSE OF YOU WHO ARE READING MY WORK FOR THE FIRST TIME, AND THOSE OF YOU WHO HAVE SUPPORTED ME FROM THE BEGINNING!! I'M TRULY GRATEFUL♡♡

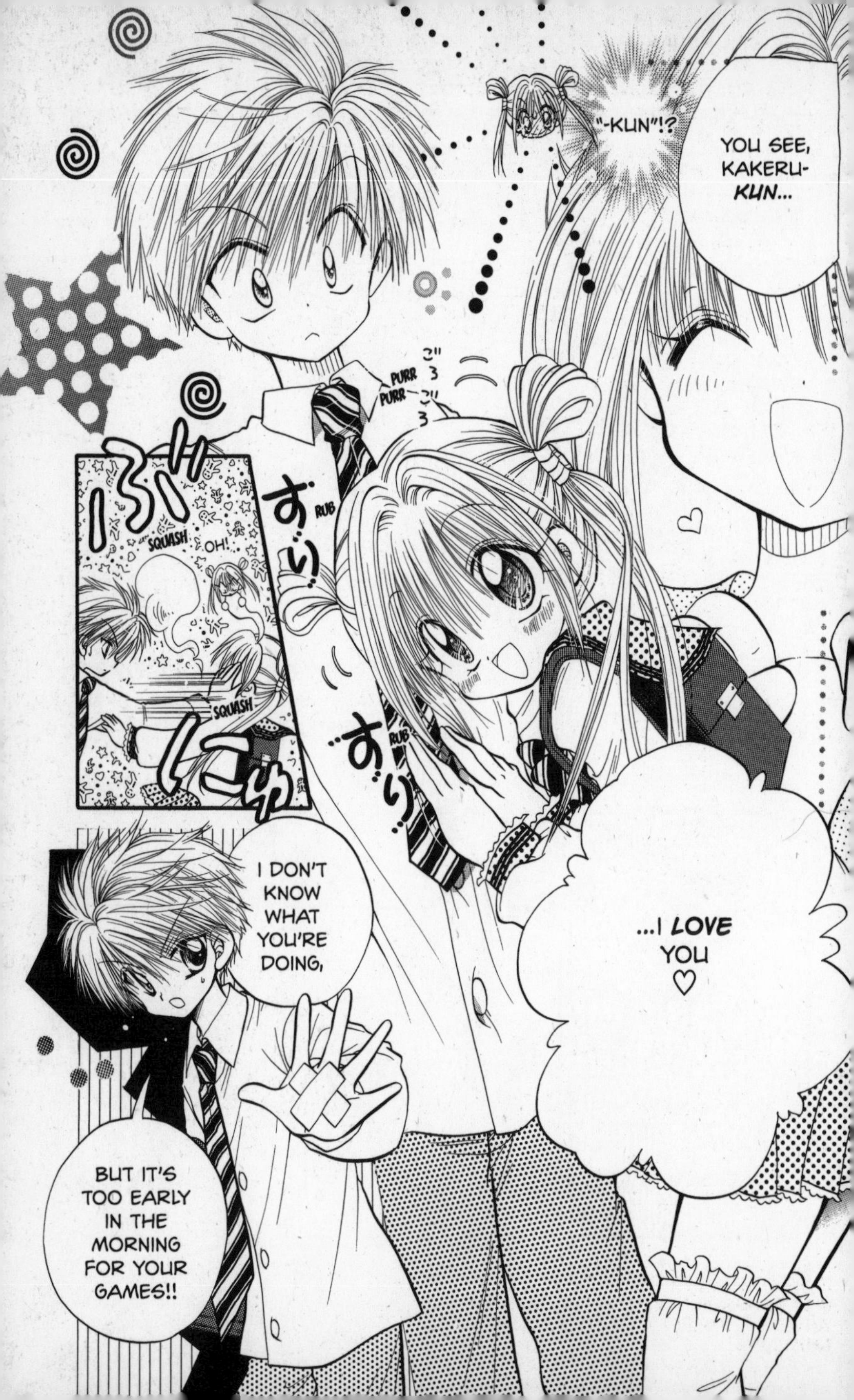
YOU SEE, KAKERU-KUN...
"-KUN"!?
ごろごろ PURR PURR
すり RUB
すり RUB
ぶにゅ
SQUASH
OH!
SQUASH
...I LOVE YOU ♡
I DON'T KNOW WHAT YOU'RE DOING,
BUT IT'S TOO EARLY IN THE MORNING FOR YOUR GAMES!!

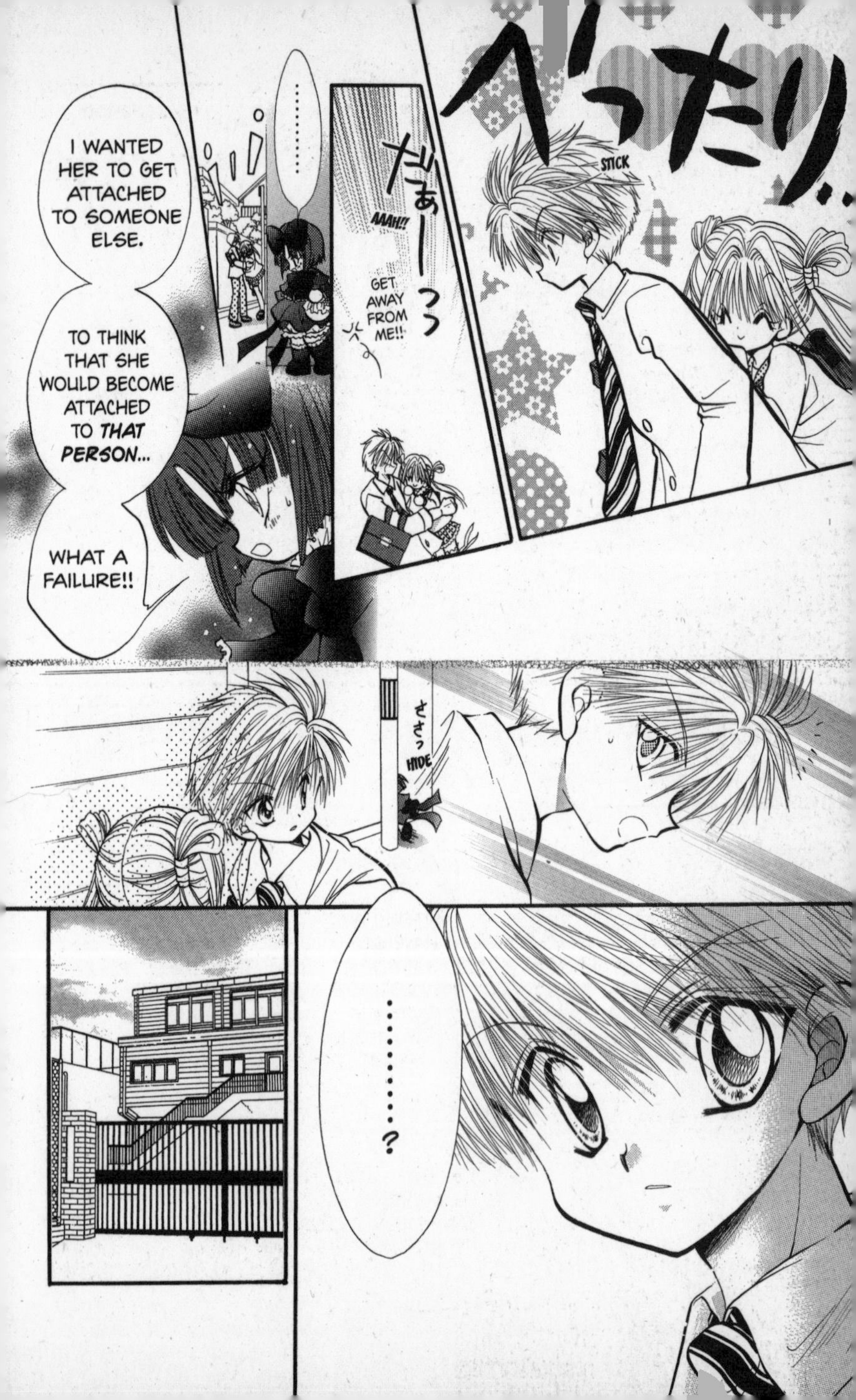
へったり…
STICK
だぁーっっ
AAAH!!
GET AWAY FROM ME!!
……
I WANTED HER TO GET ATTACHED TO SOMEONE ELSE.
TO THINK THAT SHE WOULD BECOME ATTACHED TO *THAT PERSON*...
WHAT A FAILURE!!
ささっ
HIDE
……?

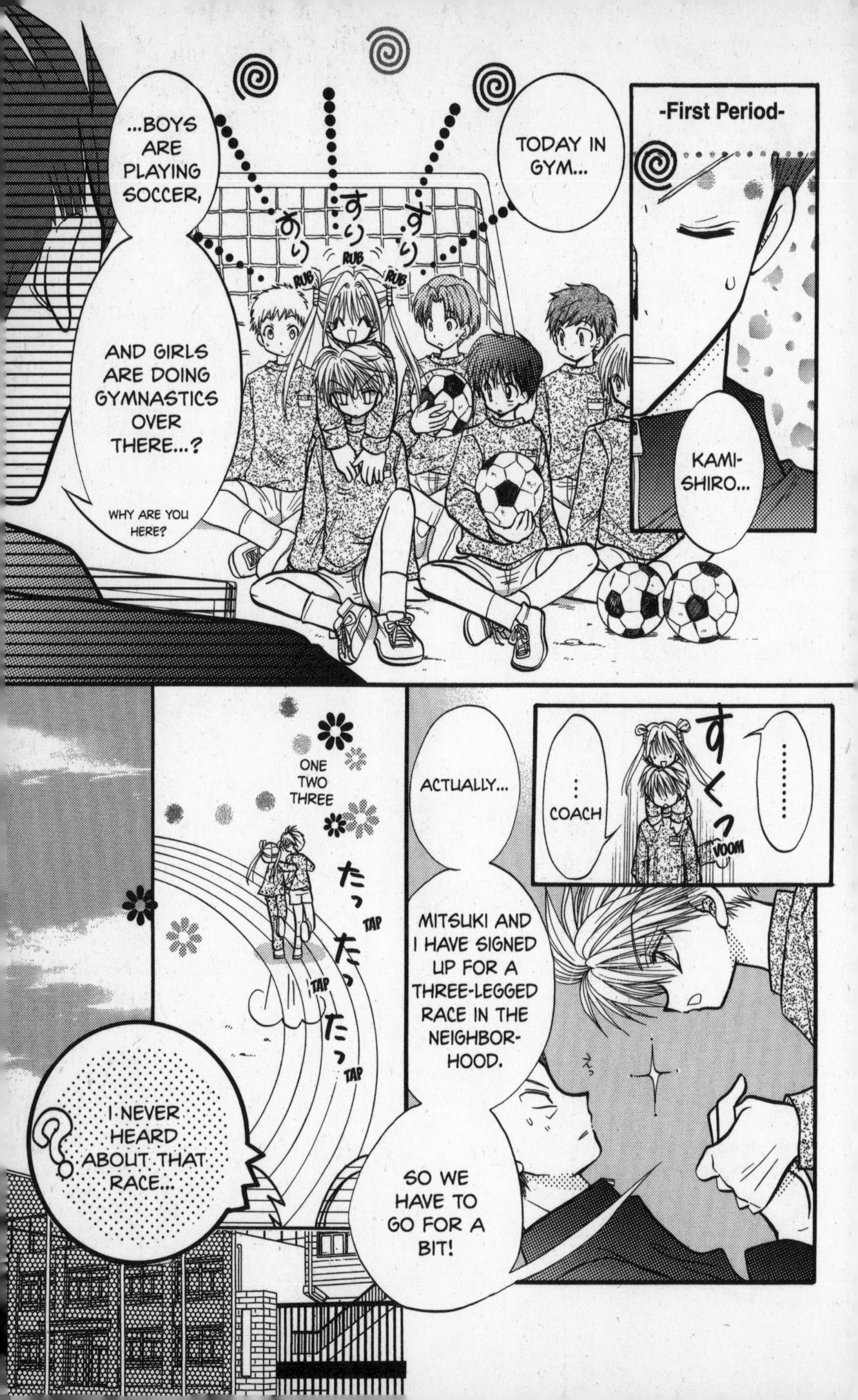
-First Period-
KAMI-SHIRO...
TODAY IN GYM...
...BOYS ARE PLAYING SOCCER,
AND GIRLS ARE DOING GYMNASTICS OVER THERE...?
WHY ARE YOU HERE?
すり RUB
すり RUB
すり RUB
......
...COACH
すくっ VOOM
ACTUALLY...
MITSUKI AND I HAVE SIGNED UP FOR A THREE-LEGGED RACE IN THE NEIGHBOR-HOOD.
SO WE HAVE TO GO FOR A BIT!
ONE TWO THREE
たっ TAP
たっ TAP
たっ TAP
I NEVER HEARD ABOUT THAT RACE...

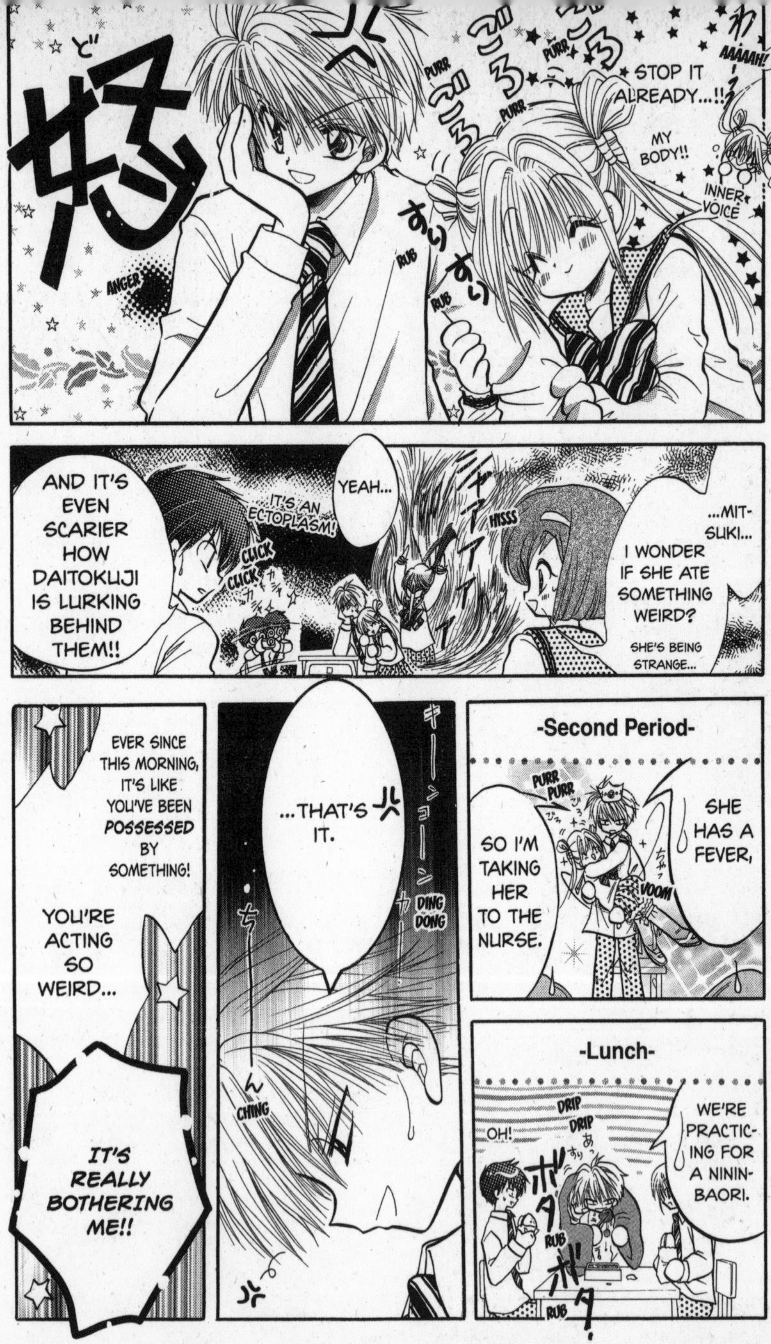
AAAAAH!
STOP IT ALREADY...!!
MY BODY!!
INNER VOICE
PURR
PURR
PURR
RUB
RUB
ANGER
...MIT-SUKI...
I WONDER IF SHE ATE SOMETHING WEIRD?
SHE'S BEING STRANGE...
HISSS
YEAH...
IT'S AN ECTOPLASM!
CLICK
CLICK
AND IT'S EVEN SCARIER HOW DAITOKUJI IS LURKING BEHIND THEM!!
-Second Period-
PURR PURR
SHE HAS A FEVER,
SO I'M TAKING HER TO THE NURSE.
VOOM
-Lunch-
WE'RE PRACTIC-ING FOR A NININ-BAORI.
DRIP
DRIP
OH!
RUB
RUB
DING DONG
...THAT'S IT.
CHING
EVER SINCE THIS MORNING, IT'S LIKE YOU'VE BEEN POSSESSED BY SOMETHING!
YOU'RE ACTING SO WEIRD...
IT'S REALLY BOTHERING ME!!

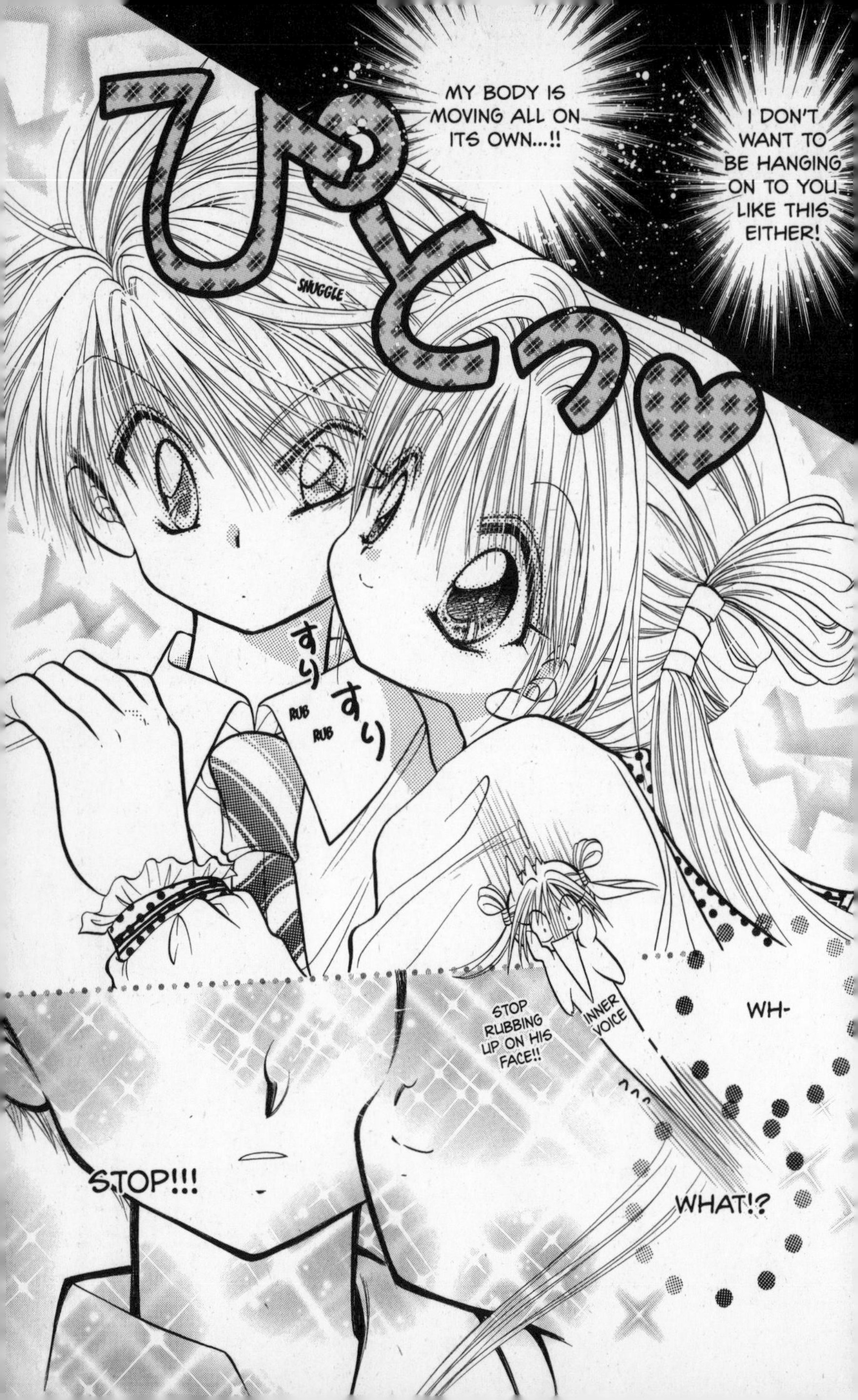
I DON'T WANT TO BE HANGING ON TO YOU LIKE THIS EITHER!
MY BODY IS MOVING ALL ON ITS OWN...!!
ぴとっ♥
SNUGGLE
すりすり
RUB RUB
WH-
WHAT!?
INNER VOICE
STOP RUBBING UP ON HIS FACE!!
STOP!!!

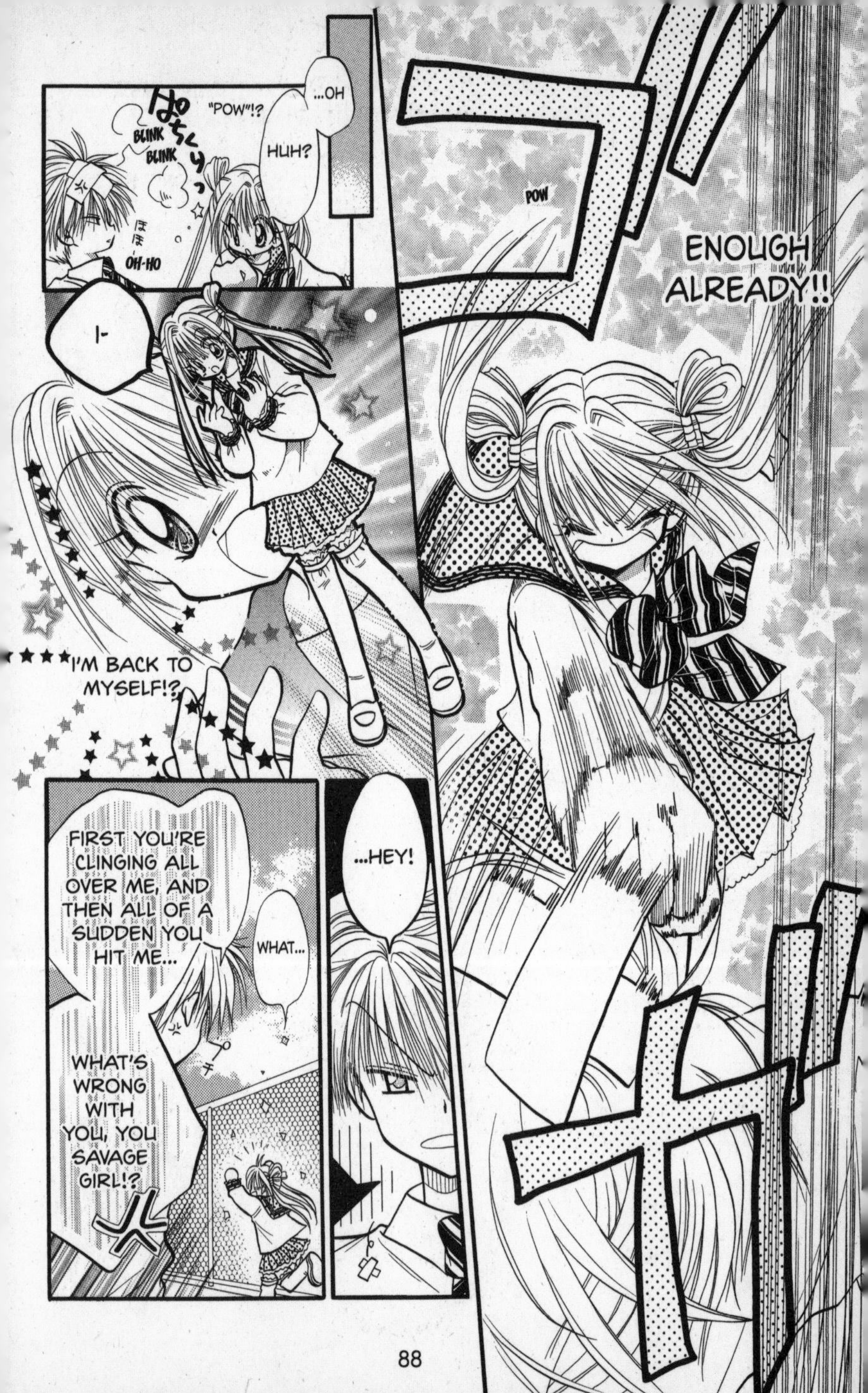
POW
ENOUGH ALREADY!!
...OH
HUH?
"POW"!?
ぱちくりっ
BLINK BLINK
ほほ
OH-HO
I'M BACK TO MYSELF!?
...HEY!
WHAT...
FIRST YOU'RE CLINGING ALL OVER ME, AND THEN ALL OF A SUDDEN YOU HIT ME...
WHAT'S WRONG WITH YOU, YOU SAVAGE GIRL!?

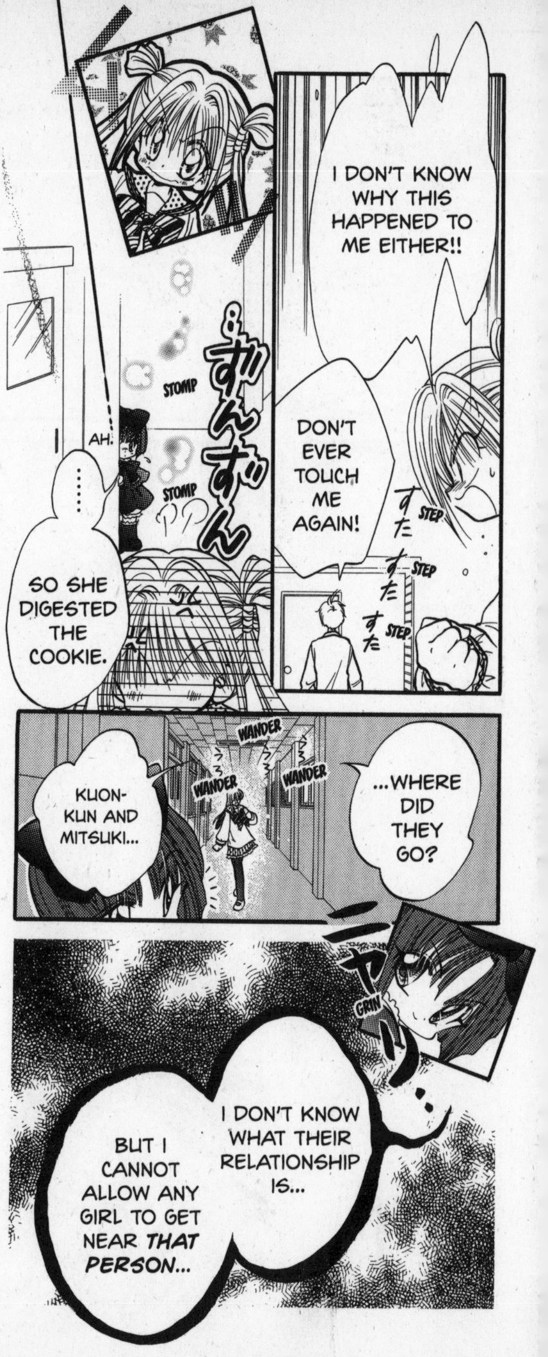
I DON'T KNOW WHY THIS HAPPENED TO ME EITHER!!
DON'T EVER TOUCH ME AGAIN!
すたすたすた
STEP
STEP
STEP
ずんずん
STOMP
STOMP
AH...
......
SO SHE DIGESTED THE COOKIE.
...WHERE DID THEY GO?
WANDER
WANDER
WANDER
KUON-KUN AND MITSUKI...
ニヤ
GRIN
I DON'T KNOW WHAT THEIR RELATIONSHIP IS...
BUT I CANNOT ALLOW ANY GIRL TO GET NEAR *THAT PERSON*...

Nobody Cares The Author's Favorite Thing To Do!

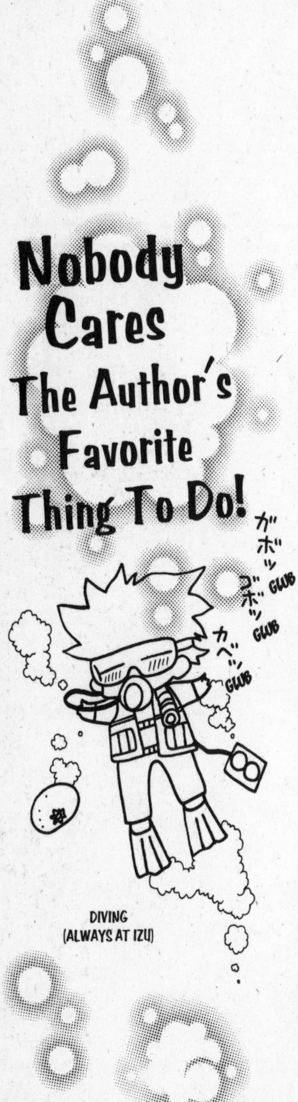
GLUB
GLUB
GLUB

DIVING
(ALWAYS AT IZU)

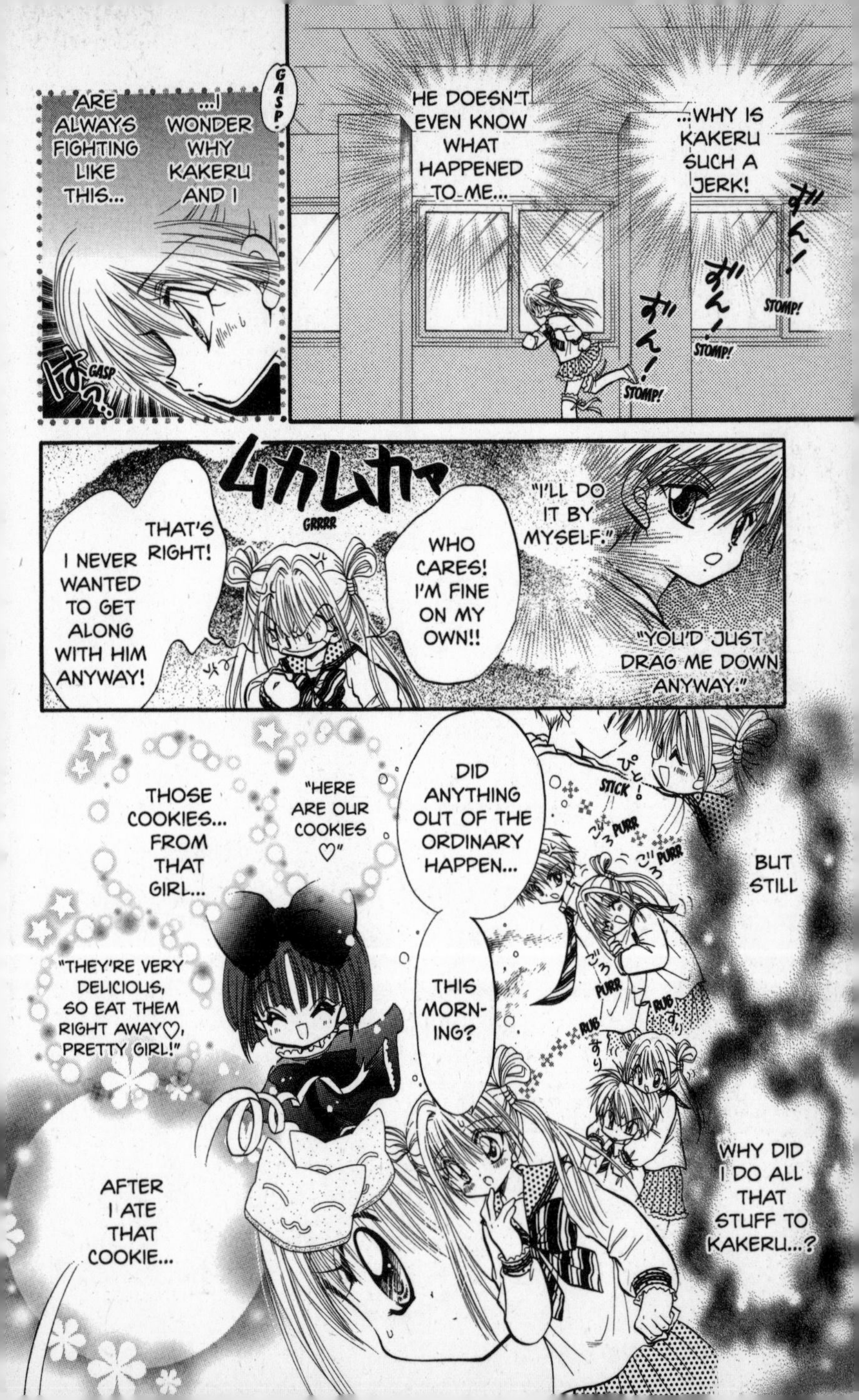
...WHY IS KAKERU SUCH A JERK!
ずん！ STOMP!
ずん！ STOMP!
ずん！ STOMP!
HE DOESN'T EVEN KNOW WHAT HAPPENED TO ME...
GASP.
...I WONDER WHY KAKERU AND I
ARE ALWAYS FIGHTING LIKE THIS...
はっ GASP
"I'LL DO IT BY MYSELF."
"YOU'D JUST DRAG ME DOWN ANYWAY."
ムカムカ GRRRR
WHO CARES! I'M FINE ON MY OWN!!
THAT'S RIGHT!
I NEVER WANTED TO GET ALONG WITH HIM ANYWAY!
BUT STILL
WHY DID I DO ALL THAT STUFF TO KAKERU...?
ぴと STICK
ごろ PURR
ごろ PURR
ごろ PURR
すり RUB
すり RUB
DID ANYTHING OUT OF THE ORDINARY HAPPEN...
THIS MORNING?
"HERE ARE OUR COOKIES ♡"
THOSE COOKIES... FROM THAT GIRL...
"THEY'RE VERY DELICIOUS, SO EAT THEM RIGHT AWAY♡, PRETTY GIRL!"
AFTER I ATE THAT COOKIE...

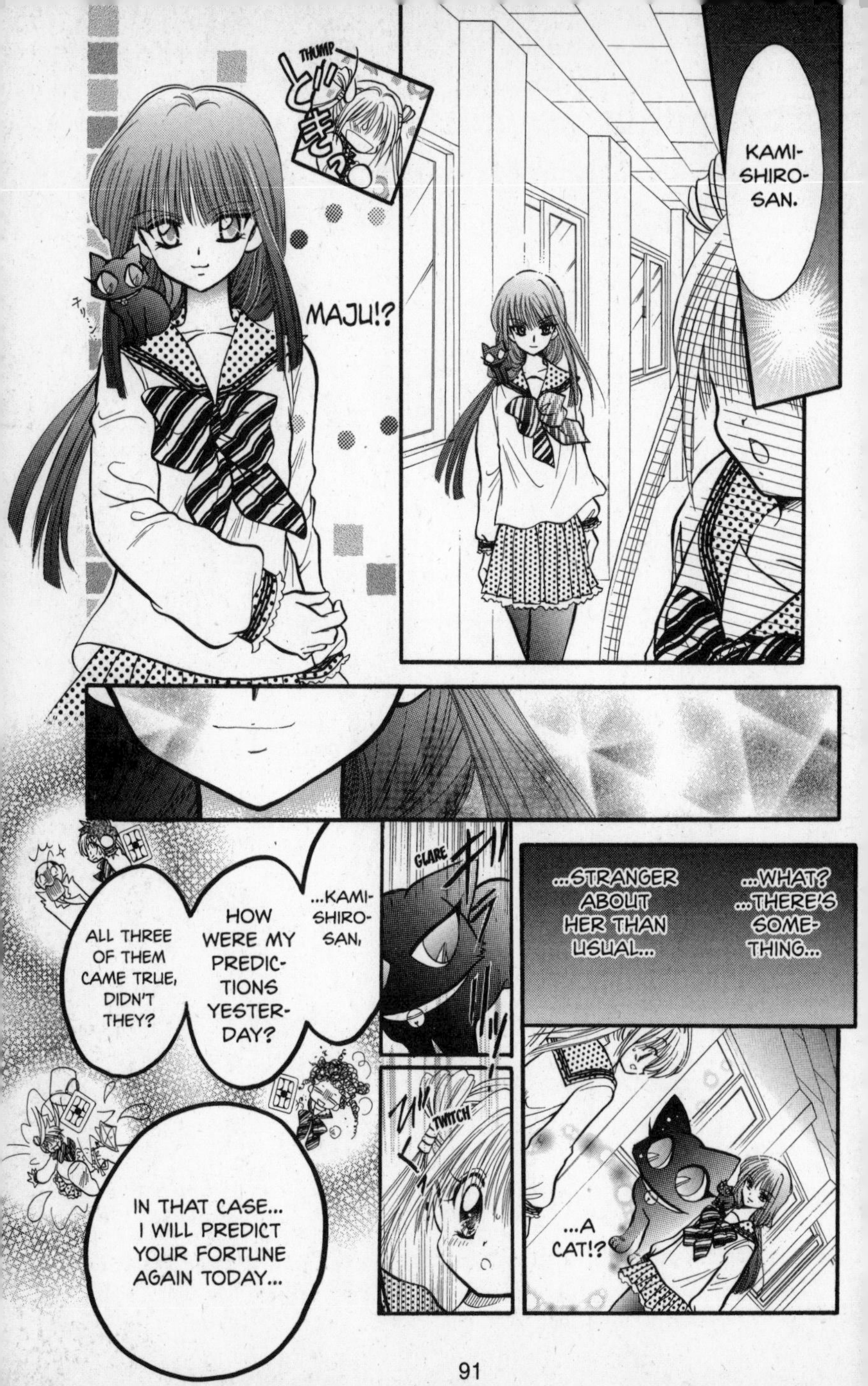
KAMI-SHIRO-SAN.
THUMP
MAJU!?
...WHAT? ...THERE'S SOME-THING...
...STRANGER ABOUT HER THAN USUAL...
GLARE
...A CAT!?
TWITCH
...KAMI-SHIRO-SAN,
HOW WERE MY PREDIC-TIONS YESTER-DAY?
ALL THREE OF THEM CAME TRUE, DIDN'T THEY?
IN THAT CASE... I WILL PREDICT YOUR FORTUNE AGAIN TODAY...

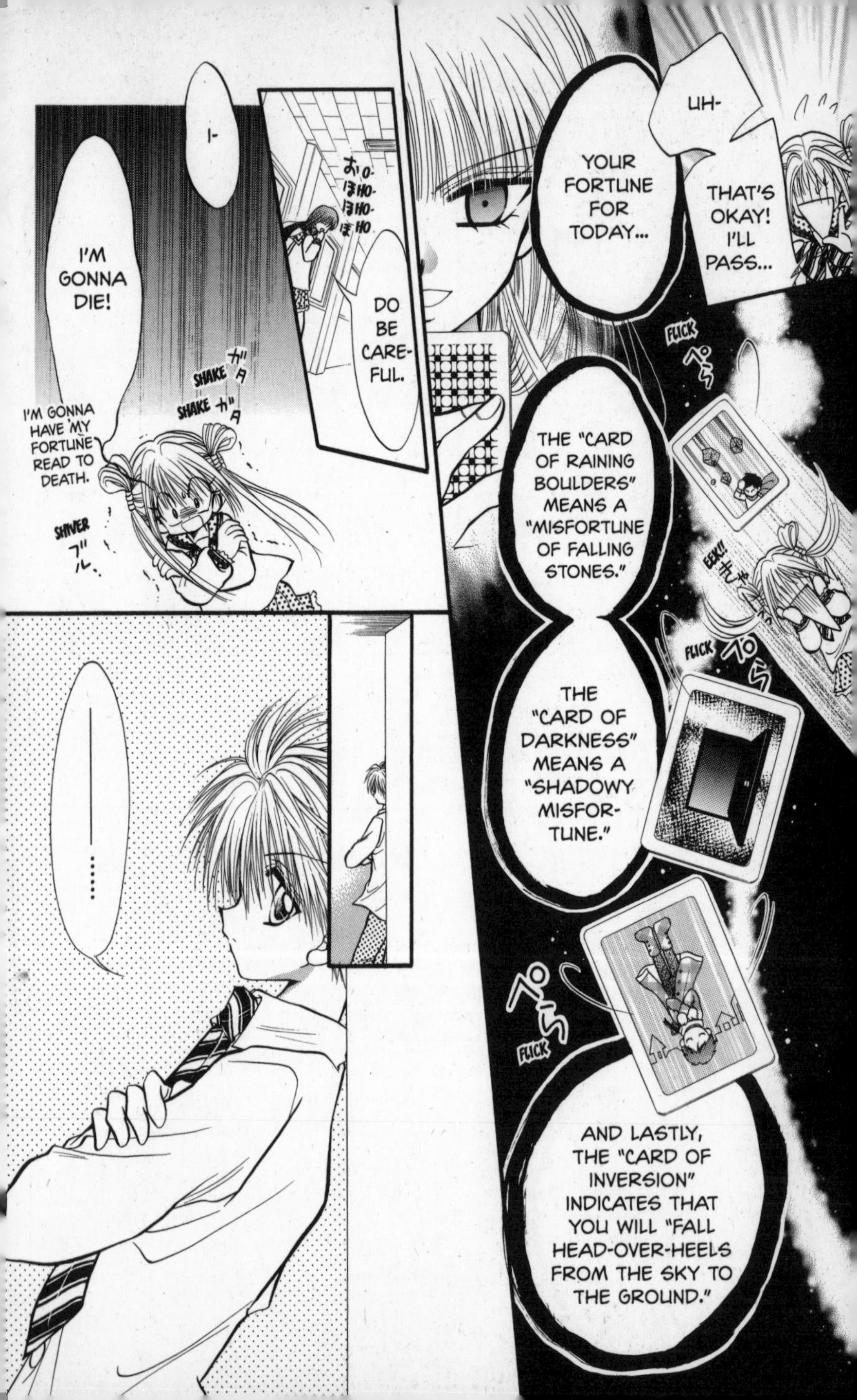
UH-
THAT'S OKAY! I'LL PASS...
YOUR FORTUNE FOR TODAY...
FLICK
THE "CARD OF RAINING BOULDERS" MEANS A "MISFORTUNE OF FALLING STONES."
EEK!!
FLICK
THE "CARD OF DARKNESS" MEANS A "SHADOWY MISFOR-TUNE."
FLICK
AND LASTLY, THE "CARD OF INVERSION" INDICATES THAT YOU WILL "FALL HEAD-OVER-HEELS FROM THE SKY TO THE GROUND."
I-
O-HO-HO-HO
DO BE CARE-FUL.
I'M GONNA DIE!
SHAKE
SHAKE
I'M GONNA HAVE MY FORTUNE READ TO DEATH.
SHIVER
—......

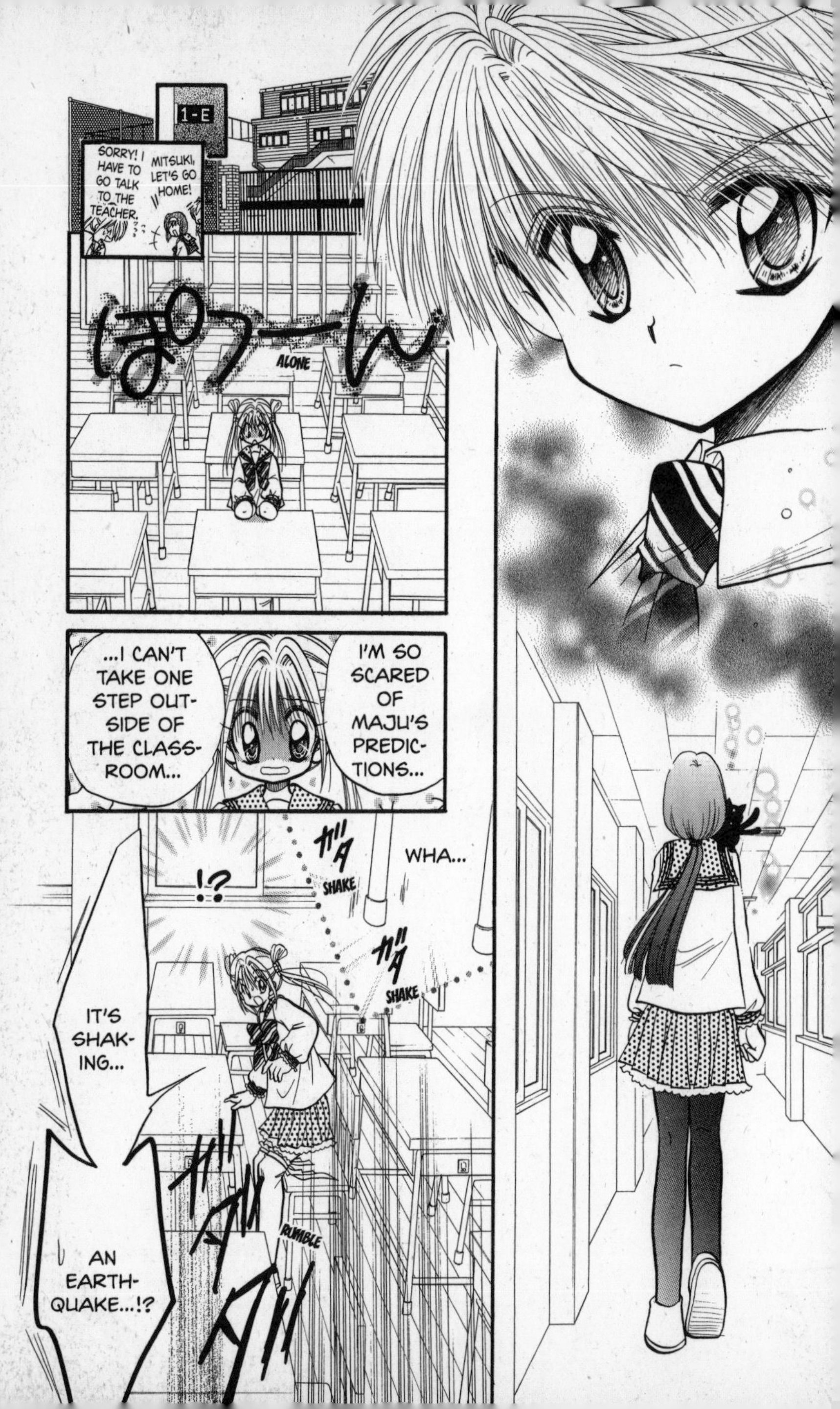
MITSUKI, LET'S GO HOME!
SORRY! I HAVE TO GO TALK TO THE TEACHER.
1-E
ぽつーん
ALONE
I'M SO SCARED OF MAJU'S PREDICTIONS...
...I CAN'T TAKE ONE STEP OUT-SIDE OF THE CLASS-ROOM...
WHA...
!?
ガタ
SHAKE
ガタ
SHAKE
IT'S SHAK-ING...
ガタガタ
RUMBLE
AN EARTH-QUAKE...!?

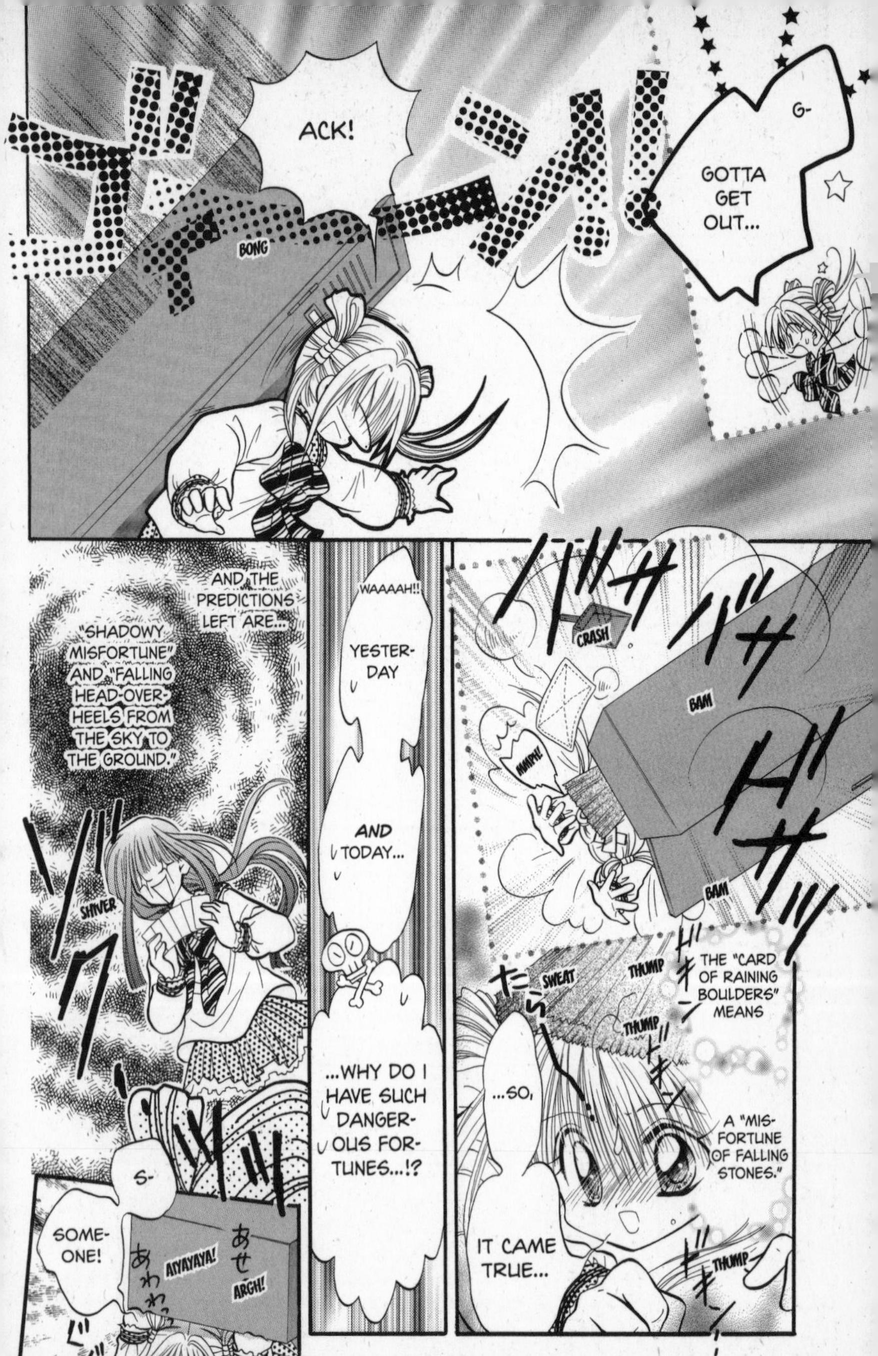
G-
GOTTA GET OUT...
ACK!
BONG
CRASH
BAM
MMPH!
BAM
THE "CARD OF RAINING BOULDERS" MEANS
THUMP
SWEAT
THUMP
A "MISFORTUNE OF FALLING STONES."
...SO,
IT CAME TRUE...
THUMP
WAAAAH!!
YESTERDAY
AND TODAY...
...WHY DO I HAVE SUCH DANGEROUS FORTUNES...!?
AND THE PREDICTIONS LEFT ARE...
"SHADOWY MISFORTUNE" AND "FALLING HEAD-OVER-HEELS FROM THE SKY TO THE GROUND."
SHIVER
S-
SOMEONE!
あせ
あわわっ
AIYAYAYA!
ARGH!
RRR...

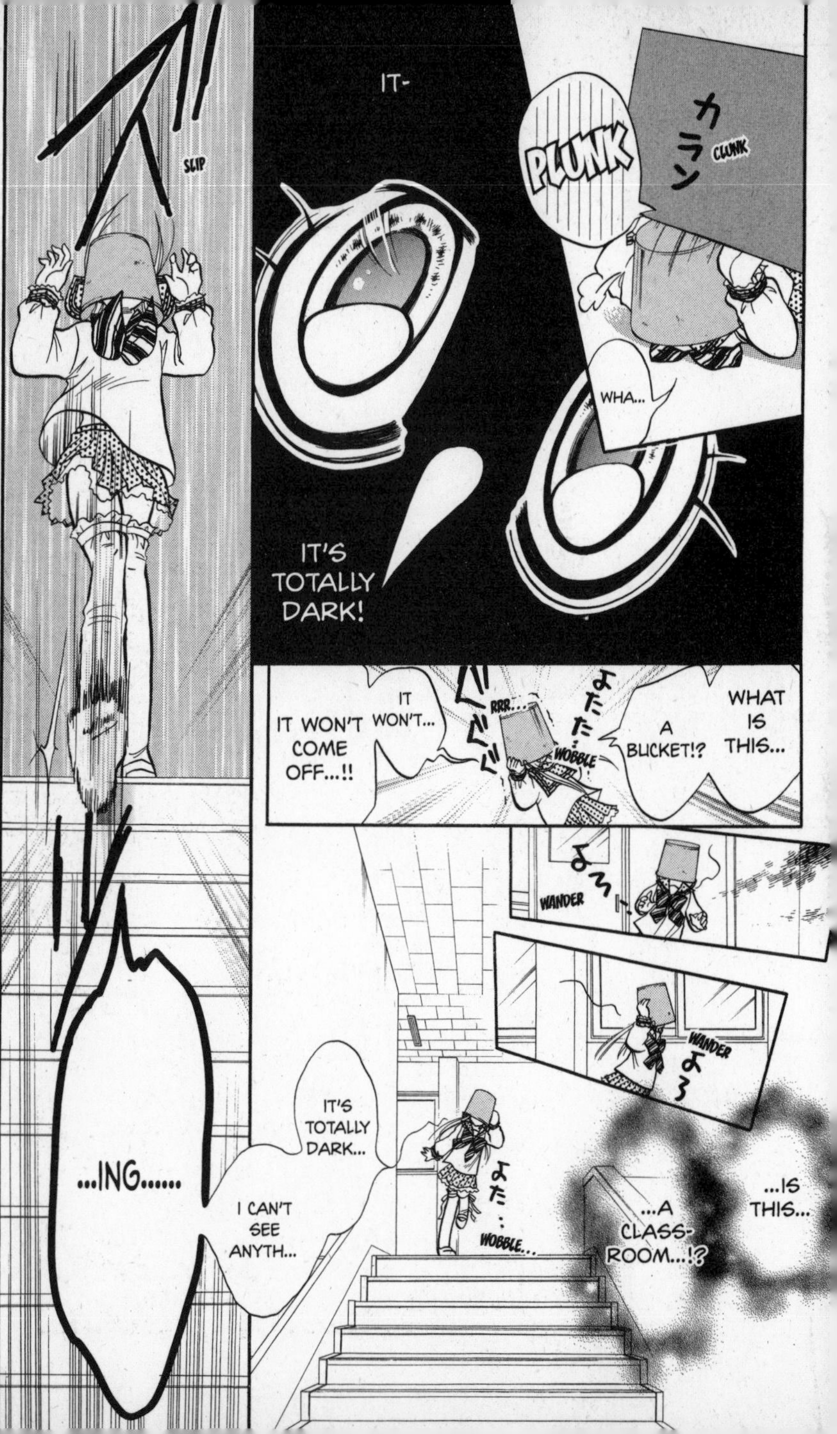
カラン
CLUNK
PLUNK
WHA...
IT-
IT'S TOTALLY DARK!
WHAT IS THIS...
A BUCKET!?
よたた
WOBBLE
ぐぐぐ
RRR...
IT WON'T...
IT WON'T COME OFF...!!
SLIP
よろ
WANDER
WANDER
よろ
...IS THIS...
...A CLASS-ROOM...!?
よた
WOBBLE...
IT'S TOTALLY DARK...
I CAN'T SEE ANYTH...
...ING......

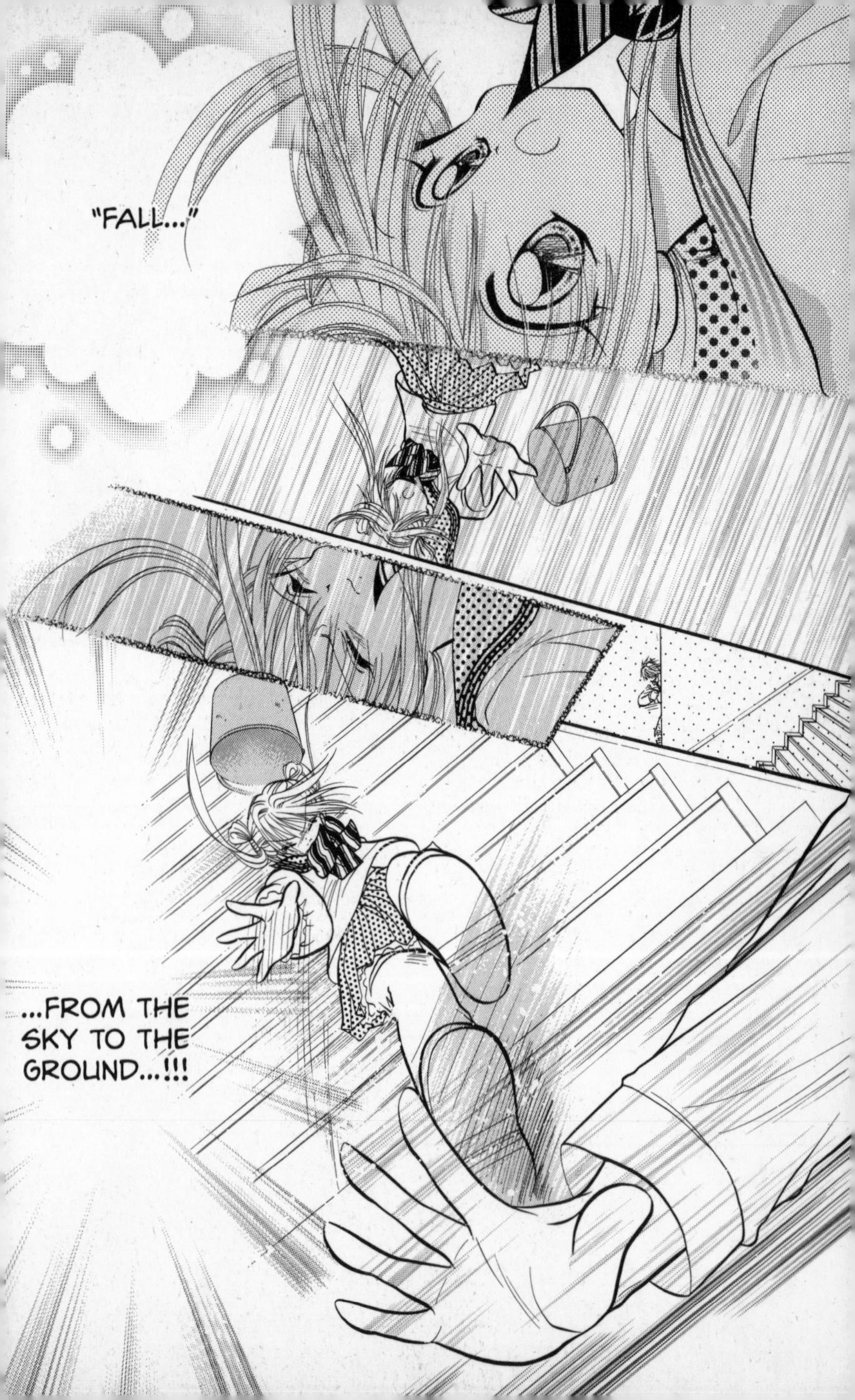
"FALL..."
...FROM THE SKY TO THE GROUND...!!!

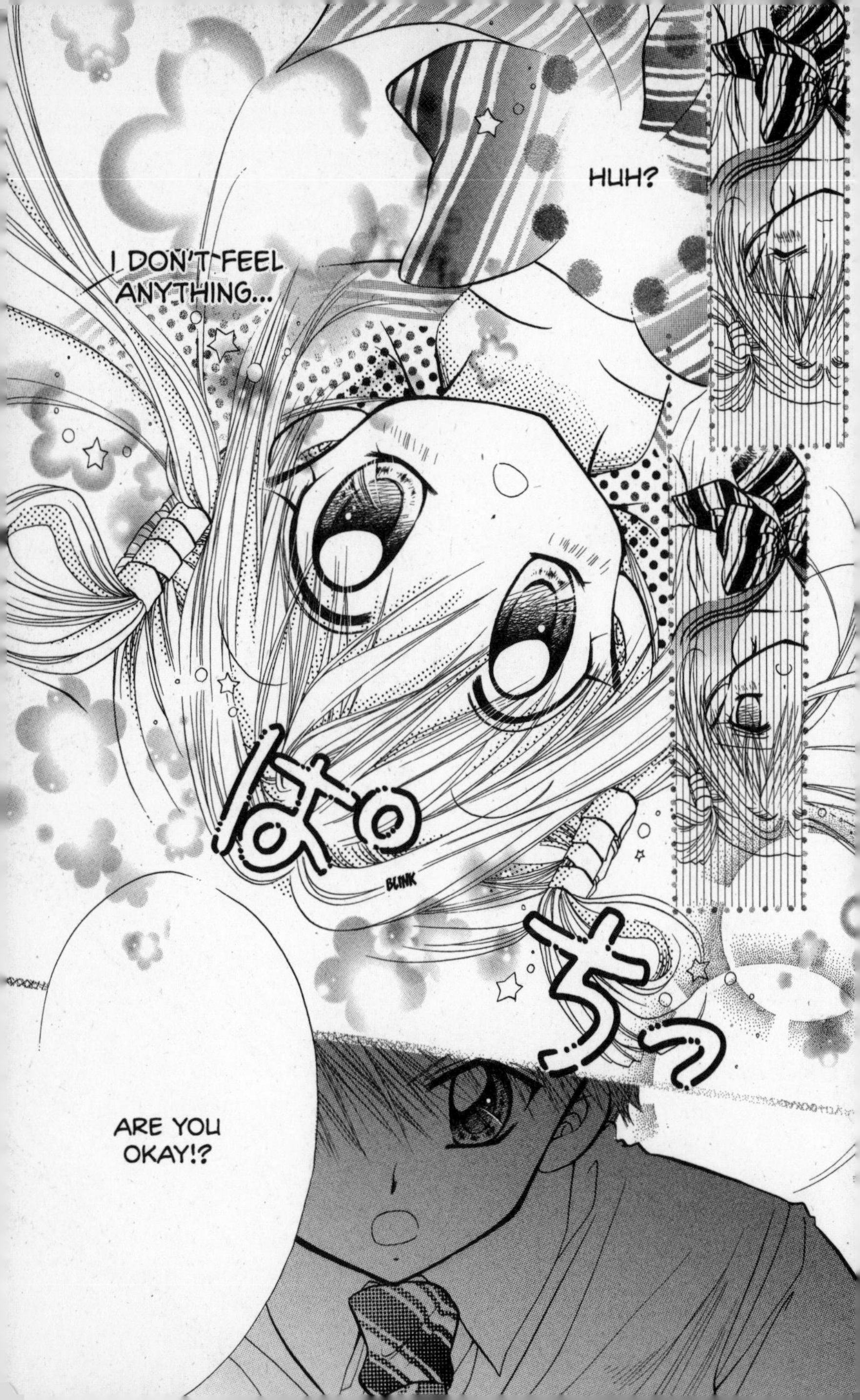
HUH?
I DON'T FEEL ANYTHING...
は
BLINK
ちっ
ARE YOU OKAY!?

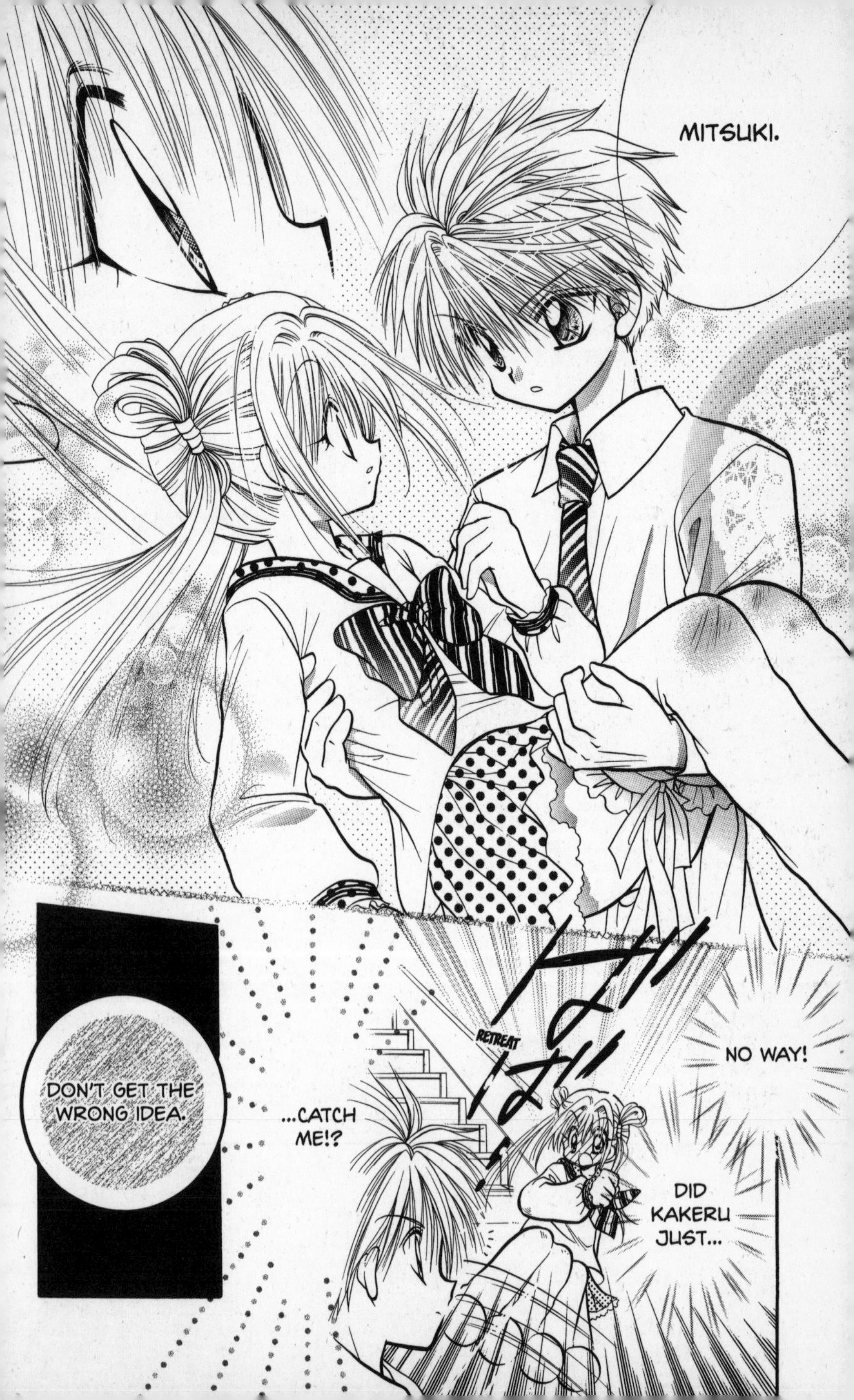
MITSUKI.
NO WAY!
DID KAKERU JUST...
...CATCH ME!?
RETREAT
DON'T GET THE WRONG IDEA.

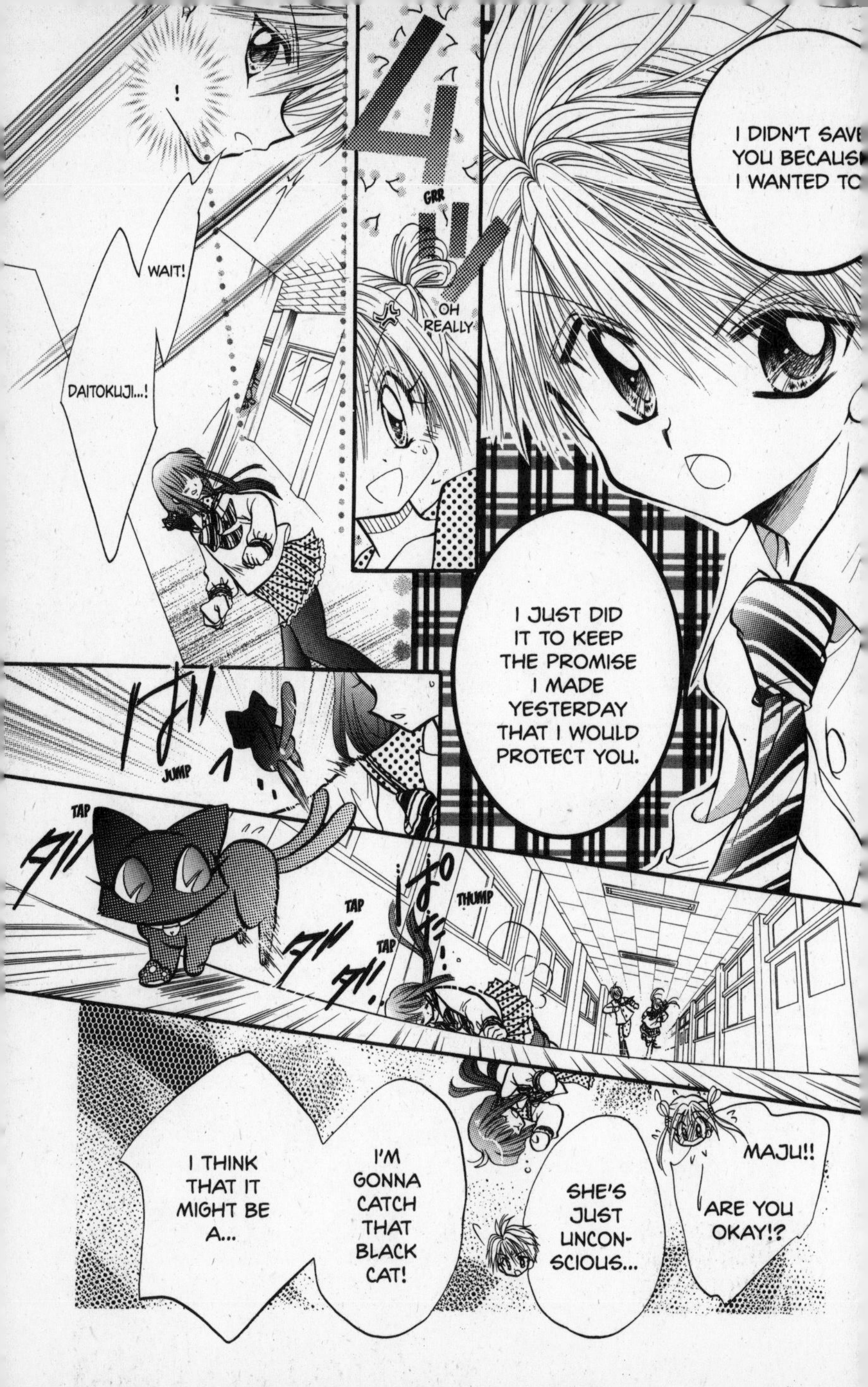
I DIDN'T SAVE YOU BECAUSE I WANTED TO
I JUST DID IT TO KEEP THE PROMISE I MADE YESTERDAY THAT I WOULD PROTECT YOU.
GRR
OH REALLY
!
WAIT!
DAITOKUJI...!
THUMP
TAP
TAP
JUMP
TAP
MAJU!!
ARE YOU OKAY!?
SHE'S JUST UNCON-SCIOUS...
I'M GONNA CATCH THAT BLACK CAT!
I THINK THAT IT MIGHT BE A...

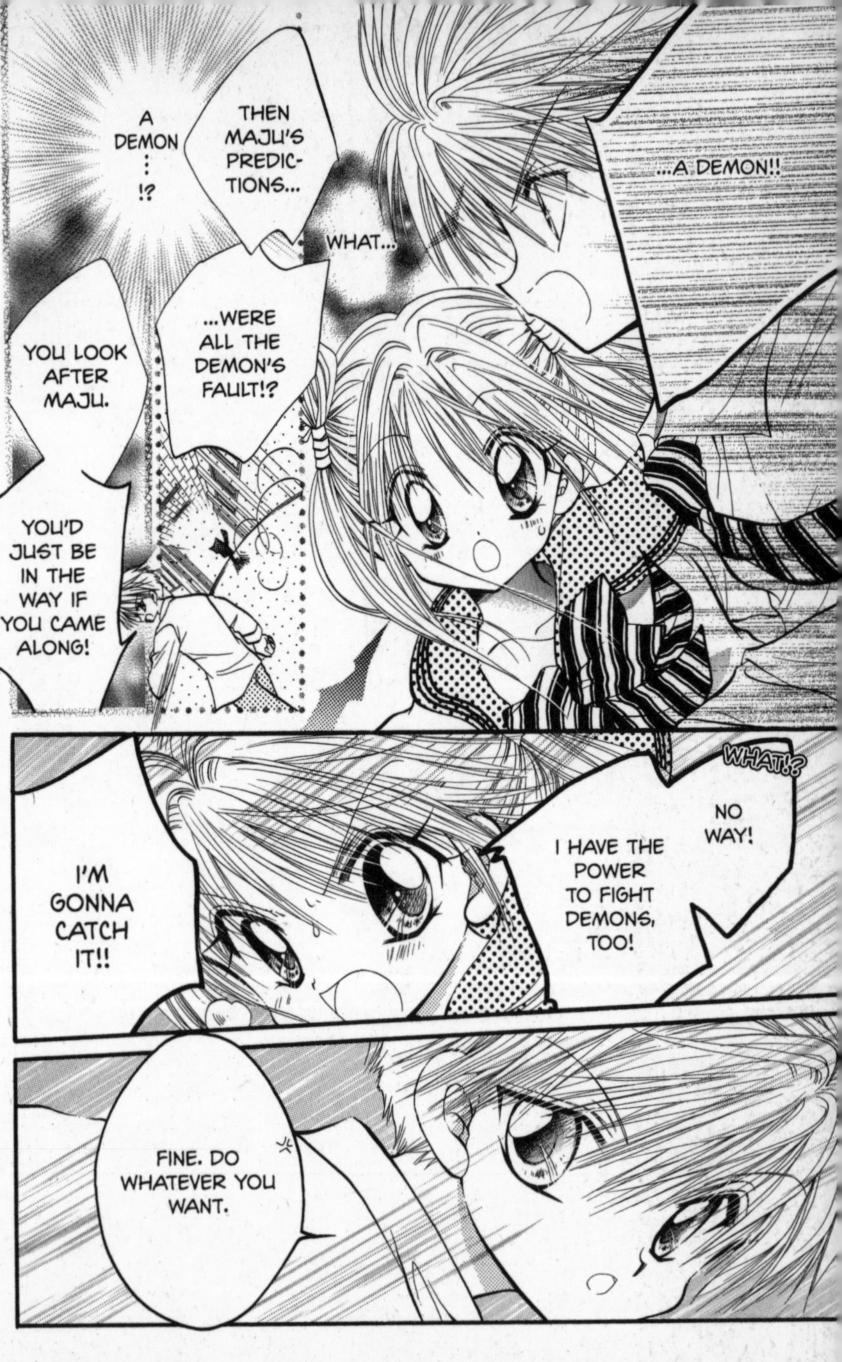

...A DEMON!!
A DEMON...!?
WHAT...
THEN MAJU'S PREDICTIONS...
...WERE ALL THE DEMON'S FAULT!?
YOU LOOK AFTER MAJU.
YOU'D JUST BE IN THE WAY IF YOU CAME ALONG!
WHAT!?
NO WAY!
I HAVE THE POWER TO FIGHT DEMONS, TOO!
I'M GONNA CATCH IT!!
FINE. DO WHATEVER YOU WANT.

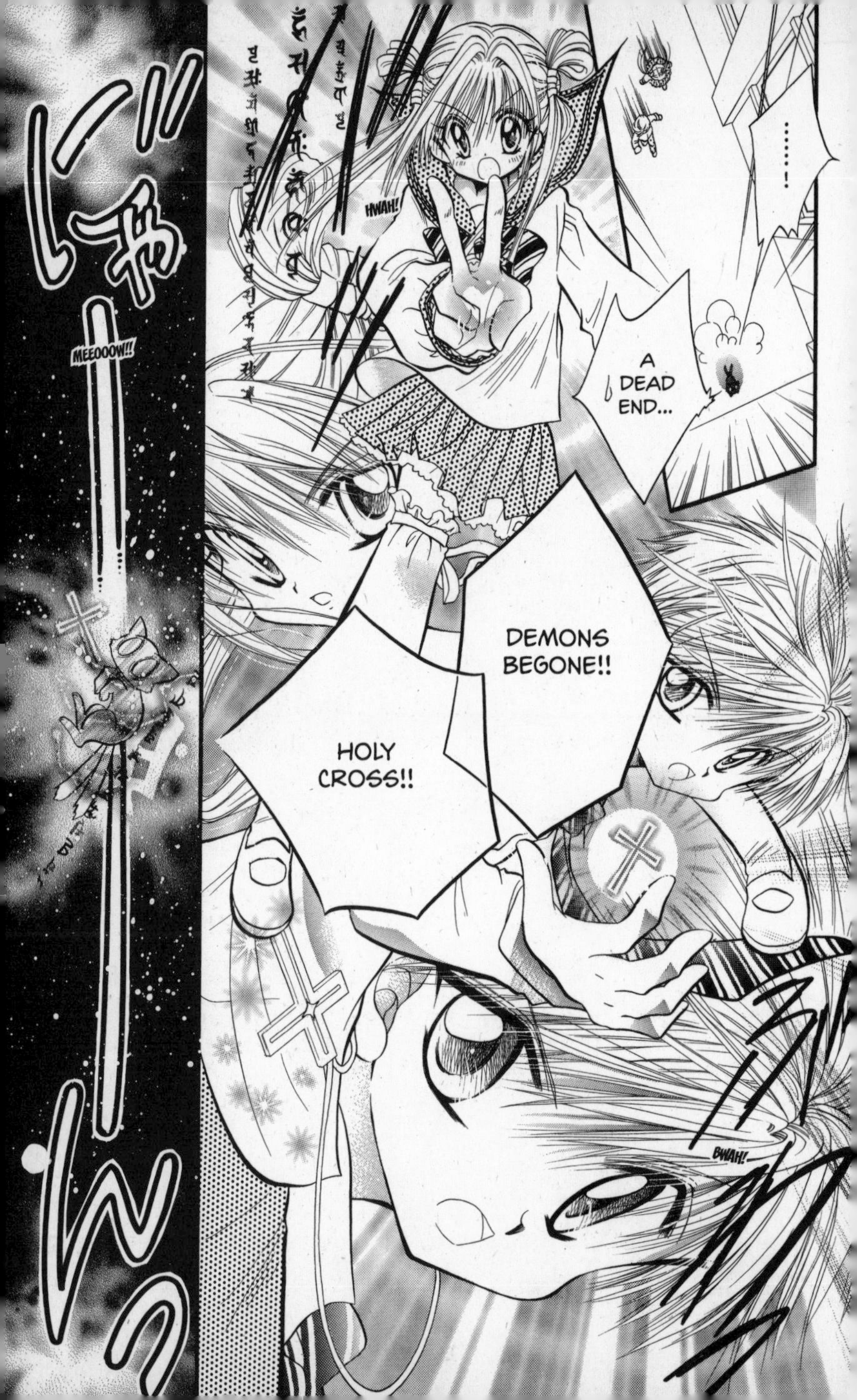
......!
A DEAD END...
HWAH!
DEMONS BEGONE!!
HOLY CROSS!!
BWAH!
MEEOOOW!!

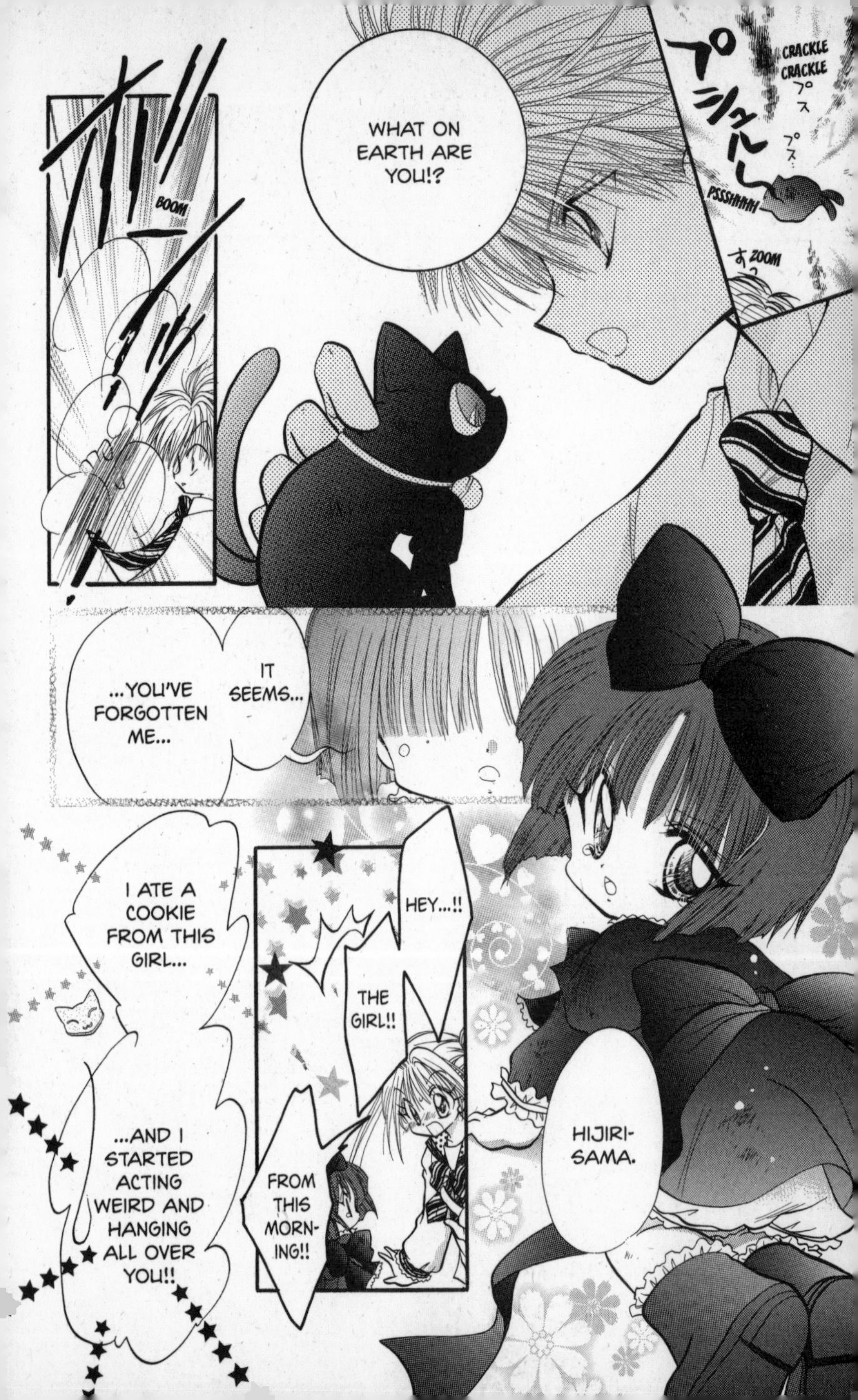
CRACKLE CRACKLE
プス プス
PSSSHHHH
すっ
ZOOM
WHAT ON EARTH ARE YOU!?
BOOM
IT SEEMS...
...YOU'VE FORGOTTEN ME...
HIJIRI-SAMA.
HEY...!!
THE GIRL!!
FROM THIS MORNING!!
I ATE A COOKIE FROM THIS GIRL...
...AND I STARTED ACTING WEIRD AND HANGING ALL OVER YOU!!

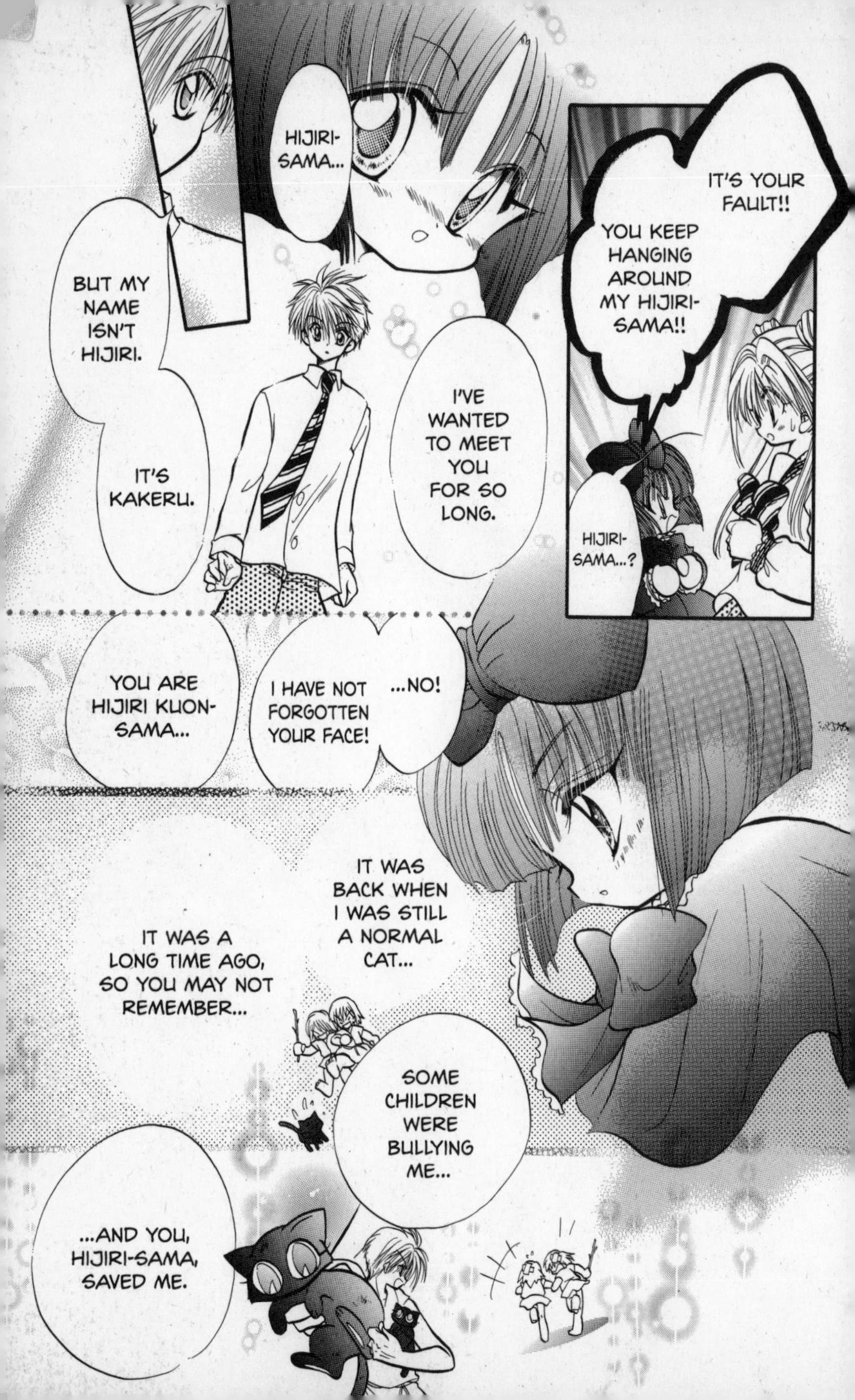
IT'S YOUR FAULT!!
YOU KEEP HANGING AROUND MY HIJIRI-SAMA!!
HIJIRI-SAMA...?
HIJIRI-SAMA...
I'VE WANTED TO MEET YOU FOR SO LONG.
BUT MY NAME ISN'T HIJIRI.
IT'S KAKERU.
...NO!
I HAVE NOT FORGOTTEN YOUR FACE!
YOU ARE HIJIRI KUON-SAMA...
IT WAS BACK WHEN I WAS STILL A NORMAL CAT...
IT WAS A LONG TIME AGO, SO YOU MAY NOT REMEMBER...
SOME CHILDREN WERE BULLYING ME...
...AND YOU, HIJIRI-SAMA, SAVED ME.

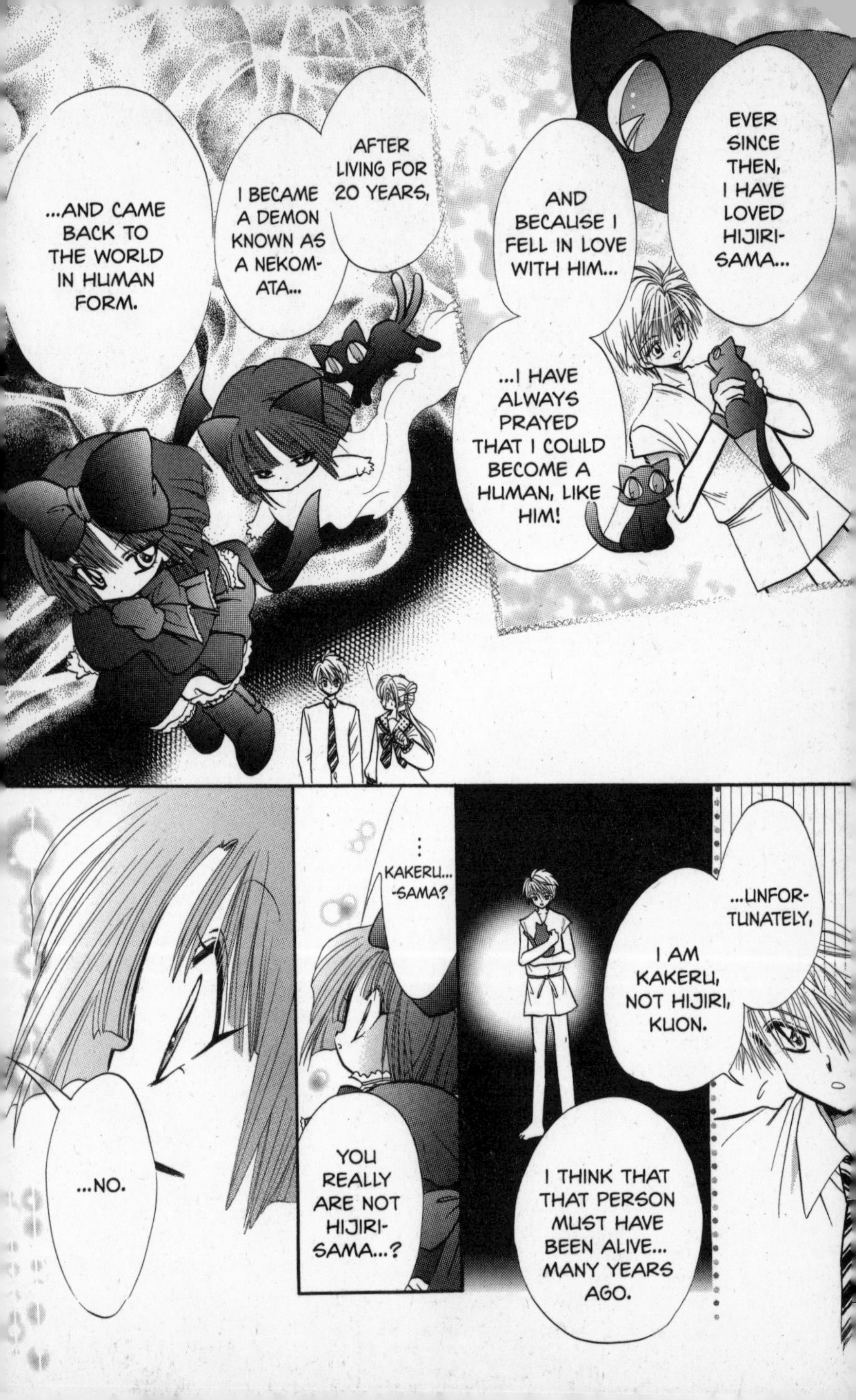
EVER SINCE THEN, I HAVE LOVED HIJIRI-SAMA...
AND BECAUSE I FELL IN LOVE WITH HIM...
...I HAVE ALWAYS PRAYED THAT I COULD BECOME A HUMAN, LIKE HIM!
AFTER LIVING FOR 20 YEARS,
I BECAME A DEMON KNOWN AS A NEKOMATA...
...AND CAME BACK TO THE WORLD IN HUMAN FORM.
...UNFORTUNATELY,
I AM KAKERU, NOT HIJIRI, KUON.
I THINK THAT THAT PERSON MUST HAVE BEEN ALIVE... MANY YEARS AGO.
... KAKERU... -SAMA?
YOU REALLY ARE NOT HIJIRI-SAMA...?
...NO.

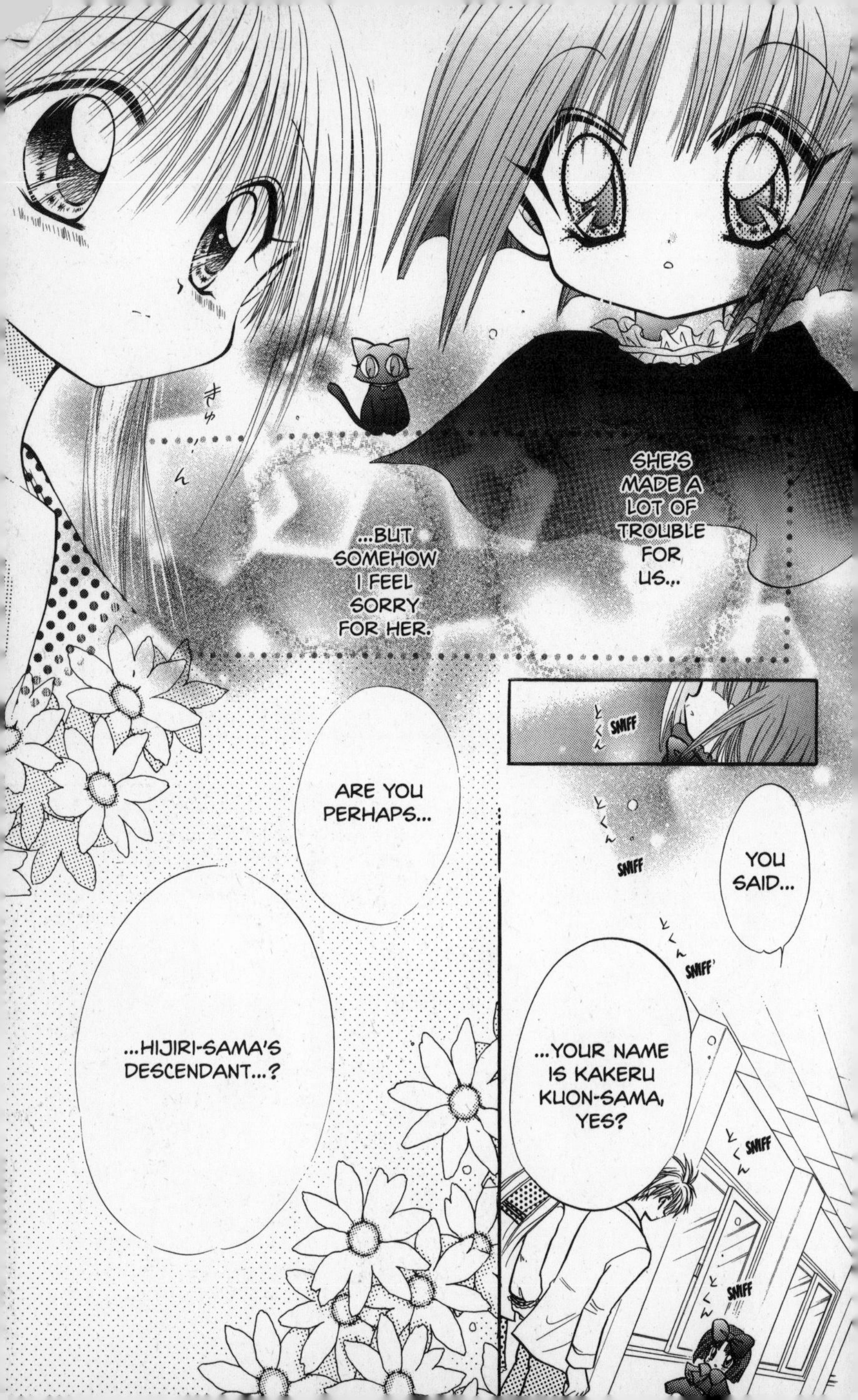
SHE'S MADE A LOT OF TROUBLE FOR US...
...BUT SOMEHOW I FEEL SORRY FOR HER.
SNIFF
SNIFF
YOU SAID...
SNIFF
...YOUR NAME IS KAKERU KUON-SAMA, YES?
SNIFF
SNIFF
ARE YOU PERHAPS...
...HIJIRI-SAMA'S DESCENDANT...?

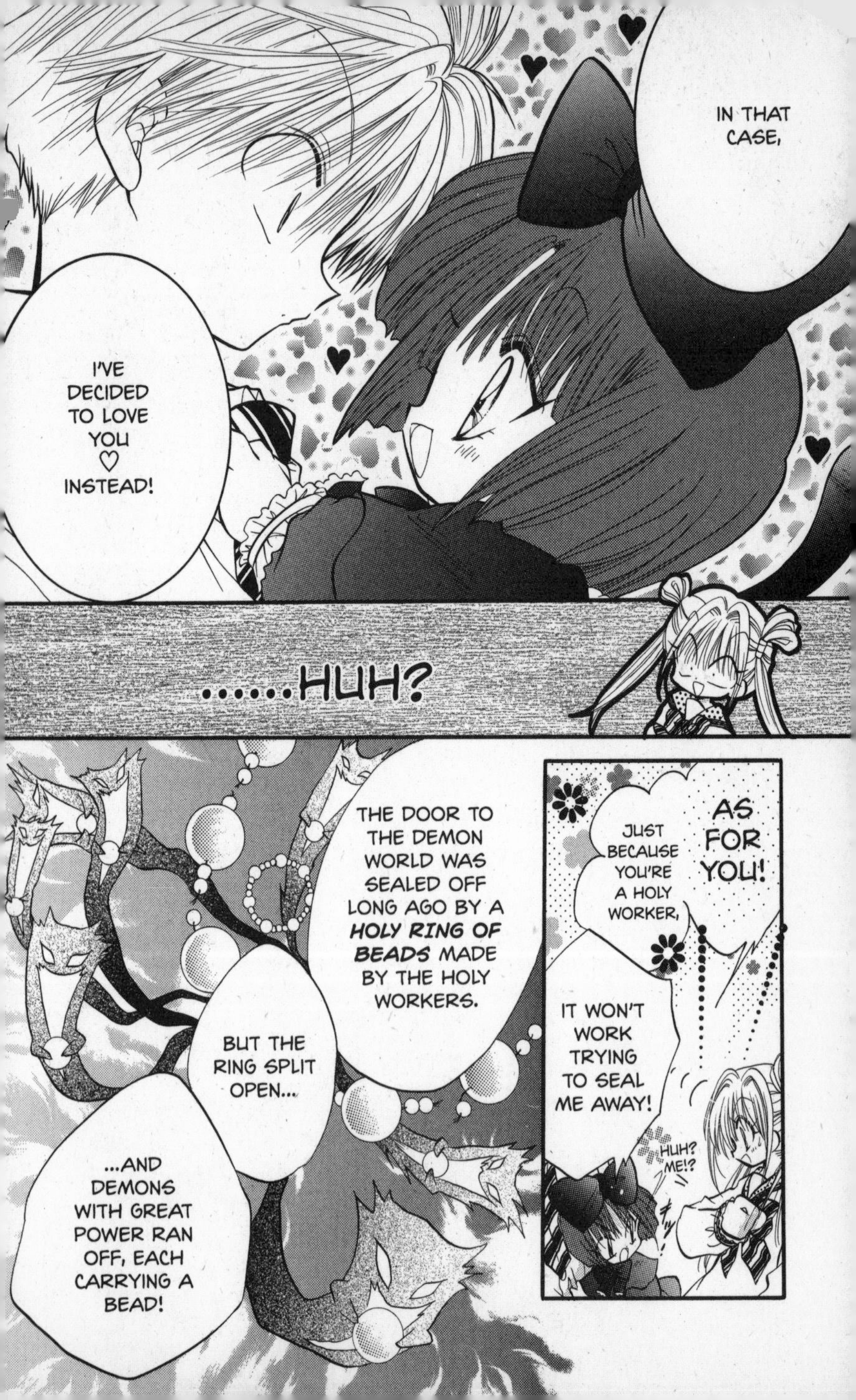
IN THAT CASE,
I'VE DECIDED TO LOVE YOU ♡ INSTEAD!
......HUH?
AS FOR YOU!
JUST BECAUSE YOU'RE A HOLY WORKER,
IT WON'T WORK TRYING TO SEAL ME AWAY!
HUH? ME!?
THE DOOR TO THE DEMON WORLD WAS SEALED OFF LONG AGO BY A ***HOLY RING OF BEADS*** MADE BY THE HOLY WORKERS.
BUT THE RING SPLIT OPEN...
...AND DEMONS WITH GREAT POWER RAN OFF, EACH CARRYING A BEAD!

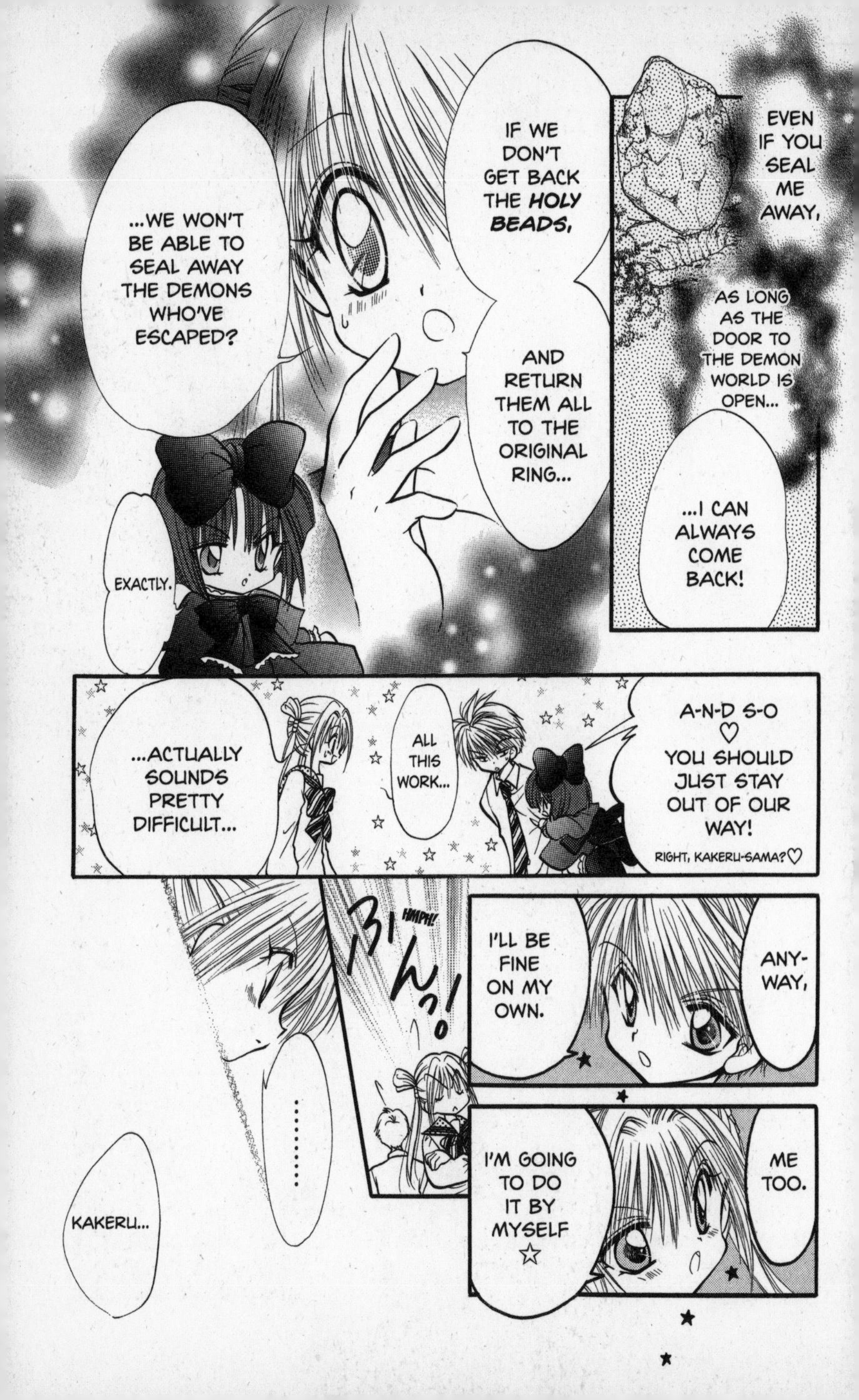
EVEN IF YOU SEAL ME AWAY,
AS LONG AS THE DOOR TO THE DEMON WORLD IS OPEN...
...I CAN ALWAYS COME BACK!
IF WE DON'T GET BACK THE HOLY BEADS,
AND RETURN THEM ALL TO THE ORIGINAL RING...
...WE WON'T BE ABLE TO SEAL AWAY THE DEMONS WHO'VE ESCAPED?
EXACTLY.
A-N-D S-O ♡ YOU SHOULD JUST STAY OUT OF OUR WAY!
RIGHT, KAKERU-SAMA?♡
ALL THIS WORK...
...ACTUALLY SOUNDS PRETTY DIFFICULT...
ANY-WAY,
I'LL BE FINE ON MY OWN.
ME TOO.
I'M GOING TO DO IT BY MYSELF ☆
HMPH!
......
KAKERU...

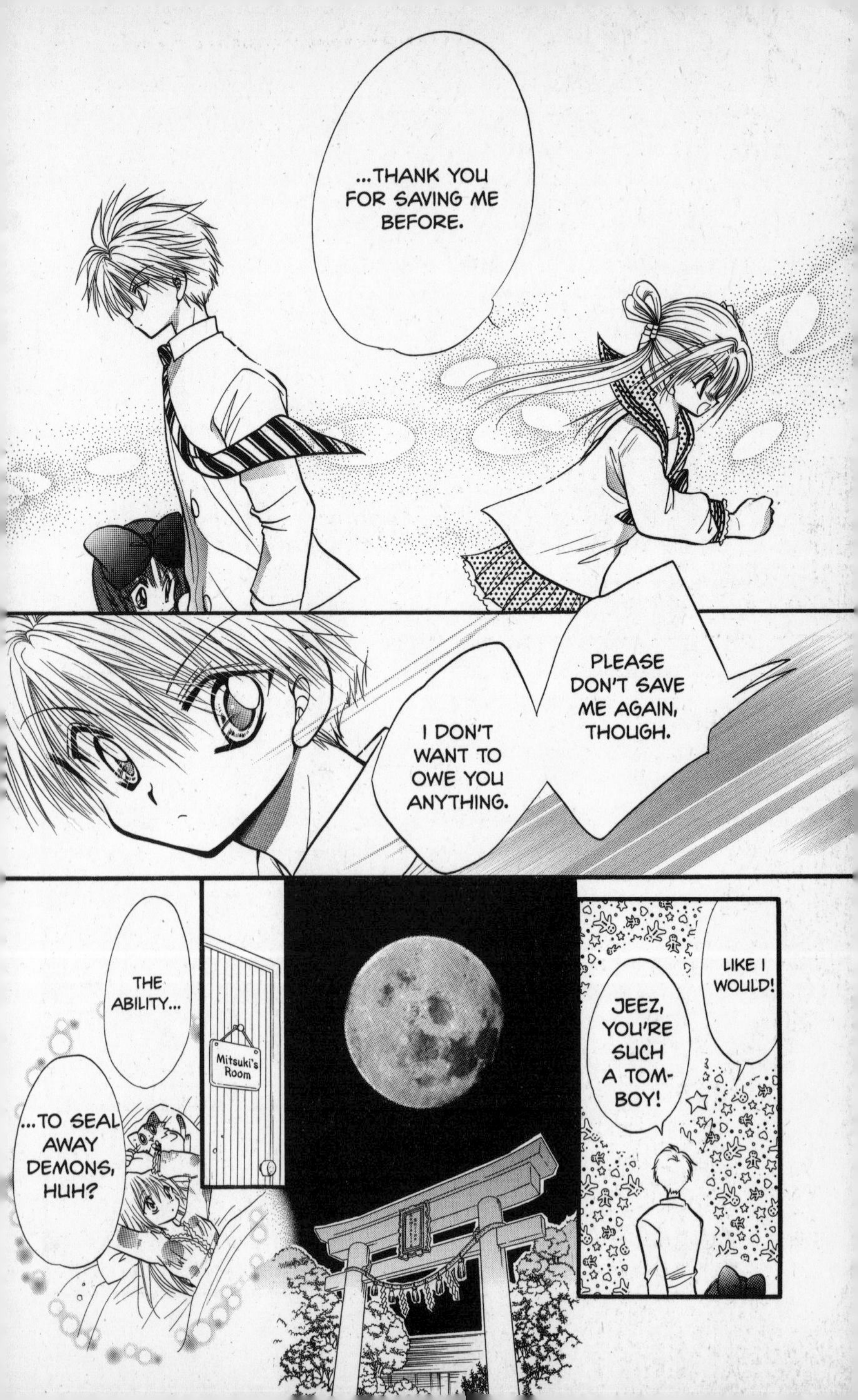
...THANK YOU FOR SAVING ME BEFORE.
PLEASE DON'T SAVE ME AGAIN, THOUGH.
I DON'T WANT TO OWE YOU ANYTHING.
LIKE I WOULD!
JEEZ, YOU'RE SUCH A TOM-BOY!
Mitsuki's Room
THE ABILITY...
...TO SEAL AWAY DEMONS, HUH?

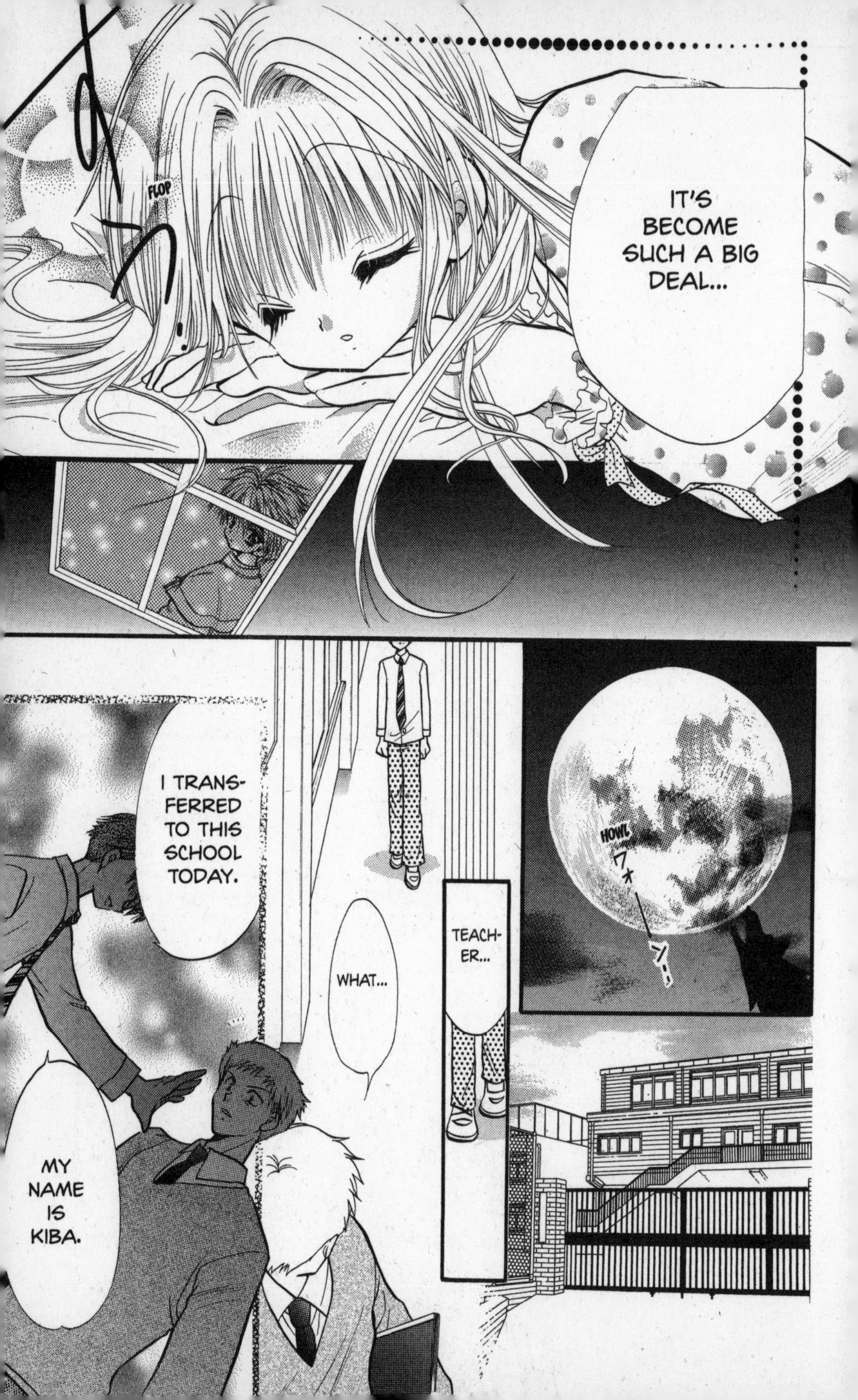
IT'S BECOME SUCH A BIG DEAL...
FLOP
HOWL
TEACH-ER...
WHAT...
I TRANS-FERRED TO THIS SCHOOL TODAY.
MY NAME IS KIBA.

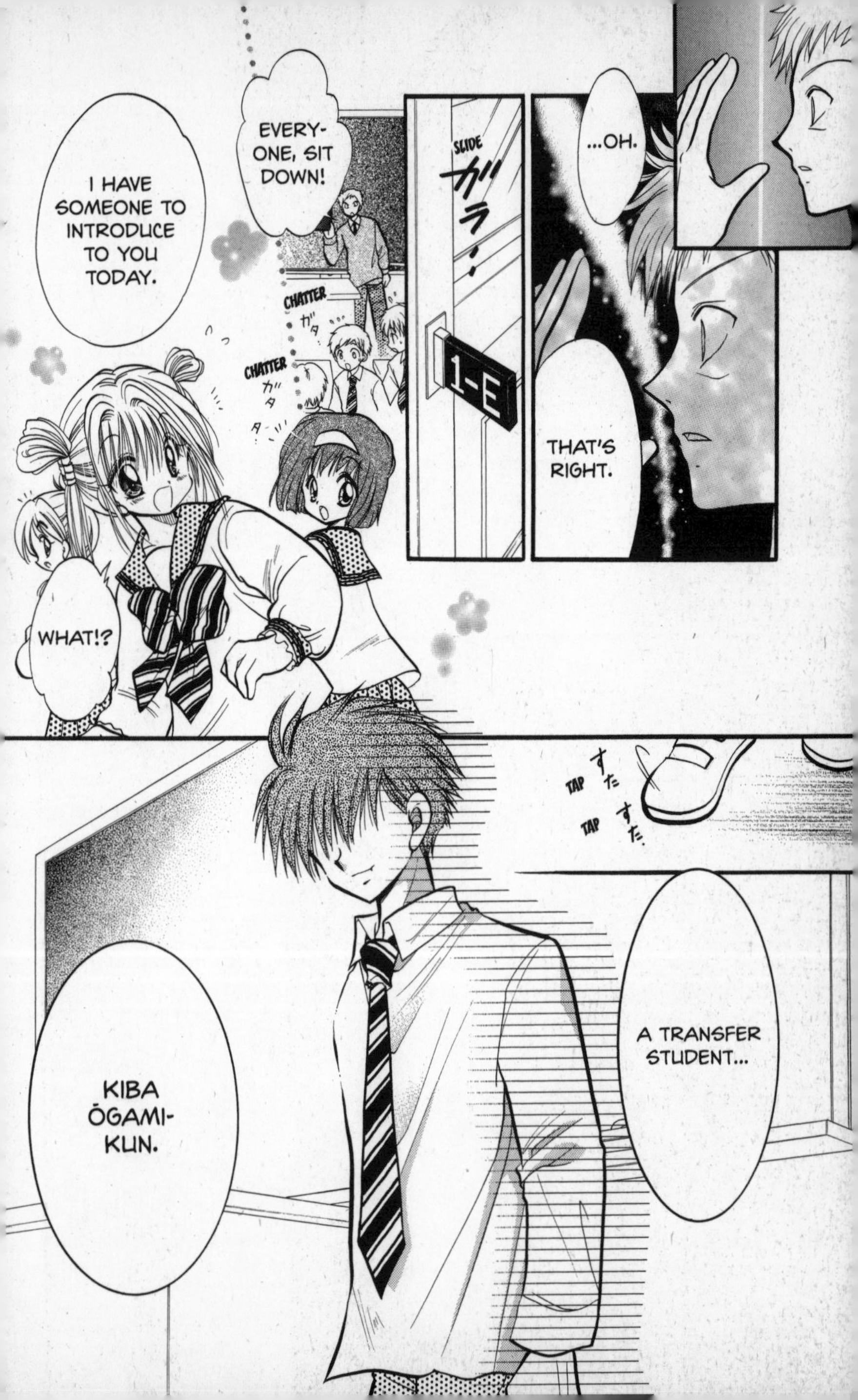
...OH.
THAT'S RIGHT.
SLIDE ガラ
1-E
EVERY-ONE, SIT DOWN!
I HAVE SOMEONE TO INTRODUCE TO YOU TODAY.
CHATTER ガタ
CHATTER ガタ
WHAT!?
TAP すた
TAP すた
A TRANSFER STUDENT...
KIBA ŌGAMI-KUN.

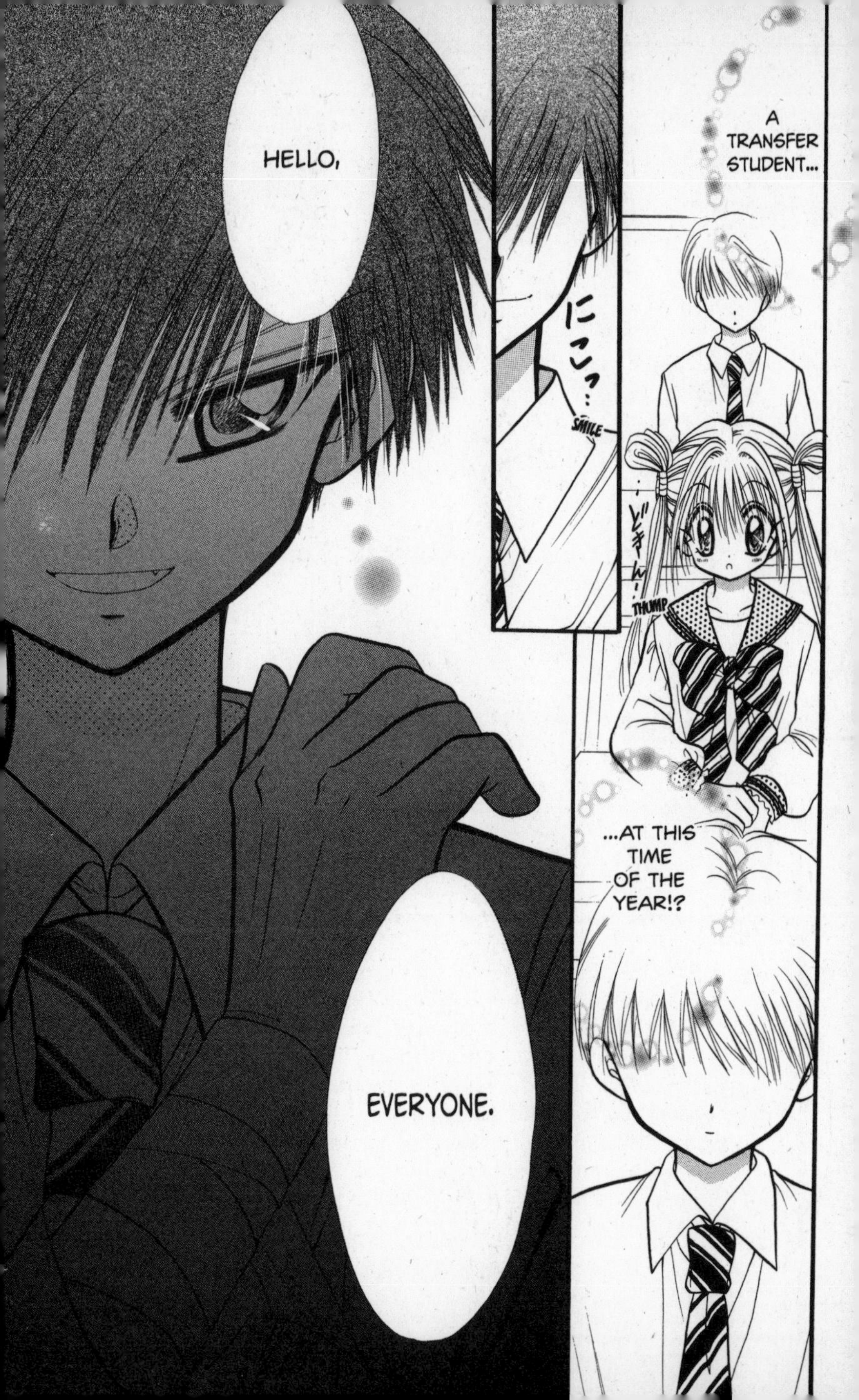
A TRANSFER STUDENT...
どきん!!
THUMP
...AT THIS TIME OF THE YEAR!?
にこっ
SMILE
HELLO,
EVERYONE.

Panic x Panic

PROFILE

VOL. 5

FROM THE AUTHOR'S ORIGINAL STORY NOTES

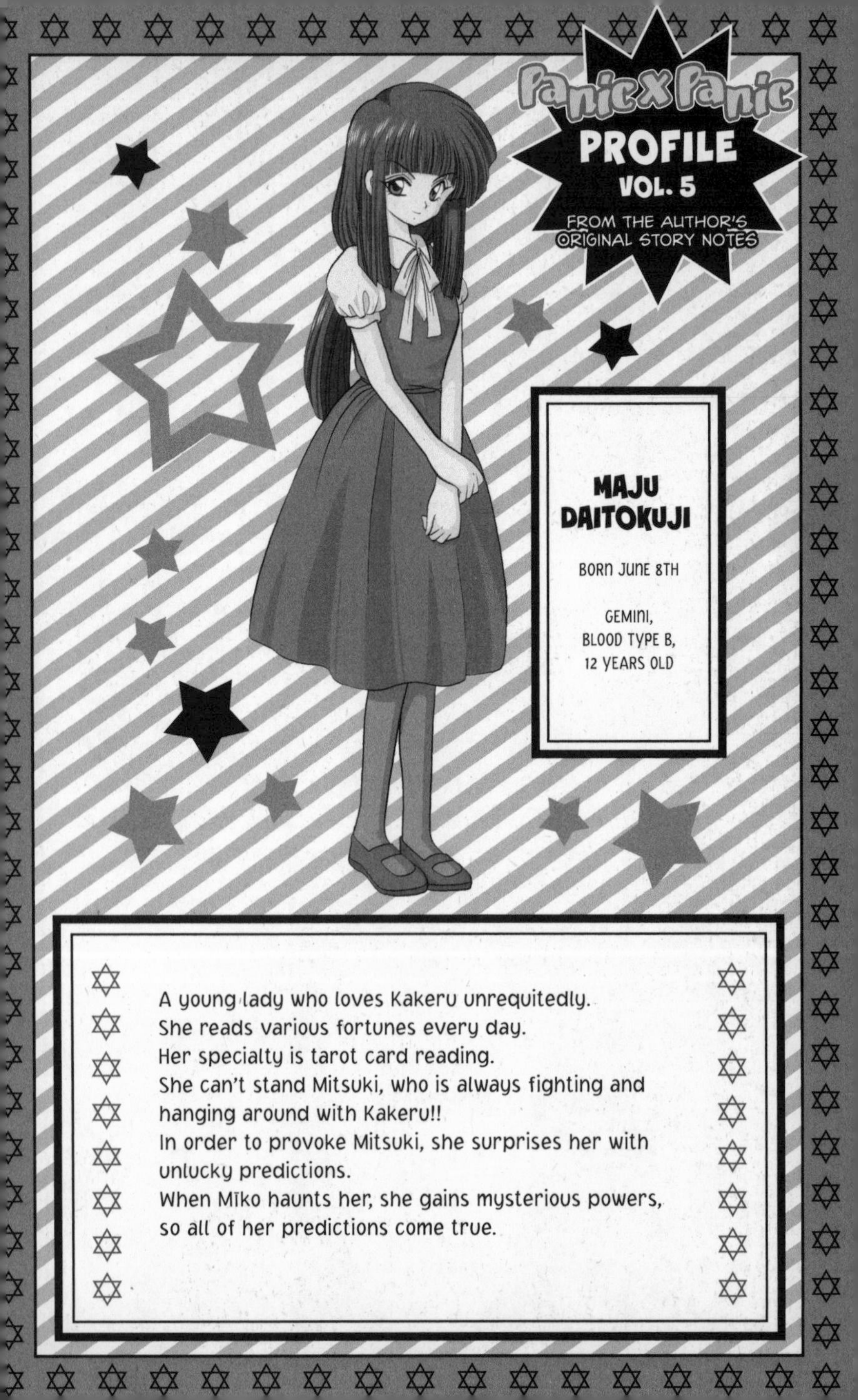

MAJU DAITOKUJI

BORN JUNE 8TH

GEMINI,
BLOOD TYPE B,
12 YEARS OLD

A young lady who loves Kakeru unrequitedly.
She reads various fortunes every day.
Her specialty is tarot card reading.
She can't stand Mitsuki, who is always fighting and hanging around with Kakeru!!
In order to provoke Mitsuki, she surprises her with unlucky predictions.
When Mīko haunts her, she gains mysterious powers, so all of her predictions come true.

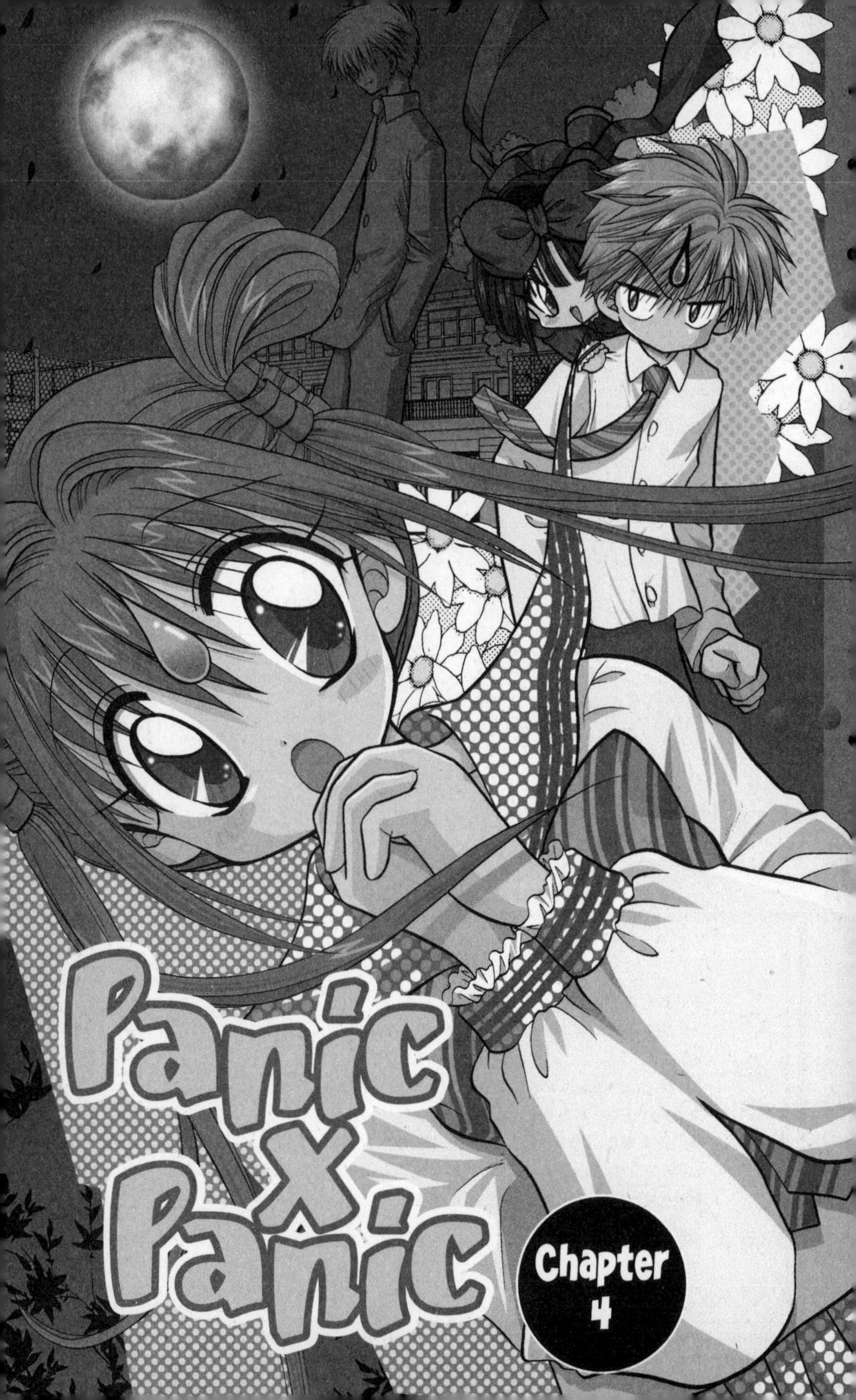

Panic
X
Panic
Chapter
4

Panic X Panic

PROFILE
VOL. 6

FROM THE AUTHOR'S
ORIGINAL STORY NOTES

MANTA AOI

BORN MARCH 20TH

PISCES,
BLOOD TYPE O,
12 YEARS OLD

Mitsuki's classmate.
He always carries a mythology encyclopedia under his arm.
He is obsessed with folklore, and his obsession is so strong that he can see demons.
But he is disappointed that no demons come to haunt him.
He is very excitable and intense.
He has had many experiences with unusual phenomena since he was very small.

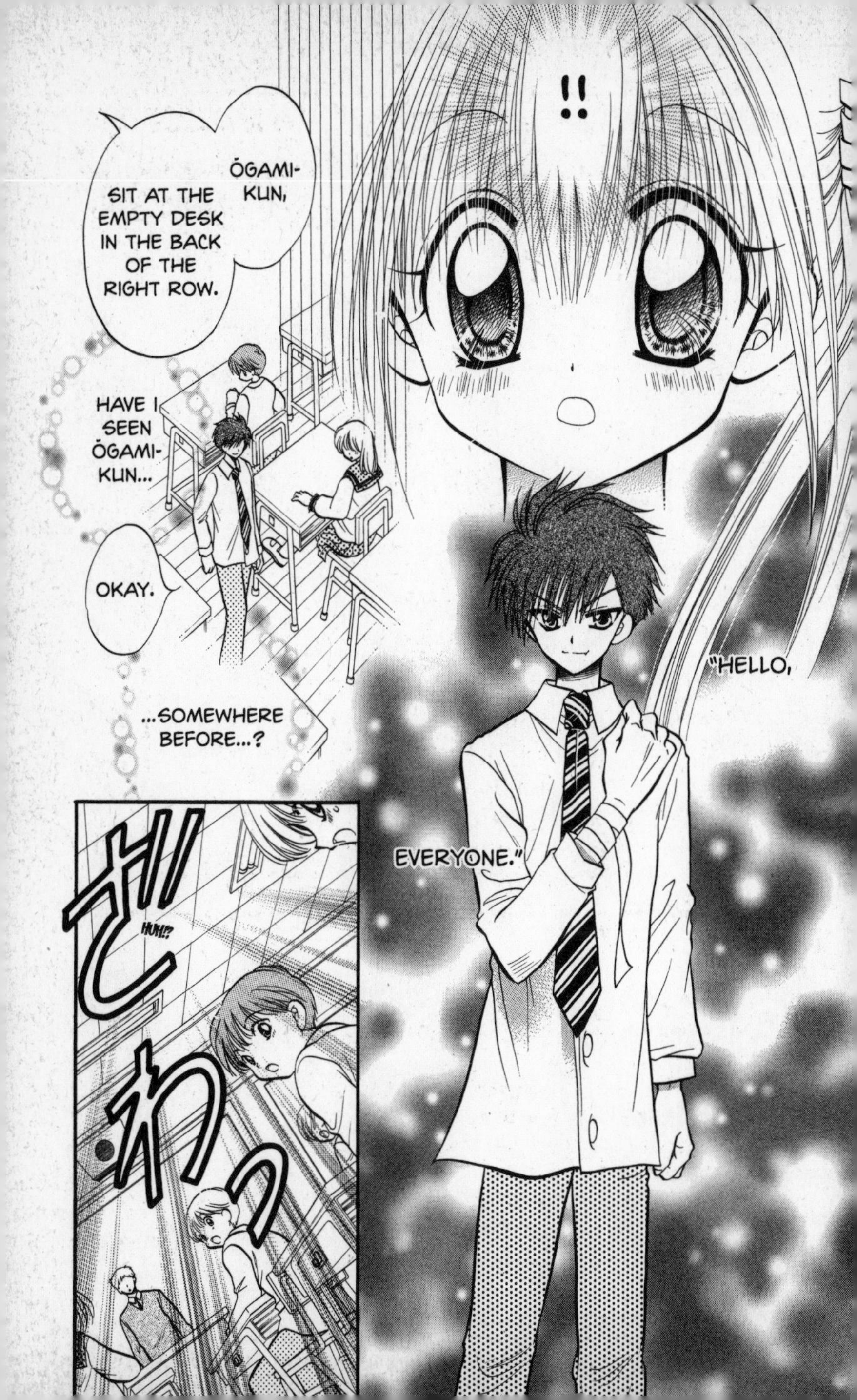
!!
"HELLO, EVERYONE."
ŌGAMI-KUN, SIT AT THE EMPTY DESK IN THE BACK OF THE RIGHT ROW.
HAVE I SEEN ŌGAMI-KUN...
OKAY.
...SOMEWHERE BEFORE...?
ざわっ
HUH!?

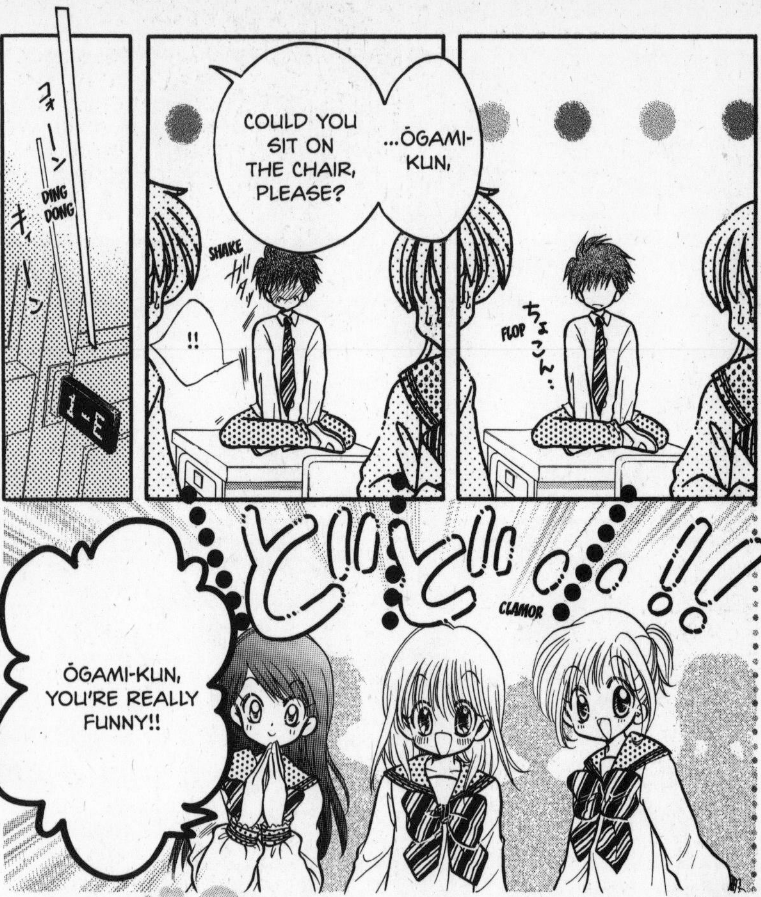
FLOP
ちょこん…
...ŌGAMI-KUN,
COULD YOU SIT ON THE CHAIR, PLEASE?
SHAKE
ガタッ
!!
DING DONG
1-E
CLAMOR
ŌGAMI-KUN, YOU'RE REALLY FUNNY!!

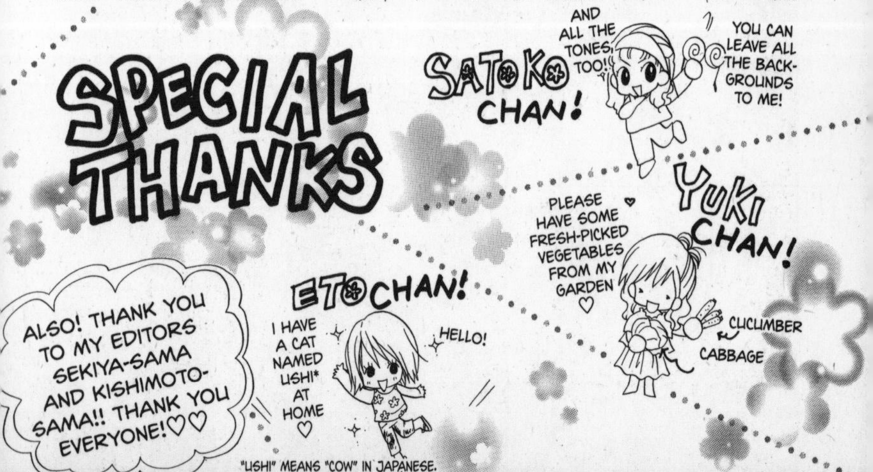
SPECIAL THANKS
SATOKO CHAN!
AND ALL THE TONES, TOO!!
YOU CAN LEAVE ALL THE BACKGROUNDS TO ME!
YUKI CHAN!
PLEASE HAVE SOME FRESH-PICKED VEGETABLES FROM MY GARDEN ♡
CUCUMBER
CABBAGE
ETO CHAN!
HELLO!
I HAVE A CAT NAMED USHI* AT HOME ♡
ALSO! THANK YOU TO MY EDITORS SEKIYA-SAMA AND KISHIMOTO-SAMA!! THANK YOU EVERYONE!♡♡

"USHI" MEANS "COW" IN JAPANESE.

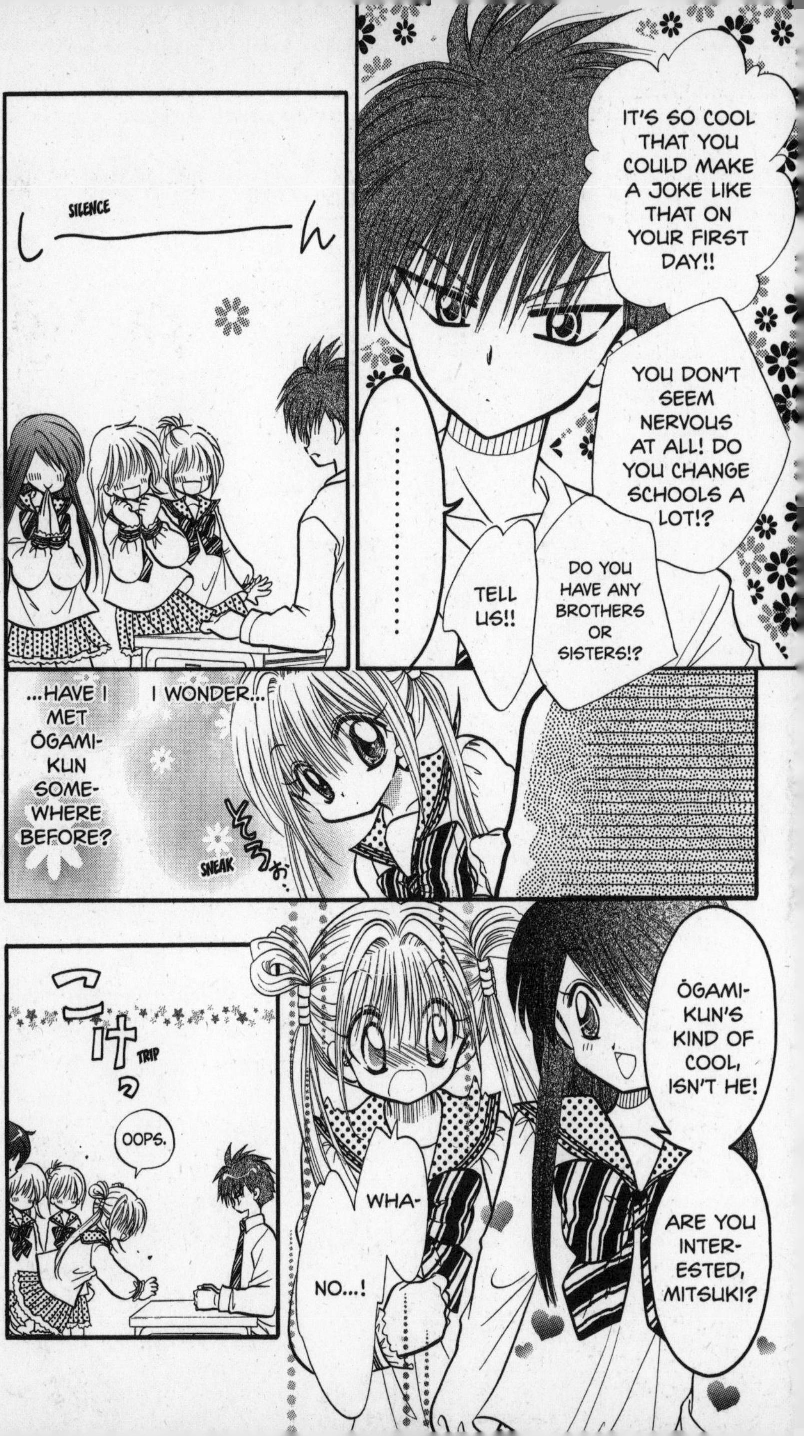
IT'S SO COOL THAT YOU COULD MAKE A JOKE LIKE THAT ON YOUR FIRST DAY!!
YOU DON'T SEEM NERVOUS AT ALL! DO YOU CHANGE SCHOOLS A LOT!?
DO YOU HAVE ANY BROTHERS OR SISTERS!?
TELL US!!
......
SILENCE
し————ん
I WONDER...
...HAVE I MET ŌGAMI-KUN SOME-WHERE BEFORE?
SNEAK
ŌGAMI-KUN'S KIND OF COOL, ISN'T HE!
ARE YOU INTER-ESTED, MITSUKI?
WHA-
NO...!
こけっ
TRIP
OOPS.

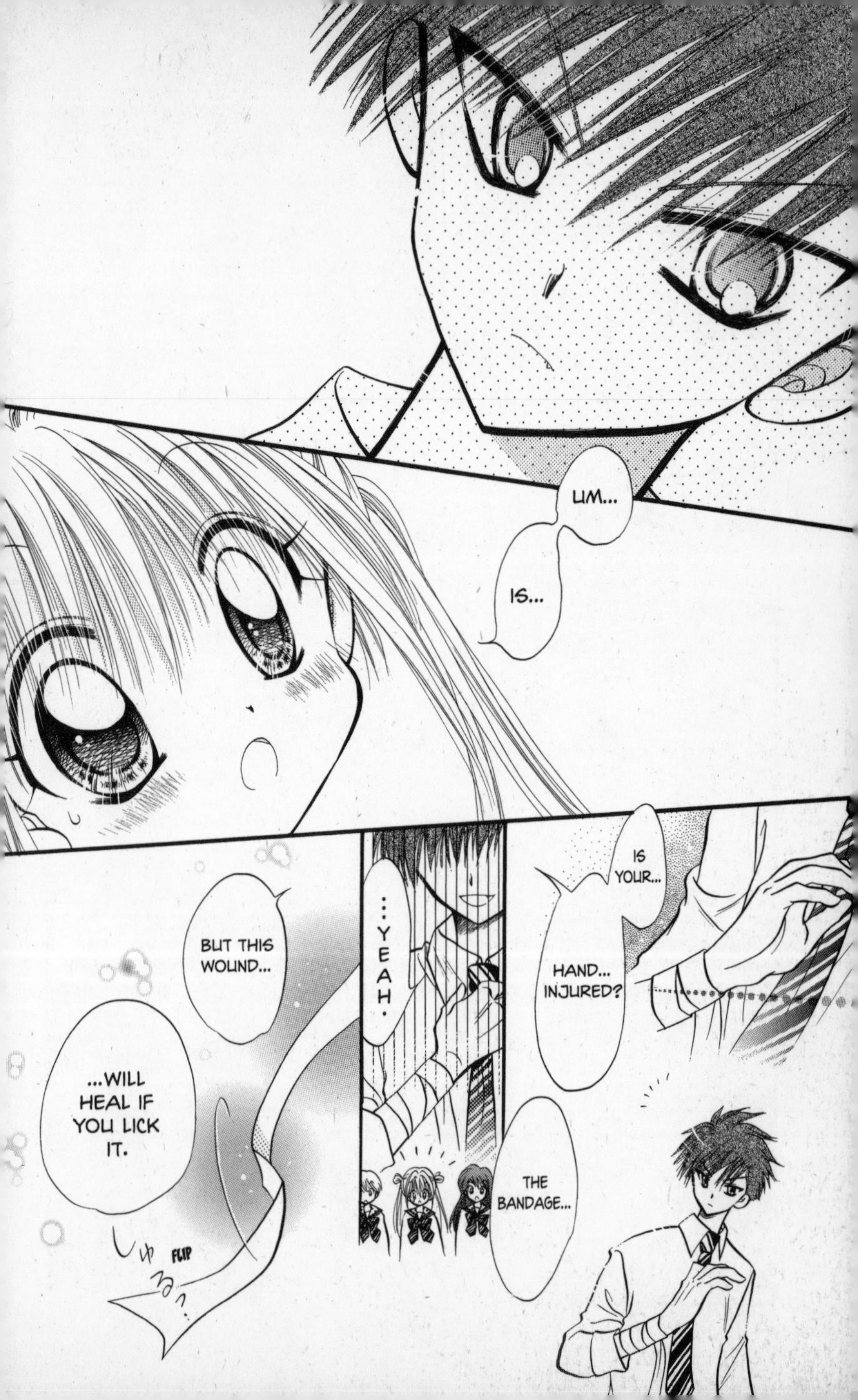

UM...
IS...
IS YOUR...
HAND... INJURED?
THE BANDAGE...
...YEAH.
BUT THIS WOUND...
...WILL HEAL IF YOU LICK IT.
FLIP

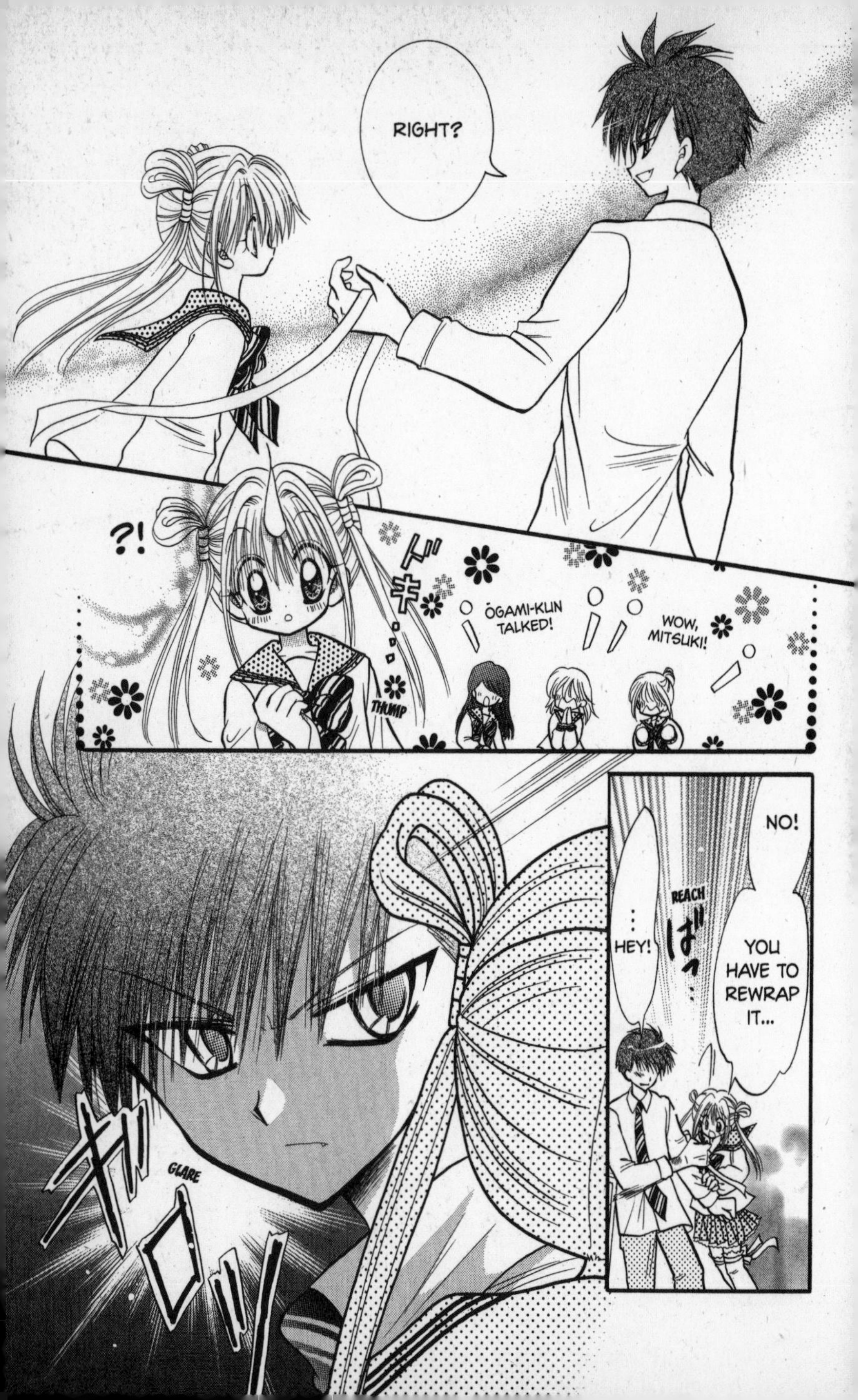
RIGHT?
?!
ÔGAMI-KUN TALKED!
WOW, MITSUKI!
THUMP
NO!
YOU HAVE TO REWRAP IT...
REACH
...HEY!
GLARE

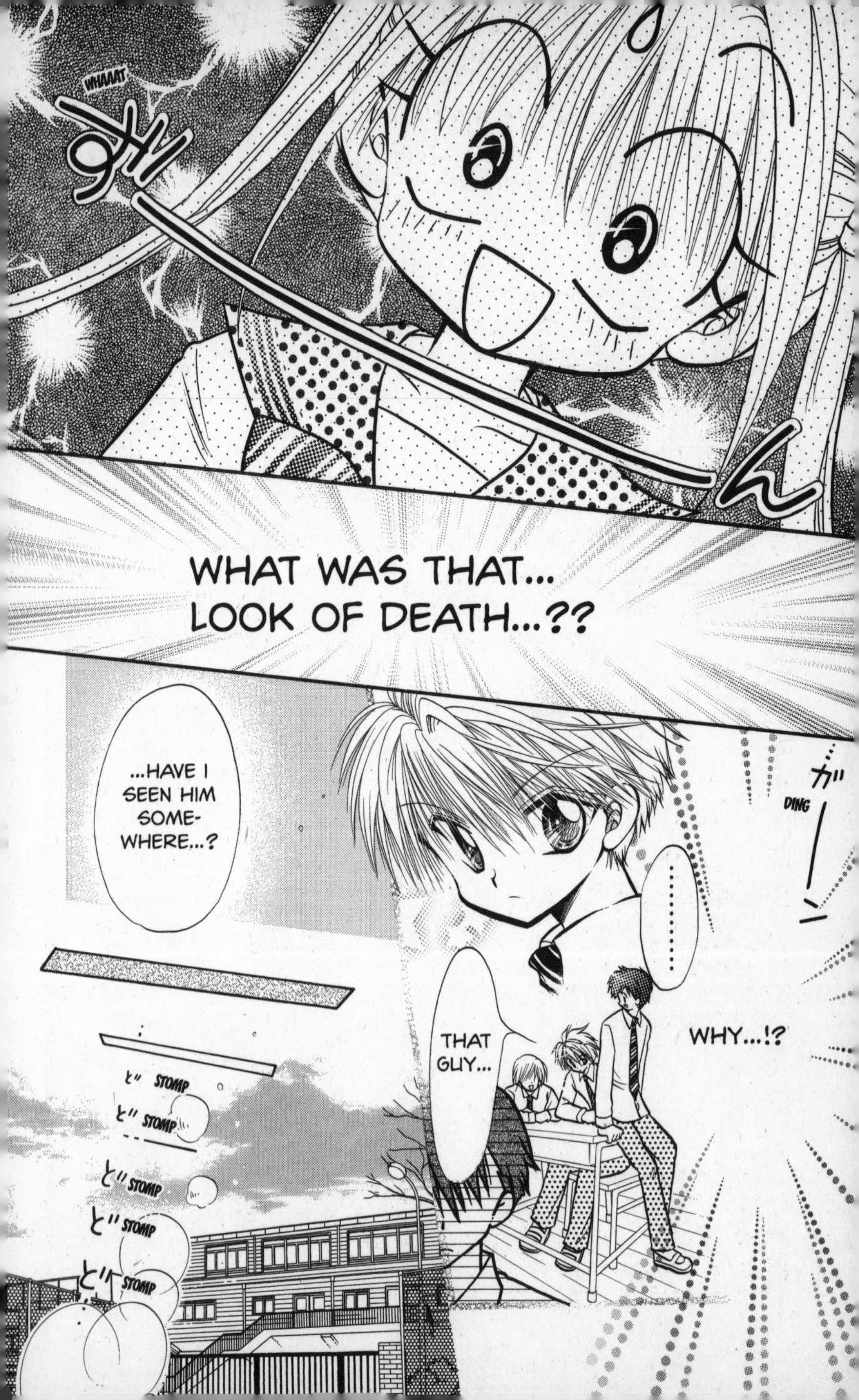

WHAAAT
WHAT WAS THAT... LOOK OF DEATH...??
DING
......
WHY...!?
THAT GUY...
...HAVE I SEEN HIM SOME- WHERE...?
STOMP
STOMP
STOMP
STOMP
STOMP

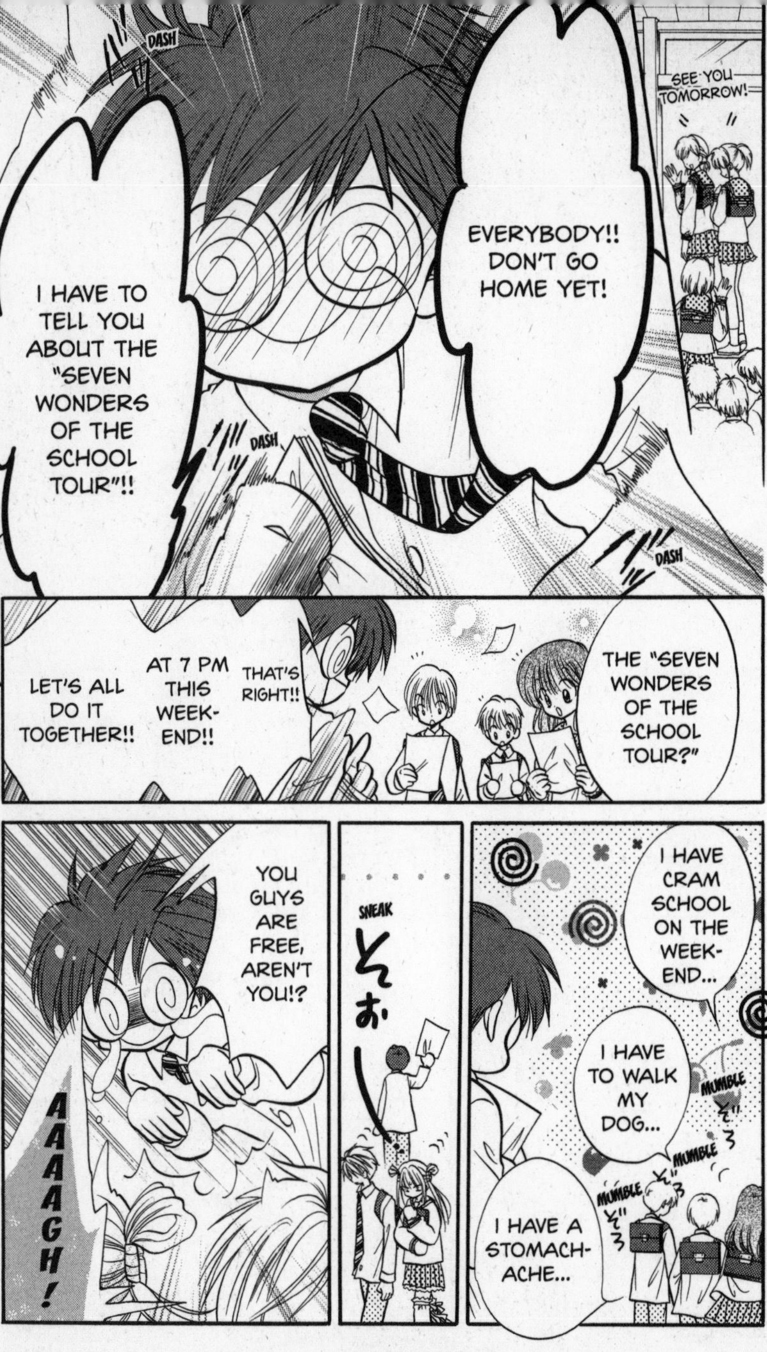
SEE YOU TOMORROW!
DASH
EVERYBODY!! DON'T GO HOME YET!
I HAVE TO TELL YOU ABOUT THE "SEVEN WONDERS OF THE SCHOOL TOUR"!!
DASH
DASH
THE "SEVEN WONDERS OF THE SCHOOL TOUR?"
THAT'S RIGHT!!
AT 7 PM THIS WEEK-END!!
LET'S ALL DO IT TOGETHER!!
I HAVE CRAM SCHOOL ON THE WEEK-END...
MUMBLE
I HAVE TO WALK MY DOG...
MUMBLE
MUMBLE
I HAVE A STOMACH-ACHE...
SNEAK
そぉー
YOU GUYS ARE FREE, AREN'T YOU!?
AAAAAGH!

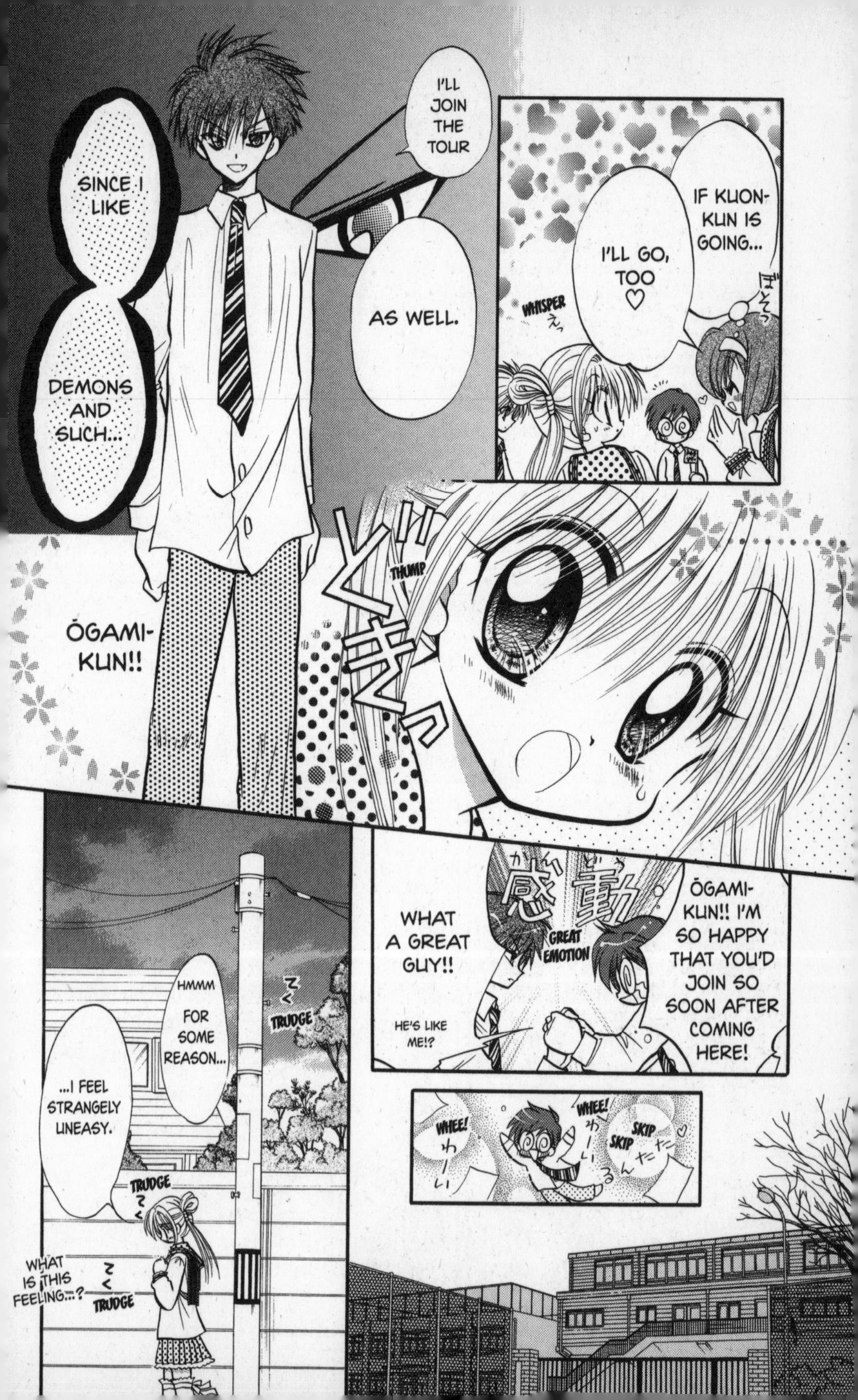
IF KUON-KUN IS GOING...
I'LL GO, TOO ♡
WHISPER
I'LL JOIN THE TOUR
AS WELL.
SINCE I LIKE
DEMONS AND SUCH...
THUMP
ŌGAMI-KUN!!
ŌGAMI-KUN!! I'M SO HAPPY THAT YOU'D JOIN SO SOON AFTER COMING HERE!
感動
GREAT EMOTION
WHAT A GREAT GUY!!
HE'S LIKE ME!?
WHEE!
WHEE!
SKIP
SKIP
HMMM
FOR SOME REASON...
...I FEEL STRANGELY UNEASY.
TRUDGE
TRUDGE
TRUDGE
WHAT IS THIS FEELING...?

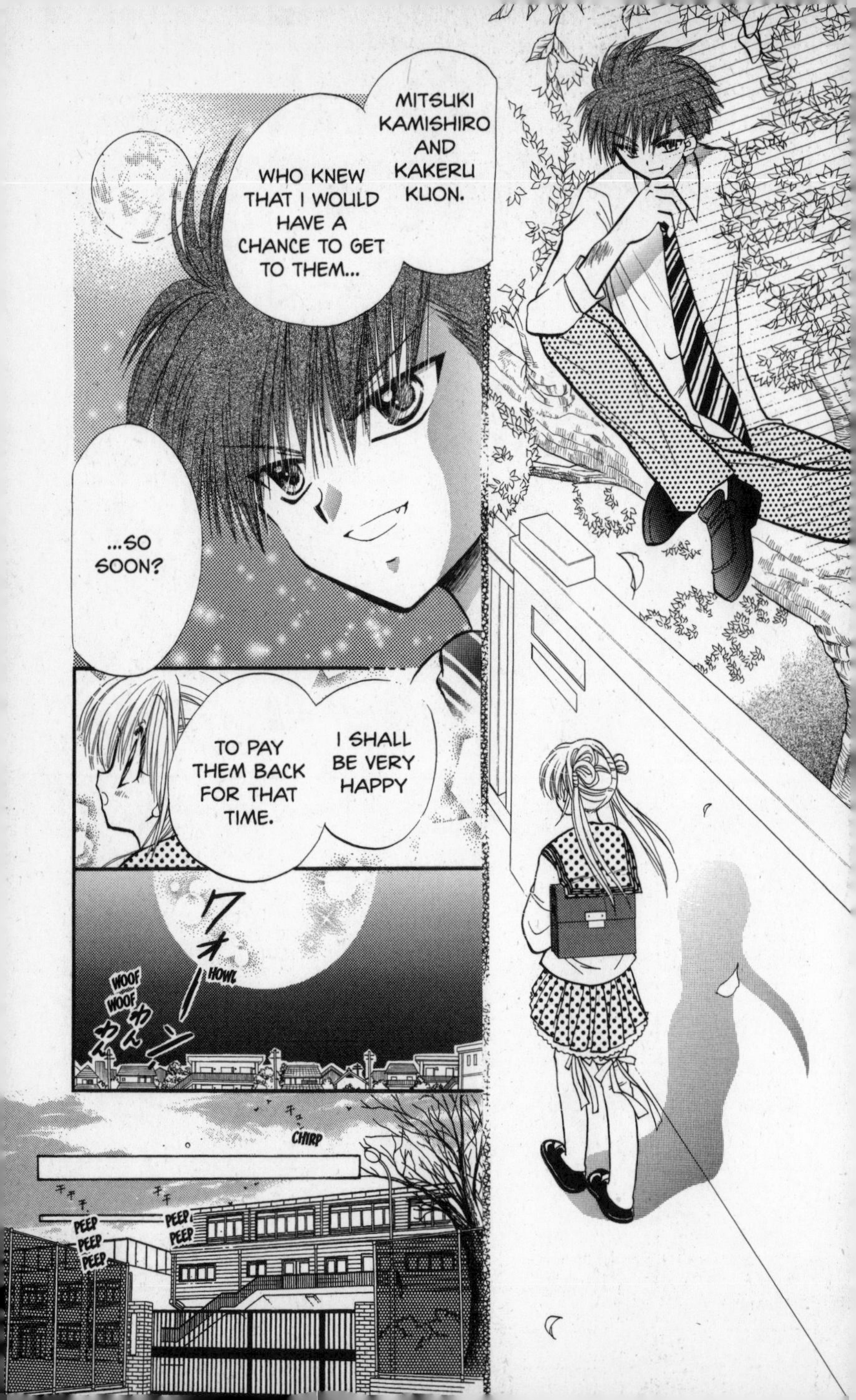
MITSUKI KAMISHIRO AND KAKERU KUON.
WHO KNEW THAT I WOULD HAVE A CHANCE TO GET TO THEM...
...SO SOON?
I SHALL BE VERY HAPPY
TO PAY THEM BACK FOR THAT TIME.
ワオーン
HOWL
わんわん
WOOF WOOF
CHIRP
PEEP PEEP
PEEP PEEP PEEP

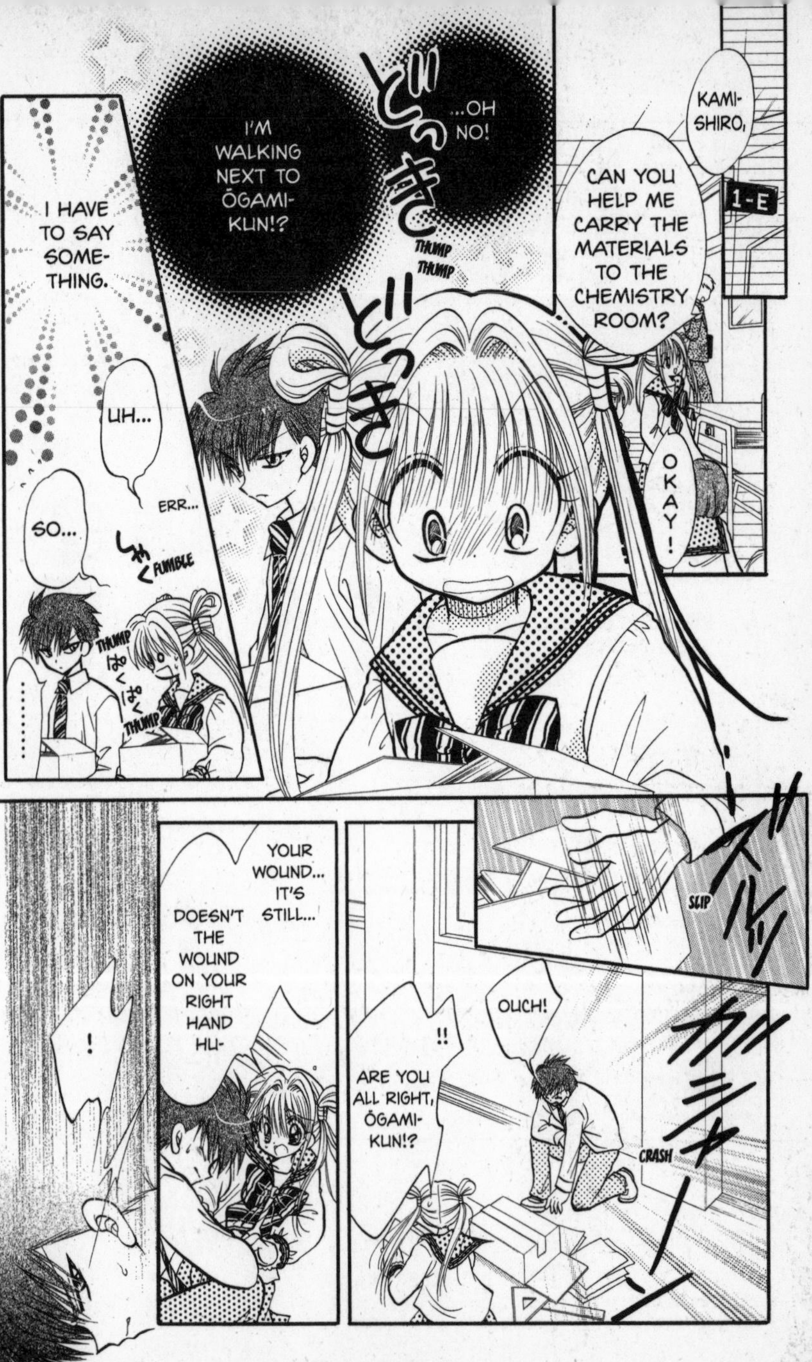
KAMI-SHIRO,
CAN YOU HELP ME CARRY THE MATERIALS TO THE CHEMISTRY ROOM?
1-E
OKAY!
...OH NO!
どっき
THUMP THUMP
どっき
I'M WALKING NEXT TO ŌGAMI-KUN!?
I HAVE TO SAY SOME-THING.
UH...
ERR...
SO...
FUMBLE
THUMP THUMP
......
ズルッ
SLIP
ガシャーン
CRASH
OUCH!
!!
ARE YOU ALL RIGHT, ŌGAMI-KUN!?
YOUR WOUND... IT'S STILL...
DOESN'T THE WOUND ON YOUR RIGHT HAND HU-
!

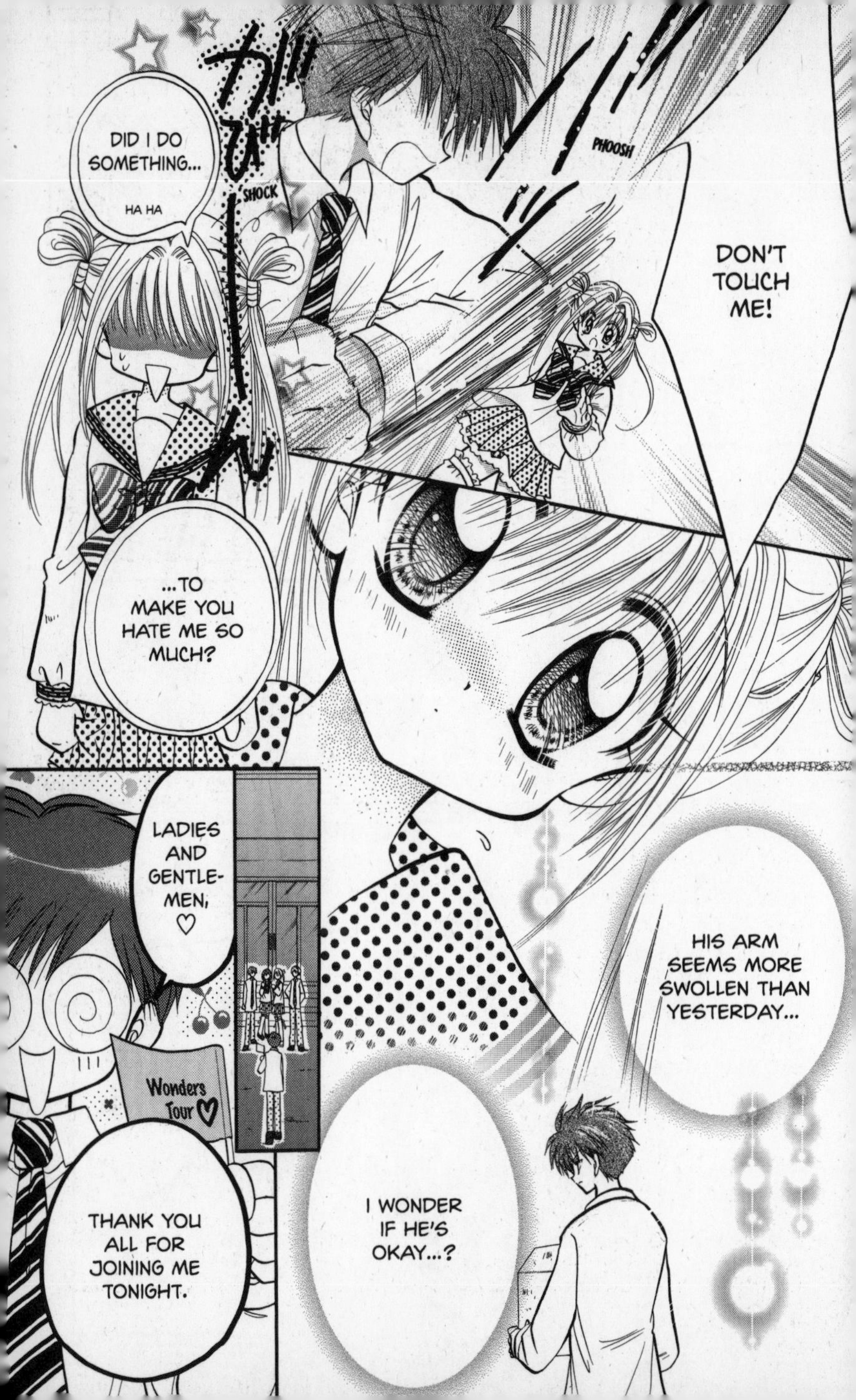
DON'T TOUCH ME!
PHOOSH
SHOCK
DID I DO SOMETHING...
HA HA
...TO MAKE YOU HATE ME SO MUCH?
HIS ARM SEEMS MORE SWOLLEN THAN YESTERDAY...
I WONDER IF HE'S OKAY...?
LADIES AND GENTLEMEN, ♡
Wonders Tour ♡
THANK YOU ALL FOR JOINING ME TONIGHT.

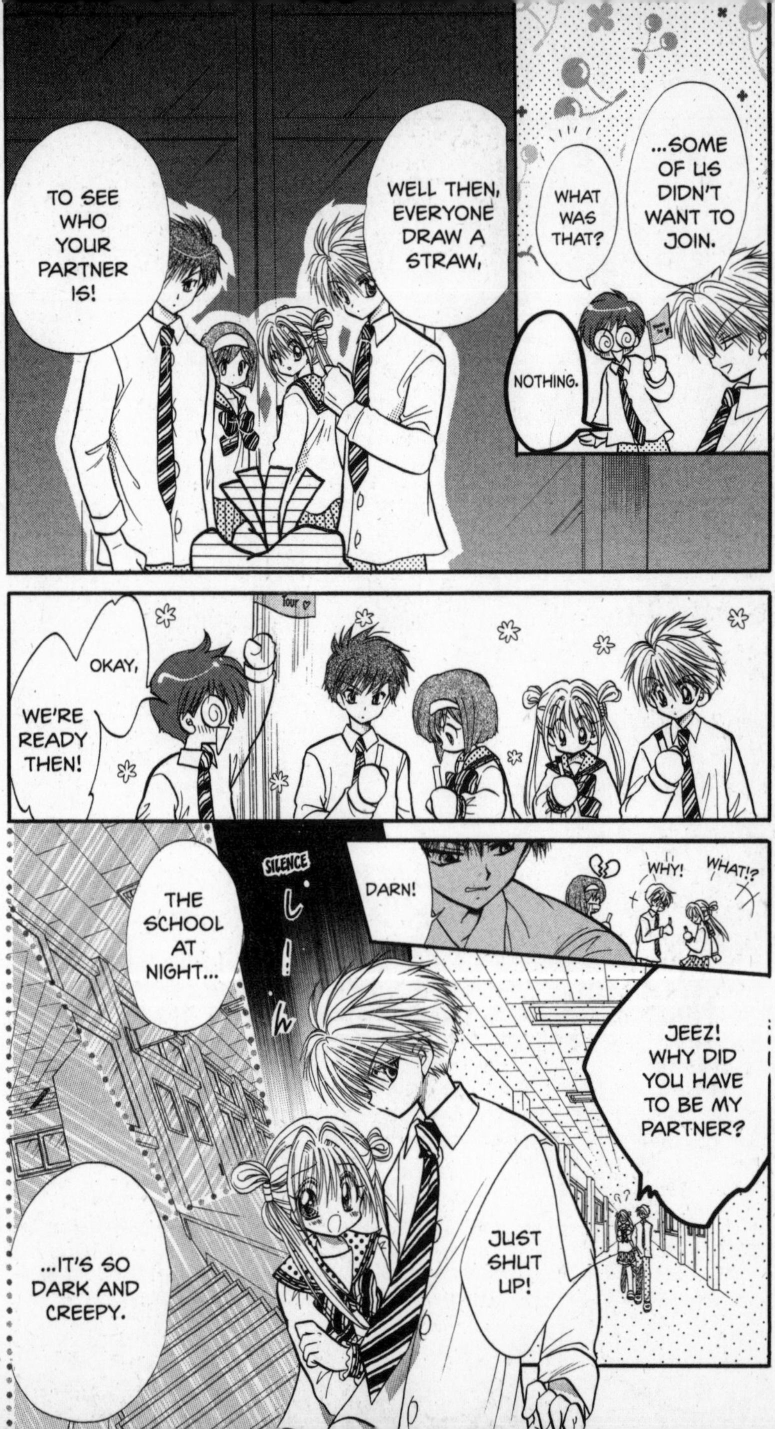
...SOME OF US DIDN'T WANT TO JOIN.
WHAT WAS THAT?
NOTHING.
WELL THEN, EVERYONE DRAW A STRAW,
TO SEE WHO YOUR PARTNER IS!
Tour
OKAY, WE'RE READY THEN!
WHAT!?
WHY!
DARN!
SILENCE
THE SCHOOL AT NIGHT...
...IT'S SO DARK AND CREEPY.
JEEZ! WHY DID YOU HAVE TO BE MY PARTNER?
JUST SHUT UP!

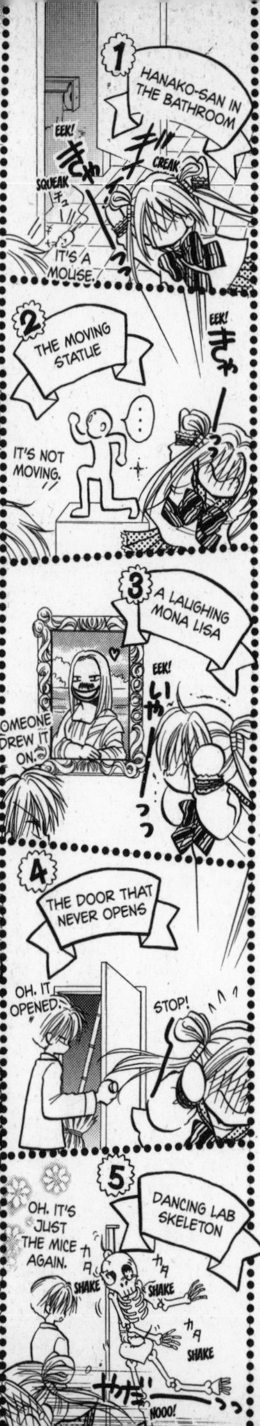
1
HANAKO-SAN IN THE BATHROOM
EEK!
CREAK
SQUEAK
IT'S A MOUSE.
2
THE MOVING STATUE
EEK!
IT'S NOT MOVING.
3
A LAUGHING MONA LISA
EEK!
SOMEONE DREW IT ON.
4
THE DOOR THAT NEVER OPENS
STOP!
OH. IT OPENED.
5
DANCING LAB SKELETON
OH. IT'S JUST THE MICE AGAIN.
SHAKE
SHAKE
SHAKE
NOOO!

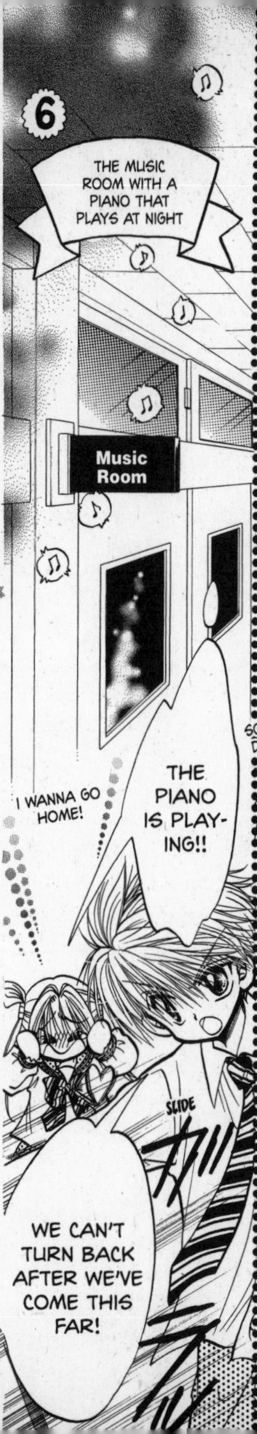
6
THE MUSIC ROOM WITH A PIANO THAT PLAYS AT NIGHT
Music Room
THE PIANO IS PLAY-ING!!
I WANNA GO HOME!
SLIDE
WE CAN'T TURN BACK AFTER WE'VE COME THIS FAR!

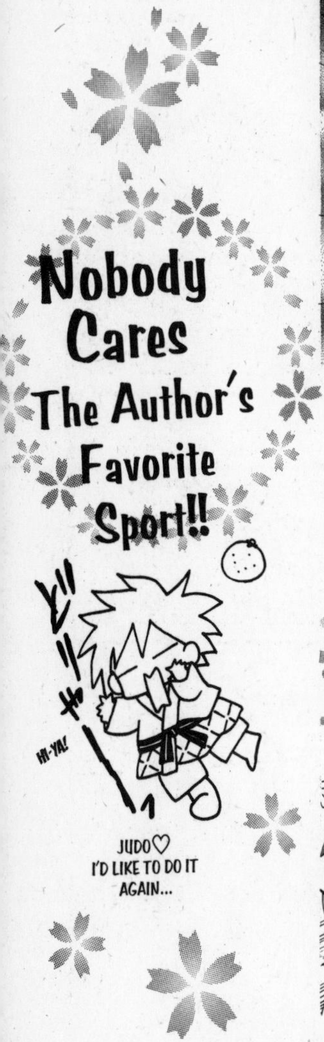
Nobody Cares The Author's Favorite Sport!!
HI-YA!
JUDO♡
I'D LIKE TO DO IT AGAIN...

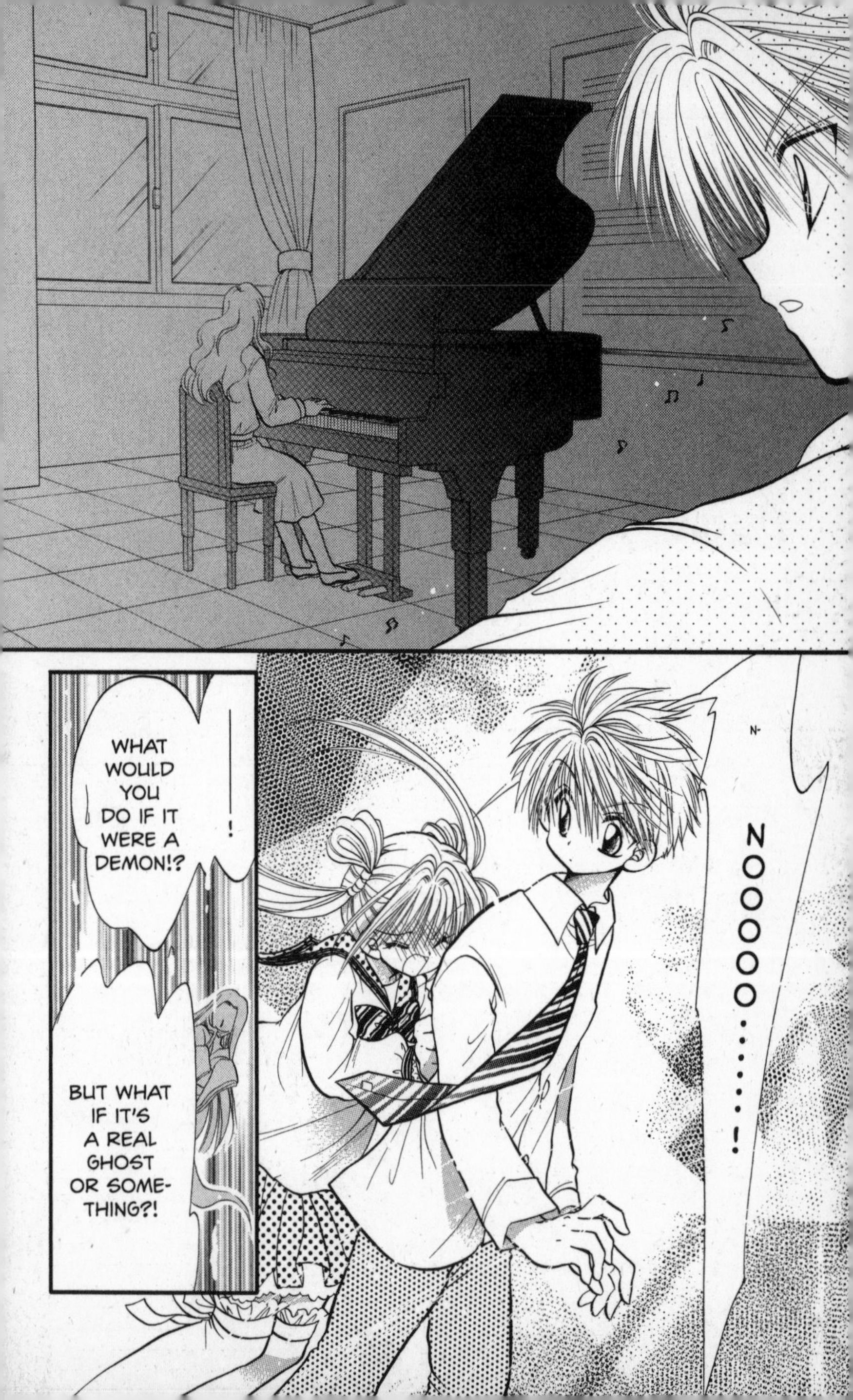
N-
NOOOOO.....!
!
WHAT WOULD YOU DO IF IT WERE A DEMON!?
BUT WHAT IF IT'S A REAL GHOST OR SOME-THING?!

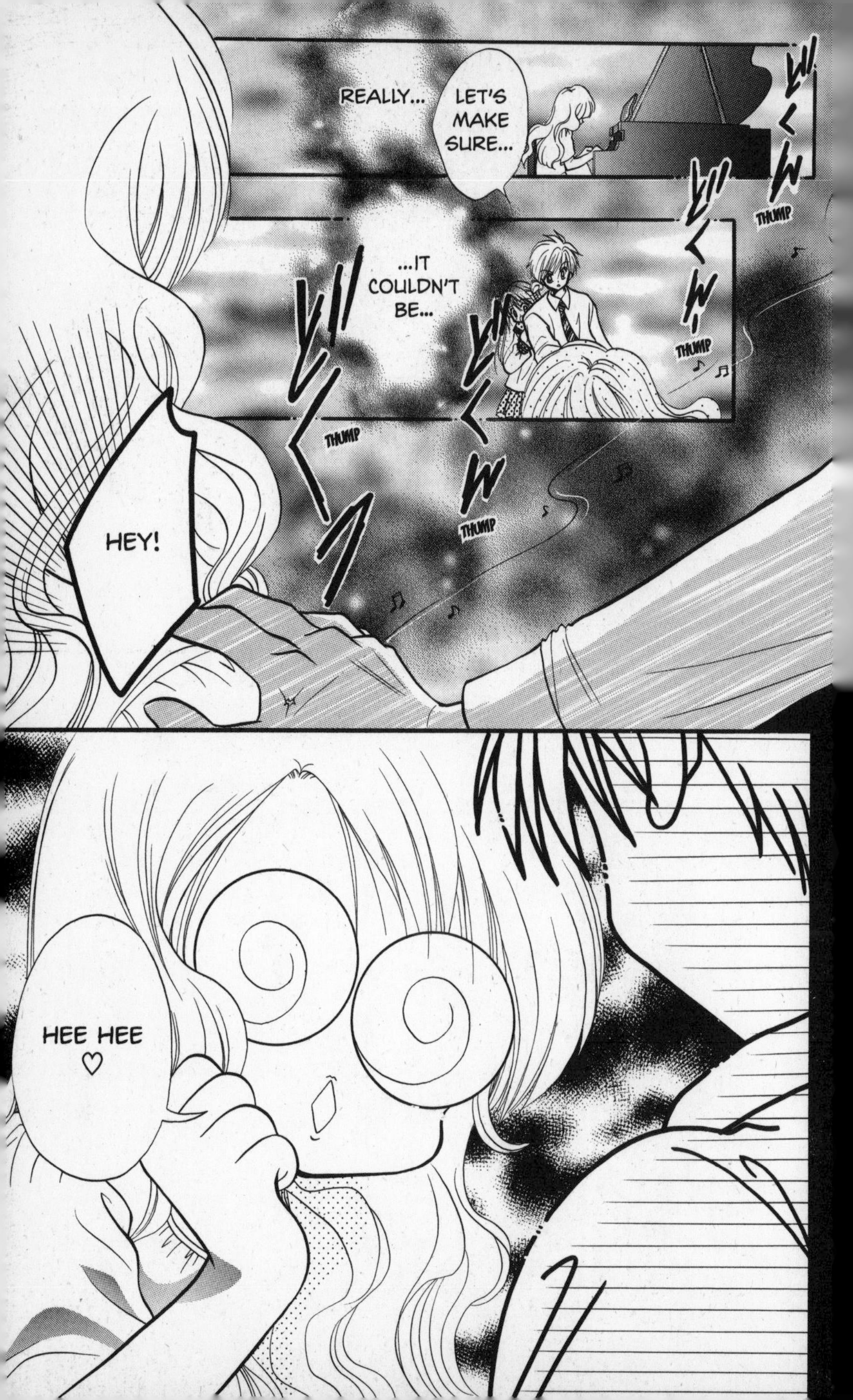
THUMP
LET'S MAKE SURE...
REALLY...
THUMP
...IT COULDN'T BE...
THUMP
THUMP
HEY!
HEE HEE ♡

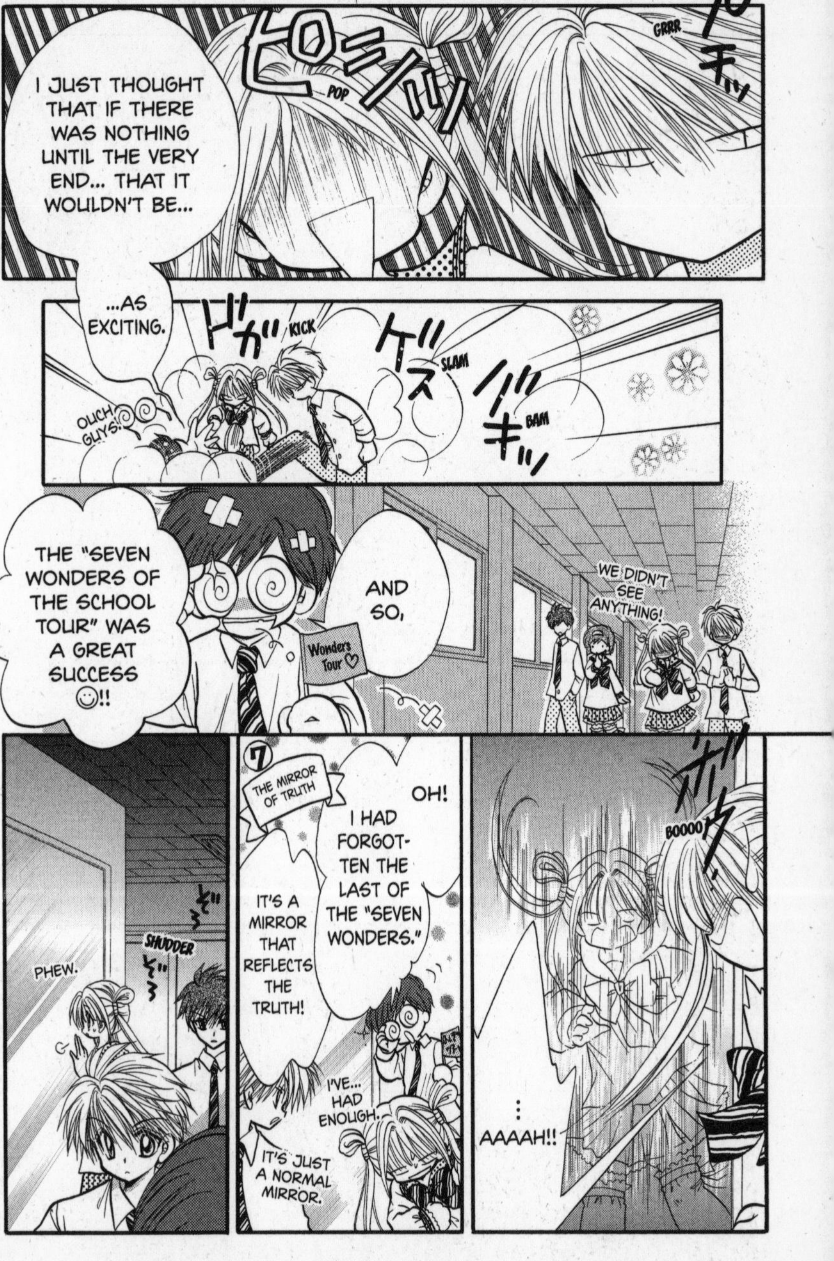
GRRR
POP
I JUST THOUGHT THAT IF THERE WAS NOTHING UNTIL THE VERY END... THAT IT WOULDN'T BE...
...AS EXCITING.
BAM
SLAM
KICK
OUCH GUYS!
WE DIDN'T SEE ANYTHING!
AND SO,
THE "SEVEN WONDERS OF THE SCHOOL TOUR" WAS A GREAT SUCCESS ☺!!
Wonders Tour ♡
BOOOO
... AAAAH!!
7 THE MIRROR OF TRUTH
OH! I HAD FORGOT-TEN THE LAST OF THE "SEVEN WONDERS."
IT'S A MIRROR THAT REFLECTS THE TRUTH!
I'VE... HAD ENOUGH.
IT'S JUST A NORMAL MIRROR.
SHUDDER
PHEW.

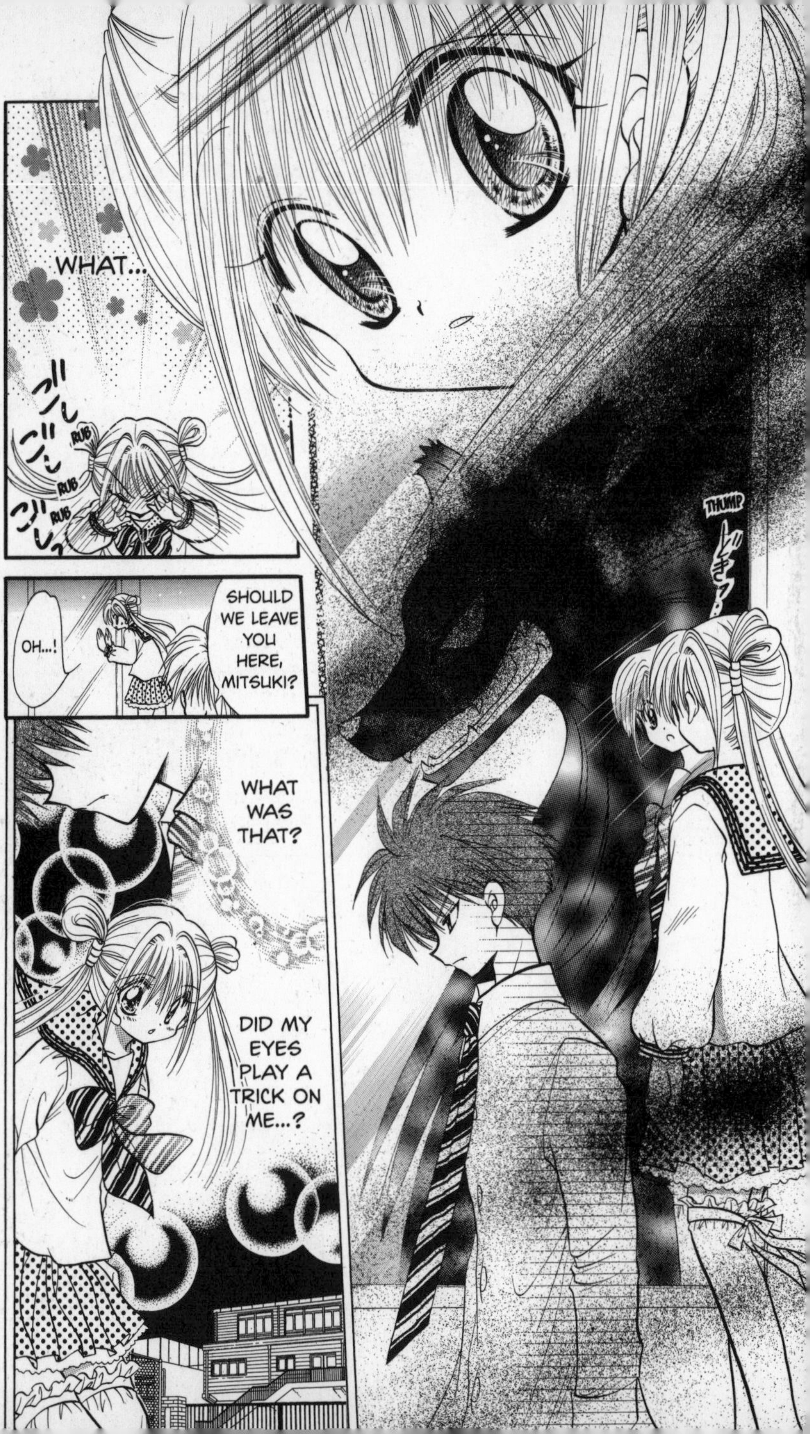
THUMP
WHAT...
RUB
RUB
RUB
SHOULD WE LEAVE YOU HERE, MITSUKI?
OH...!
WHAT WAS THAT?
DID MY EYES PLAY A TRICK ON ME...?

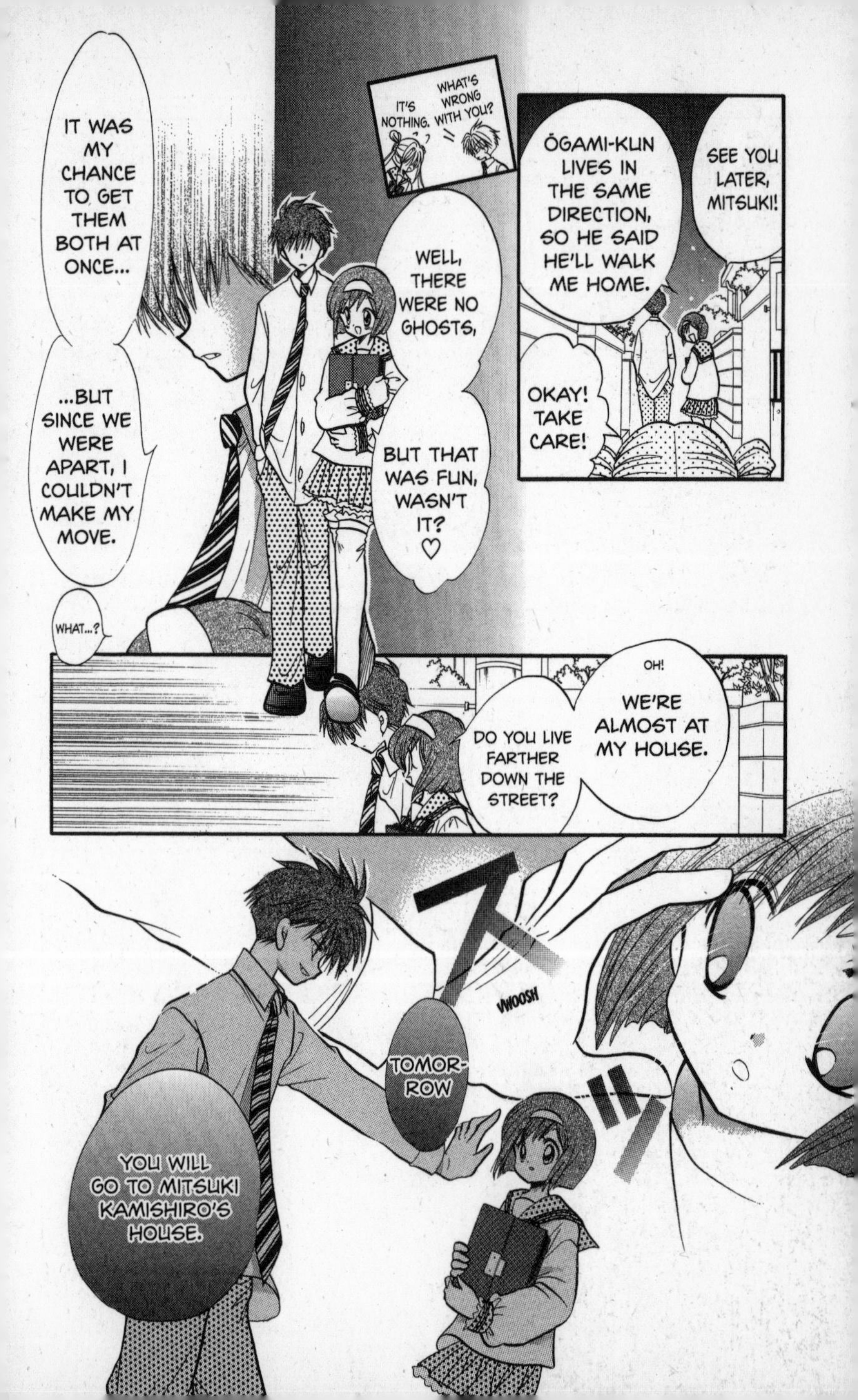
SEE YOU LATER, MITSUKI!
ŌGAMI-KUN LIVES IN THE SAME DIRECTION, SO HE SAID HE'LL WALK ME HOME.
OKAY! TAKE CARE!
WHAT'S WRONG WITH YOU?
IT'S NOTHING.
WELL, THERE WERE NO GHOSTS,
BUT THAT WAS FUN, WASN'T IT? ♡
IT WAS MY CHANCE TO GET THEM BOTH AT ONCE...
...BUT SINCE WE WERE APART, I COULDN'T MAKE MY MOVE.
WHAT...?
OH!
WE'RE ALMOST AT MY HOUSE.
DO YOU LIVE FARTHER DOWN THE STREET?
VWOOSH
TOMOR-ROW
YOU WILL GO TO MITSUKI KAMISHIRO'S HOUSE.

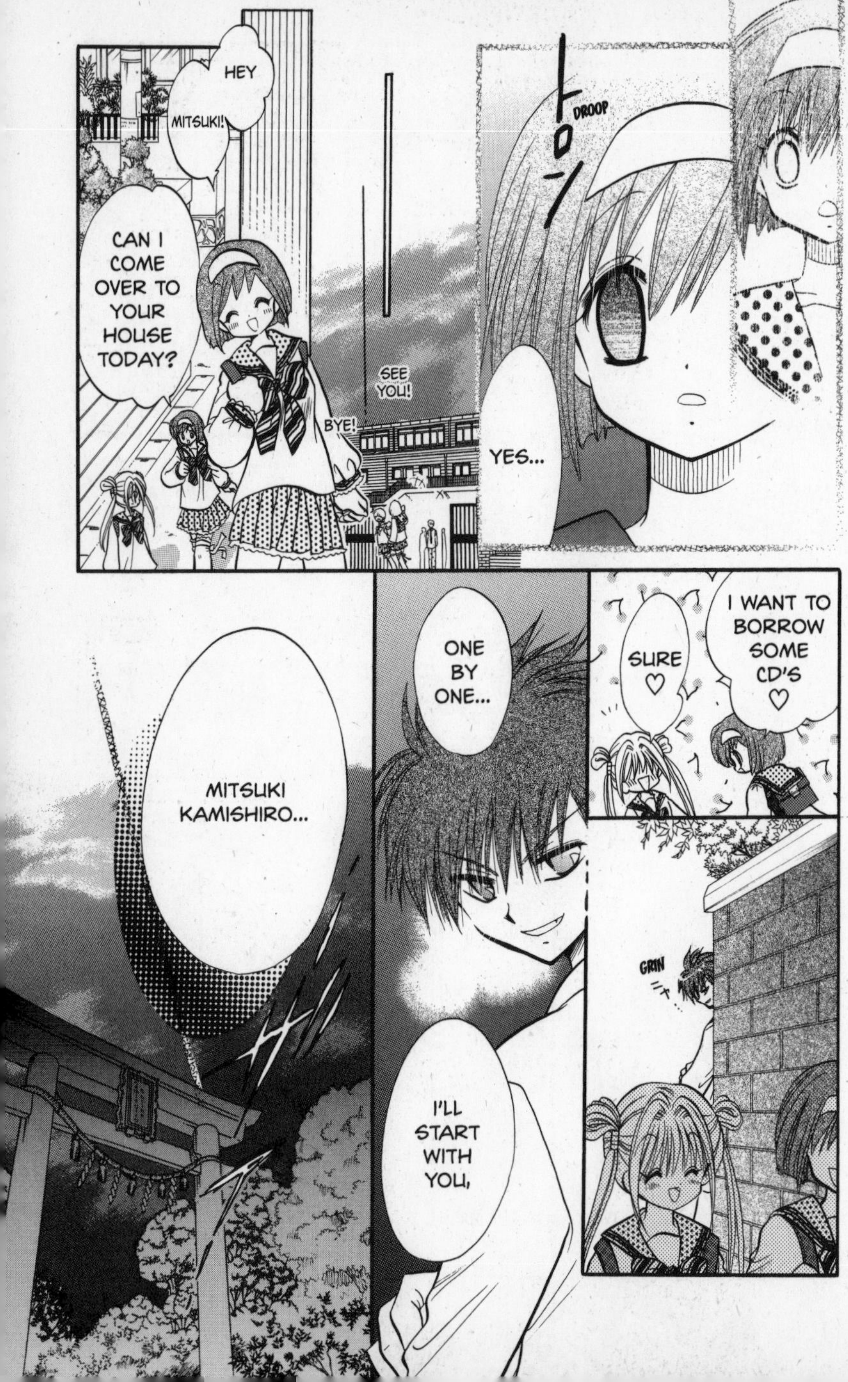
DROOP
YES...
HEY
MITSUKI!
CAN I COME OVER TO YOUR HOUSE TODAY?
SEE YOU!
BYE!
I WANT TO BORROW SOME CD'S ♡
SURE ♡
GRIN
ONE BY ONE...
I'LL START WITH YOU,
MITSUKI KAMISHIRO...

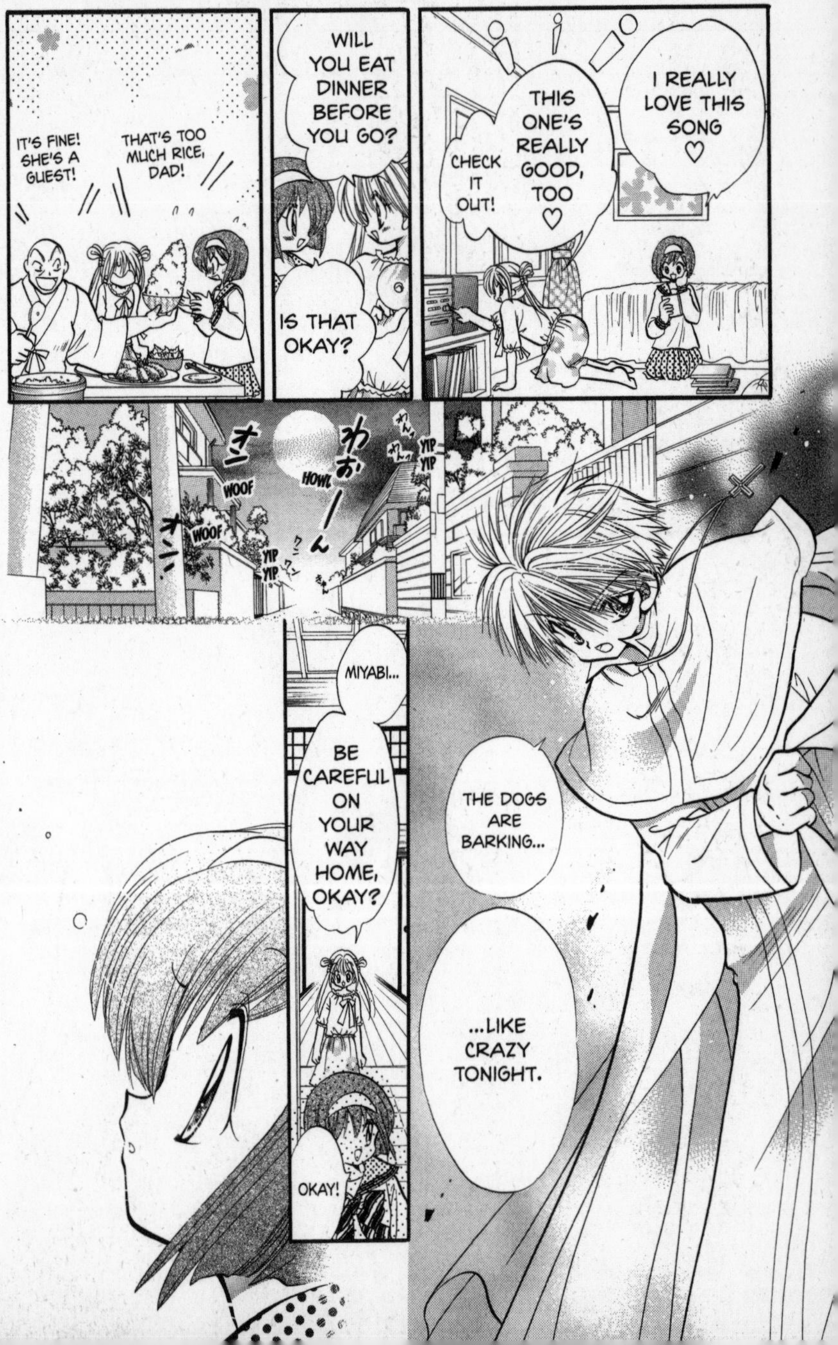
I REALLY LOVE THIS SONG ♡
THIS ONE'S REALLY GOOD, TOO ♡
CHECK IT OUT!
WILL YOU EAT DINNER BEFORE YOU GO?
IS THAT OKAY?
THAT'S TOO MUCH RICE, DAD!
IT'S FINE! SHE'S A GUEST!
THE DOGS ARE BARKING...
...LIKE CRAZY TONIGHT.
YIP YIP
HOWL
WOOF
WOOF
YIP YIP
MIYABI...
BE CAREFUL ON YOUR WAY HOME, OKAY?
OKAY!

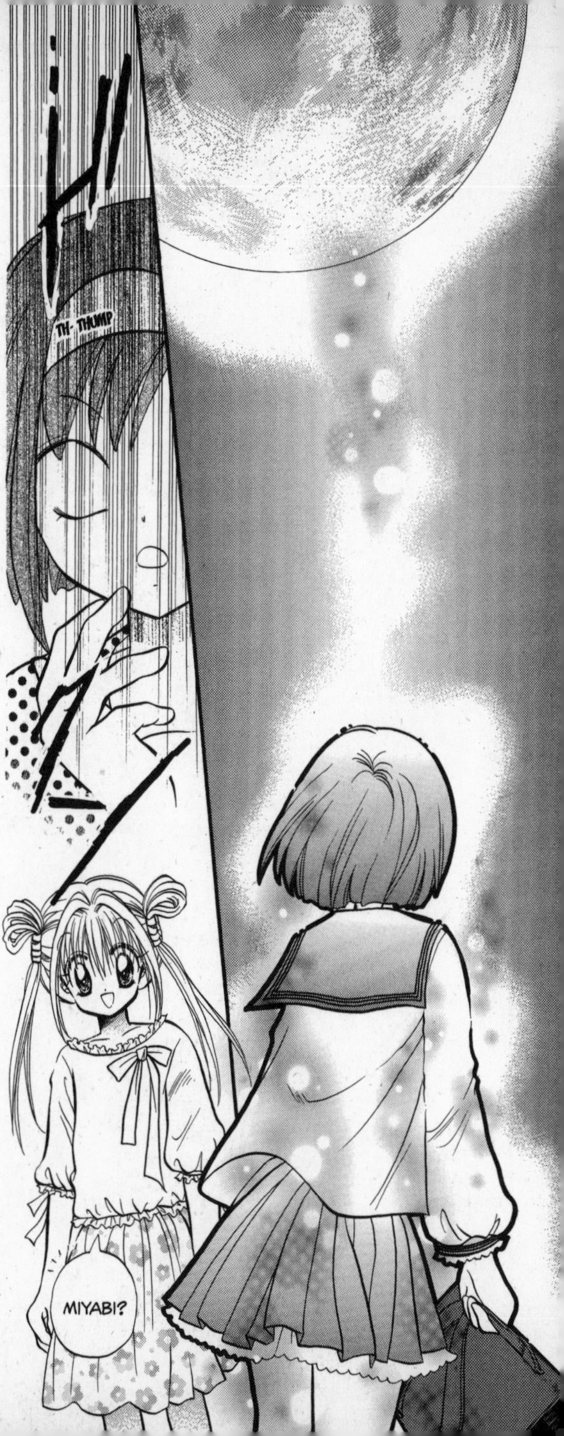
TH-THUMP
MIYABI?

Nobody Cares The Author's Favorite Ride!!

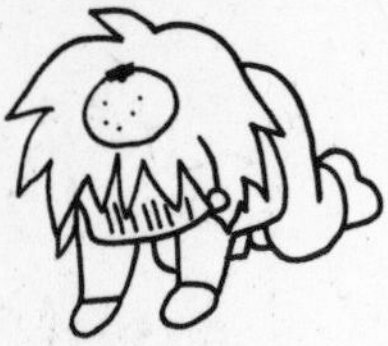

NONE...

THEY ALL MAKE ME SICK...

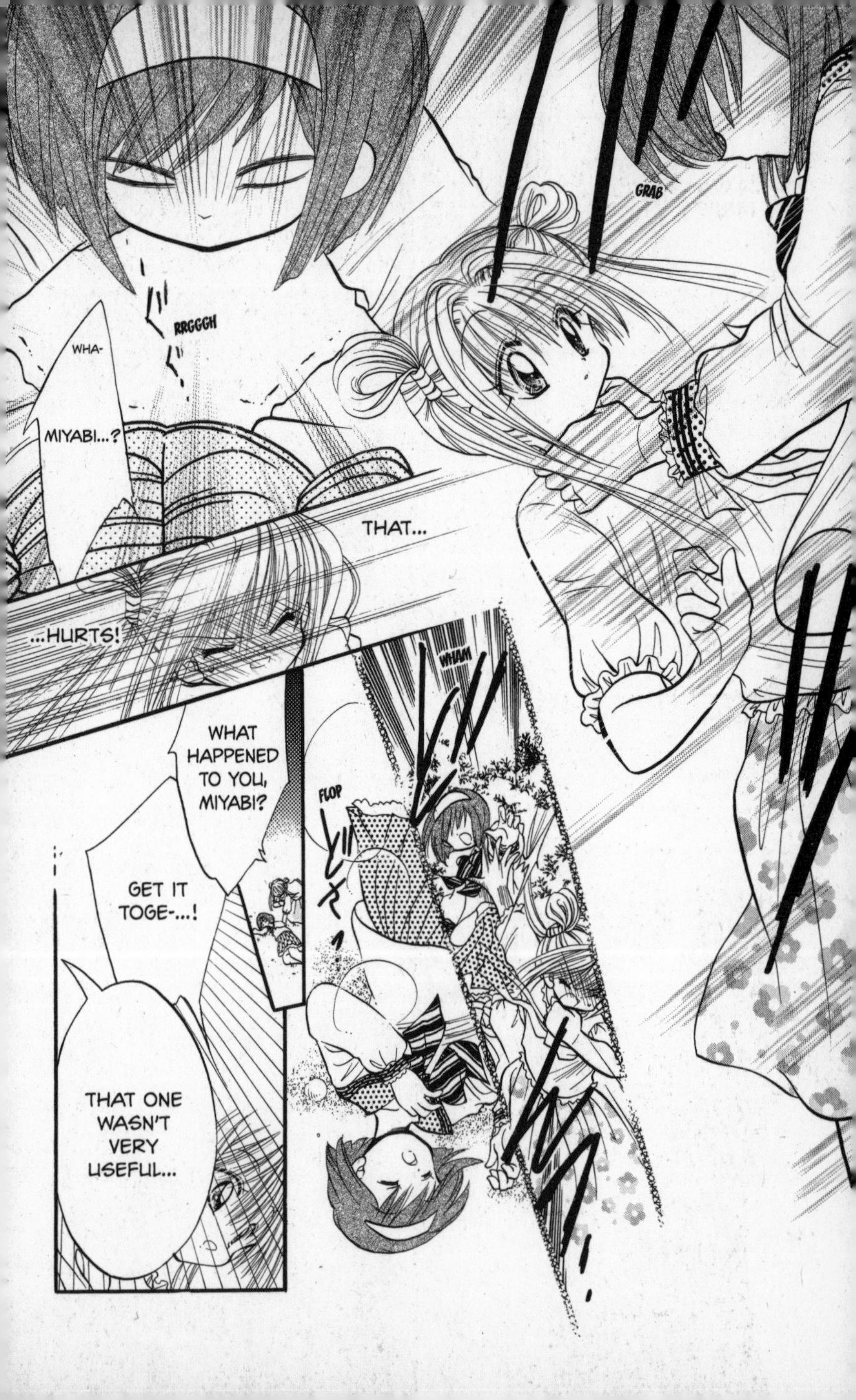
GRAB
RRGGGH
WHA-
MIYABI...?
THAT...
...HURTS!
WHAM
FLOP
WHAT HAPPENED TO YOU, MIYABI?
GET IT TOGE-...!
THAT ONE WASN'T VERY USEFUL...

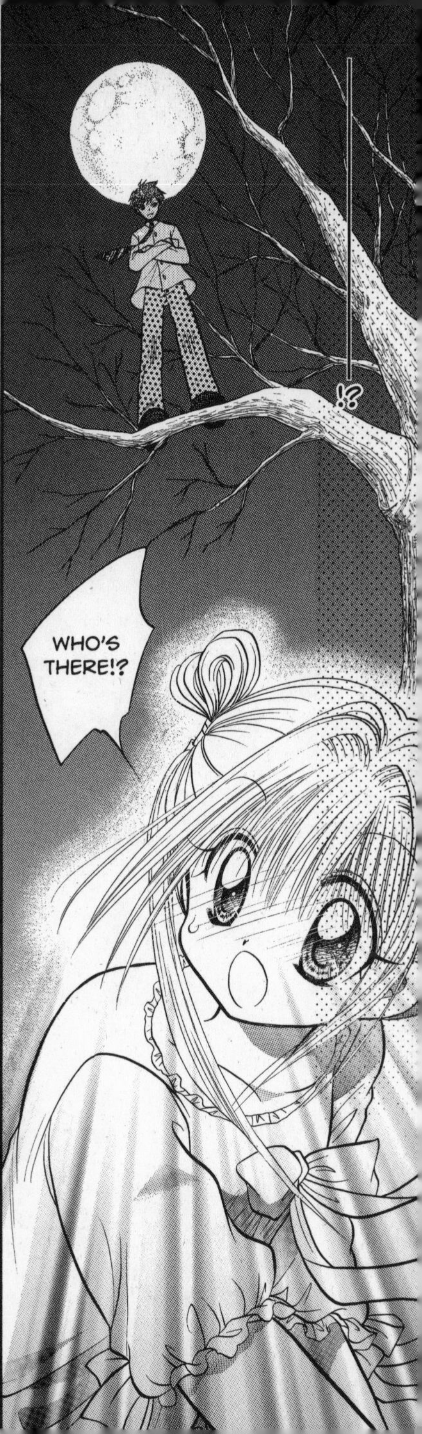
!?
WHO'S THERE!?

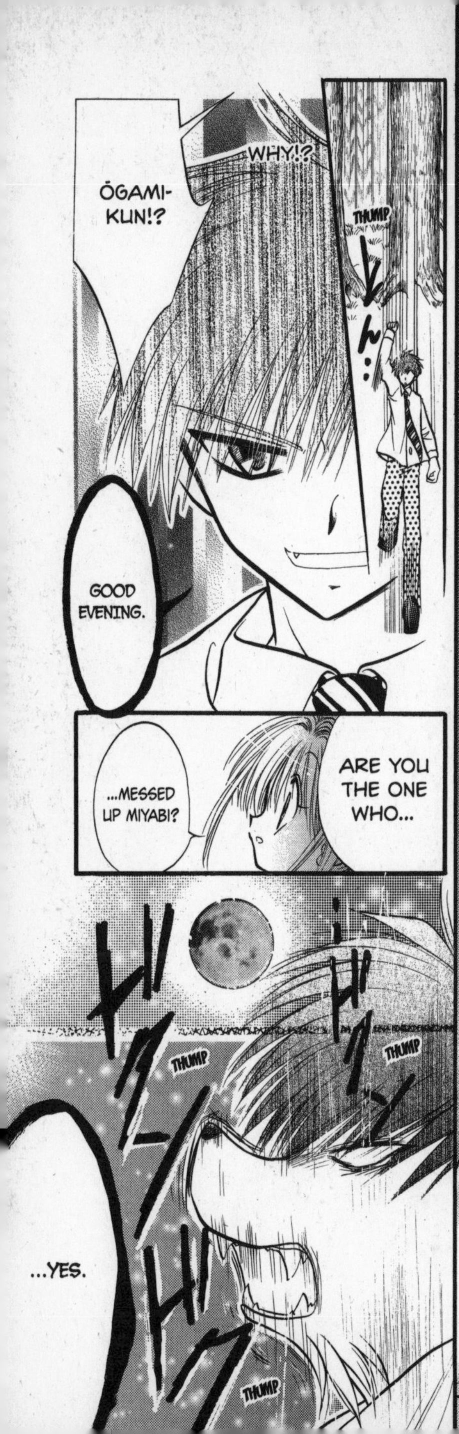
THUMP
WHY!?
ŌGAMI-KUN!?
GOOD EVENING.
ARE YOU THE ONE WHO...
...MESSED UP MIYABI?
THUMP
THUMP
...YES.
THUMP

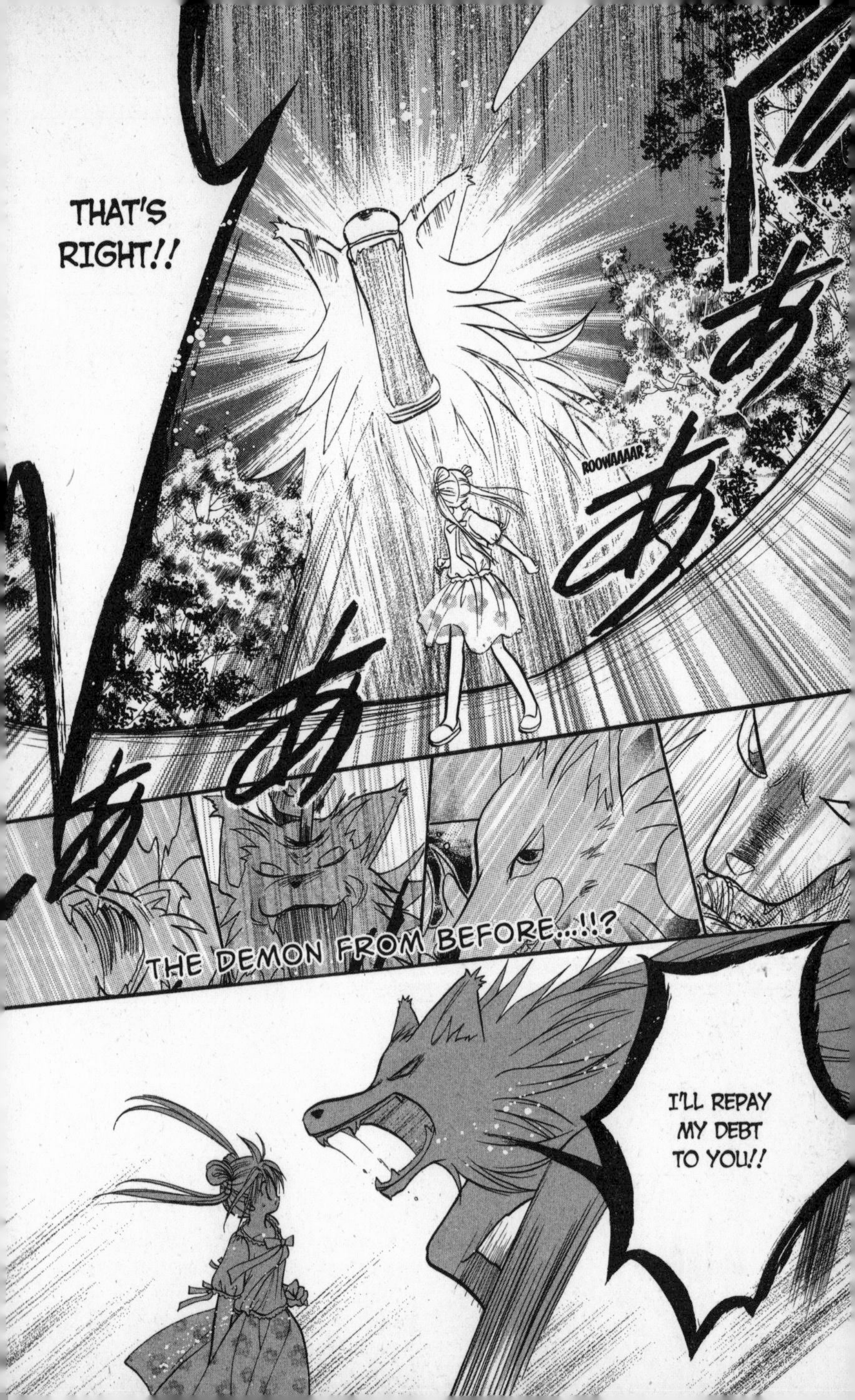
THAT'S RIGHT!!
ROOWAAAAR
THE DEMON FROM BEFORE...!!?
I'LL REPAY MY DEBT TO YOU!!

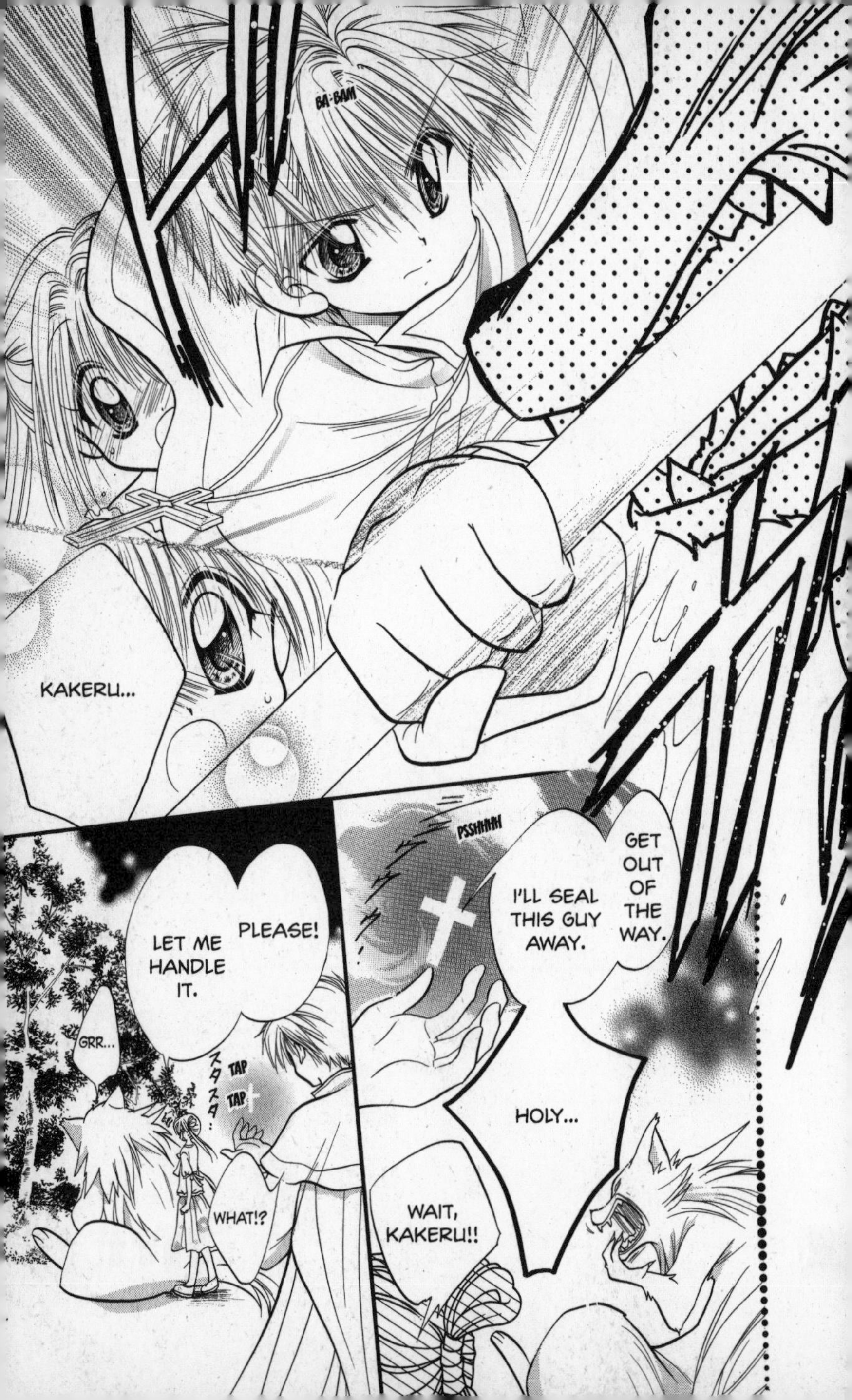
BA-BAM
KAKERU...
PSSHHHH
GET OUT OF THE WAY.
I'LL SEAL THIS GUY AWAY.
HOLY...
WAIT, KAKERU!!
PLEASE!
LET ME HANDLE IT.
GRR...
TAP TAP
スタスタ
WHAT!?

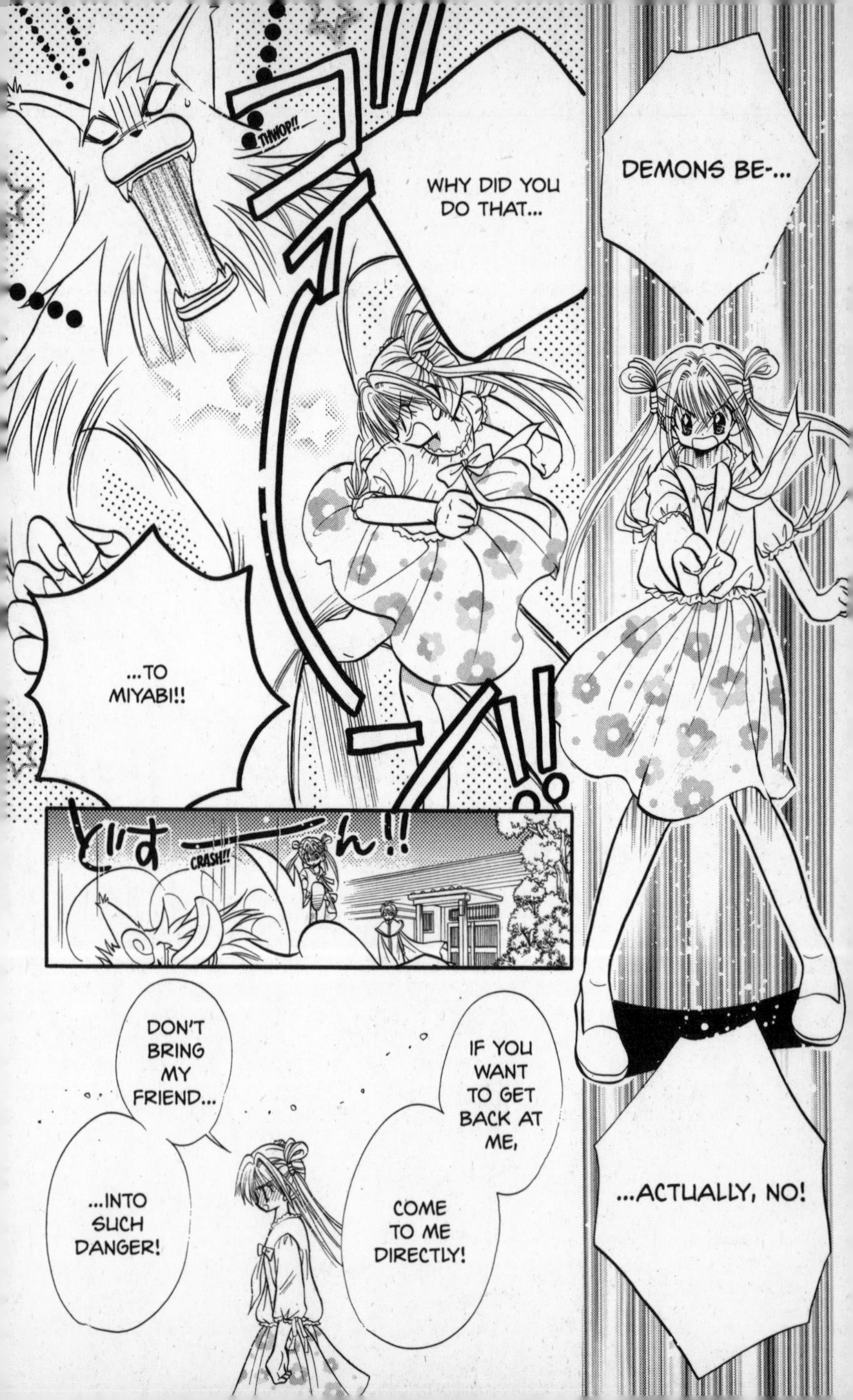
DEMONS BE-...
...ACTUALLY, NO!
THWOP!!
WHY DID YOU DO THAT...
...TO MIYABI!!
どすーん!!
CRASH!!
IF YOU WANT TO GET BACK AT ME,
COME TO ME DIRECTLY!
DON'T BRING MY FRIEND...
...INTO SUCH DANGER!

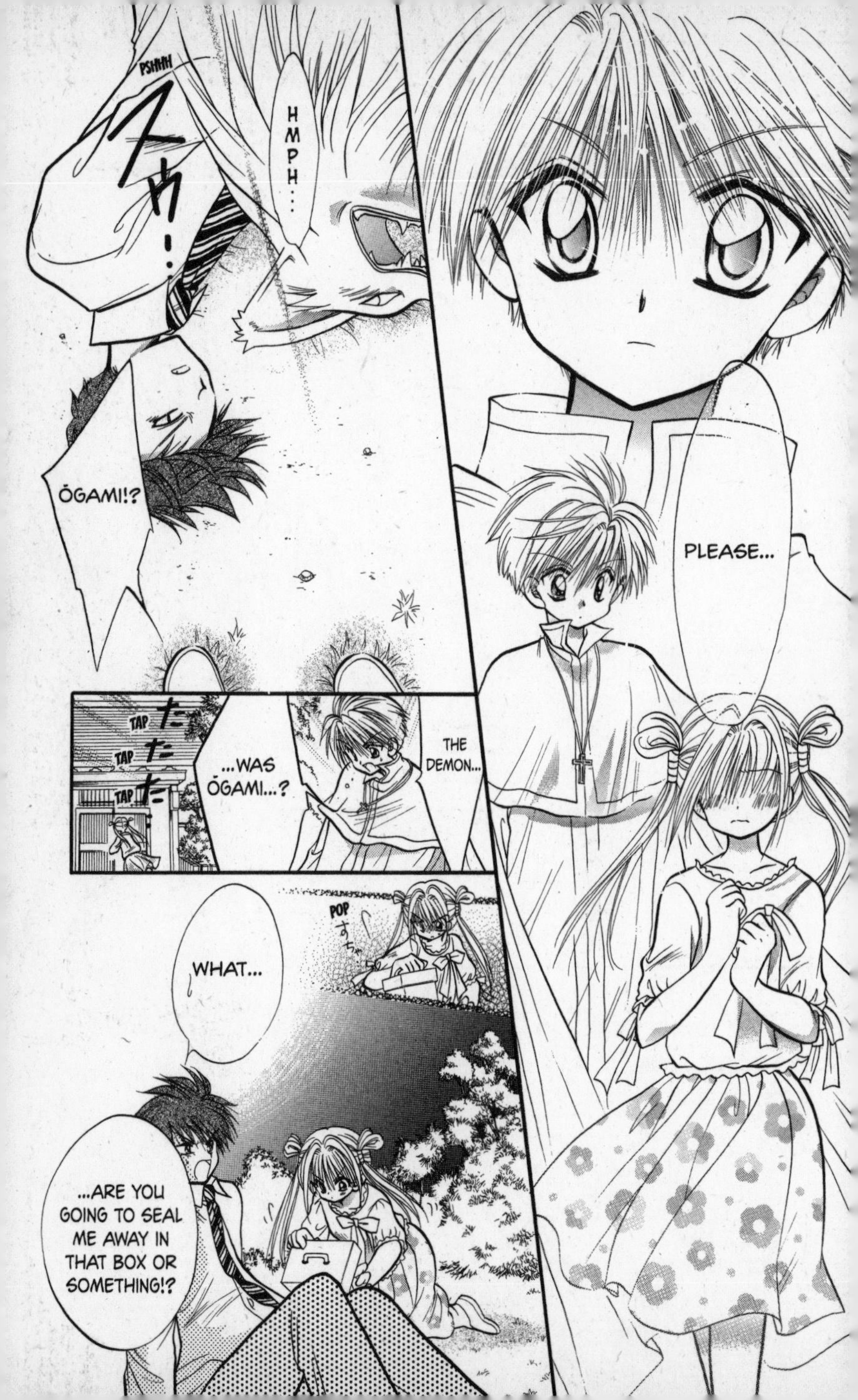
PLEASE...
HMPH...
PSHHH
ŌGAMI!?
THE DEMON...
...WAS ŌGAMI...?
TAP
TAP
TAP
POP
WHAT...
...ARE YOU GOING TO SEAL ME AWAY IN THAT BOX OR SOMETHING!?

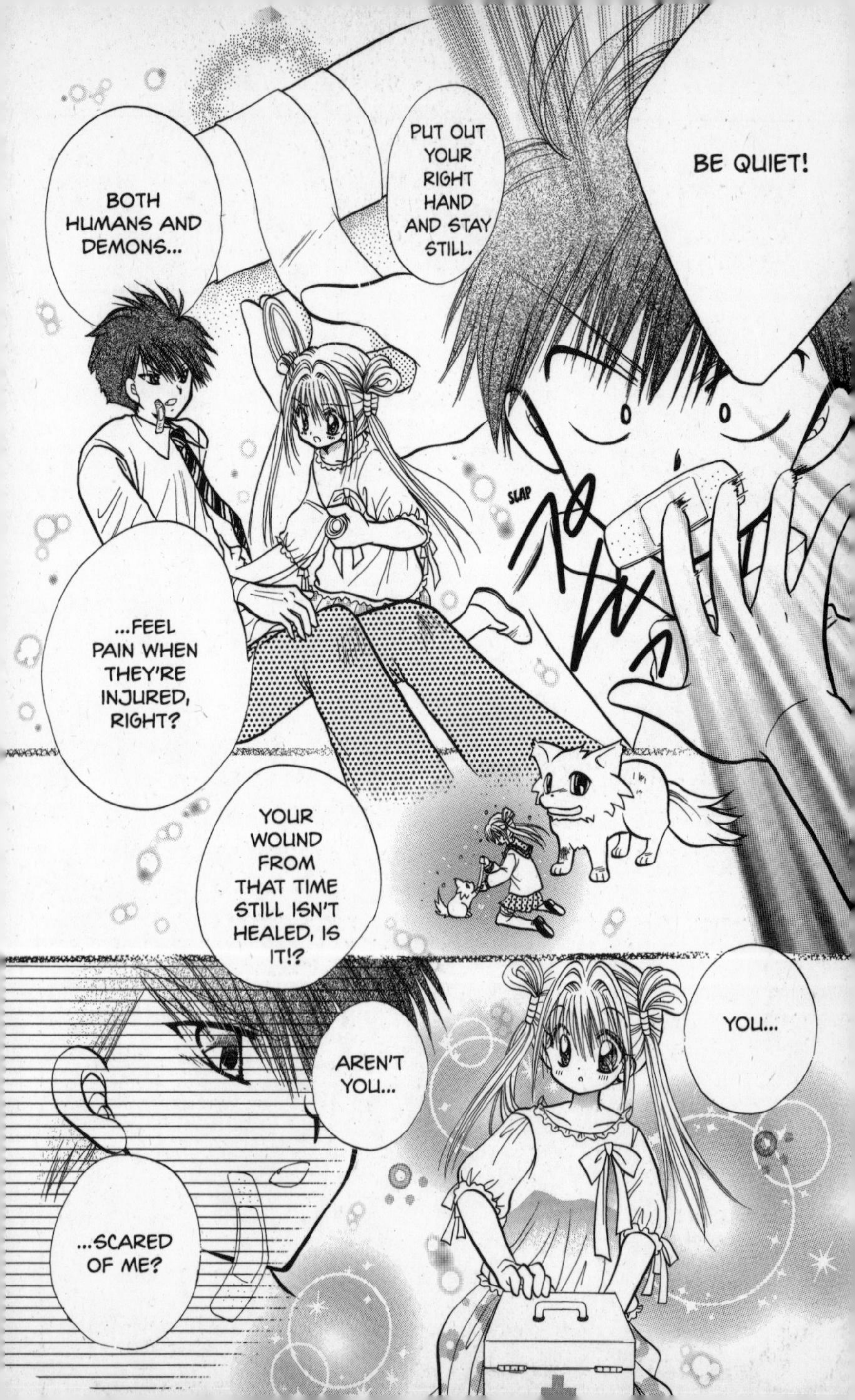
BE QUIET!
SLAP
PUT OUT YOUR RIGHT HAND AND STAY STILL.
BOTH HUMANS AND DEMONS...
...FEEL PAIN WHEN THEY'RE INJURED, RIGHT?
YOUR WOUND FROM THAT TIME STILL ISN'T HEALED, IS IT!?
YOU...
AREN'T YOU...
...SCARED OF ME?

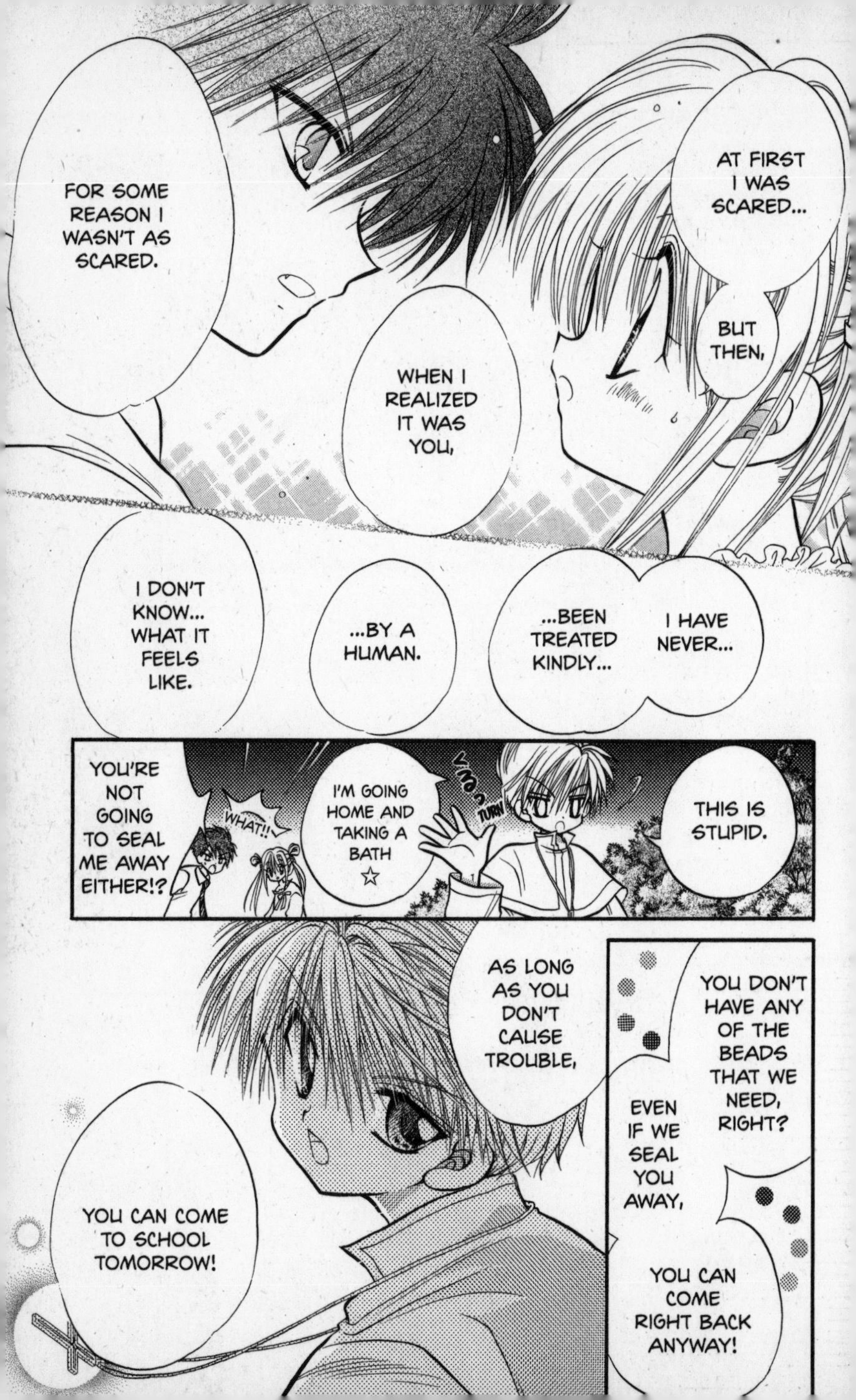
AT FIRST I WAS SCARED...
BUT THEN,
WHEN I REALIZED IT WAS YOU,
FOR SOME REASON I WASN'T AS SCARED.
I HAVE NEVER...
...BEEN TREATED KINDLY...
...BY A HUMAN.
I DON'T KNOW... WHAT IT FEELS LIKE.
THIS IS STUPID.
TURN
I'M GOING HOME AND TAKING A BATH ☆
WHAT!!
YOU'RE NOT GOING TO SEAL ME AWAY EITHER!?
YOU DON'T HAVE ANY OF THE BEADS THAT WE NEED, RIGHT?
EVEN IF WE SEAL YOU AWAY,
YOU CAN COME RIGHT BACK ANYWAY!
AS LONG AS YOU DON'T CAUSE TROUBLE,
YOU CAN COME TO SCHOOL TOMORROW!

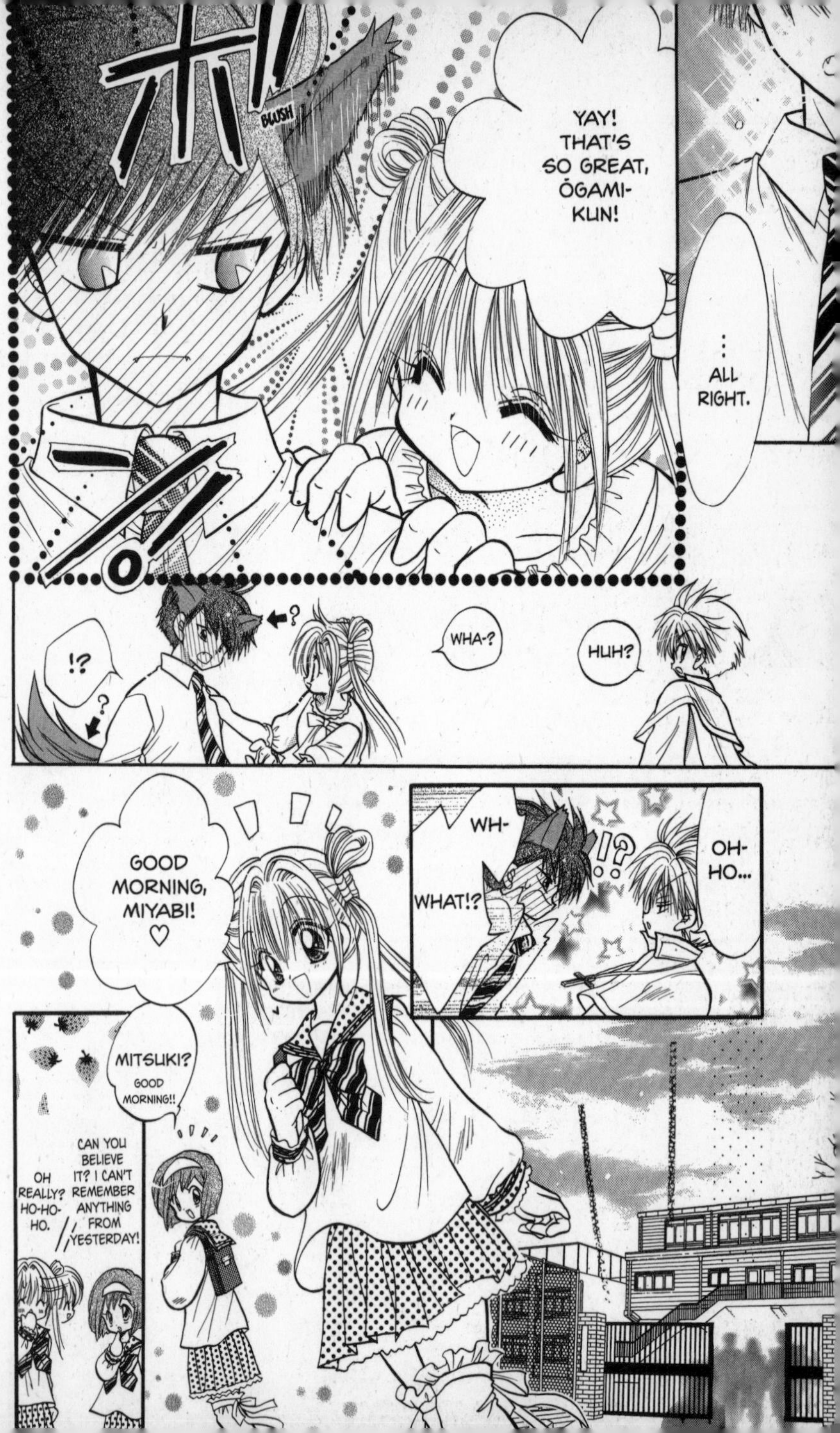
...ALL RIGHT.
YAY! THAT'S SO GREAT, ŌGAMI-KUN!
BLUSH
HUH?
WHA-?
!?
OH-HO...
WH- WHAT!?
GOOD MORNING, MIYABI! ♡
MITSUKI? GOOD MORNING!!
CAN YOU BELIEVE IT? I CAN'T REMEMBER ANYTHING FROM YESTERDAY!
OH REALLY? HO-HO-HO.

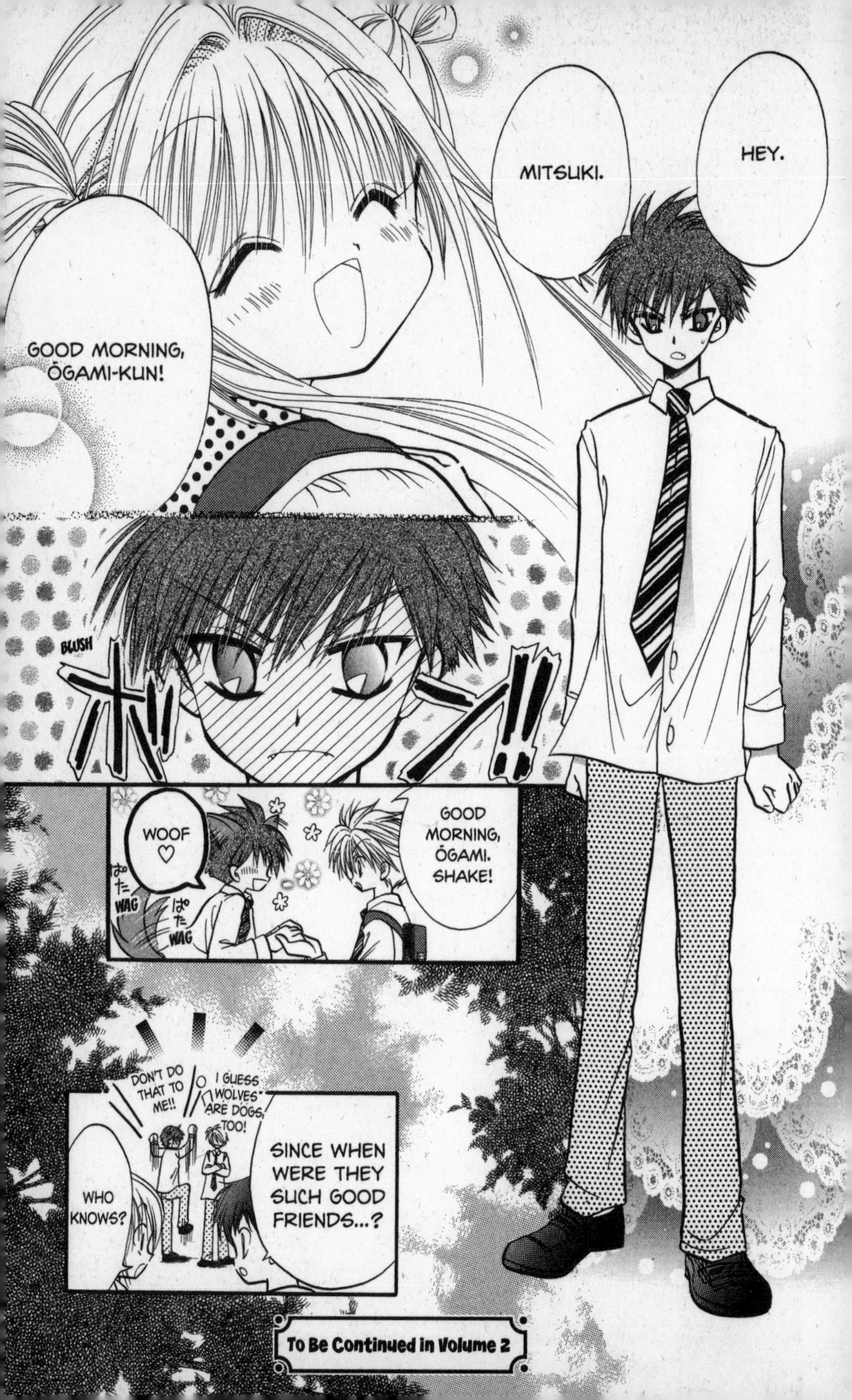
HEY.
MITSUKI.
GOOD MORNING, ŌGAMI-KUN!
BLUSH
GOOD MORNING, ŌGAMI. SHAKE!
WOOF ♡
ぱた WAG
ぱた WAG
SINCE WHEN WERE THEY SUCH GOOD FRIENDS...?
I GUESS WOLVES ARE DOGS, TOO!
DON'T DO THAT TO ME!!
WHO KNOWS?
To Be Continued in Volume 2

Panic x Panic
PROFILE
VOL. 7
FROM THE AUTHOR'S ORIGINAL STORY NOTES

PARTING OF WAYS BLACK CAT MIKO

DATE OF BIRTH unknown

Many years ago she fell in love with a human who saved her life, and lived many years in unrequited love. When she died, she turned into a demon cat. Her wish to become a person came true after becoming a demon, and she can change between human and cat form.
Now she mistakenly chases after Kakeru, the descendant of her original love.
She is jealous of all humans who are close to Kakeru. When she is in black cat form, she acts from her perch on Maju's shoulder.

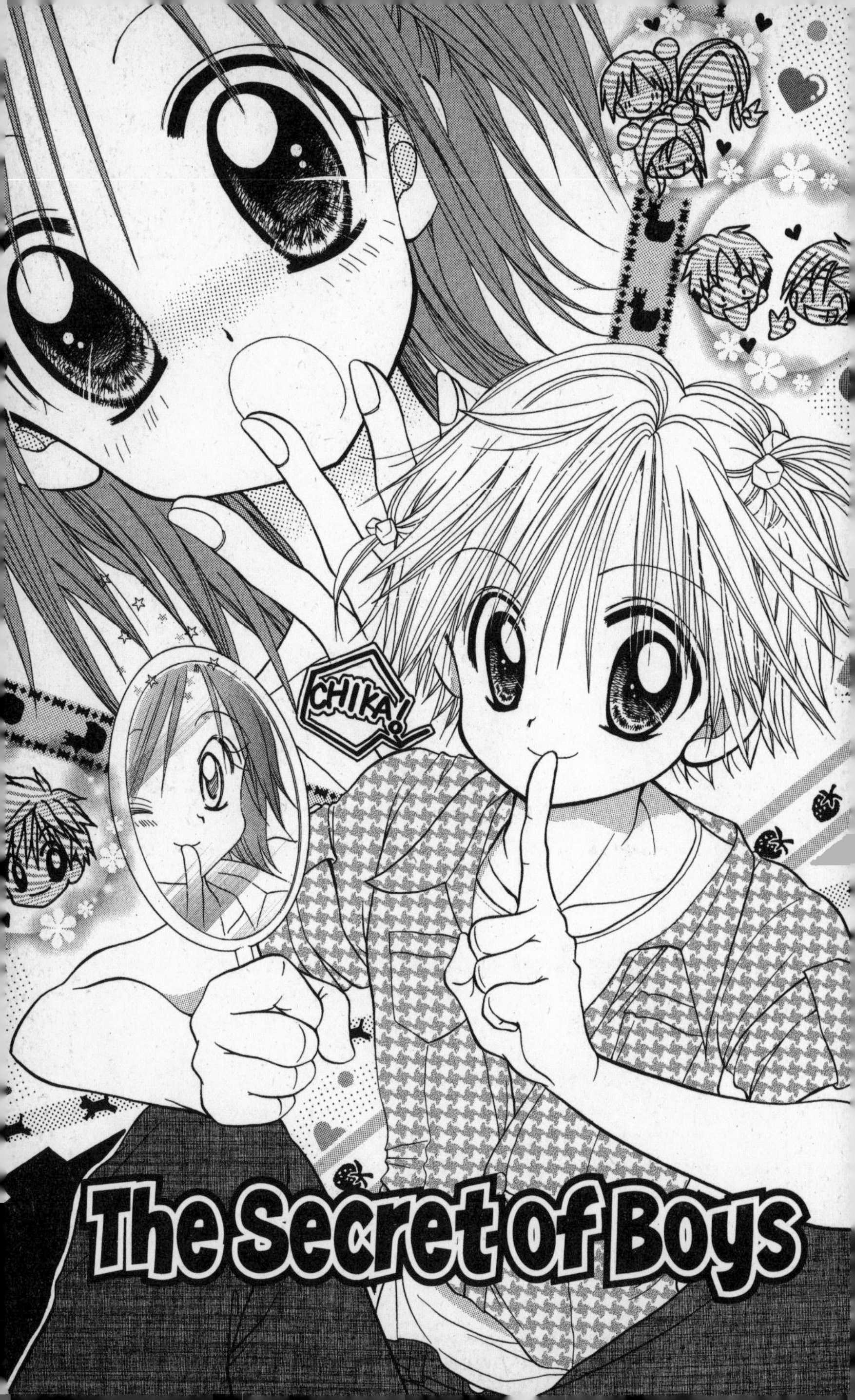
CHIKA!
The Secret of Boys

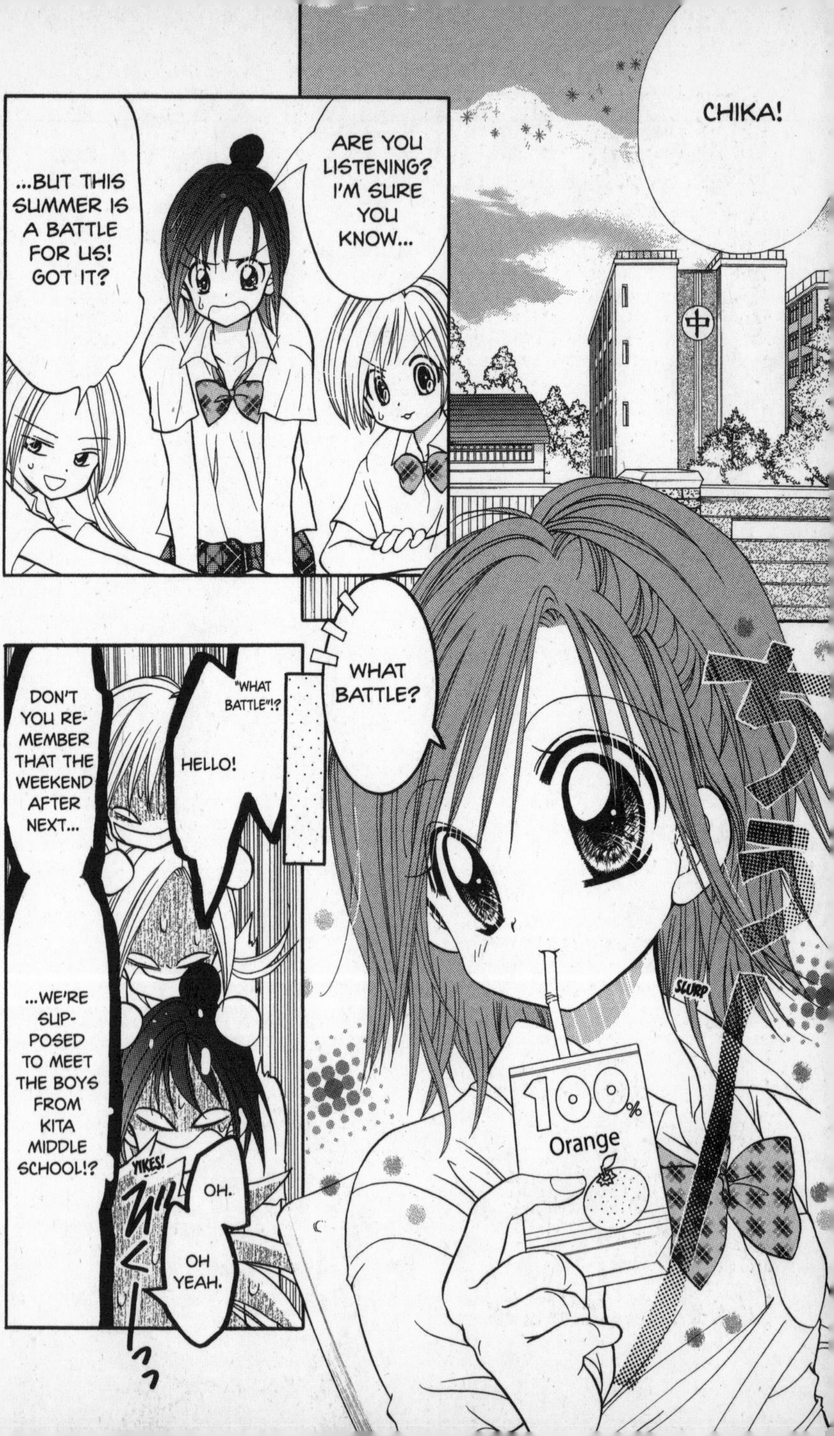
CHIKA!
WHAT BATTLE?
SLURP
100% Orange
ARE YOU LISTENING? I'M SURE YOU KNOW...
...BUT THIS SUMMER IS A BATTLE FOR US! GOT IT?
"WHAT BATTLE"!?
HELLO!
DON'T YOU RE-MEMBER THAT THE WEEKEND AFTER NEXT...
...WE'RE SUP-POSED TO MEET THE BOYS FROM KITA MIDDLE SCHOOL!?
YIKES!
OH.
OH YEAH.

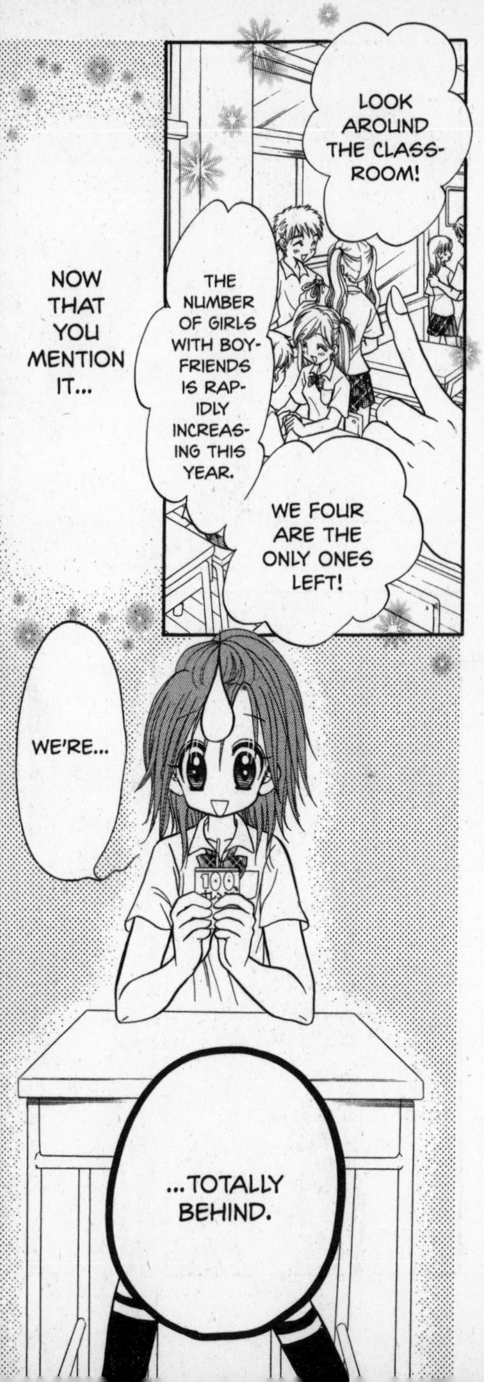
LOOK AROUND THE CLASS-ROOM!
THE NUMBER OF GIRLS WITH BOY-FRIENDS IS RAP-IDLY INCREAS-ING THIS YEAR.
WE FOUR ARE THE ONLY ONES LEFT!
NOW THAT YOU MENTION IT...
WE'RE...
...TOTALLY BEHIND.
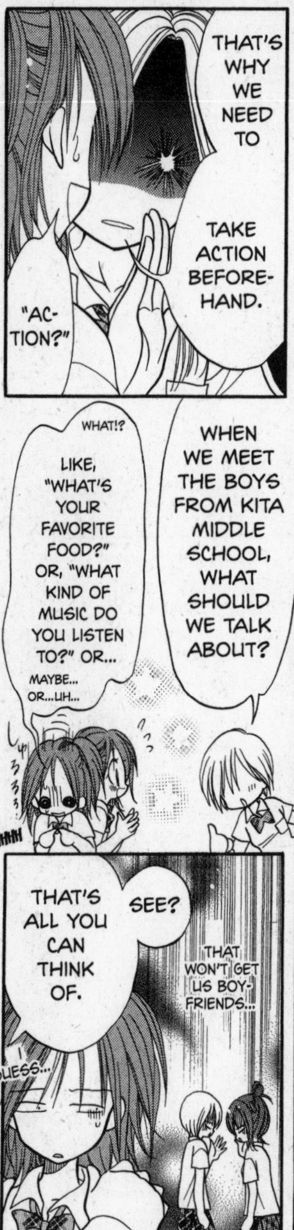
THAT'S WHY WE NEED TO
TAKE ACTION BEFORE-HAND.
"AC-TION?"
WHEN WE MEET THE BOYS FROM KITA MIDDLE SCHOOL, WHAT SHOULD WE TALK ABOUT?
WHAT!?
LIKE, "WHAT'S YOUR FAVORITE FOOD?" OR, "WHAT KIND OF MUSIC DO YOU LISTEN TO?" OR...
MAYBE... OR...UH...
PSHHHH
SEE?
THAT'S ALL YOU CAN THINK OF.
THAT WON'T GET US BOY-FRIENDS...
I GUESS...

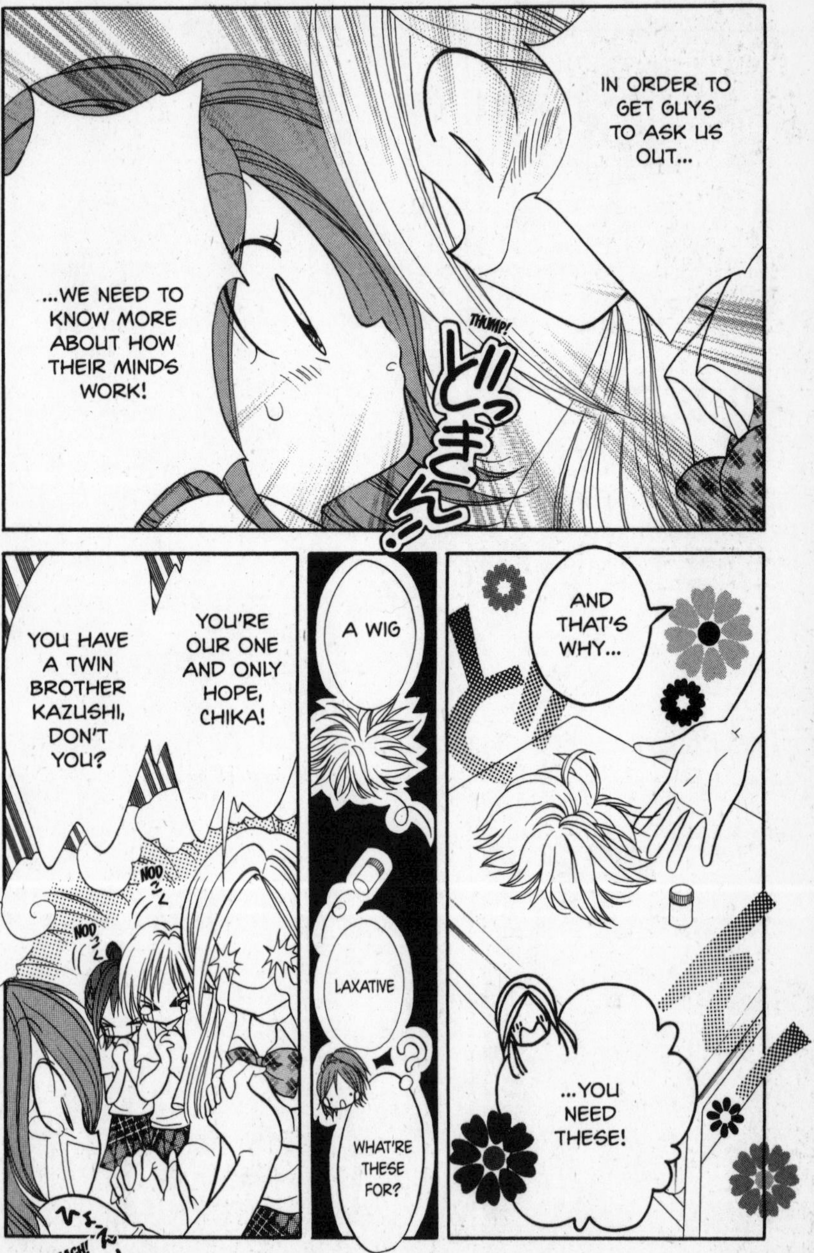
IN ORDER TO GET GUYS TO ASK US OUT...
...WE NEED TO KNOW MORE ABOUT HOW THEIR MINDS WORK!
THUMP!
AND THAT'S WHY...
...YOU NEED THESE!
A WIG
LAXATIVE
WHAT'RE THESE FOR?
YOU'RE OUR ONE AND ONLY HOPE, CHIKA!
YOU HAVE A TWIN BROTHER KAZUSHI, DON'T YOU?
NOD
NOD
AAAGH!

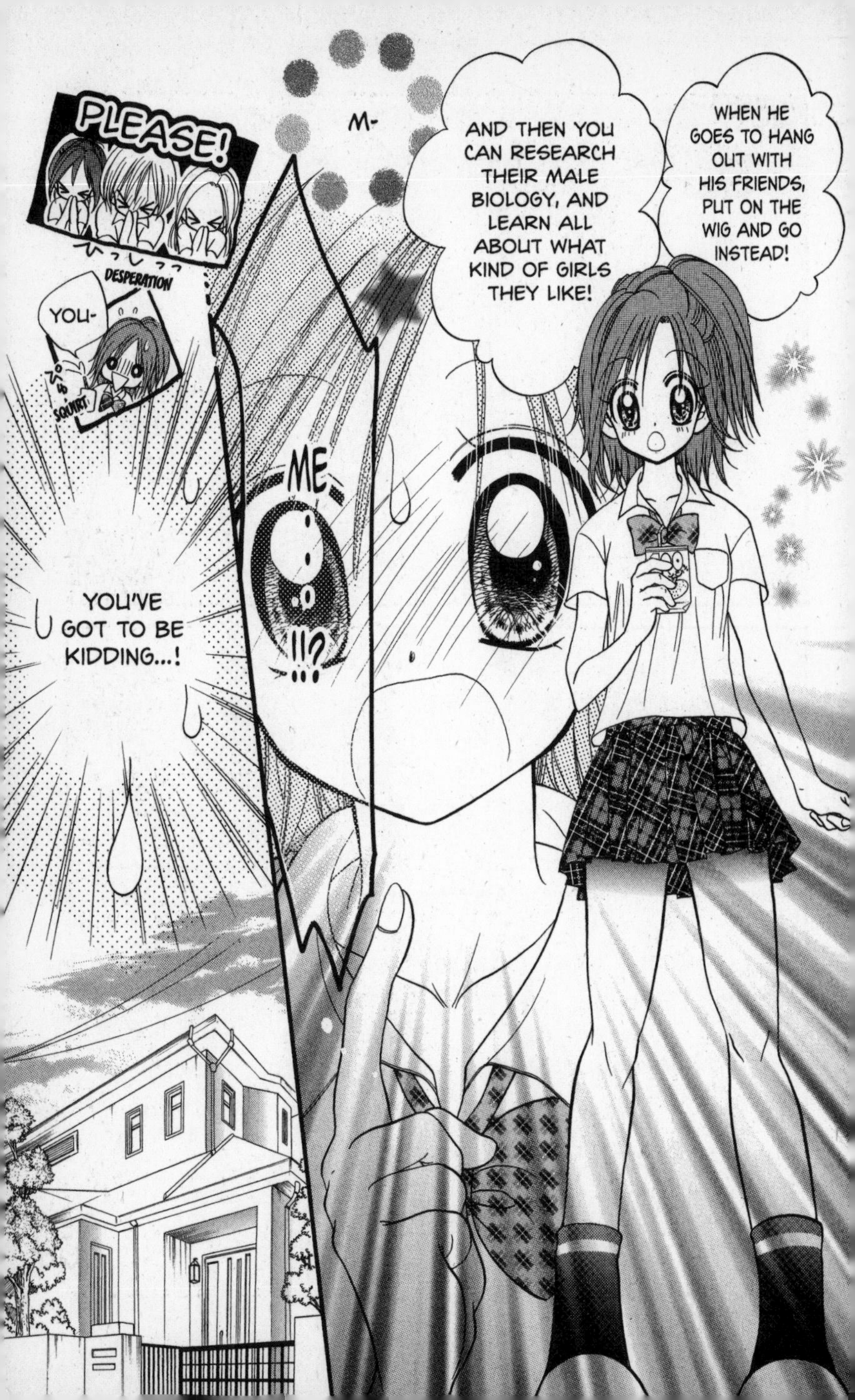
WHEN HE GOES TO HANG OUT WITH HIS FRIENDS, PUT ON THE WIG AND GO INSTEAD!
AND THEN YOU CAN RESEARCH THEIR MALE BIOLOGY, AND LEARN ALL ABOUT WHAT KIND OF GIRLS THEY LIKE!
M-
ME-
!!?
PLEASE!
DESPERATION
YOU-
SQUIRT
YOU'VE GOT TO BE KIDDING...!

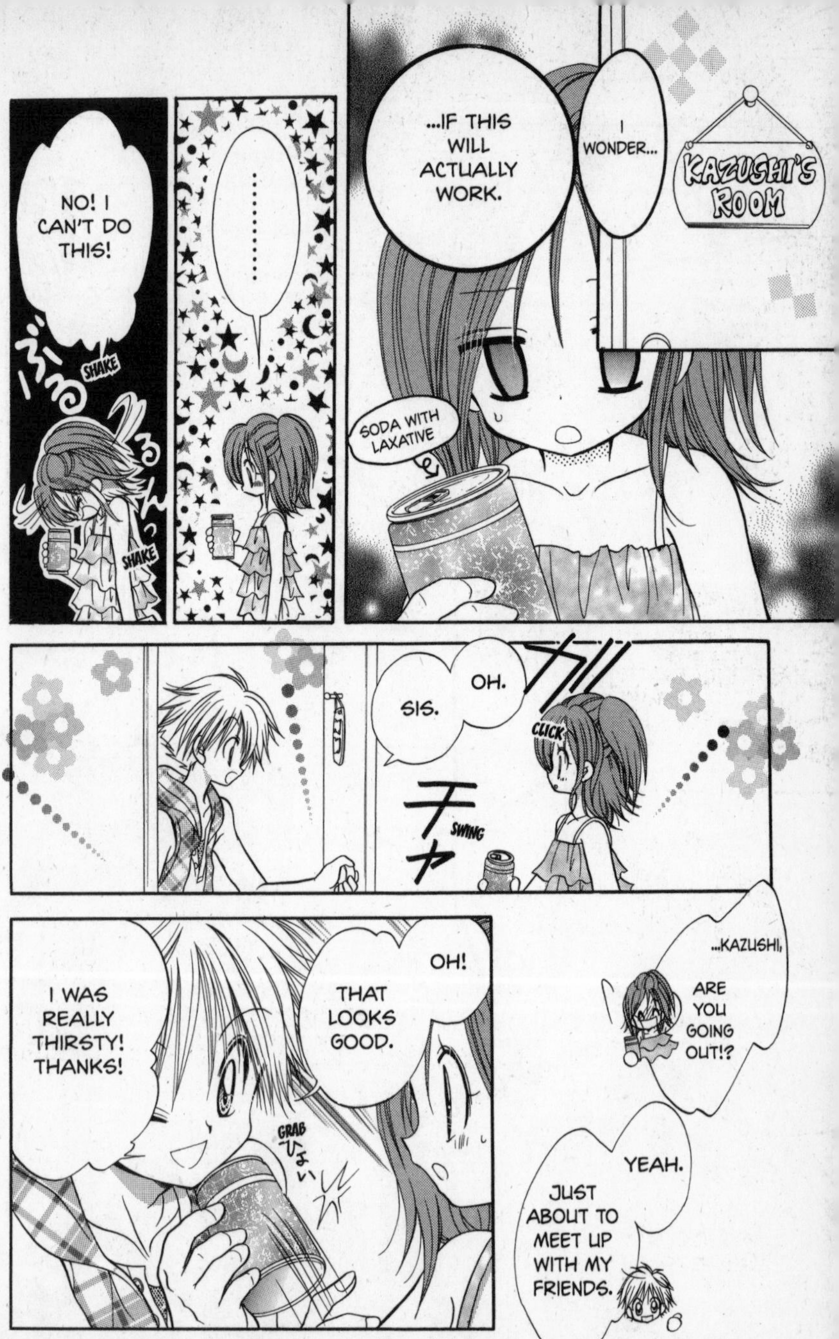
KAZUSHI'S ROOM
I WONDER...
...IF THIS WILL ACTUALLY WORK.
SODA WITH LAXATIVE
......
NO! I CAN'T DO THIS!
SHAKE
SHAKE
CLICK
OH. SIS.
SWING
...KAZUSHI, ARE YOU GOING OUT!?
YEAH. JUST ABOUT TO MEET UP WITH MY FRIENDS.
OH! THAT LOOKS GOOD.
I WAS REALLY THIRSTY! THANKS!
GRAB

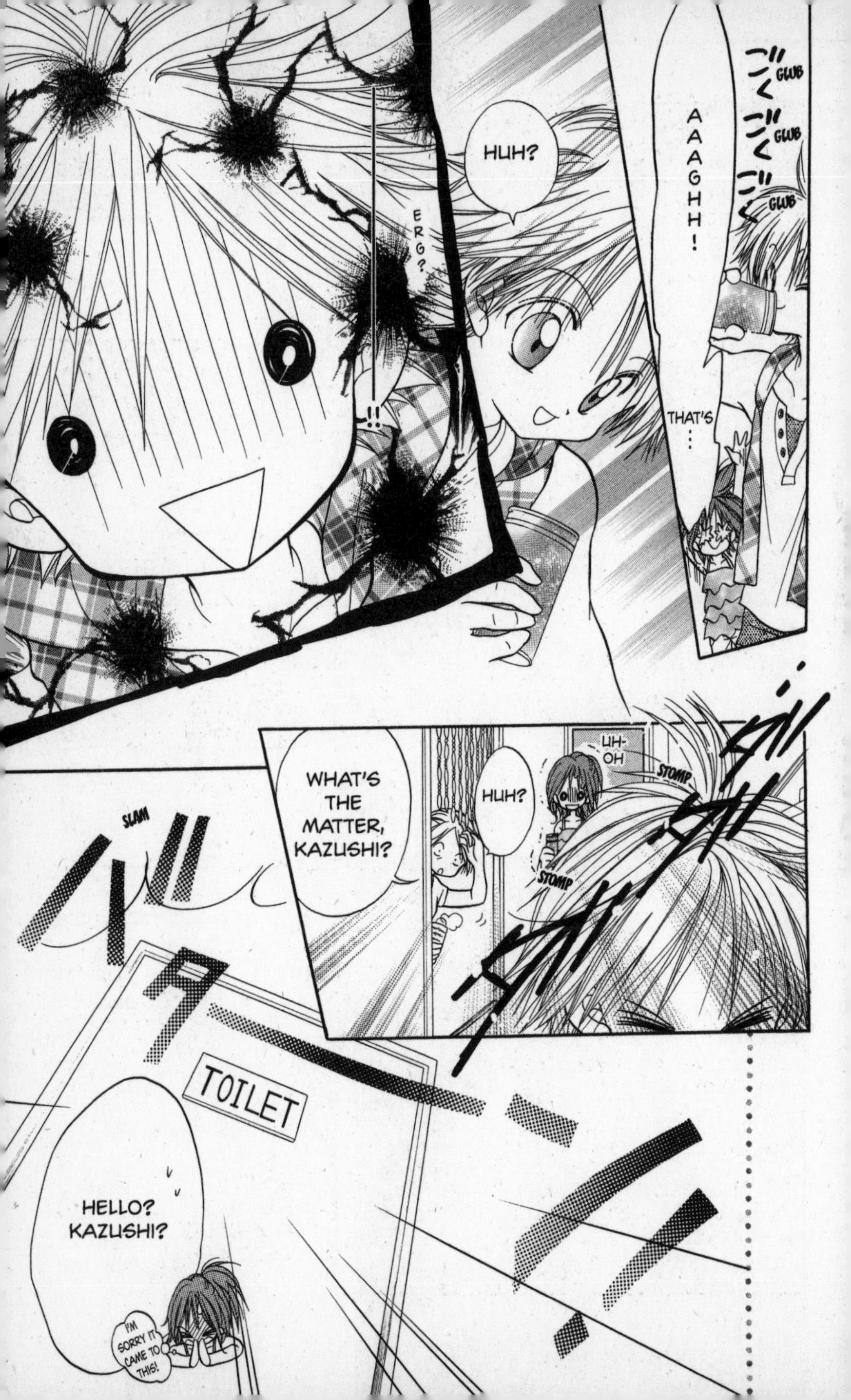
GLUB
GLUB
GLUB
AAAAGH!
THAT'S...
HUH?
ERG?
!!
UH-OH
STOMP
STOMP
HUH?
WHAT'S THE MATTER, KAZUSHI?
SLAM
TOILET
HELLO? KAZUSHI?
I'M SORRY IT CAME TO THIS!

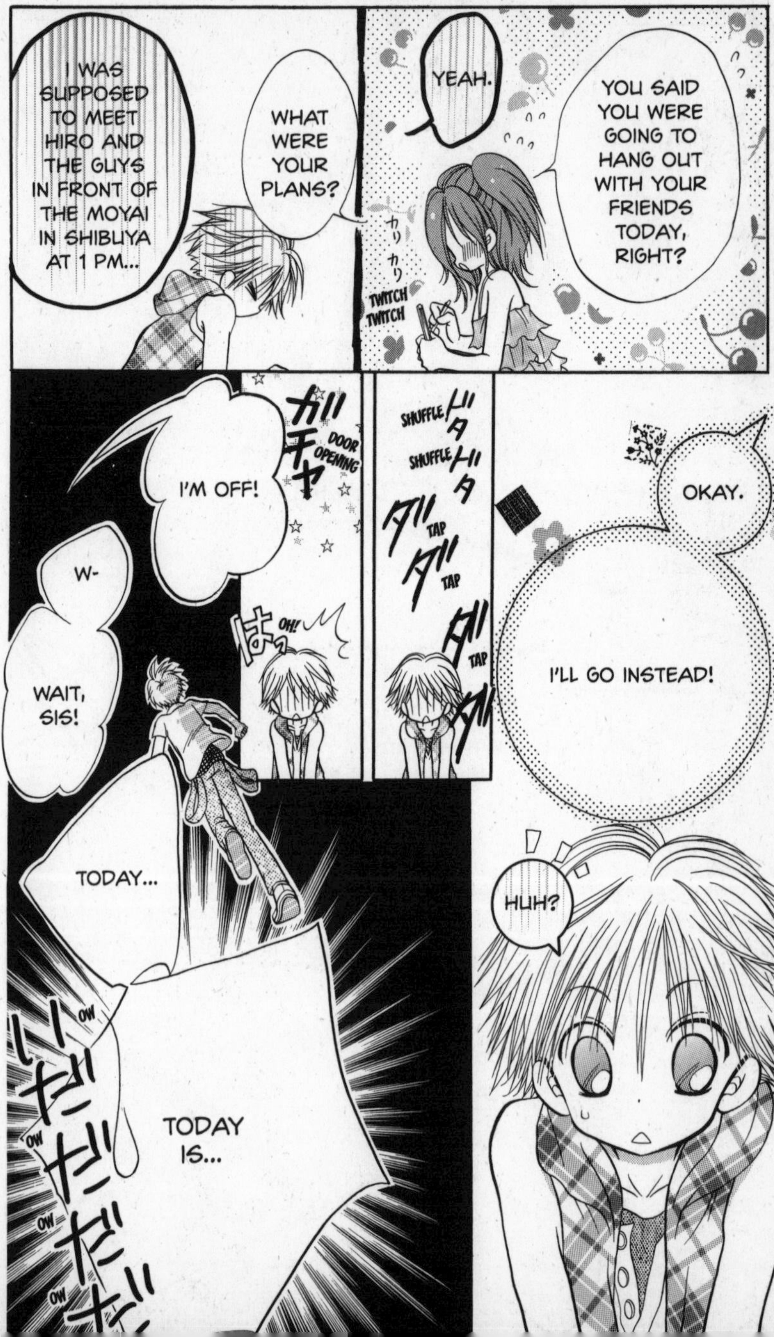

YOU SAID YOU WERE GOING TO HANG OUT WITH YOUR FRIENDS TODAY, RIGHT?
YEAH.
カリ カリ
TWITCH TWITCH
WHAT WERE YOUR PLANS?
I WAS SUPPOSED TO MEET HIRO AND THE GUYS IN FRONT OF THE MOYAI IN SHIBUYA AT 1 PM...
OKAY.
I'LL GO INSTEAD!
HUH?
ダダ
SHUFFLE SHUFFLE
ダダダ
TAP TAP TAP
はっ
OH!
ガチャ
DOOR OPENING
I'M OFF!
W-
WAIT, SIS!
TODAY...
TODAY IS...
OW OW OW OW

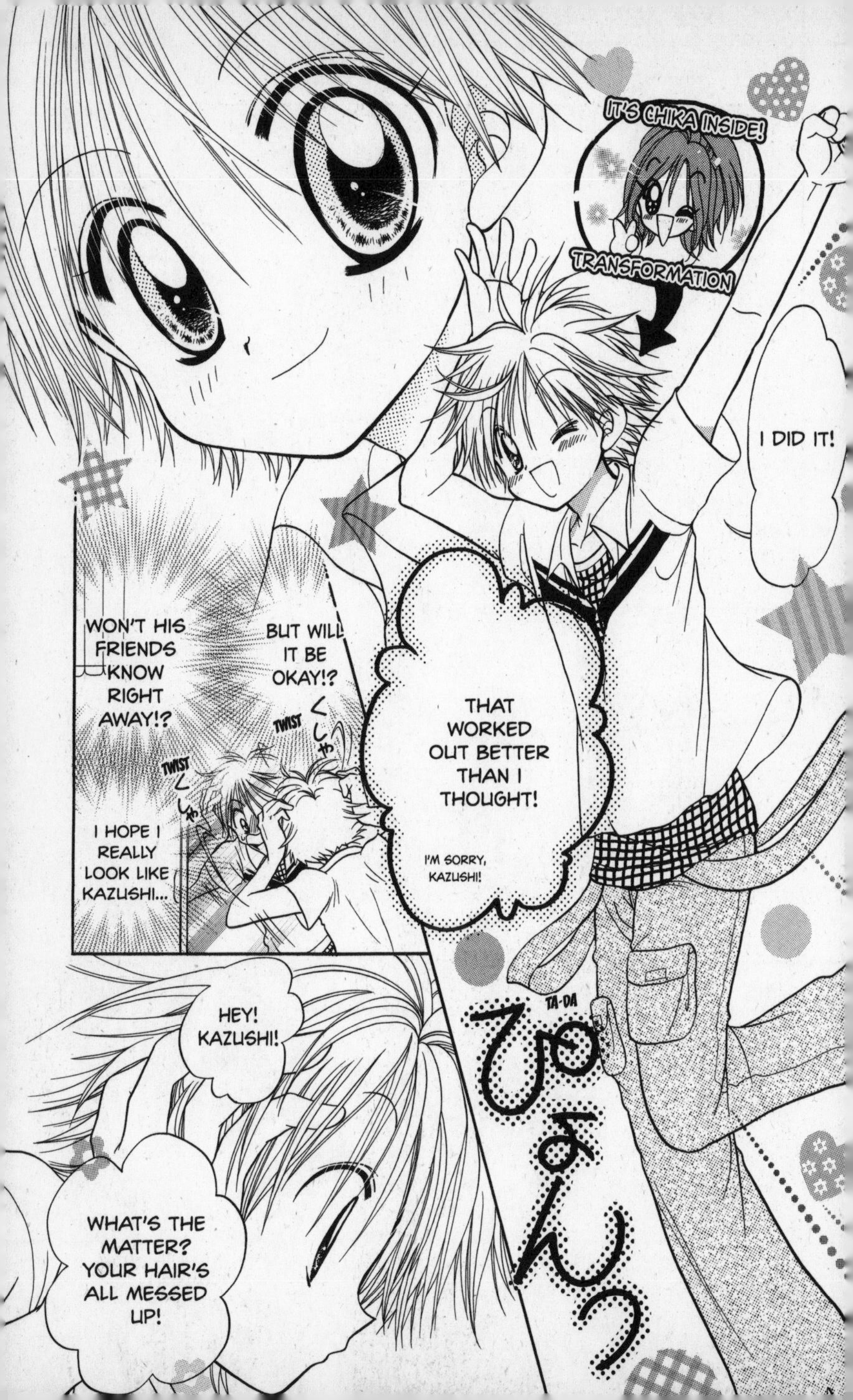
IT'S CHIKA INSIDE!
TRANSFORMATION
I DID IT!
THAT WORKED OUT BETTER THAN I THOUGHT!
I'M SORRY, KAZUSHI!
TA-DA
BUT WILL IT BE OKAY!?
WON'T HIS FRIENDS KNOW RIGHT AWAY!?
TWIST
TWIST
I HOPE I REALLY LOOK LIKE KAZUSHI...
HEY! KAZUSHI!
WHAT'S THE MATTER? YOUR HAIR'S ALL MESSED UP!

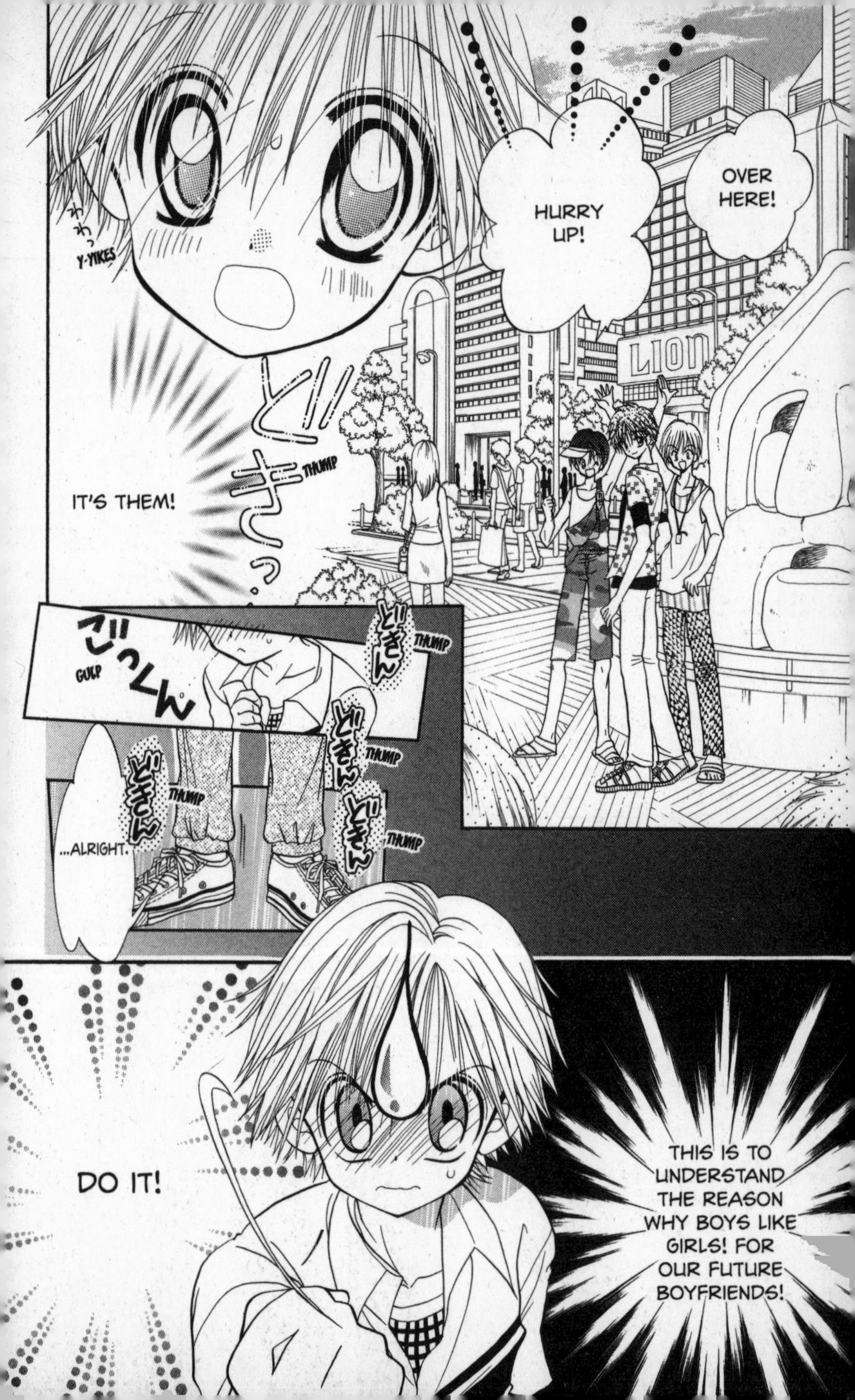
OVER HERE!
HURRY UP!
わわっ
Y-YIKES
どきっ
THUMP
IT'S THEM!
ごっくん
GULP
どきん
THUMP
どきん
THUMP
どきん
THUMP
どきん
THUMP
...ALRIGHT.
THIS IS TO UNDERSTAND THE REASON WHY BOYS LIKE GIRLS! FOR OUR FUTURE BOYFRIENDS!
DO IT!

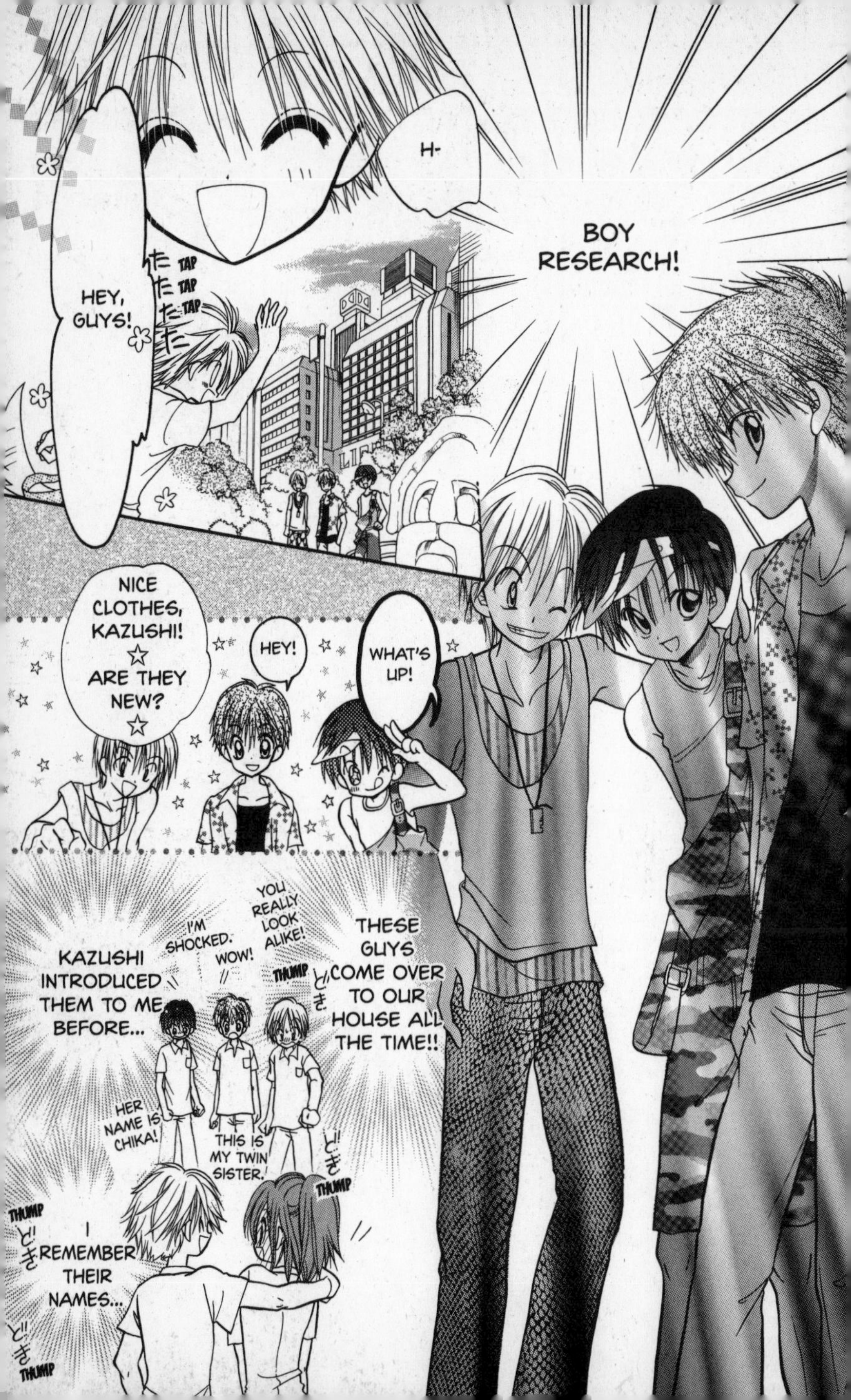

H-
BOY RESEARCH!
たたたた TAP TAP TAP
HEY, GUYS!
WHAT'S UP!
HEY!
NICE CLOTHES, KAZUSHI! ☆ ARE THEY NEW? ☆
THESE GUYS COME OVER TO OUR HOUSE ALL THE TIME!!
どき THUMP
YOU REALLY LOOK ALIKE!
WOW!
I'M SHOCKED.
KAZUSHI INTRODUCED THEM TO ME BEFORE...
どき!! THUMP
THIS IS MY TWIN SISTER.
HER NAME IS CHIKA!
THUMP どき
I REMEMBER THEIR NAMES...
どき!! THUMP

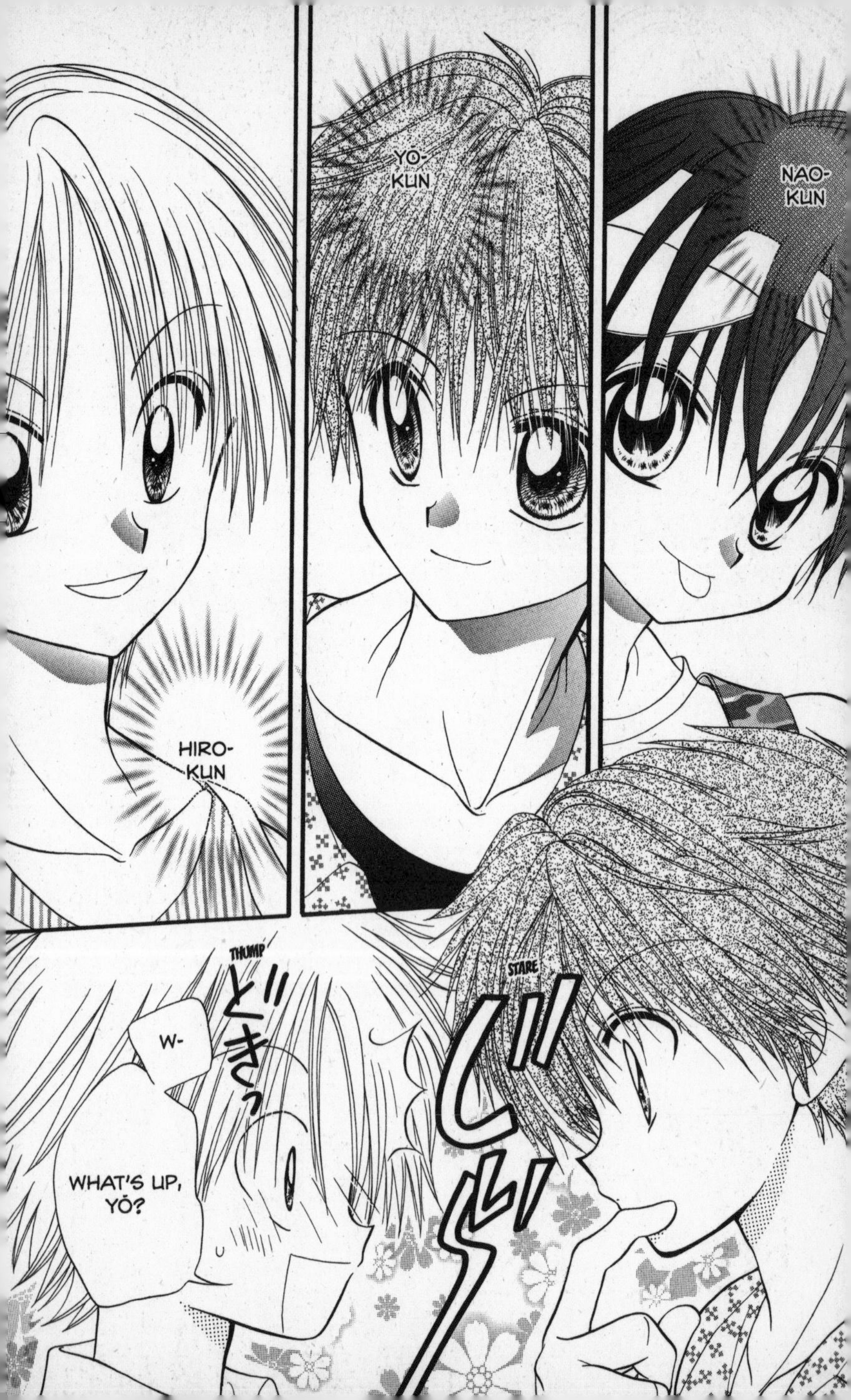
NAO-KUN
YŌ-KUN
HIRO-KUN
STARE
じーっ
THUMP
どきっ
W-
WHAT'S UP, YŌ?

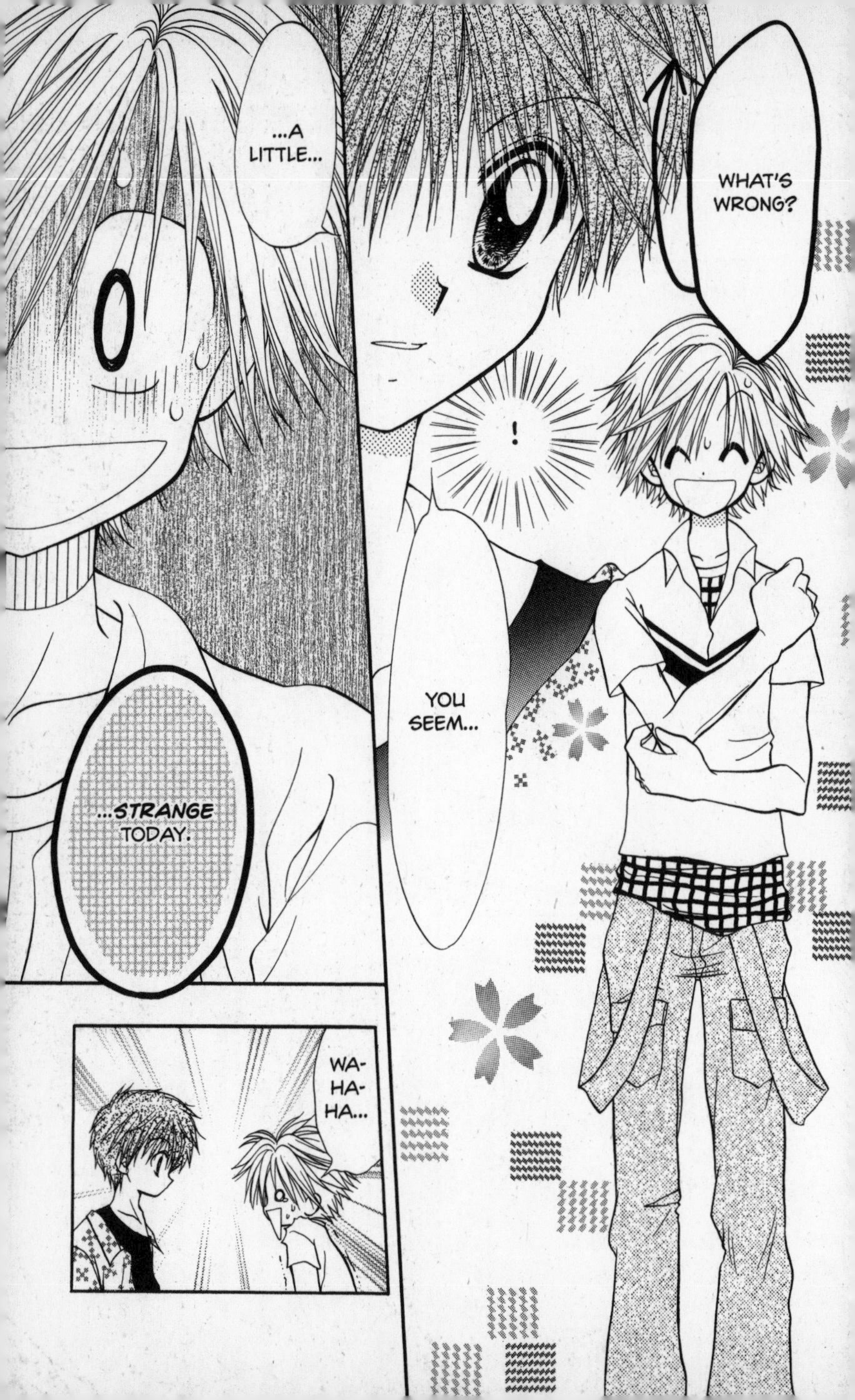
WHAT'S WRONG?
!
YOU SEEM...
...A LITTLE...
...STRANGE TODAY.
WA-HA-HA...

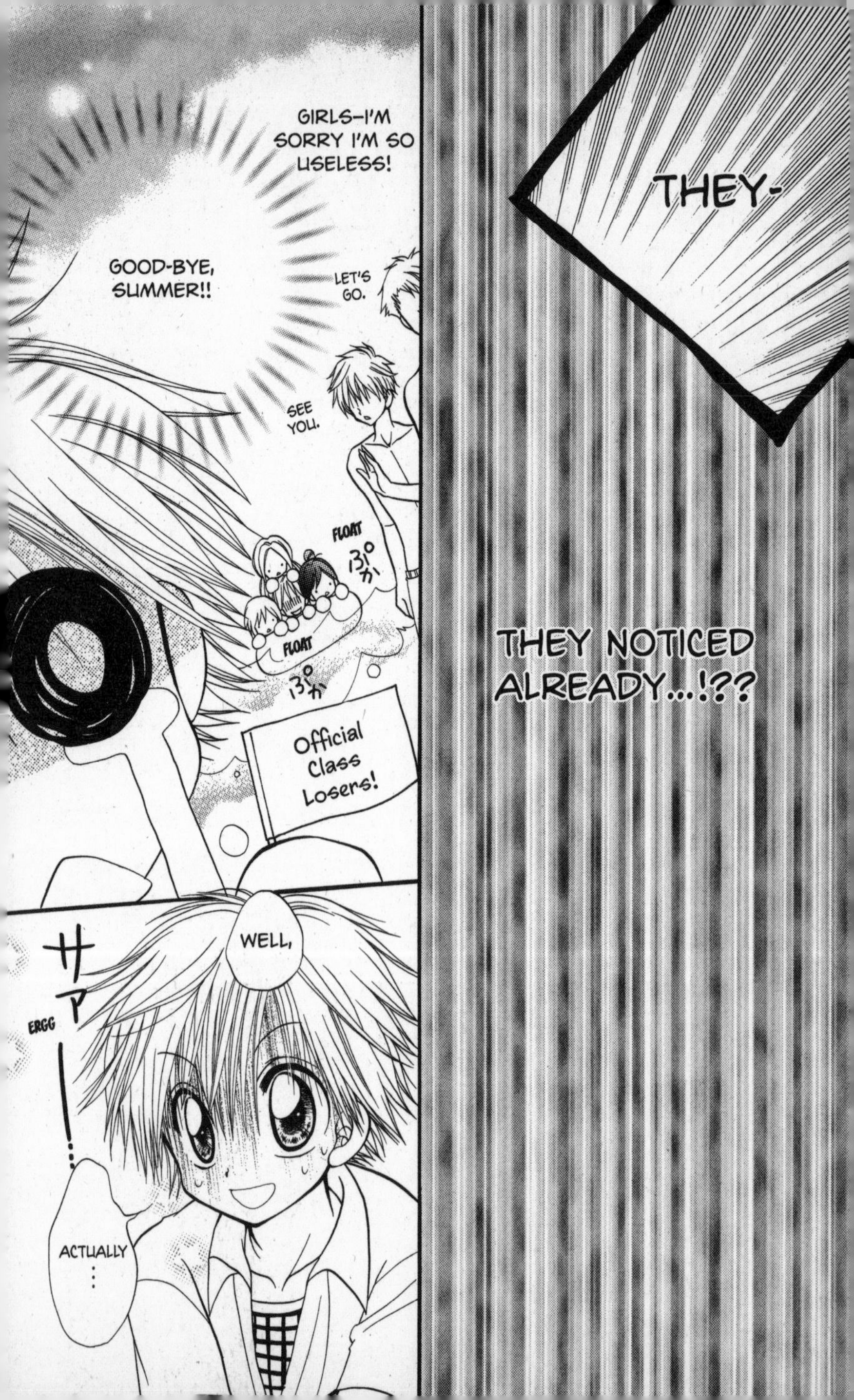
THEY-
THEY NOTICED ALREADY...!??
GIRLS—I'M SORRY I'M SO USELESS!
LET'S GO.
GOOD-BYE, SUMMER!!
SEE YOU.
FLOAT
FLOAT
Official Class Losers!
WELL,
ERGG
ACTUALLY
...

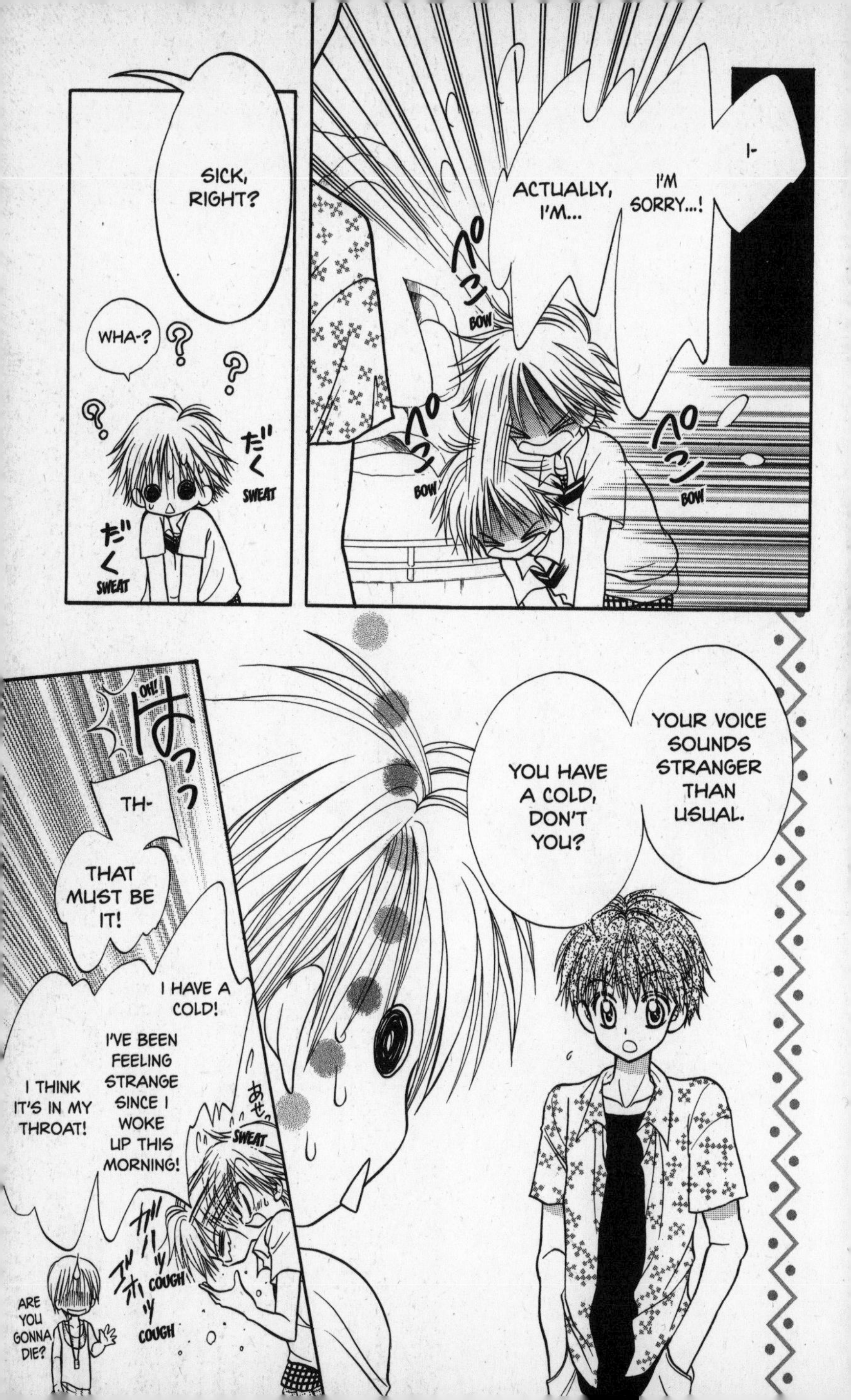

I-
I'M SORRY...!
ACTUALLY, I'M...
BOW
BOW
BOW
SICK, RIGHT?
WHA-?
SWEAT
SWEAT
YOUR VOICE SOUNDS STRANGER THAN USUAL.
YOU HAVE A COLD, DON'T YOU?
OH!
TH-
THAT MUST BE IT!
I HAVE A COLD!
I'VE BEEN FEELING STRANGE SINCE I WOKE UP THIS MORNING!
I THINK IT'S IN MY THROAT!
SWEAT
COUGH
COUGH
ARE YOU GONNA DIE?

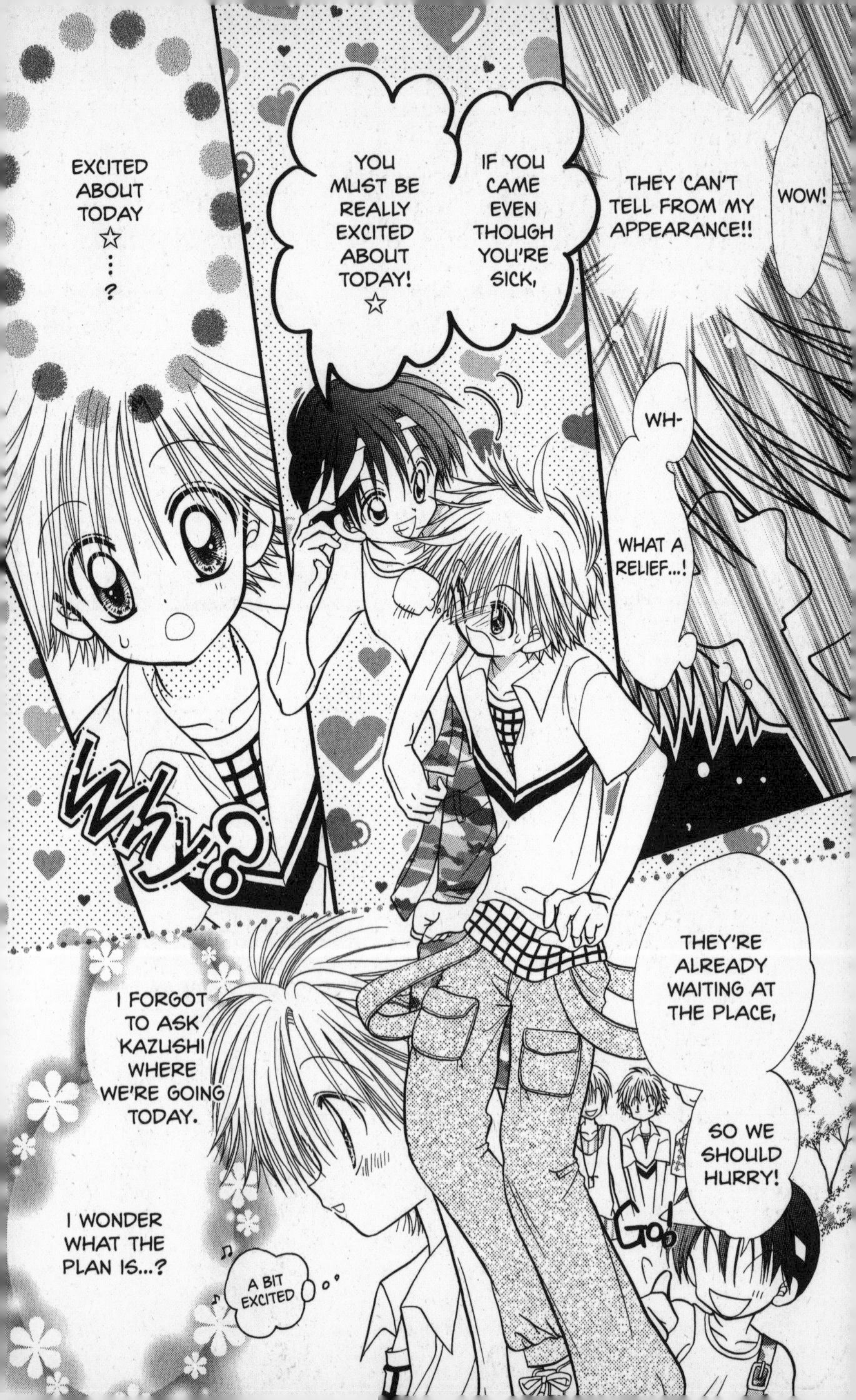
WOW!
THEY CAN'T TELL FROM MY APPEARANCE!!
WH-
WHAT A RELIEF...!
IF YOU CAME EVEN THOUGH YOU'RE SICK,
YOU MUST BE REALLY EXCITED ABOUT TODAY! ☆
EXCITED ABOUT TODAY ☆ ...?
Why?
THEY'RE ALREADY WAITING AT THE PLACE,
SO WE SHOULD HURRY!
Go!
I FORGOT TO ASK KAZUSHI WHERE WE'RE GOING TODAY.
I WONDER WHAT THE PLAN IS...?
A BIT EXCITED

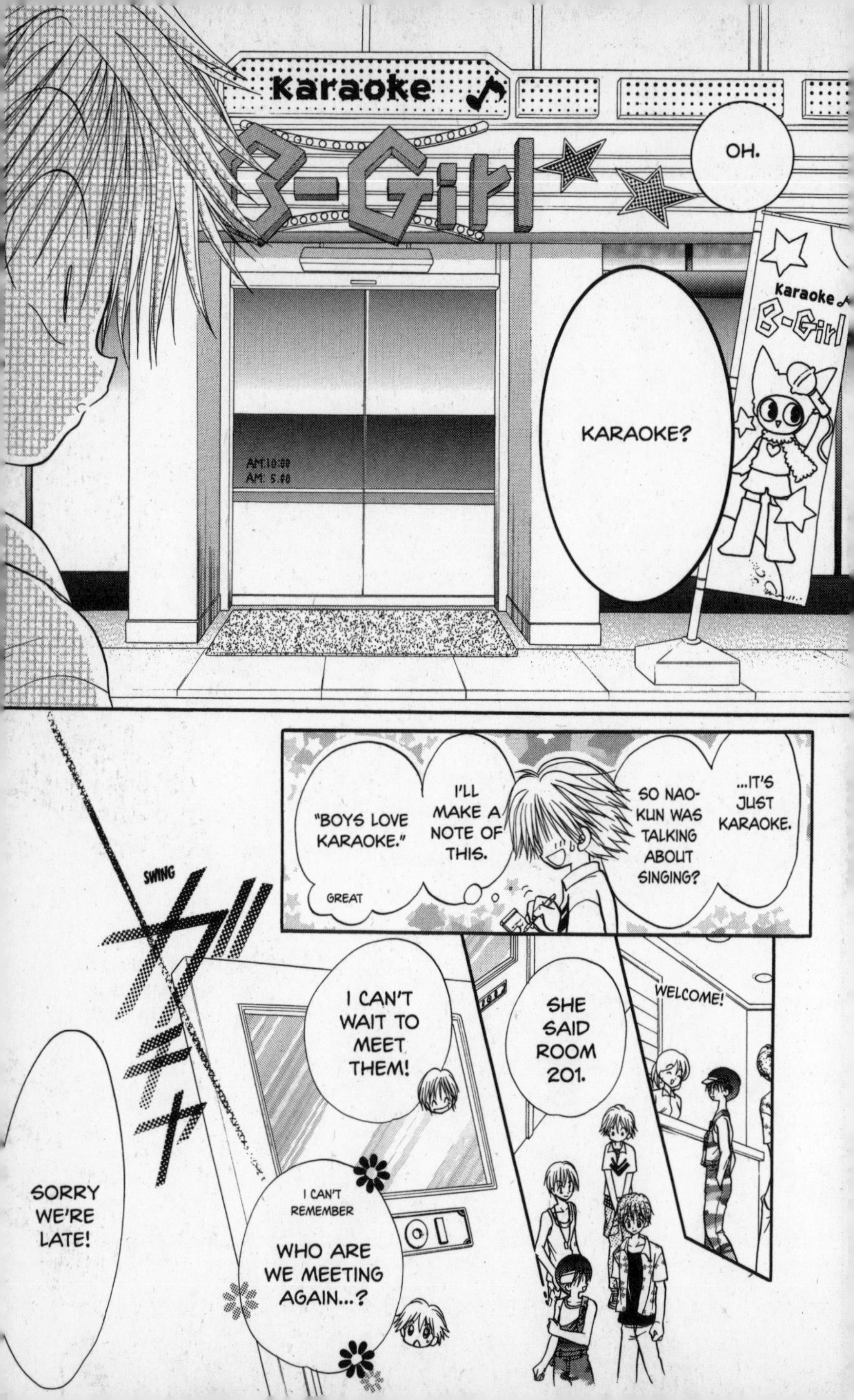
Karaoke
B-Girl
AM 10:00
AM 5:00
Karaoke
B-Girl
OH.
KARAOKE?
...IT'S JUST KARAOKE.
SO NAO-KUN WAS TALKING ABOUT SINGING?
I'LL MAKE A NOTE OF THIS.
"BOYS LOVE KARAOKE."
GREAT
WELCOME!
SHE SAID ROOM 201.
I CAN'T WAIT TO MEET THEM!
WHO ARE WE MEETING AGAIN...?
I CAN'T REMEMBER
SWING
SORRY WE'RE LATE!

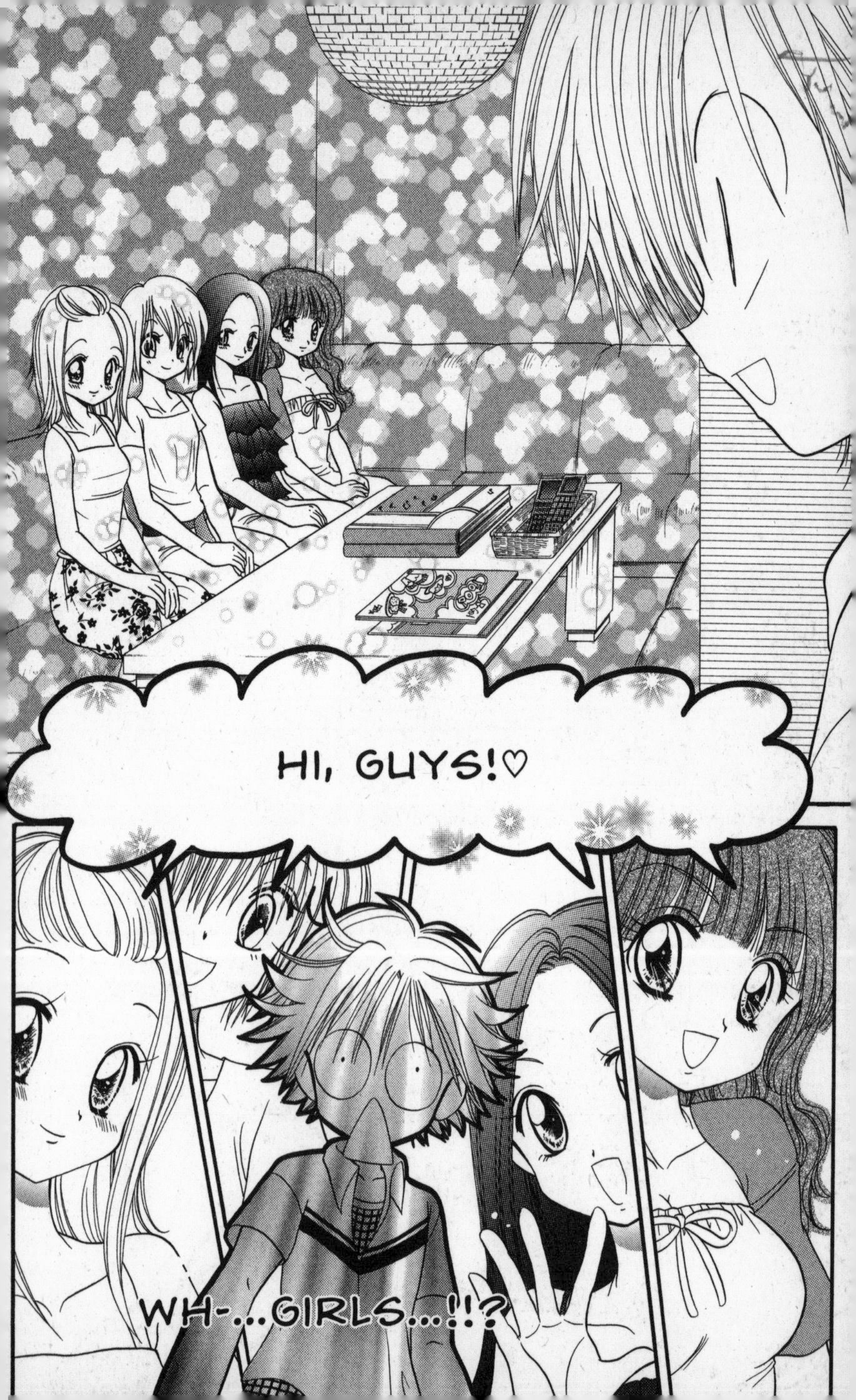
HI, GUYS!♡
WH-...GIRLS...!!?

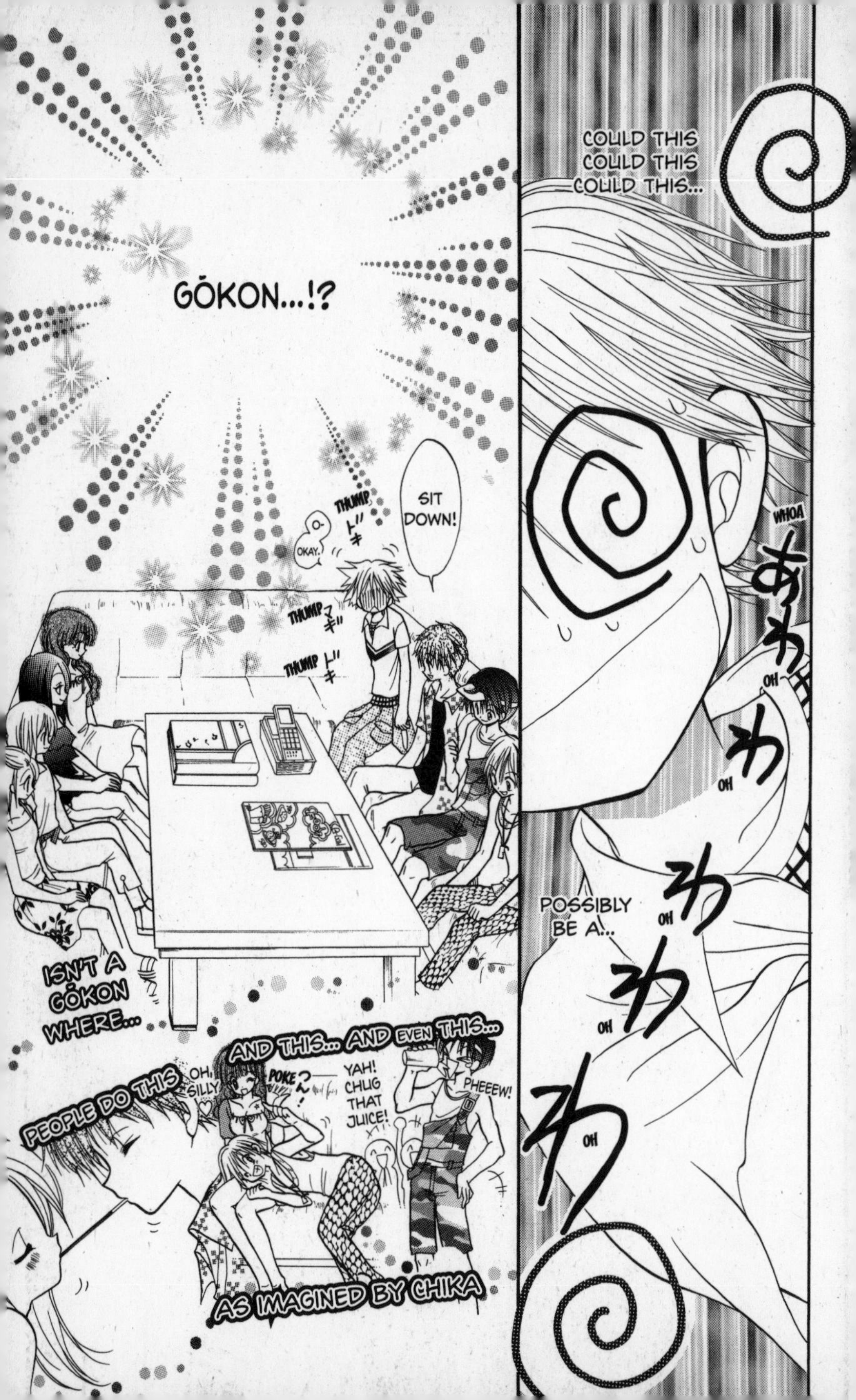
COULD THIS COULD THIS COULD THIS...
WHOA
OH
OH
OH
OH
OH
POSSIBLY BE A...
GŌKON...!?
SIT DOWN!
THUMP
O-OKAY.
THUMP
THUMP
ISN'T A GŌKON WHERE...
PEOPLE DO THIS
AND THIS... AND EVEN THIS...
PHEEEW!
YAH! CHUG THAT JUICE!
POKE
OH, SILLY ♡
AS IMAGINED BY CHIKA

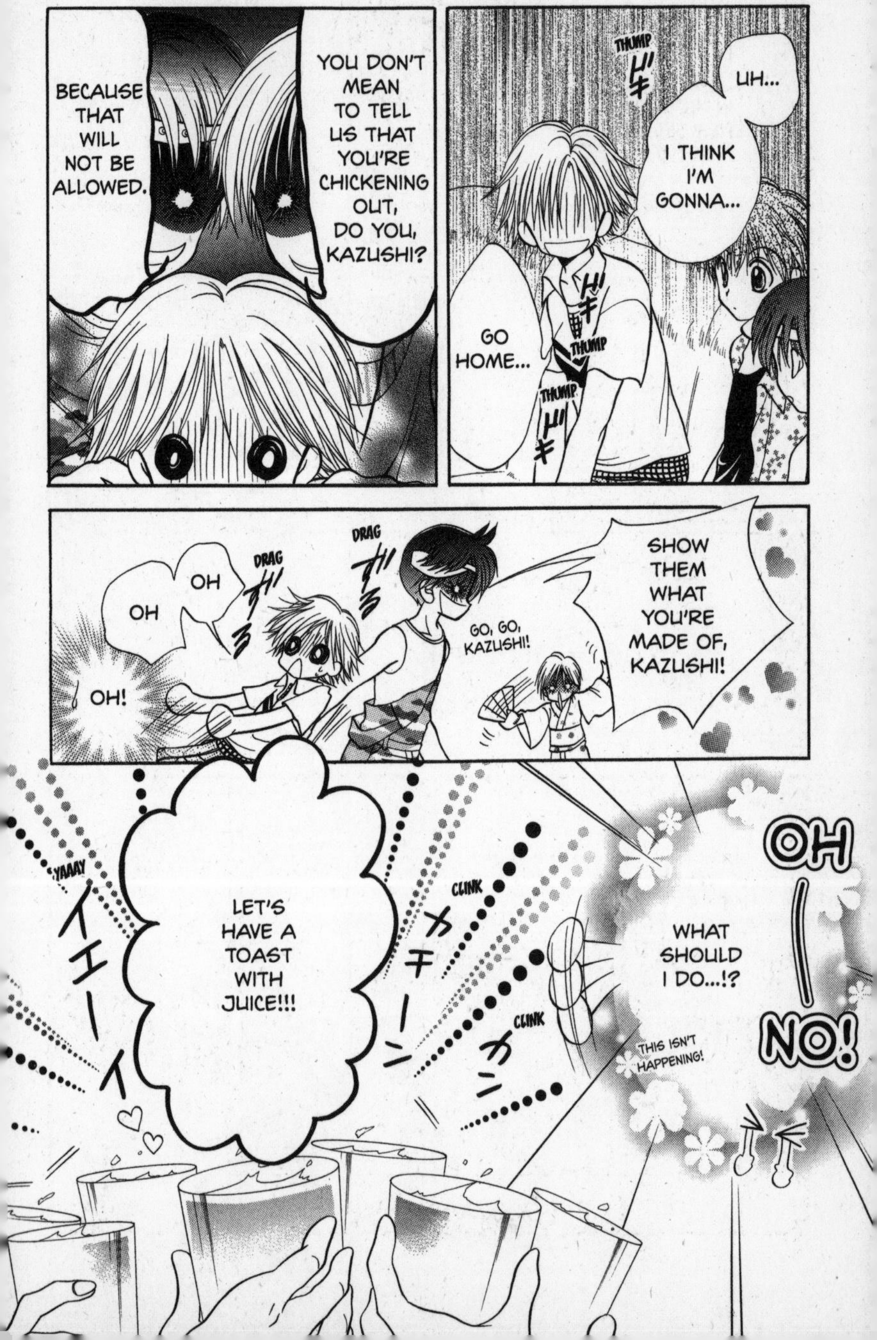
THUMP
UH...
I THINK I'M GONNA...
GO HOME...
THUMP
THUMP
YOU DON'T MEAN TO TELL US THAT YOU'RE CHICKENING OUT, DO YOU, KAZUSHI?
BECAUSE THAT WILL NOT BE ALLOWED.
SHOW THEM WHAT YOU'RE MADE OF, KAZUSHI!
GO, GO, KAZUSHI!
DRAG
DRAG
OH
OH
OH!
OH—NO!
WHAT SHOULD I DO...!?
THIS ISN'T HAPPENING!
CLINK
CLINK
LET'S HAVE A TOAST WITH JUICE!!!
YAAAY

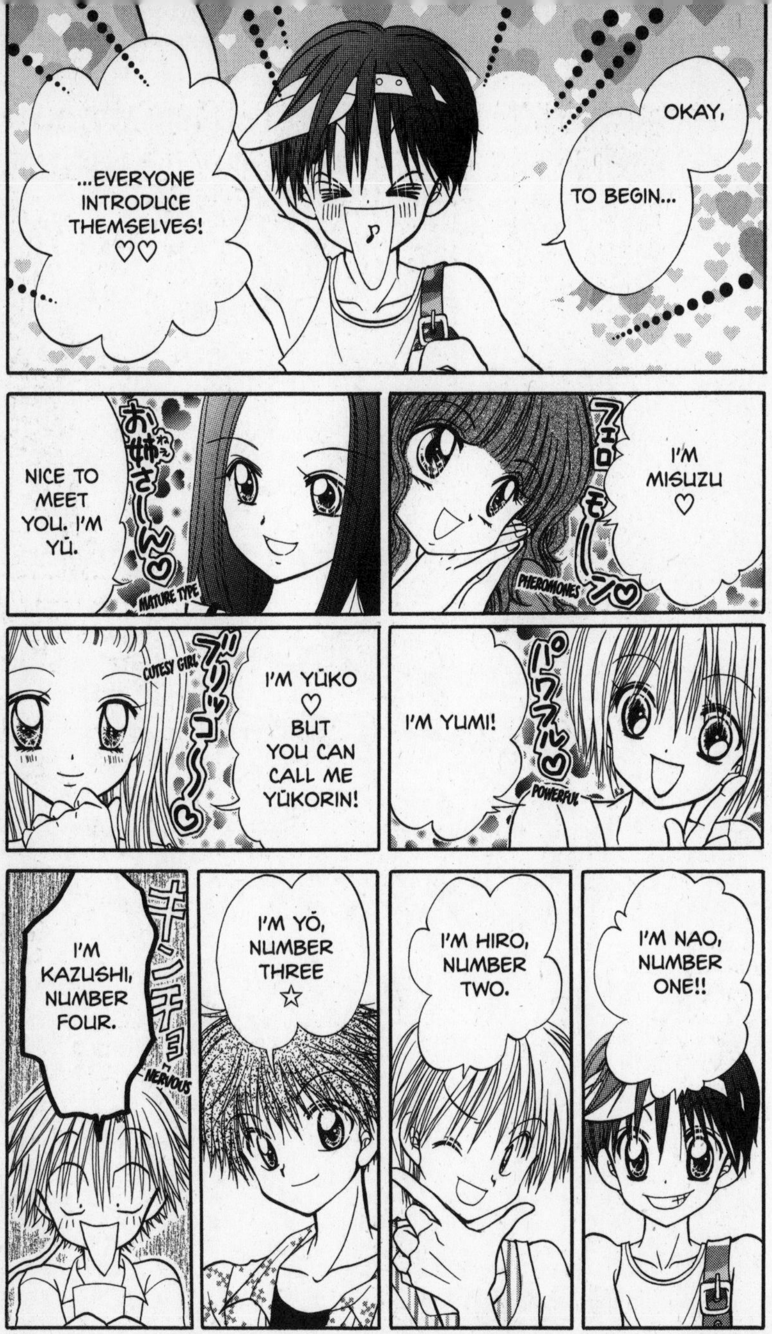
OKAY, TO BEGIN...
...EVERYONE INTRODUCE THEMSELVES! ♡♡
フェロモーン♡
PHEROMONES
I'M MISUZU ♡
お姉さーん♡
MATURE TYPE
NICE TO MEET YOU. I'M YŪ.
パワフル♡
POWERFUL
I'M YUMI!
ブリッコ～♡
CUTESY GIRL
I'M YŪKO ♡ BUT YOU CAN CALL ME YŪKORIN!
I'M NAO, NUMBER ONE!!
I'M HIRO, NUMBER TWO.
I'M YŌ, NUMBER THREE ☆
キンチョ
NERVOUS
I'M KAZUSHI, NUMBER FOUR.

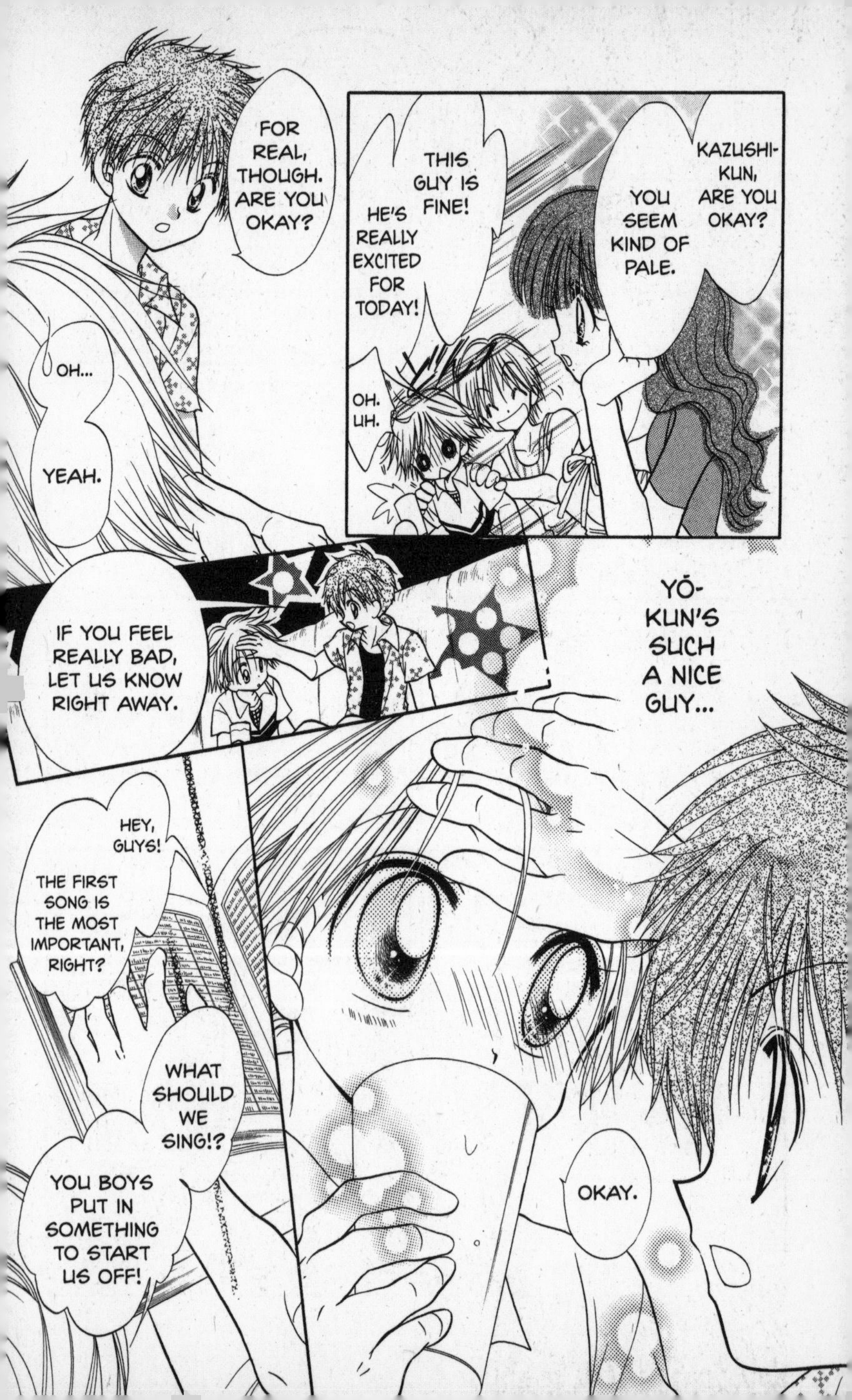
KAZUSHI-KUN, ARE YOU OKAY?
YOU SEEM KIND OF PALE.
THIS GUY IS FINE!
HE'S REALLY EXCITED FOR TODAY!
OH. UH.
FOR REAL, THOUGH. ARE YOU OKAY?
OH...
YEAH.
IF YOU FEEL REALLY BAD, LET US KNOW RIGHT AWAY.
YŌ-KUN'S SUCH A NICE GUY...
HEY, GUYS!
THE FIRST SONG IS THE MOST IMPORTANT, RIGHT?
WHAT SHOULD WE SING!?
OKAY.
YOU BOYS PUT IN SOMETHING TO START US OFF!

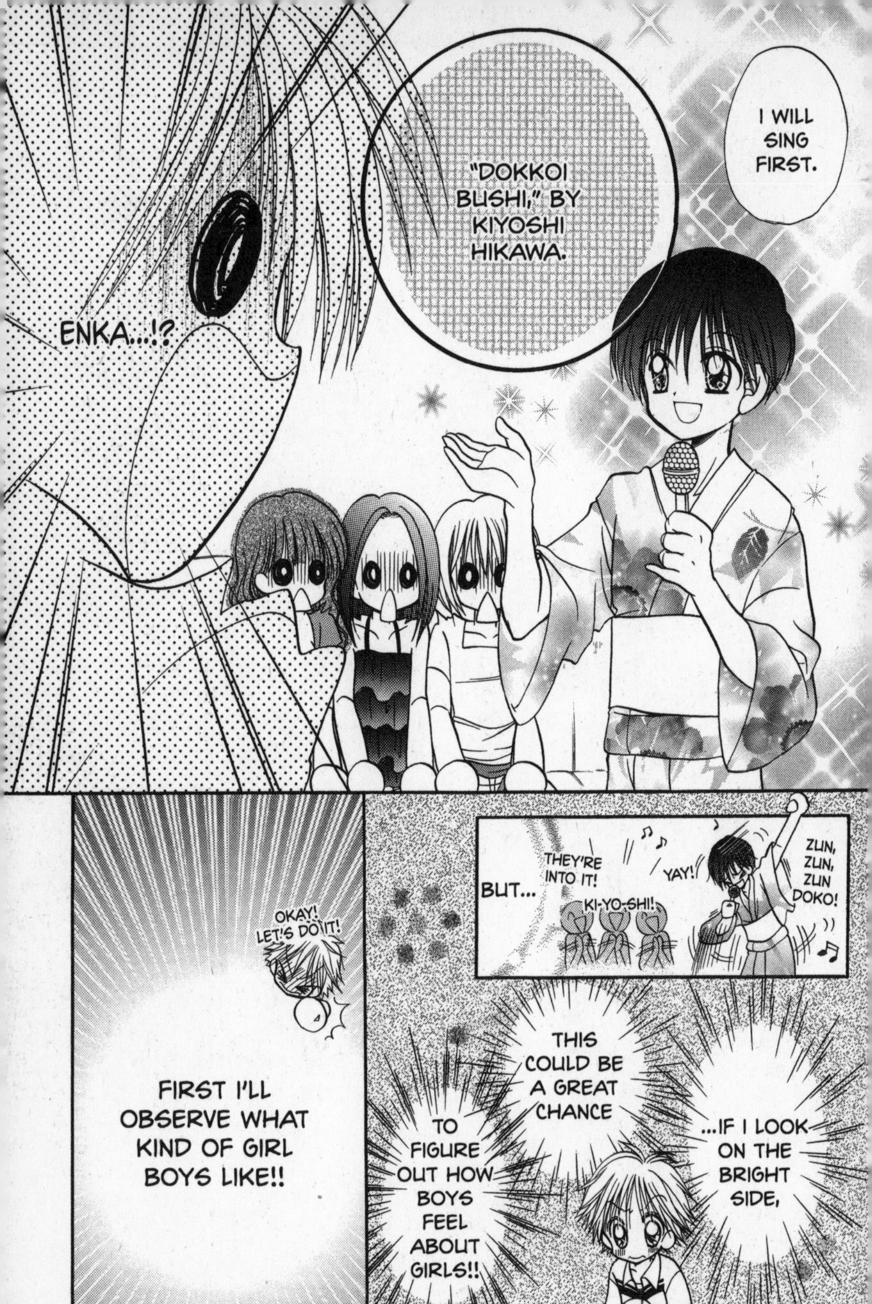
I WILL SING FIRST.
"DOKKOI BUSHI," BY KIYOSHI HIKAWA.
ENKA...!?
ZUN, ZUN, ZUN DOKO!
YAY!
KI-YO-SHI!
THEY'RE INTO IT!
BUT...
...IF I LOOK ON THE BRIGHT SIDE,
THIS COULD BE A GREAT CHANCE
TO FIGURE OUT HOW BOYS FEEL ABOUT GIRLS!!
OKAY! LET'S DO IT!
FIRST I'LL OBSERVE WHAT KIND OF GIRL BOYS LIKE!!

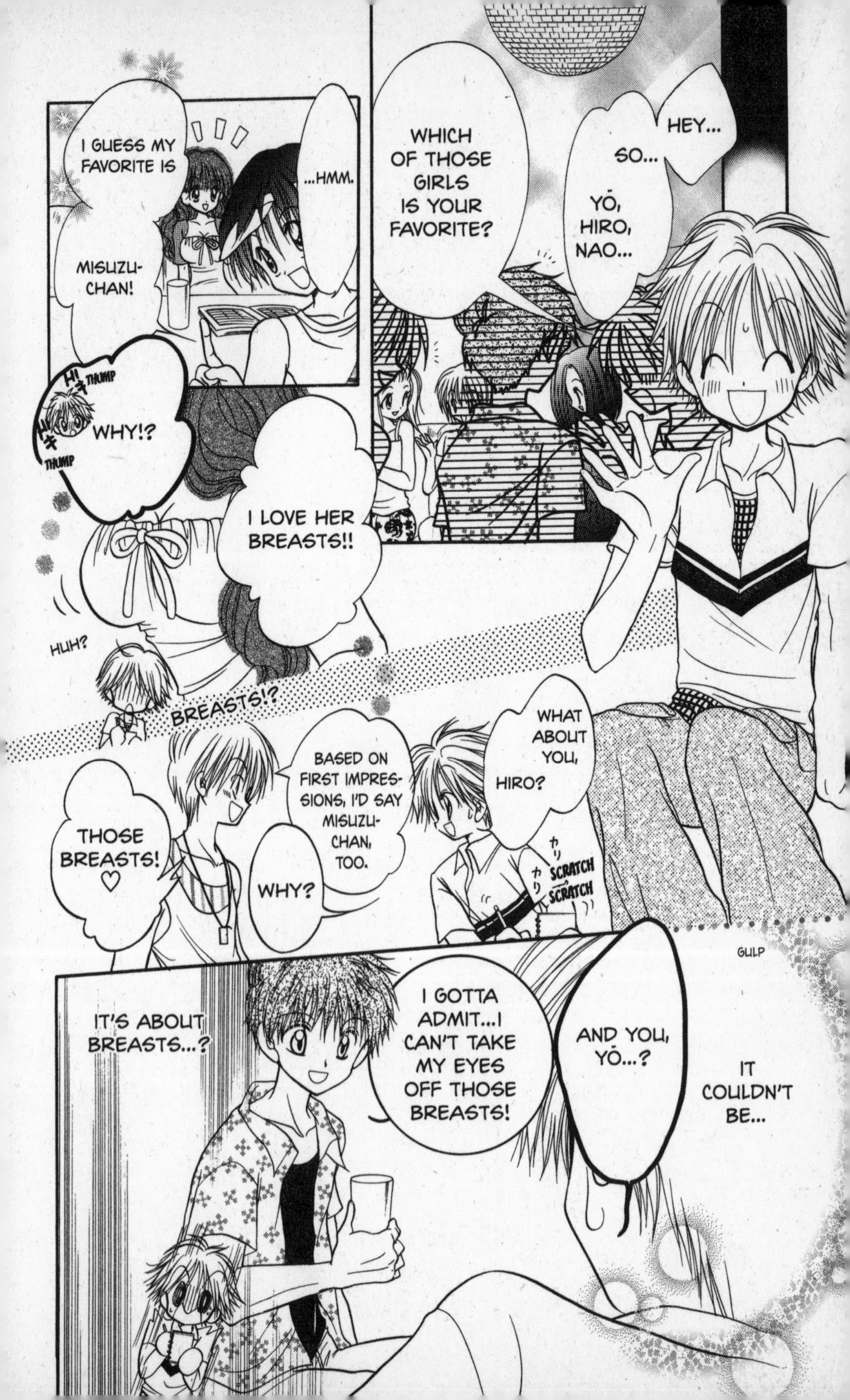

HEY...
SO...
YŌ, HIRO, NAO...
WHICH OF THOSE GIRLS IS YOUR FAVORITE?
...HMM.
I GUESS MY FAVORITE IS
MISUZU-CHAN!
THUMP
THUMP
WHY!?
I LOVE HER BREASTS!!
HUH?
BREASTS!?
WHAT ABOUT YOU,
HIRO?
SCRATCH
SCRATCH
BASED ON FIRST IMPRESSIONS, I'D SAY MISUZU-CHAN, TOO.
WHY?
THOSE BREASTS! ♡
GULP
IT COULDN'T BE...
AND YOU, YŌ...?
I GOTTA ADMIT...I CAN'T TAKE MY EYES OFF THOSE BREASTS!
IT'S ABOUT BREASTS...?

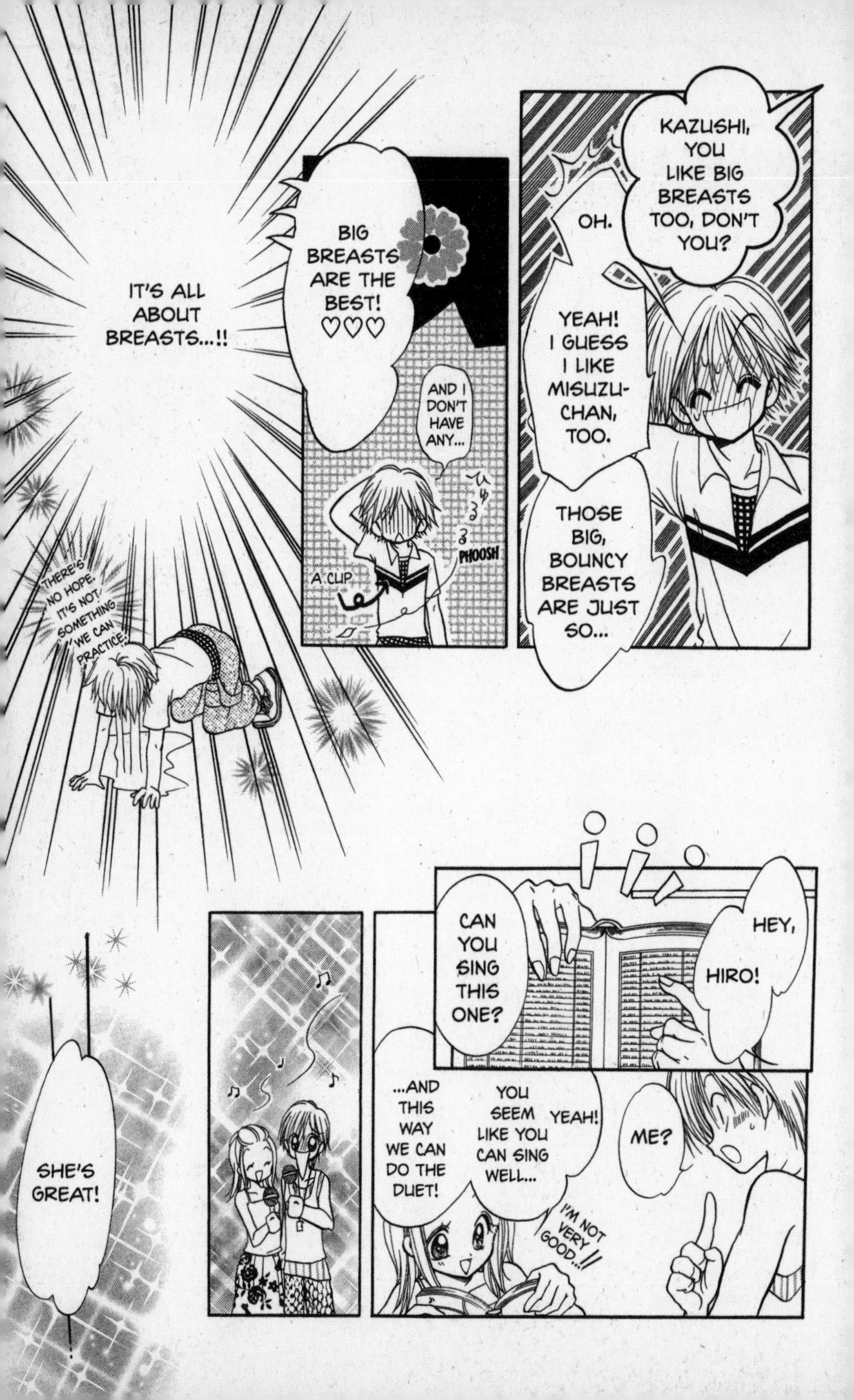
KAZUSHI, YOU LIKE BIG BREASTS TOO, DON'T YOU?
OH.
YEAH! I GUESS I LIKE MISUZU-CHAN, TOO.
THOSE BIG, BOUNCY BREASTS ARE JUST SO...
BIG BREASTS ARE THE BEST! ♡♡♡
AND I DON'T HAVE ANY...
ひゅるる
PHOOSH
A CUP
IT'S ALL ABOUT BREASTS...!!
THERE'S NO HOPE. IT'S NOT SOMETHING WE CAN PRACTICE.
HEY, HIRO!
CAN YOU SING THIS ONE?
ME?
YEAH!
YOU SEEM LIKE YOU CAN SING WELL...
I'M NOT VERY GOOD...!!
...AND THIS WAY WE CAN DO THE DUET!
SHE'S GREAT!

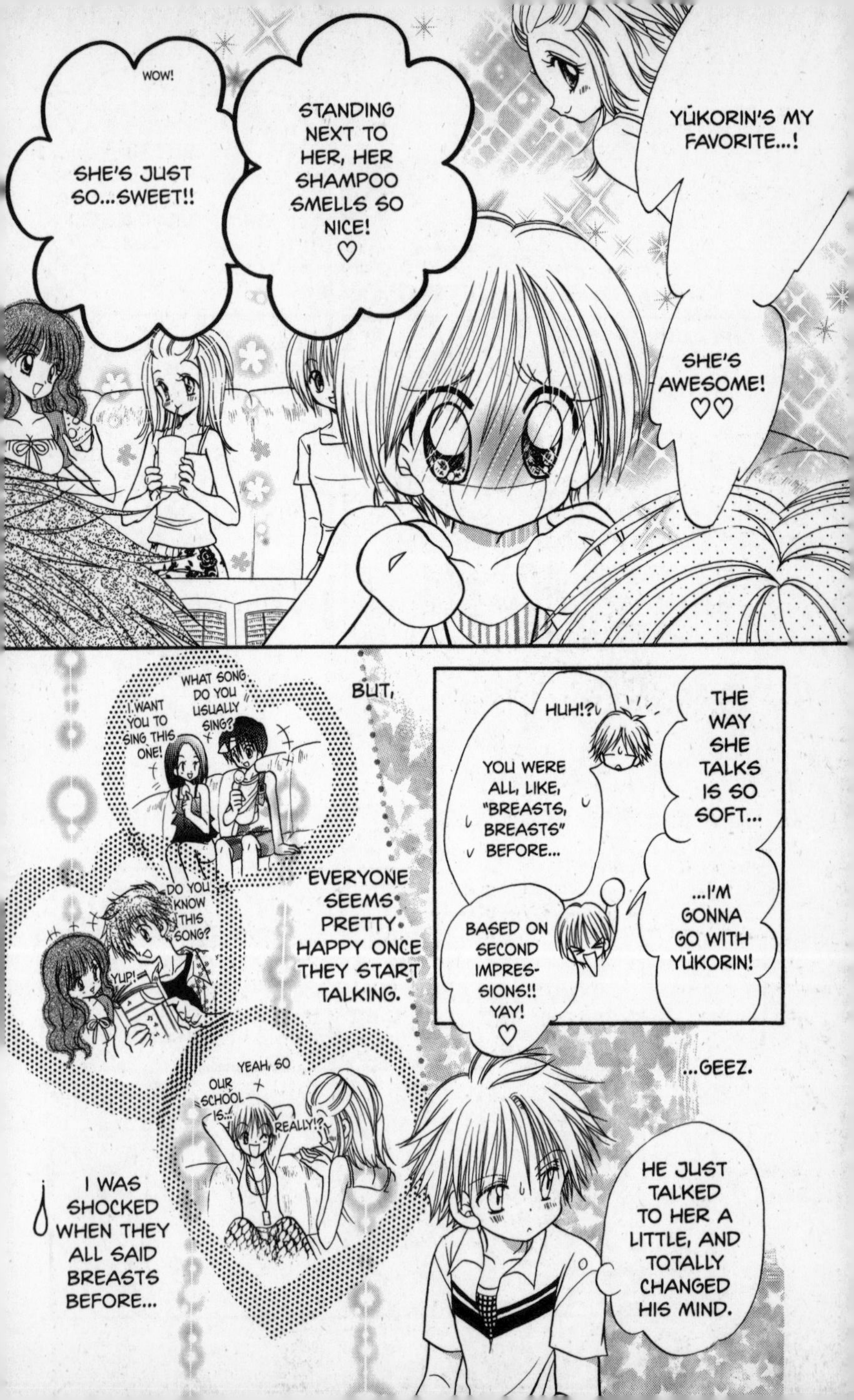
YŪKORIN'S MY FAVORITE...!
SHE'S AWESOME! ♡♡
STANDING NEXT TO HER, HER SHAMPOO SMELLS SO NICE! ♡
WOW!
SHE'S JUST SO...SWEET!!
THE WAY SHE TALKS IS SO SOFT...
...I'M GONNA GO WITH YŪKORIN!
HUH!?
YOU WERE ALL, LIKE, "BREASTS, BREASTS" BEFORE...
BASED ON SECOND IMPRESSIONS!! YAY! ♡
...GEEZ.
HE JUST TALKED TO HER A LITTLE, AND TOTALLY CHANGED HIS MIND.
BUT,
WHAT SONG DO YOU USUALLY SING?
I WANT YOU TO SING THIS ONE!
EVERYONE SEEMS PRETTY HAPPY ONCE THEY START TALKING.
DO YOU KNOW THIS SONG?
YUP!
YEAH, SO OUR SCHOOL IS...
REALLY!?
I WAS SHOCKED WHEN THEY ALL SAID BREASTS BEFORE...

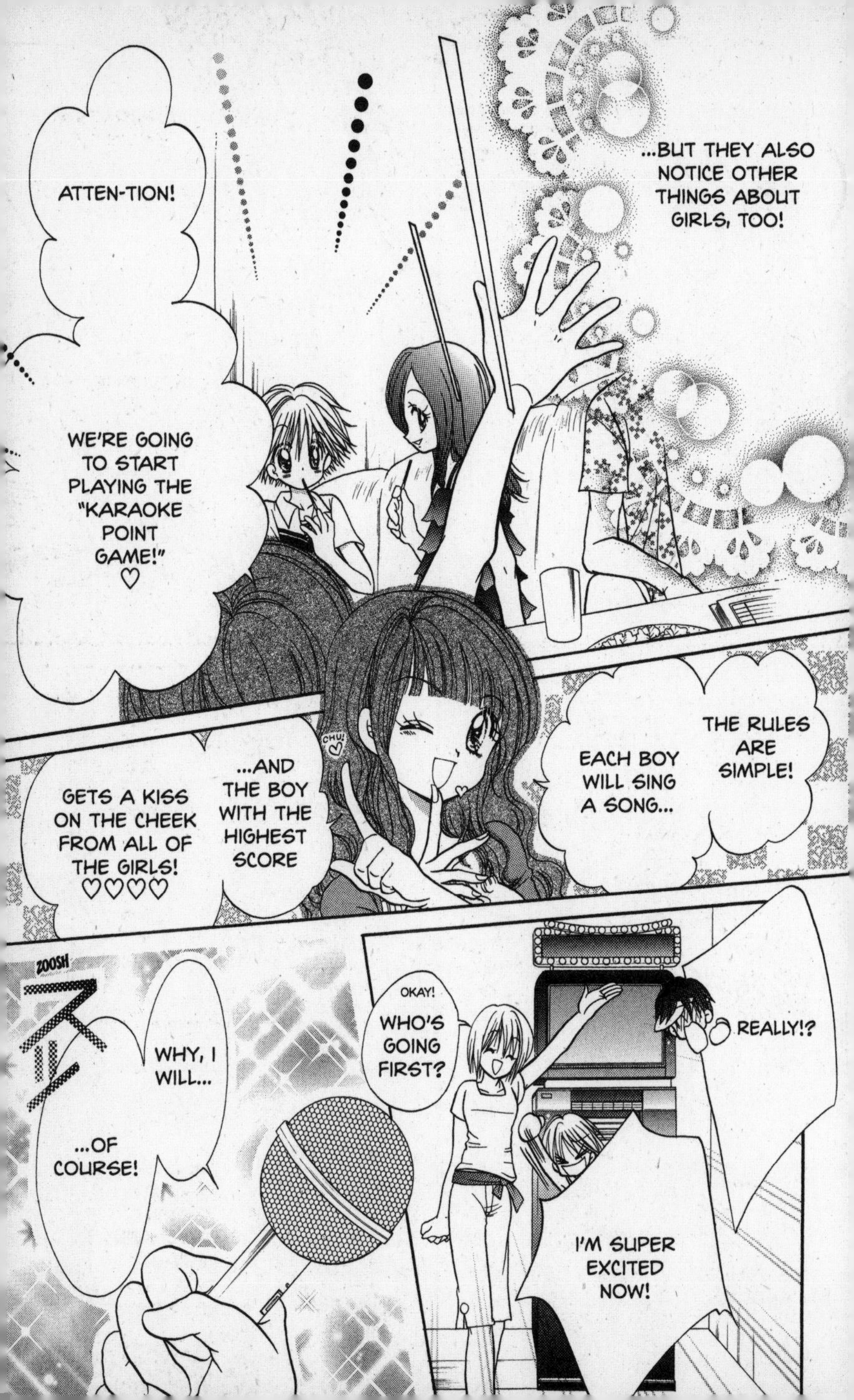
...BUT THEY ALSO NOTICE OTHER THINGS ABOUT GIRLS, TOO!
ATTEN-TION!
WE'RE GOING TO START PLAYING THE "KARAOKE POINT GAME!" ♡
THE RULES ARE SIMPLE!
EACH BOY WILL SING A SONG...
CHU! ♡
...AND THE BOY WITH THE HIGHEST SCORE
GETS A KISS ON THE CHEEK FROM ALL OF THE GIRLS! ♡♡♡♡
REALLY!?
I'M SUPER EXCITED NOW!
OKAY!
WHO'S GOING FIRST?
ZOOSH
WHY, I WILL...
...OF COURSE!

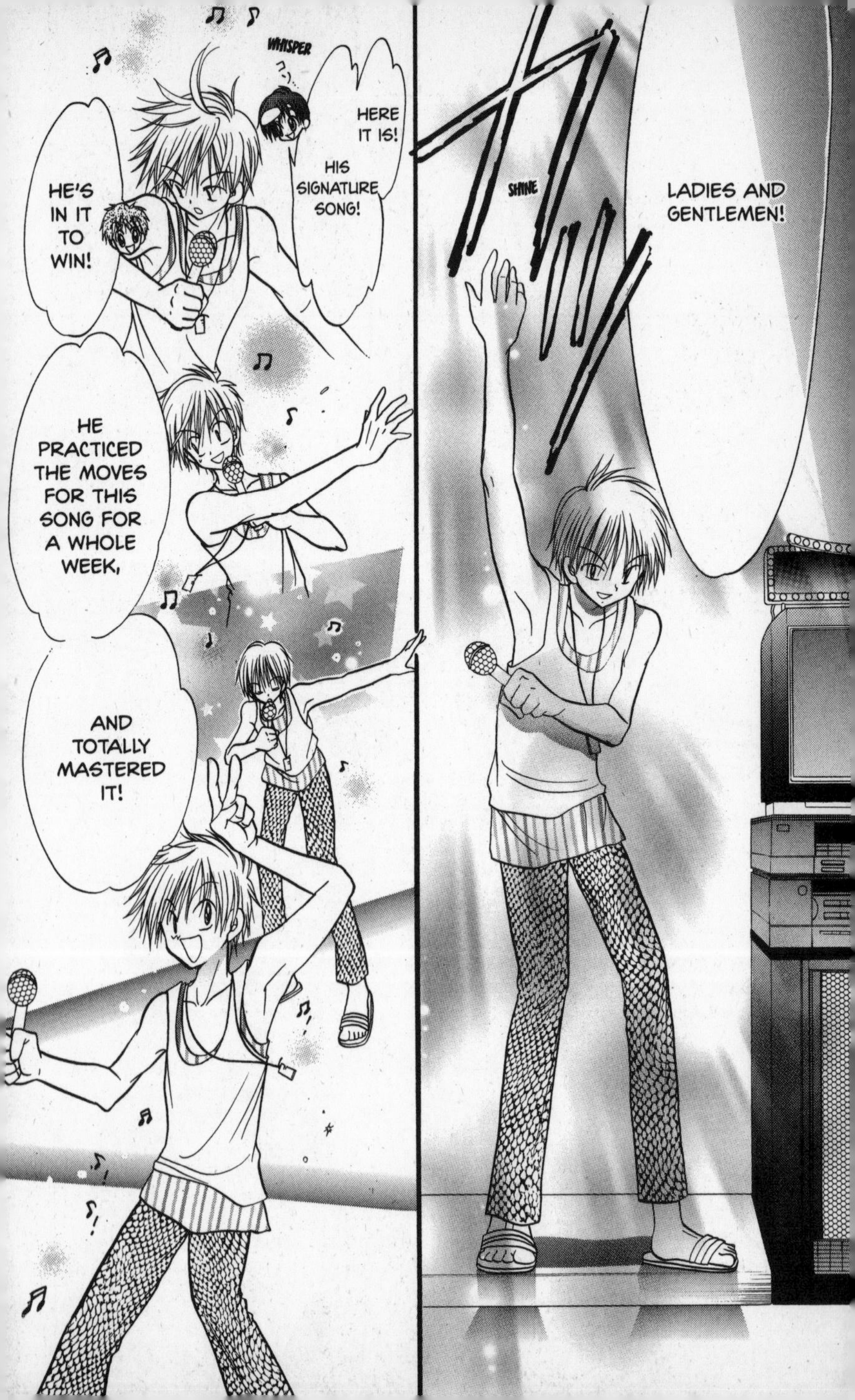
SHINE
LADIES AND GENTLEMEN!
WHISPER
HERE IT IS!
HIS SIGNATURE SONG!
HE'S IN IT TO WIN!
HE PRACTICED THE MOVES FOR THIS SONG FOR A WHOLE WEEK,
AND TOTALLY MASTERED IT!

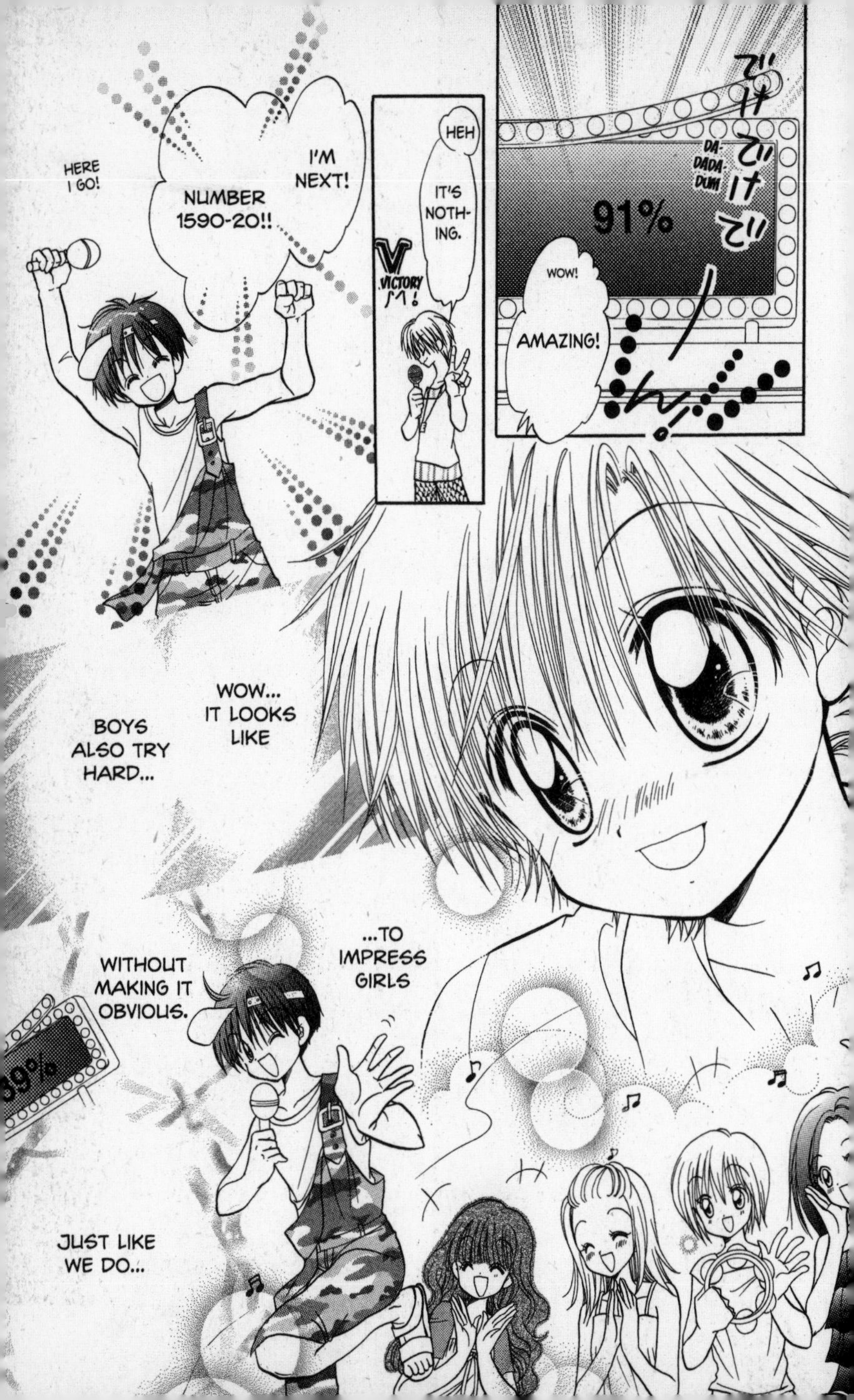
でけでけでーん!
DA-DADADA-DUM
91%
WOW!
AMAZING!
HEH
IT'S NOTHING.
VICTORY
ブイ!
HERE I GO!
I'M NEXT!
NUMBER 1590-20!!
WOW... IT LOOKS LIKE
BOYS ALSO TRY HARD...
...TO IMPRESS GIRLS
WITHOUT MAKING IT OBVIOUS.
JUST LIKE WE DO...

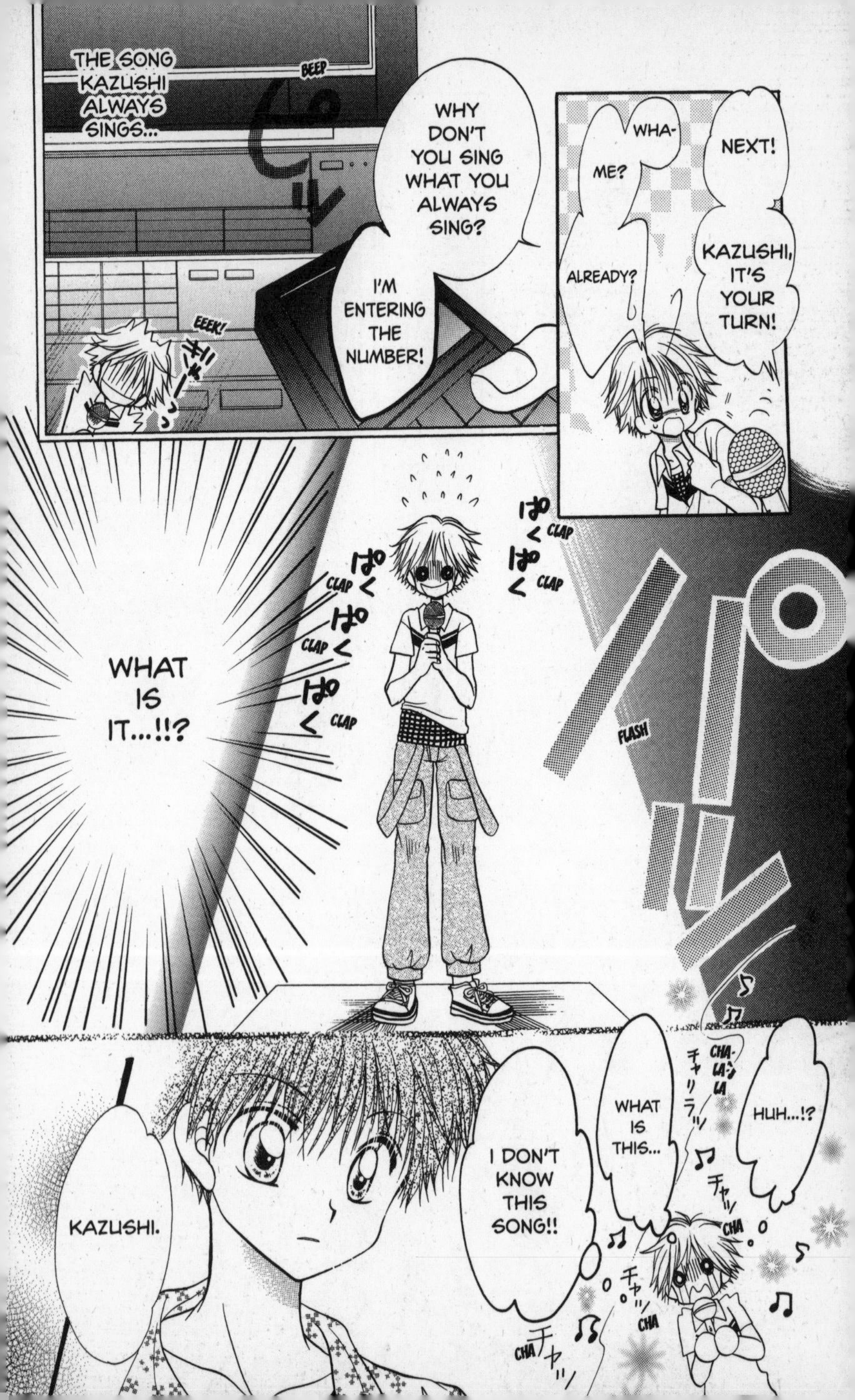
NEXT!
KAZUSHI, IT'S YOUR TURN!
WHA- ME?
ALREADY?
WHY DON'T YOU SING WHAT YOU ALWAYS SING?
I'M ENTERING THE NUMBER!
BEEP
EEEK!
THE SONG KAZUSHI ALWAYS SINGS...
FLASH
CLAP
CLAP
CLAP
CLAP
CLAP
WHAT IS IT...!!?
HUH...!?
CHA-LA-LA
WHAT IS THIS...
I DON'T KNOW THIS SONG!!
CHA
CHA
CHA
KAZUSHI.

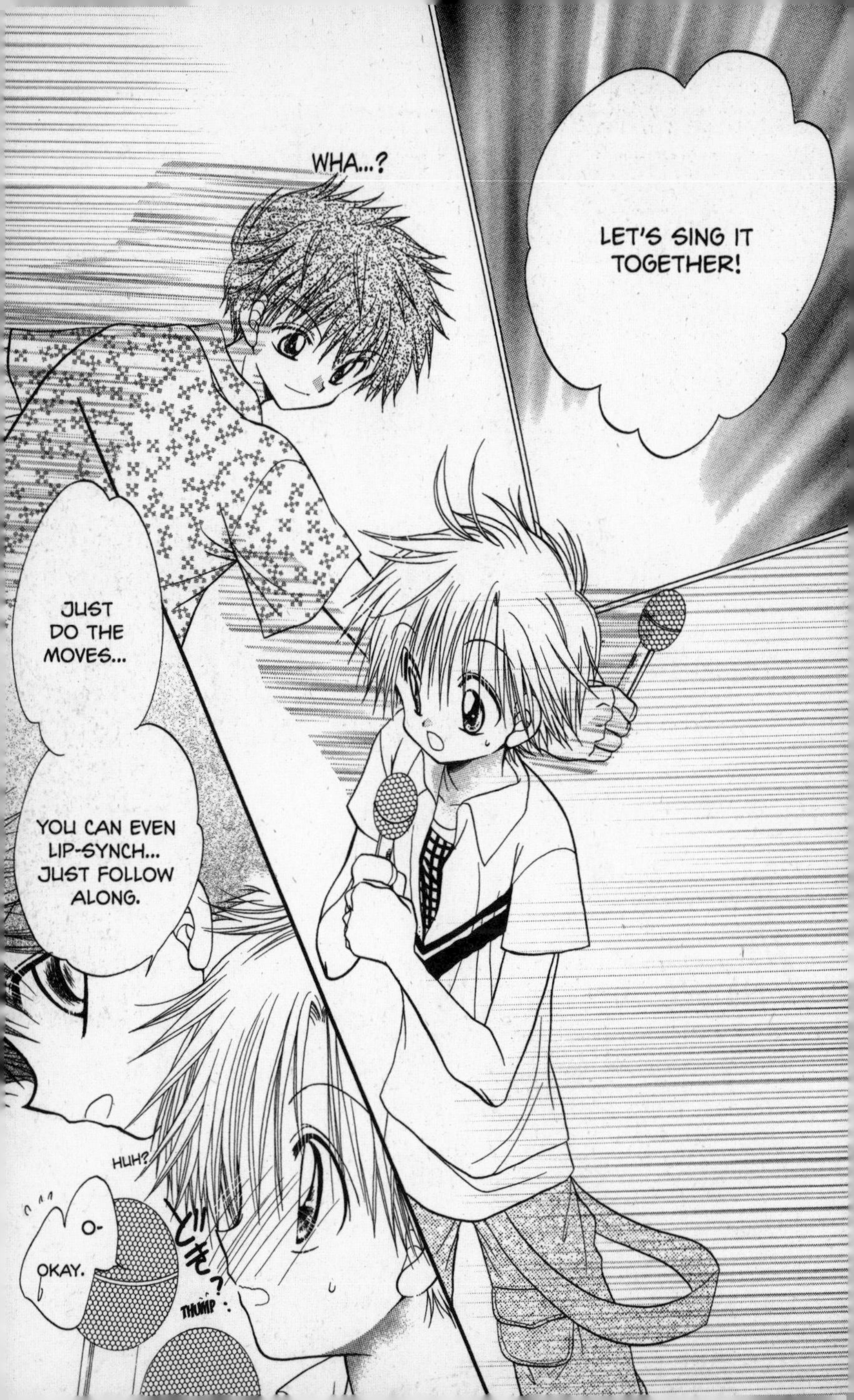
LET'S SING IT TOGETHER!
WHA...?
JUST DO THE MOVES...
YOU CAN EVEN LIP-SYNCH... JUST FOLLOW ALONG.
HUH?
どき
THUMP
O- OKAY.

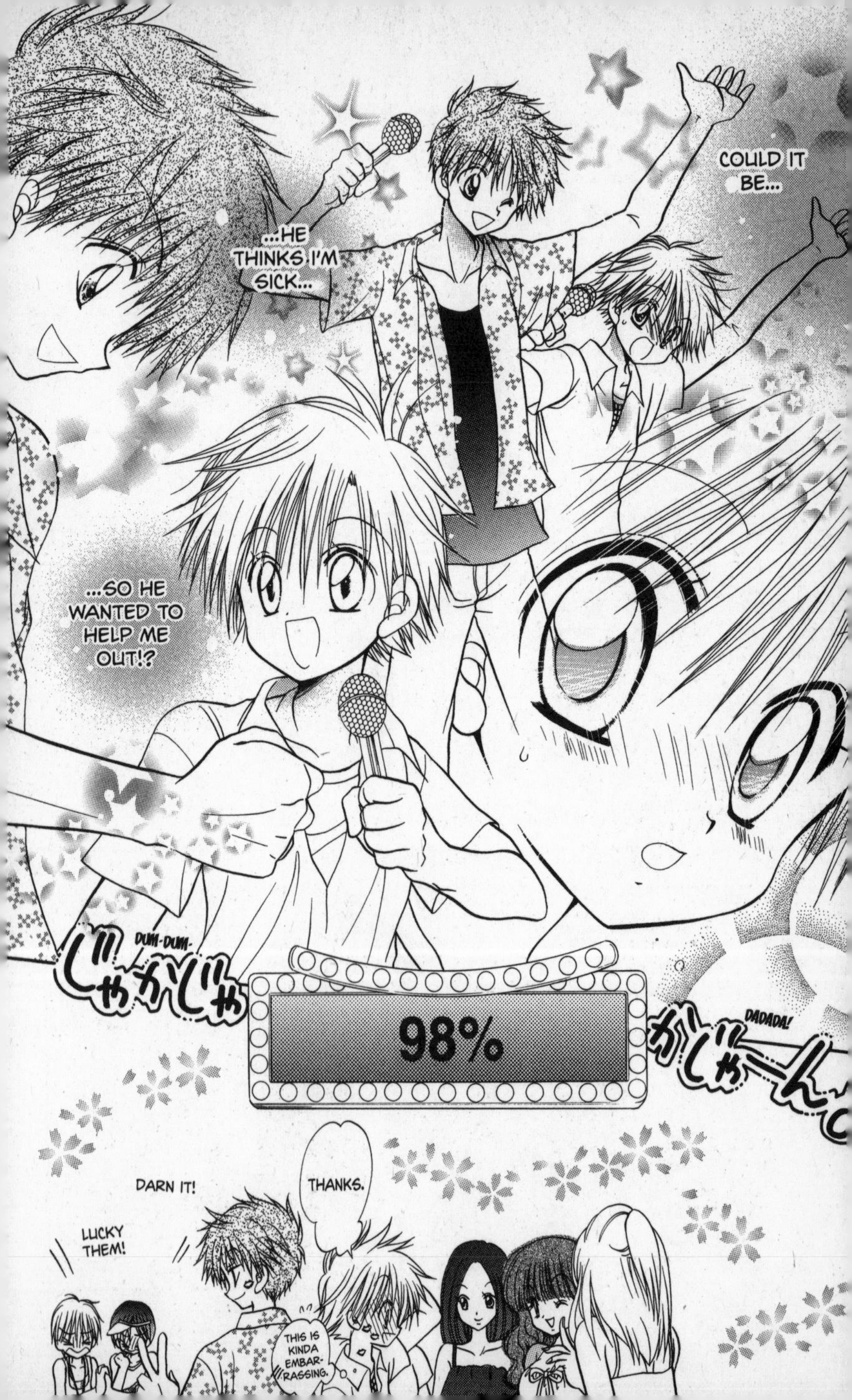
COULD IT BE...
...HE THINKS I'M SICK...
...SO HE WANTED TO HELP ME OUT!?
DUM-DUM-
98%
DADADA!
THANKS.
THIS IS KINDA EMBARRASSING.
DARN IT!
LUCKY THEM!

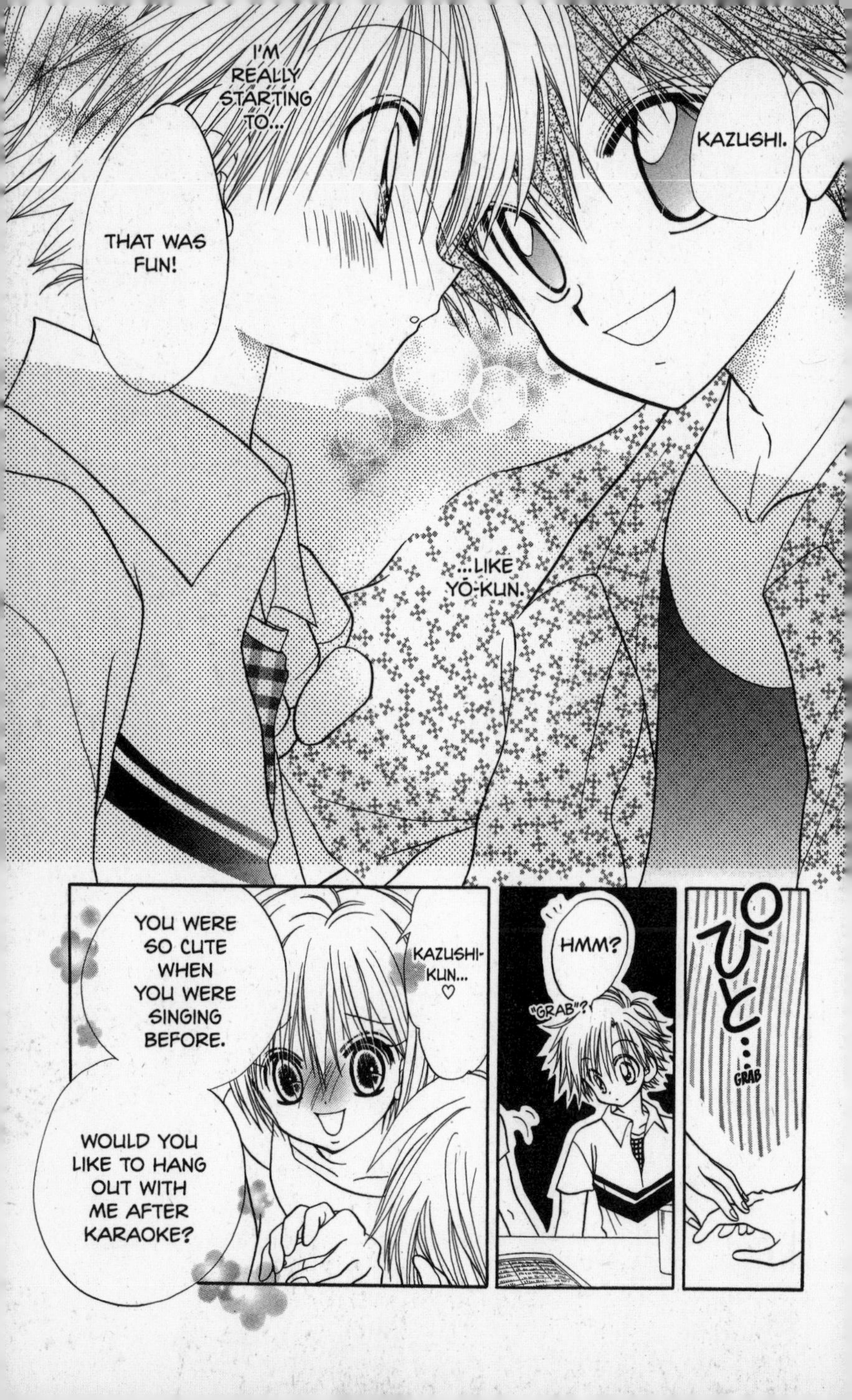
KAZUSHI.
I'M REALLY STARTING TO...
THAT WAS FUN!
...LIKE YŌ-KUN.
ぴと…
GRAB
HMM?
"GRAB"?
KAZUSHI-KUN... ♡
YOU WERE SO CUTE WHEN YOU WERE SINGING BEFORE.
WOULD YOU LIKE TO HANG OUT WITH ME AFTER KARAOKE?

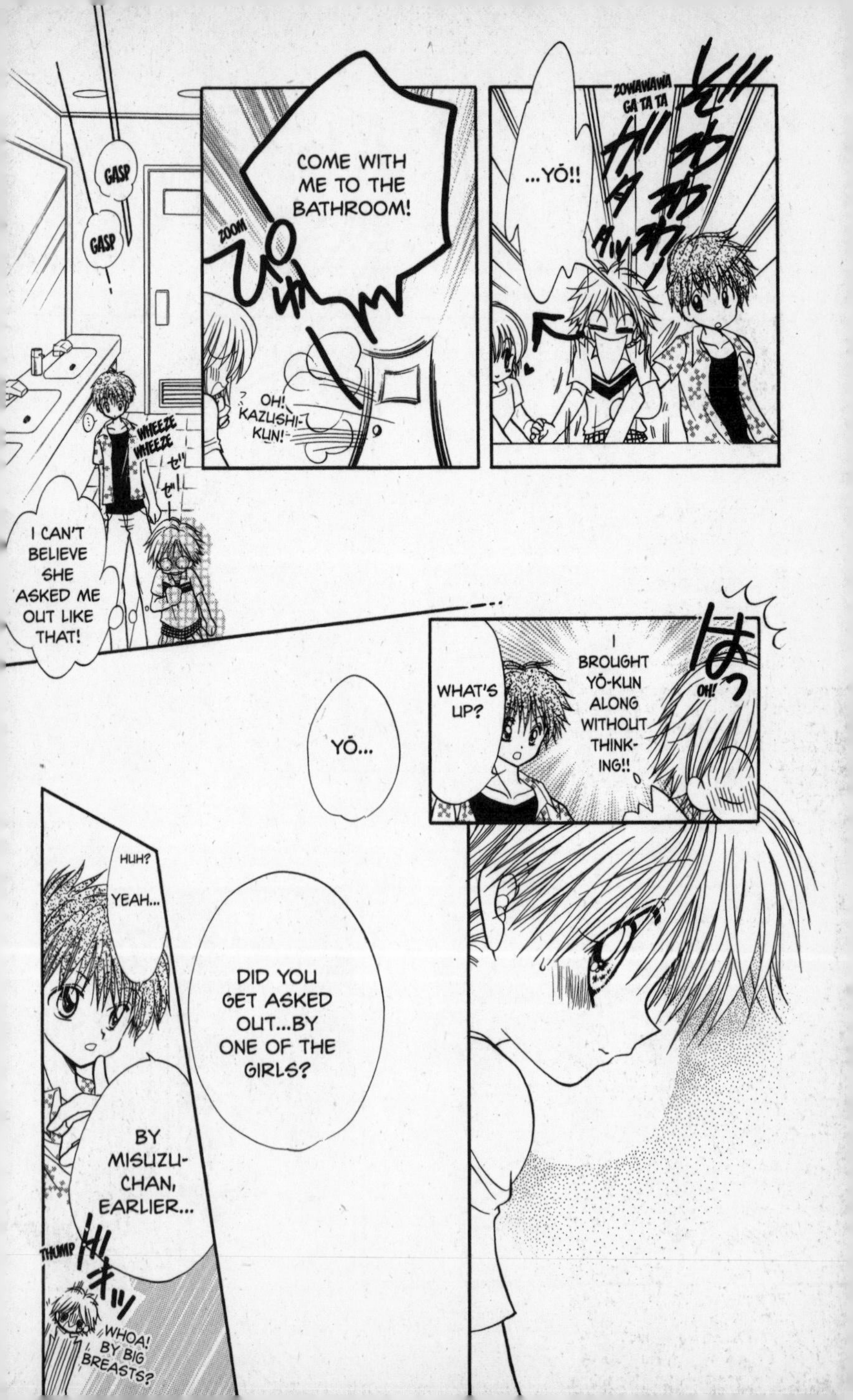
ZOWAWAWA
GA TA TA
...YŌ!!
COME WITH ME TO THE BATHROOM!
ZOOM
OH! KAZUSHI-KUN!
GASP
GASP
WHEEZE WHEEZE
I CAN'T BELIEVE SHE ASKED ME OUT LIKE THAT!
OH!
I BROUGHT YŌ-KUN ALONG WITHOUT THINKING!!
WHAT'S UP?
YŌ...
DID YOU GET ASKED OUT...BY ONE OF THE GIRLS?
HUH?
YEAH...
BY MISUZU-CHAN, EARLIER...
THUMP
WHOA! BY BIG BREASTS?

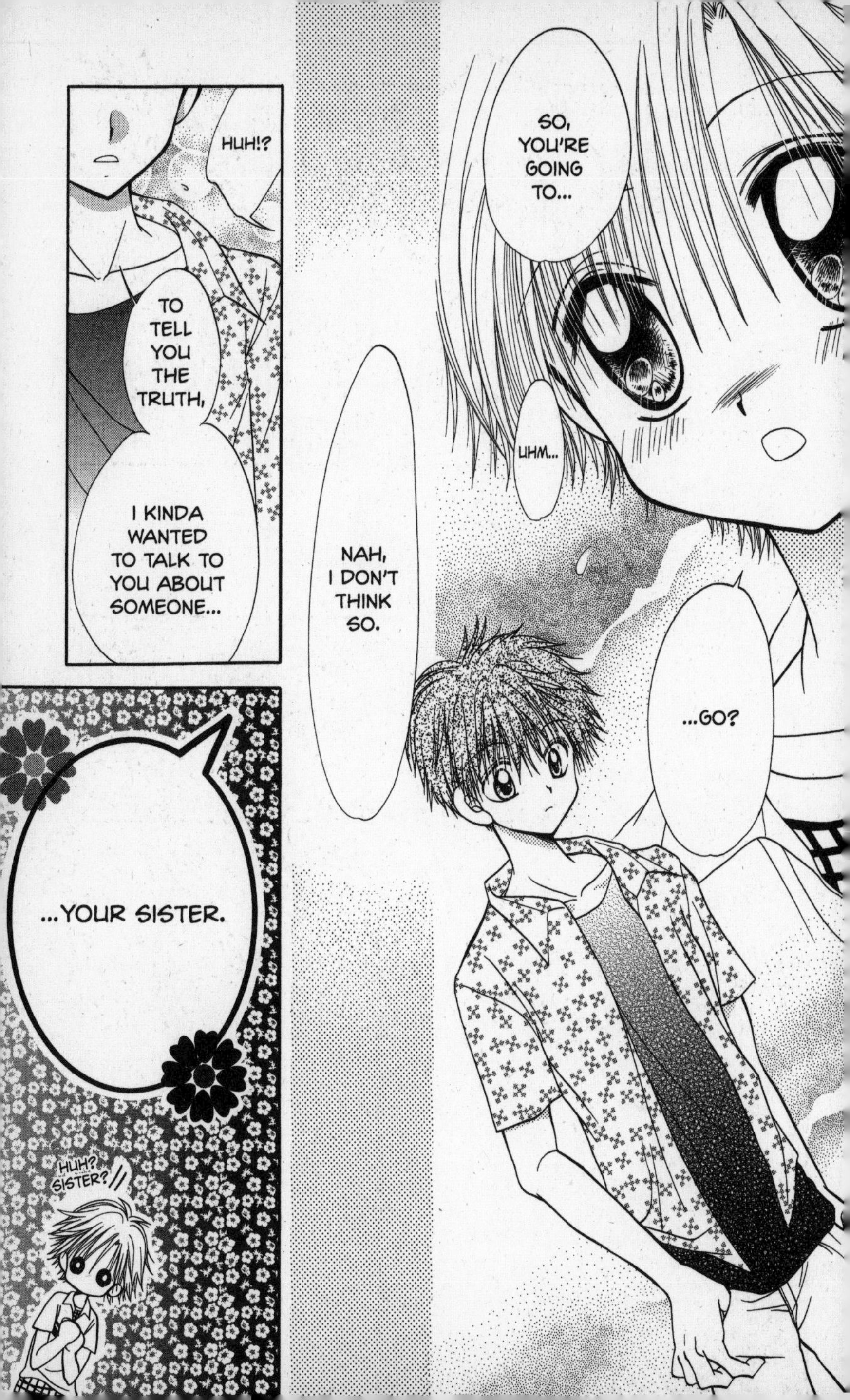
SO, YOU'RE GOING TO...
UHM...
...GO?
NAH, I DON'T THINK SO.
HUH!?
TO TELL YOU THE TRUTH,
I KINDA WANTED TO TALK TO YOU ABOUT SOMEONE...
...YOUR SISTER.
HUH? SISTER?

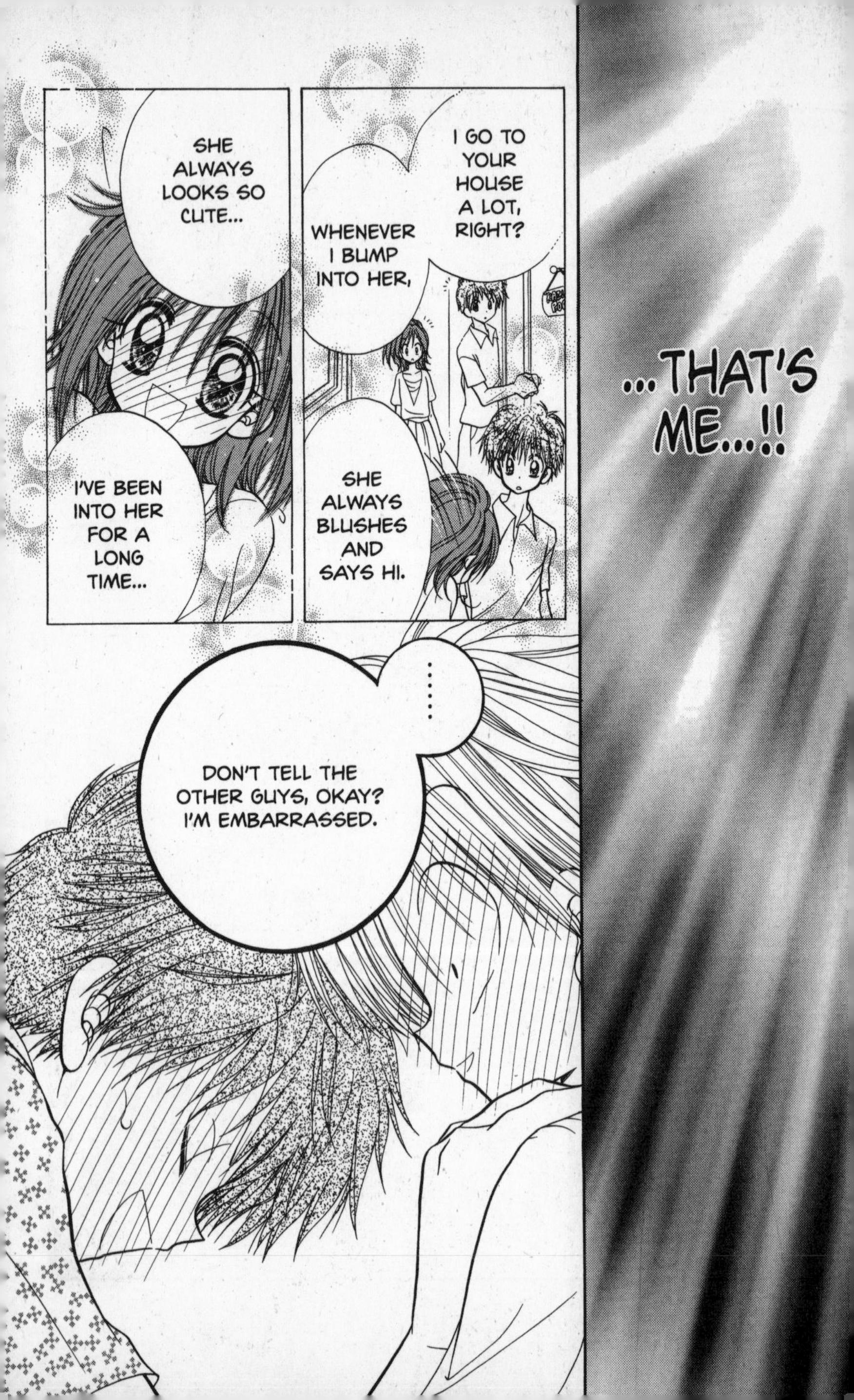
...THAT'S ME...!!
I GO TO YOUR HOUSE A LOT, RIGHT?
WHENEVER I BUMP INTO HER,
SHE ALWAYS BLUSHES AND SAYS HI.
SHE ALWAYS LOOKS SO CUTE...
I'VE BEEN INTO HER FOR A LONG TIME...
......
DON'T TELL THE OTHER GUYS, OKAY? I'M EMBARRASSED.

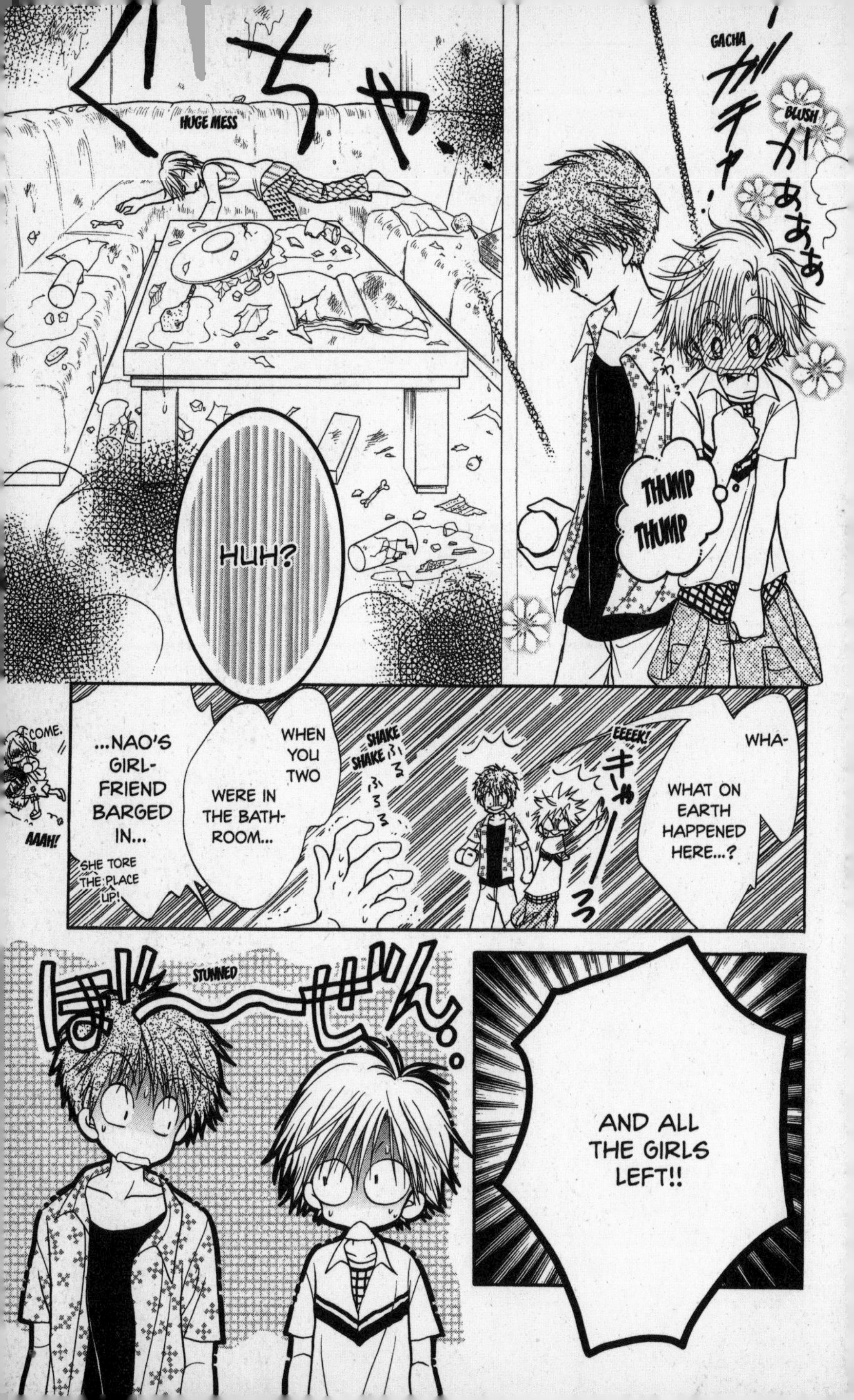

GACHA
ガチャ!
BLUSH
かあああ
THUMP THUMP
HUGE MESS
ぐちゃ
HUH?
WHA-
WHAT ON EARTH HAPPENED HERE...?
EEEEK!
SHAKE SHAKE
ふるふる
WHEN YOU TWO WERE IN THE BATHROOM...
...NAO'S GIRLFRIEND BARGED IN...
SHE TORE THE PLACE UP!
COME.
AAAH!
AND ALL THE GIRLS LEFT!!
STUNNED

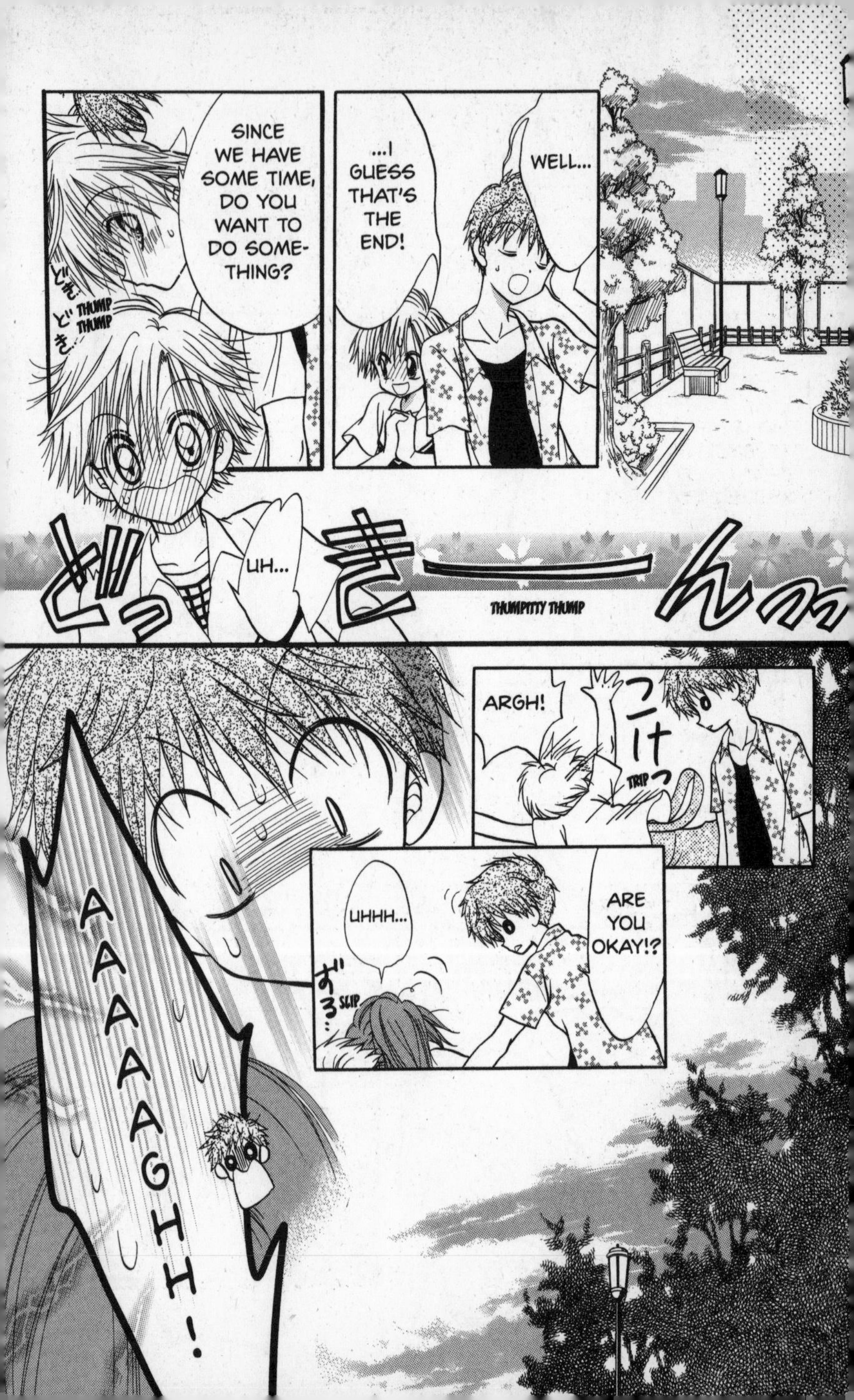
WELL...
...I GUESS THAT'S THE END!
SINCE WE HAVE SOME TIME, DO YOU WANT TO DO SOME-THING?
どき どき…
THUMP THUMP
UH...
どっきーーん
THUMPITTY THUMP
ARGH!
こけっ
TRIP
ARE YOU OKAY!?
UHHH...
ずる…
SLIP
AAAAAAGHH!

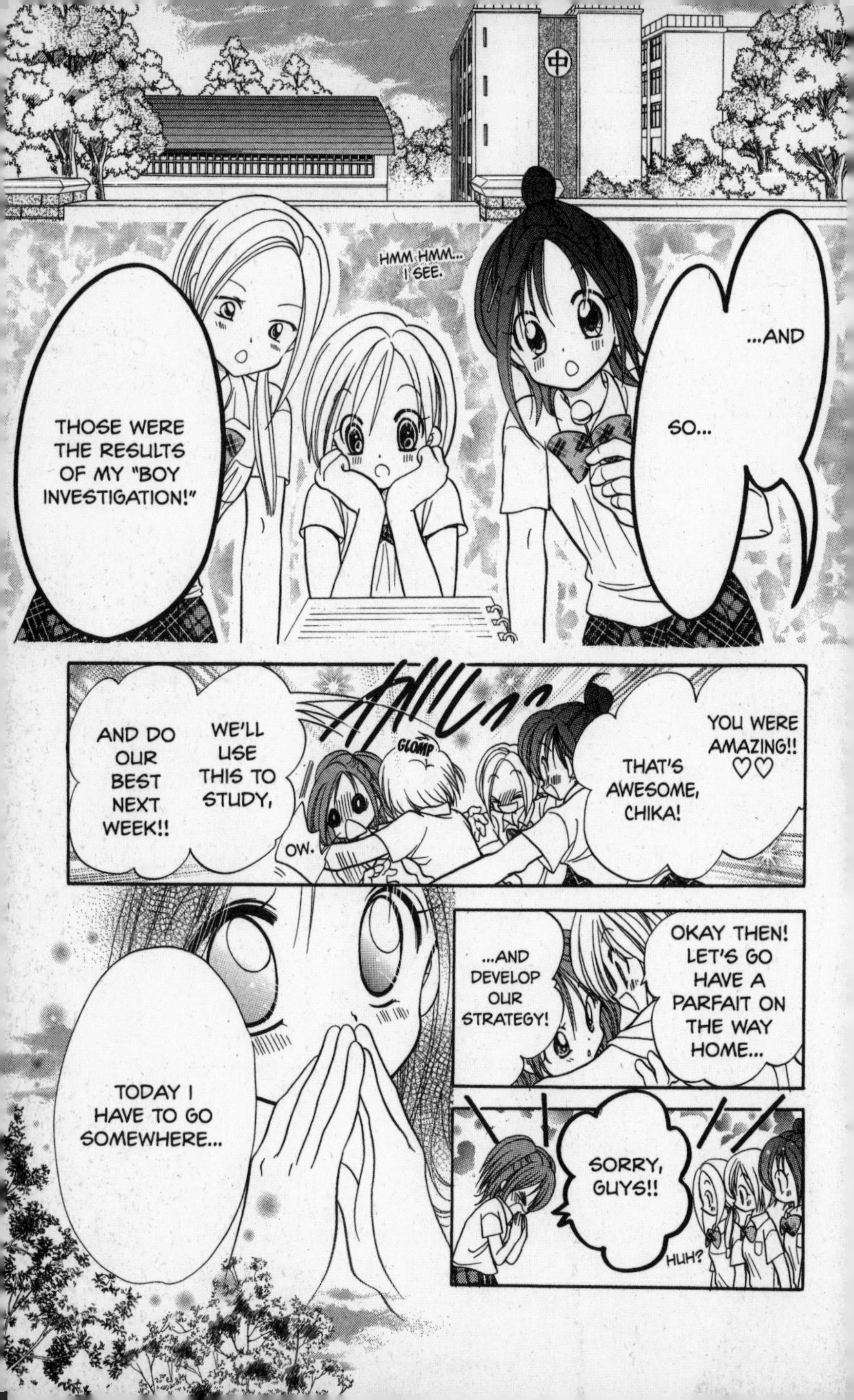
...AND SO...
HMM HMM... I SEE.
THOSE WERE THE RESULTS OF MY "BOY INVESTIGATION!"
YOU WERE AMAZING!! ♡♡
THAT'S AWESOME, CHIKA!
GLOMP
OW.
WE'LL USE THIS TO STUDY,
AND DO OUR BEST NEXT WEEK!!
OKAY THEN! LET'S GO HAVE A PARFAIT ON THE WAY HOME...
...AND DEVELOP OUR STRATEGY!
SORRY, GUYS!!
HUH?
TODAY I HAVE TO GO SOMEWHERE...

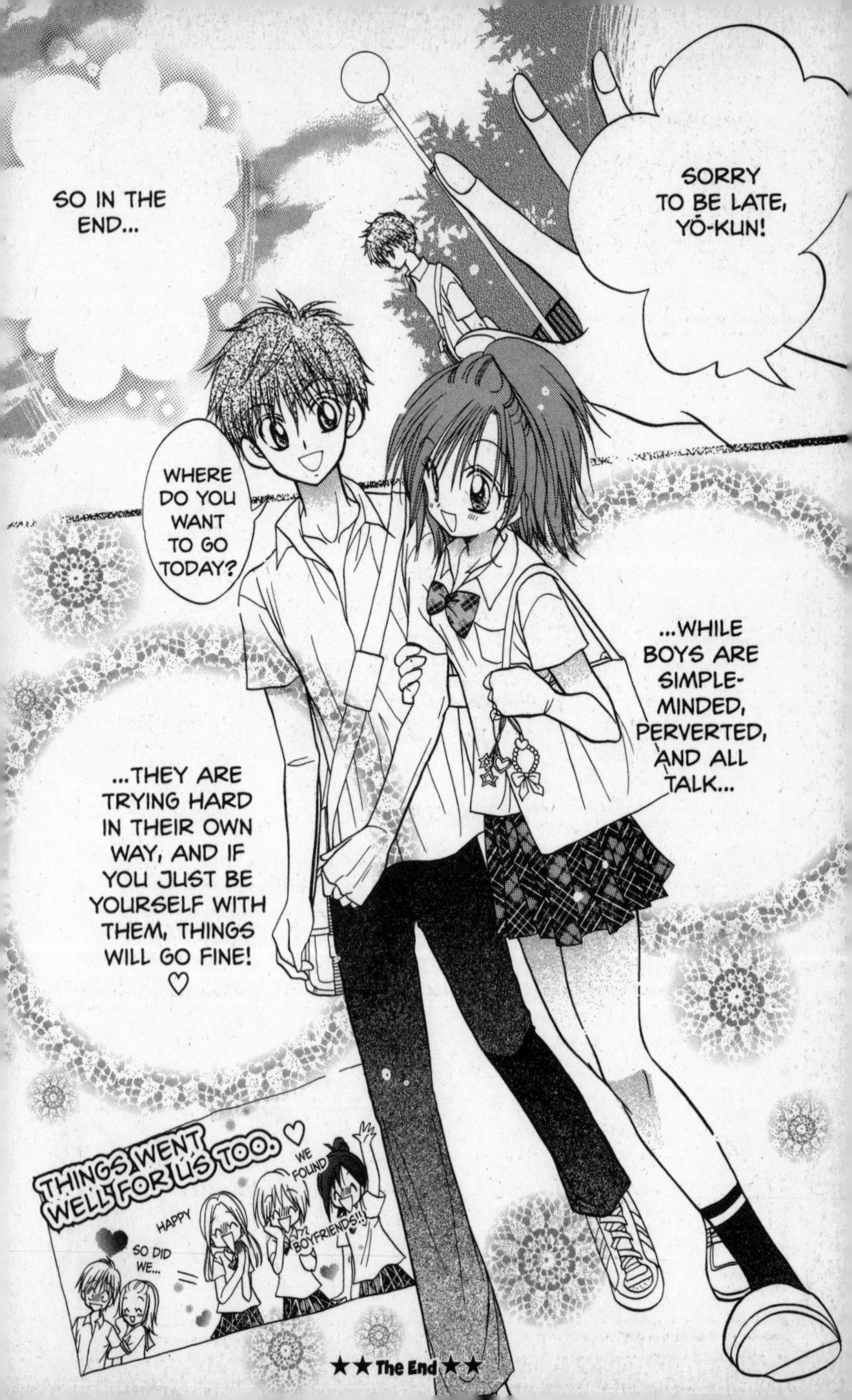

SORRY TO BE LATE, YŌ-KUN!
SO IN THE END...
WHERE DO YOU WANT TO GO TODAY?
...WHILE BOYS ARE SIMPLE-MINDED, PERVERTED, AND ALL TALK...
...THEY ARE TRYING HARD IN THEIR OWN WAY, AND IF YOU JUST BE YOURSELF WITH THEM, THINGS WILL GO FINE! ♡
THINGS WENT WELL FOR US TOO. ♡
WE FOUND
BOYFRIENDS!!
HAPPY
SO DID WE...
★★ The End ★★

Panic X Panic
PROFILE
VOL. 8
FROM THE AUTHOR'S ORIGINAL STORY NOTES

KIBA ŌGAMI

DATE OF BIRTH
unknown

Mitsuki's classmate.
A mysterious transfer student with incredible reflexes!
...But actually he's a werewolf!!!
He changes shape at the full moon.
He's fallen in love with Mitsuki, and is very aggressive.
He'll hug you in public without caring if people see.
Second-most popular guy in the class.

Translation Notes

Japanese is a tricky language for most Westerners, and translation is often more art than science. For your edification and reading pleasure, here are notes on some of the places where we could have gone in a different direction with our translation of the work, or where a Japanese cultural reference is used.

***Shokupan*, page 17**

Shokupan is a Japanese twist on Western-style bread. It is typically baked in a rectangular shape, and cut into thick slices. One slice with butter or jam is a meal in itself, hence the name *shoku* ("meal") plus *pan* ("bread").

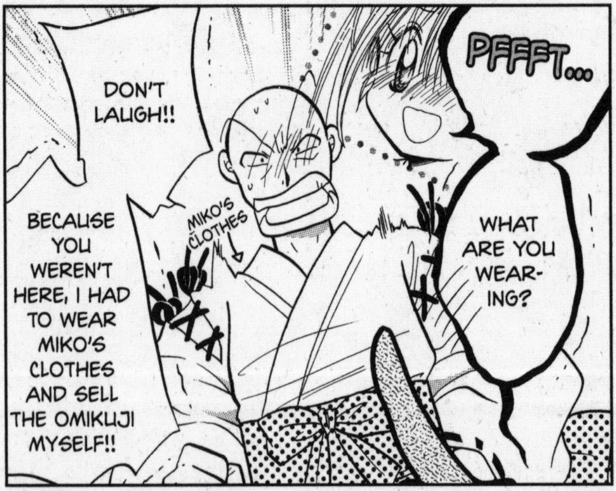
PFFFT...
WHAT ARE YOU WEAR-ING?
DON'T LAUGH!!
MIKO'S CLOTHES
BECAUSE YOU WEREN'T HERE, I HAD TO WEAR MIKO'S CLOTHES AND SELL THE OMIKUJI MYSELF!!

***Miko*'s Clothes / *Omikuji*, page 18**

Miko, literally "shrine maiden," are the female attendants at Shinto shrines. *Omikuji* are small strips of paper sold at shrines on which visitors write wishes and then hang on branches, praying they will come true. (Common wishes include entrance to school of choice, luck in love, etc.) In the Kamishiro Shrine, Mitsuki usually wears the *miko*'s clothes to help her dad by selling the *omikuji* to visitors, but this time Benkei had to do it himself.

Mount Tenpō, page 18

Mount Tenpō is located in Osaka, and is commonly recognized as Japan's *lowest* mountain, therefore making this a humorous reference.

Japanese Demons: *Amefurashi, Zashiki-Warashi, Rokuro-Kubi, Kappa,* and the *Nine-Tailed Fox,* page 20–22

There are many demons, or *yōkai,* in Japanese folklore, and most of them are characterized by a particular appearance or story. *Amefurashi* ("rain bringer") is a demon who takes the form of a young child. *Zashiki-warashi* ("child of the house") is also a child, and haunts peoples' homes. *Rokuro-kubi* ("potter's wheel neck") are usually women who can stretch their necks to great lengths. *Kappa* are child-sized humanoids with the body of a monkey or frog. The nine-tailed fox is a magical fox with healing powers.

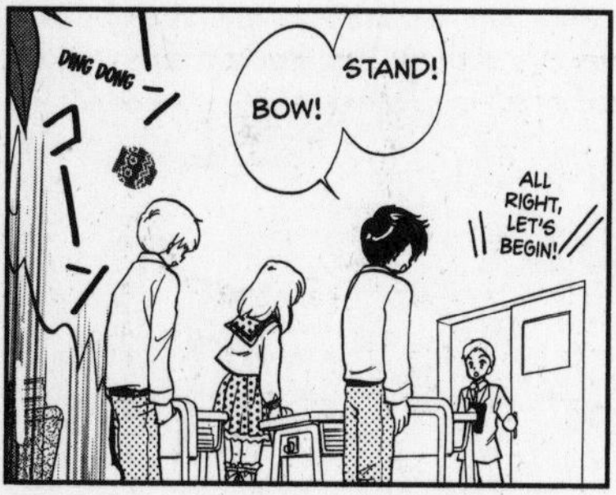
STAND!
BOW!
ALL RIGHT, LET'S BEGIN!
DING DONG

Classroom Rituals, page 22

In Japan, it is customary for the students to stand and bow when the teacher enters the room and starts the class.

Maybe the Sky Will Fall Today, page 33

It is a common joke in Japan to mention that it might rain (or snow) when something extremely unexpected happens—in this case, Mitsuki doing something as smart as carry around a first-aid kit.

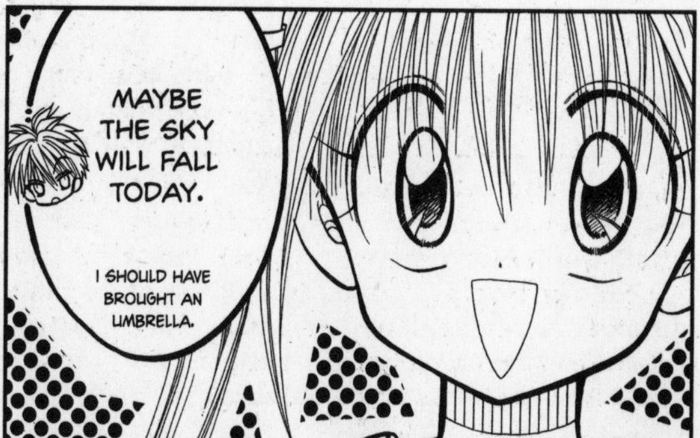
MAYBE THE SKY WILL FALL TODAY.
I SHOULD HAVE BROUGHT AN UMBRELLA.

Effigy, page 53
Japanese readers would recognize this doll as an effigy doll of Mitsuki. Effigy dolls are common props in manga—usually used by one character hoping to curse another. In this case Maju likely hopes to cast a curse on Mitsuki.

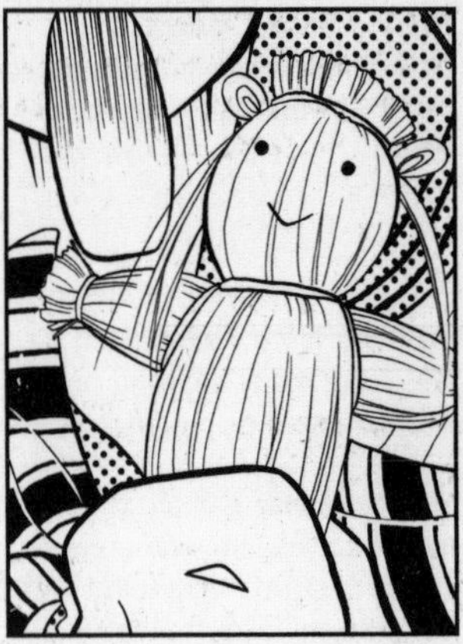

Cram School, page 54, 121
In Japan, a significant percentage of students attend cram school in the evening and on weekends, even students in elementary school! The greatest attendance rate (roughly 60 percent) is in middle school—the age-range of the characters in this comic.

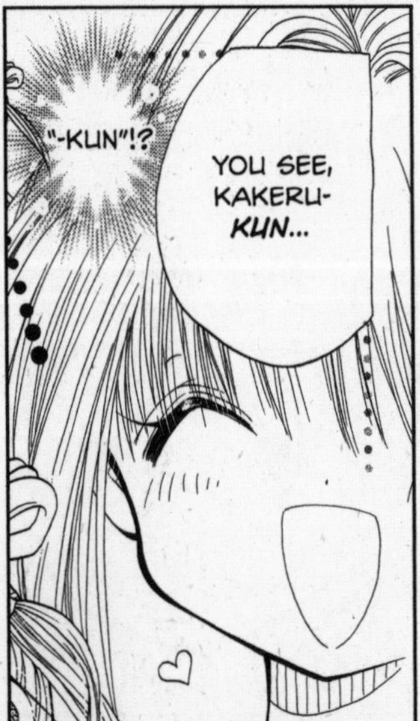
YOU SEE, KAKERU-KUN...
"-KUN"!?

Kakeru-"Kun," page 83
Whereas Mitsuki usually calls Kakeru with no suffix, indicating a completely equal and even contentious relationship, suddenly adding a "-kun" to his name suggests a new-found admiration and respect.

***Ninin-Baori*, page 86**

Ninin-baori is a Japanese comedic act where two people *(ninin)* wear the same large coat *(baori)* and pretend to be one hunchbacked person.

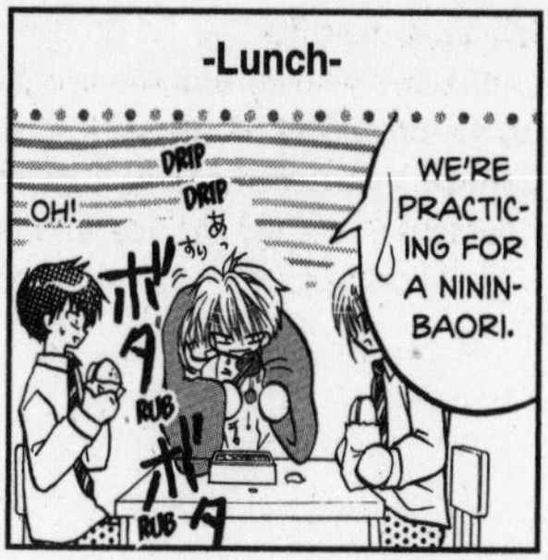
-Lunch-
WE'RE PRACTIC-ING FOR A NININ-BAORI.
DRIP
DRIP
OH!
RUB
RUB

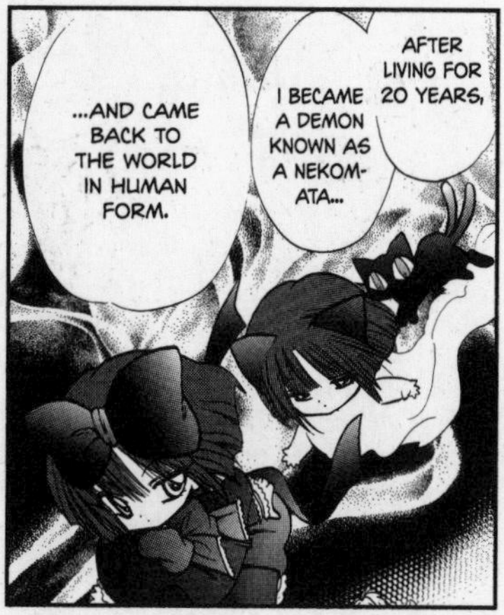
AFTER LIVING FOR 20 YEARS,
I BECAME A DEMON KNOWN AS A NEKOM-ATA...
...AND CAME BACK TO THE WORLD IN HUMAN FORM.

***Nekomata*, page 104**

Nekomata (literally "cat-again") are the second incarnation of the *bakeneko* ("monster cat") class of demon. They can be evil or good, and have special powers.

Kiba Ōgami, page 110

Kiba means "fang," and Ōgami, though a real Japanese surname, sounds very similar to *ōkami,* which means "wolf." Japanese readers would know at once that something is up with this guy!

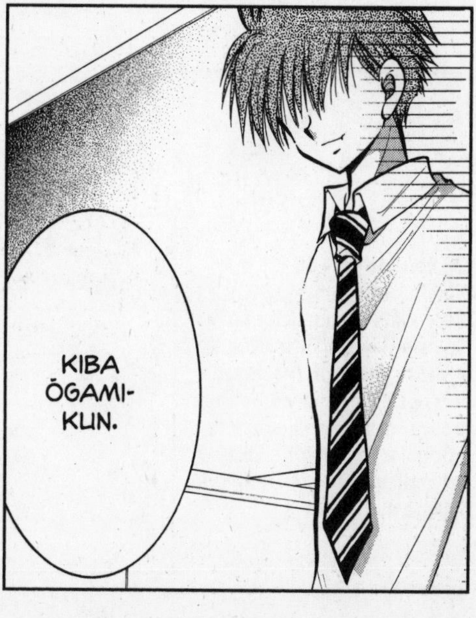
KIBA ŌGAMI-KUN.

Hanako-san in the Bathroom, page 127
"Hanako-san" is the name of a girl said to haunt bathrooms. She recurs in several Japanese movies, comics, and other pop culture media.

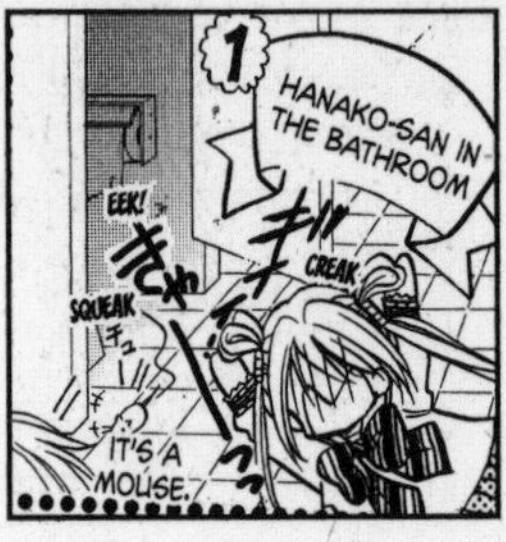
1
HANAKO-SAN IN THE BATHROOM
CREAK
EEK!
SQUEAK
IT'S A MOUSE.

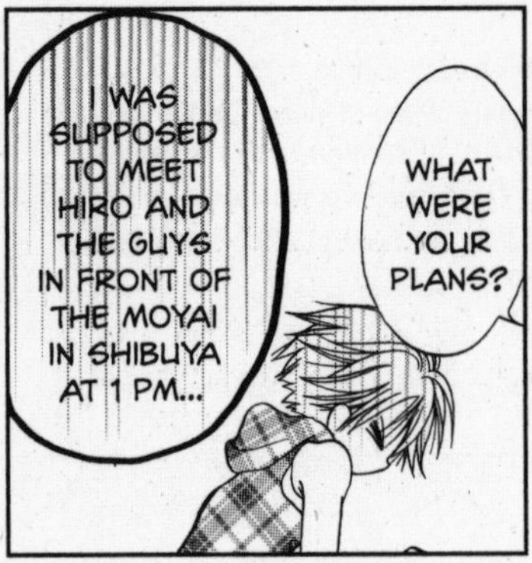
WHAT WERE YOUR PLANS?
I WAS SUPPOSED TO MEET HIRO AND THE GUYS IN FRONT OF THE MOYAI IN SHIBUYA AT 1 PM...

Moyai at Shibuya, page 154
The Moyai statue is a large statue in Shibuya, one of the popular neighborhoods for young people to hang out in Japan. It is based on the Moai statues of Easter Island, and is the second-most famous meeting spot after the Hachiko dog statue.

***Gōkon*, page 165**
Gōkon (literally "combined party") is a group blind date, typically used to overcome shyness and form friendships and possibly romance between groups of boys and girls. It is a popular format for social networking, particularly among college students.

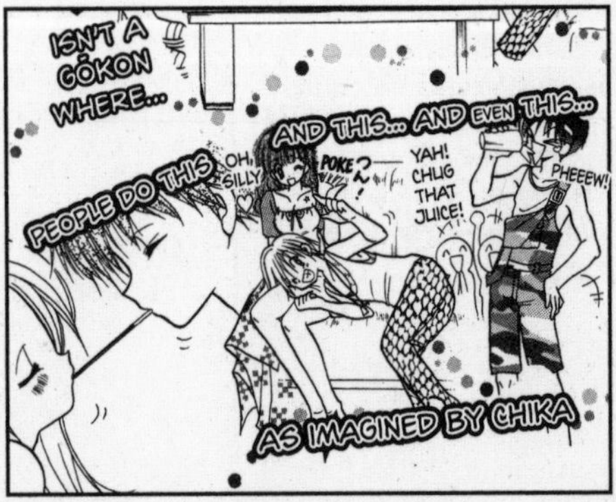
ISN'T A GŌKON WHERE...
PEOPLE DO THIS
AND THIS... AND EVEN THIS...
PHEEEW!
YAH! CHUG THAT JUICE!
POKE
OH, SILLY
AS IMAGINED BY CHIKA

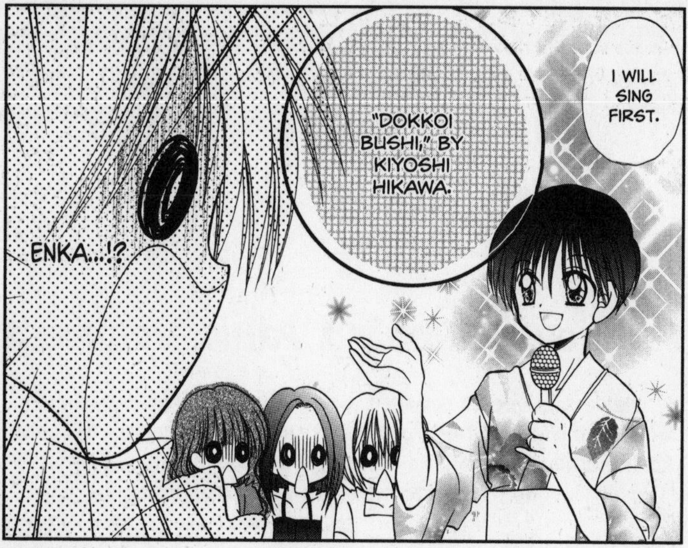
I WILL SING FIRST.
"DOKKOI BUSHI," BY KIYOSHI HIKAWA.
ENKA...!?

***Enka*, page 169**

Enka is a balladic music of Japanese popular songs developed in the postwar period. It is considered old-fashioned and out of style among young people. Kiyoshi Hikawa is a famous *enka* singer.

Preview of *Panic X Panic*, volume 2

We're pleased to present a preview from *Panic X Panic*,
volume 2. Please check our website (www.delreymanga.com)
to see when this volume will be available in English. For now
you'll have to make do with Japanese!

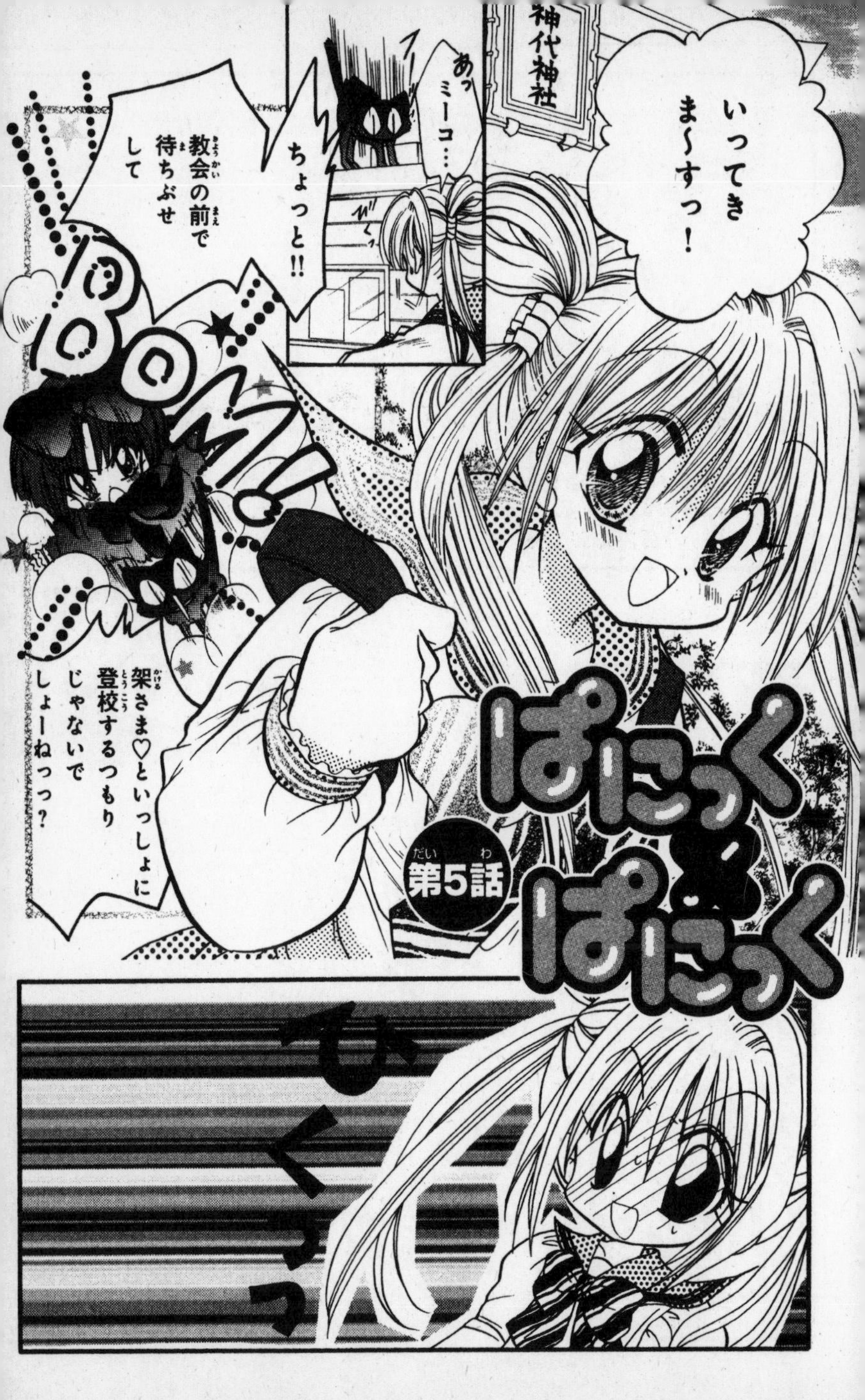
いってきま〜すっ!
神代神社
あっミーコ…
ちょっと!!
ビクッ
教会の前で待ちぶせして
BOOM!!
架さま♡といっしょに登校するつもりじゃないでしょーねっっ?
ぱにっく&ぱにっく
第5話
ひくっっ

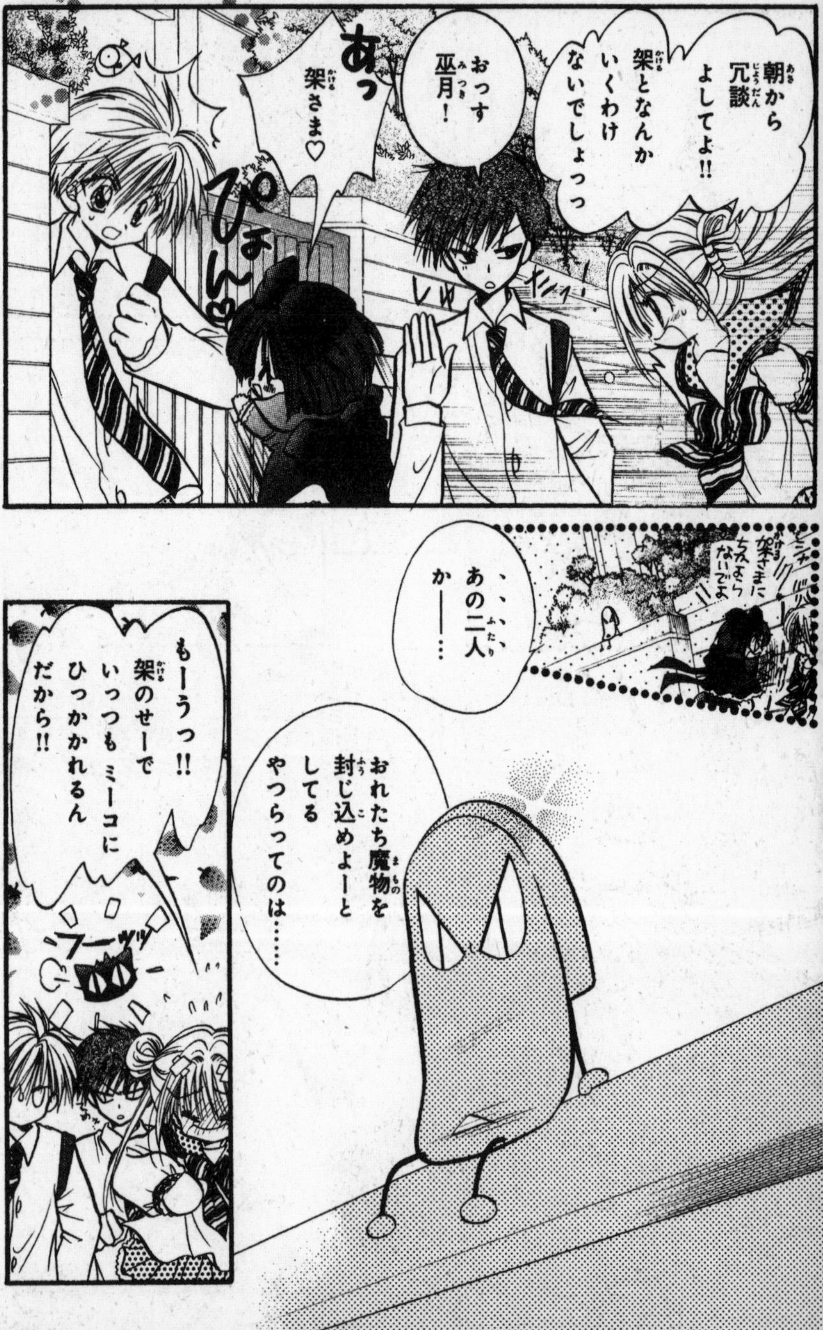
朝から冗談よしてよ!!
架となんかいくわけないでしょっっ
おっす巫月!
あっ
架さま♡
ぴょん〜♡
架さまにちかよらないでよ
、、、、あの二人か——…
おれたち魔物を封じ込めよーとしてるやつらってのは……
もーうっ!!
架のせーでいっつもミーコにひっかかれるんだから!!
フーッ

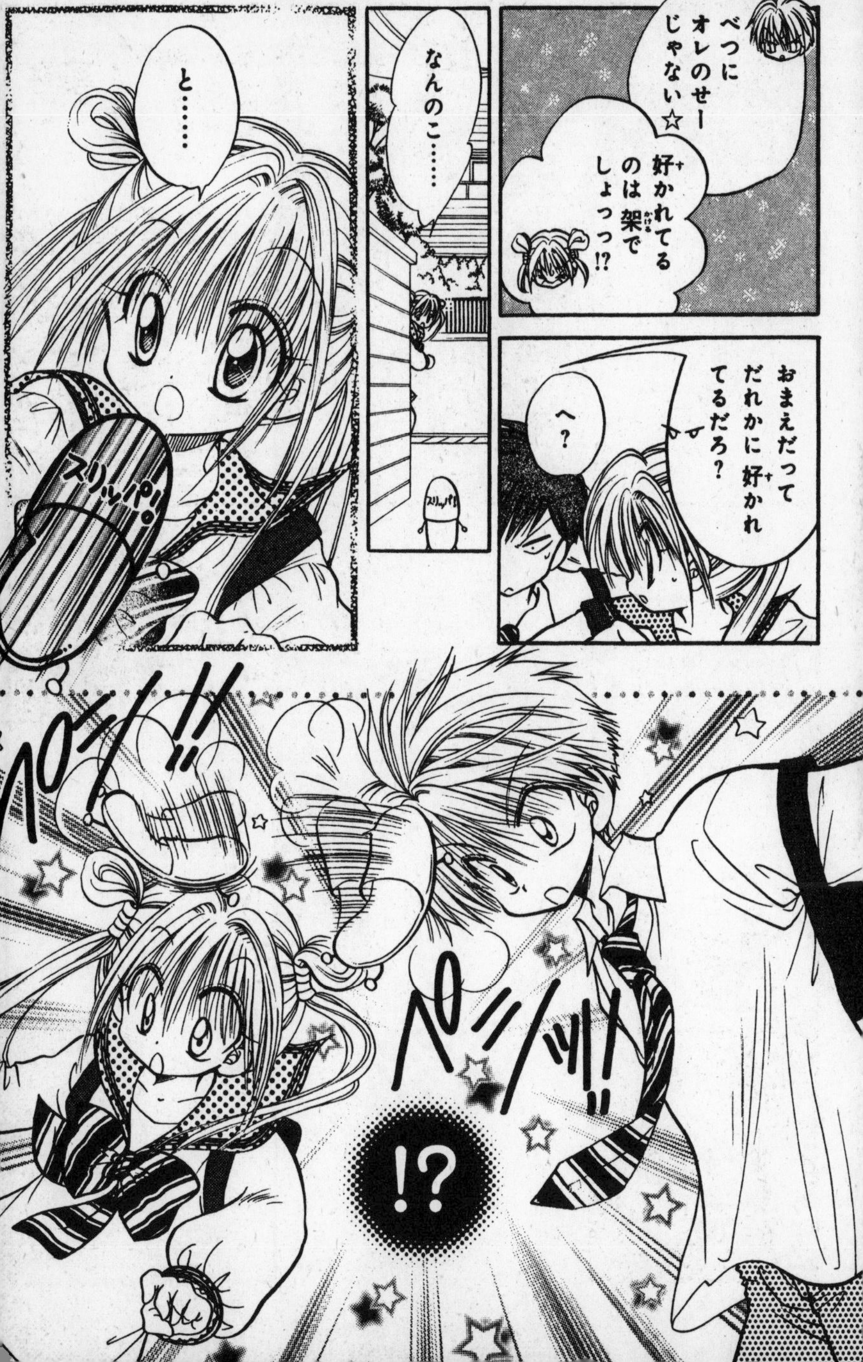
べつにオレのせーじゃない☆
好かれてるのは架でしょっっ!?
おまえだってだれかに好かれてるだろ?
へ?
なんのこ……
スリッパ!!
と……
スリッパ!!
ペシッ!!
!?
パン!!

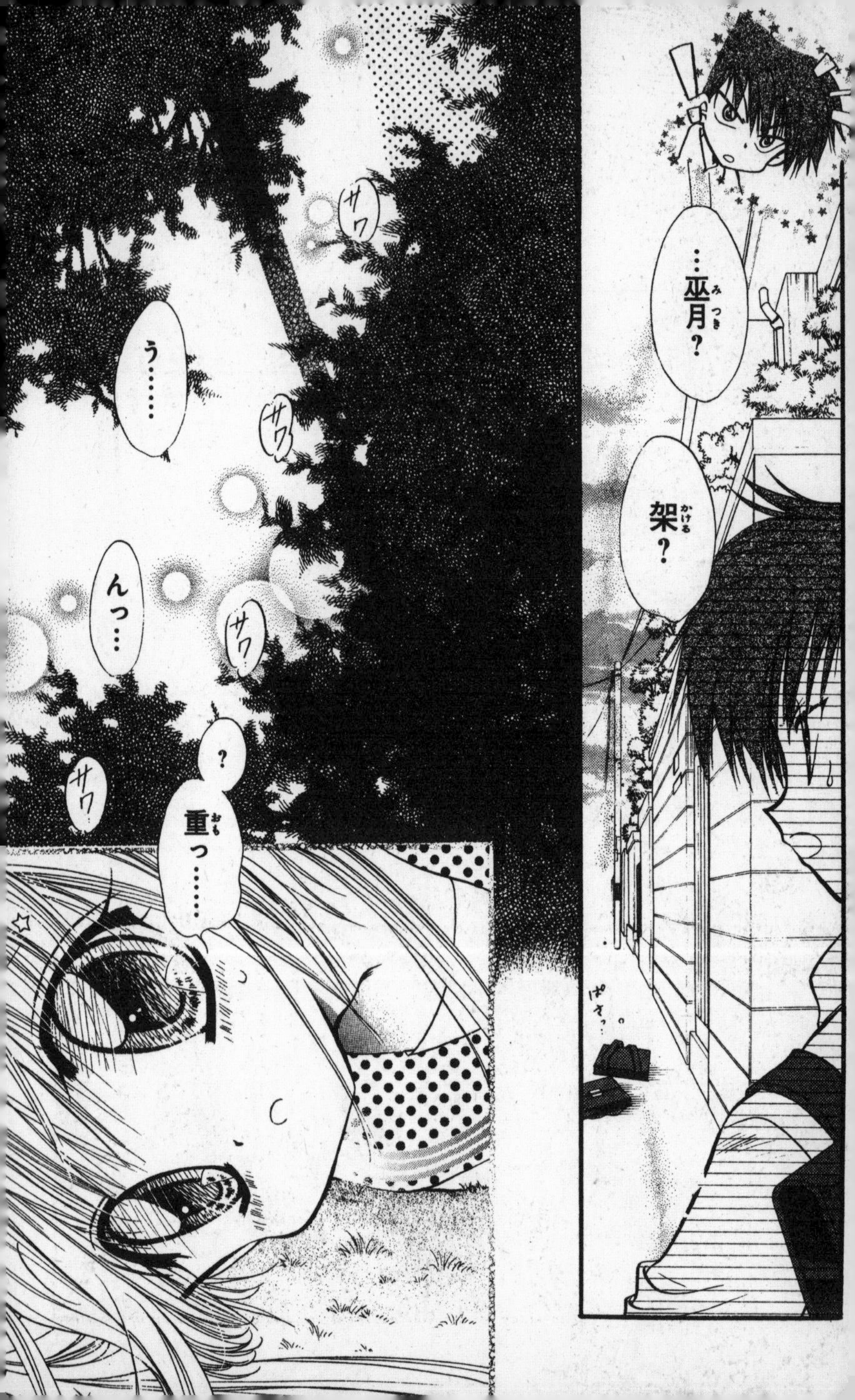

…巫月？
架？
ぱさっ…
サワ
う……
サワ
サワ
んっ…
サワ
？
重っ……

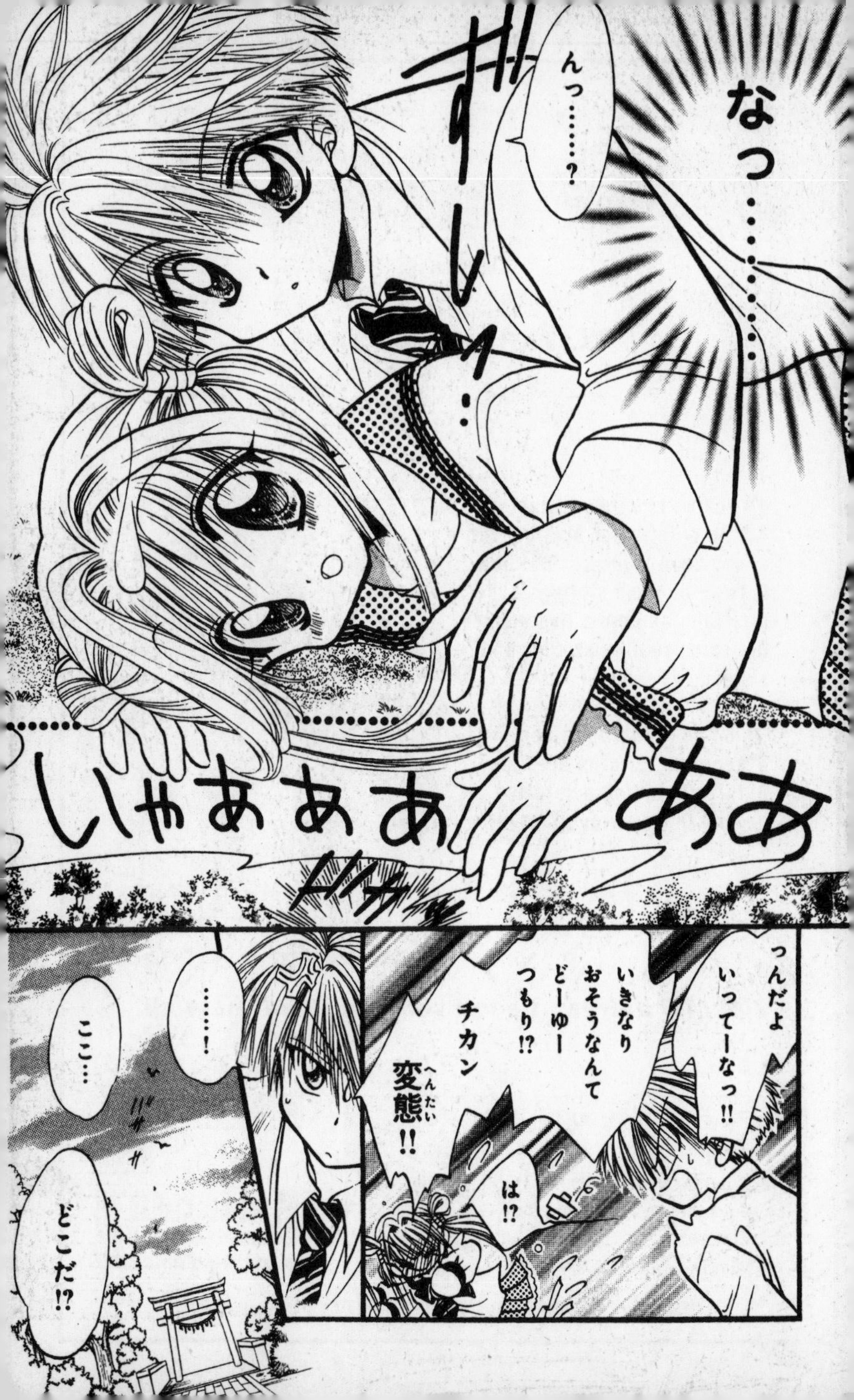
なっ……
んっ……？
ずしっ…
いゃあああ
ああ
つんだよ
いってーなっ!!
いきなりおそうなんてどーゆーつもり!?
チカン
変態!!
は!?
……！
ここ…
どこだ!?

TOMARE!

[STOP!]

You're going the wrong way!

Manga is a completely different type of reading experience.

To start at the *beginning*, go to the end!

That's right! Authentic manga is read the traditional Japanese way—from right to left. Exactly the opposite of how American books are read. It's easy to follow: Just go to the other end of the book, and read each page—and each panel—from right side to left side, starting at the top right. Now you're experiencing manga as it was meant to be!